Models of Cognitive Aging

DEBATES IN PSYCHOLOGY

Series Editor Dianne C. Berry
Series advisor Lawrence Weiskrantz

Martin Conway (ed.) Recovered Memories and False Memories
Dianne C. Berry (ed.) How Implicit is Implicit Learning?
Timothy J. Perfect and Elizabeth A. Maylor (ed.) Models of Cognitive Aging

Models of Cognitive Aging

Edited by

TIMOTHY J. PERFECT

Department of Psychology,
University of Plymouth

and

ELIZABETH A. MAYLOR

Department of Psychology,
University of Warwick

OXFORD
UNIVERSITY PRESS

OXFORD

UNIVERSITY PRESS

Great Clarendon Street, Oxford OX2 6DP

Oxford University Press is a department of the University of Oxford.
It furthers the University's objective of excellence in research, scholarship,
and education by publishing worldwide in

Oxford New York

Athens Auckland Bangkok Bogotá Buenos Aires Calcutta
Cape Town Chennai Dar es Salaam Delhi Florence Hong Kong Istanbul
Karachi Kuala Lumpur Madrid Melbourne Mexico City Mumbai
Nairobi Paris São Paulo Singapore Taipei Tokyo Toronto Warsaw

and associated companies in Berlin Ibadan

Published in the United States
by Oxford University Press Inc., New York

A catalogue record for this book is available from the British Library

Library of Congress Cataloging in Publication Data

Models of cognitive aging / edited by Timothy J. Perfect and Elizabeth
A. Maylor
    p.   cm. — (Debates in psychology)
Includes index.
    1. Cognition—Age factors. 2. Aging—Psychological aspects.
I. Perfect, Timothy J. II. Maylor, Elizabeth A. III. Series.
BF724.55.C63M63   2000   155.67'13—dc21   99-15924

ISBN 0 19 852438 2 (Hbk)
ISBN 0 19 852437 4 (Pbk)

Typeset by Bibliocraft Ltd, Dundee
Printed in India by
Thomson Press Ltd

Preface

Demographic pressures mean that we live in an era in which both expected longevity and the proportion of people in society living beyond retirement are increasing. Consequently, there is a growing interest in older adults, their capabilities, and changes in their functioning. The amount of research examining cognitive functioning in older adults is growing rapidly. This book represents both a taking stock of that research and an attempt to address some fundamental theoretical issues in the area. Whilst there is an enormous amount known about the average performance of younger and older adults across a range of cognitive abilities, there is rather less agreement as to how such data should be understood.

This book was written as part of the 'Theoretical Debates in Psychology' series, with the deliberate aim of producing a unique book on cognitive aging. Previous books in the area have generally been one of two kinds – either an introductory textbook or a 'Handbook' research volume, with each chapter written by a different author, dedicated to a different topic. Here we deliberately cast our net wide, with the intention not of providing a comprehensive review of cognitive change across many domains, but instead of getting a comprehensive picture of the theoretical perspectives that researchers in cognitive aging have adopted. Hence this book does not contain chapters on attention, memory, language, reasoning, etc., but instead has chapters on single factor models, mathematical modelling, time-accuracy functions, meta-analysis, and others. We believe the novelty of the 'Debates' series is the key reason we were able to recruit such excellent contributors, all of whom agreed with us that a theoretical book on aging would have something unique to say. In turn, we believe that the excellence of the contributors means that we were able to achieve this aim.

We would like to thank the staff at Oxford University Press for their support and encouragement. Without their help this book would never have seen the light of day. We would also like to acknowledge the financial support of the Medical Research Council and the Economic and Social Research Council during the genesis of the book.

This book is dedicated to our parents
Timothy J. Perfect   Elizabeth A. Maylor
17 February 1999

Contents

List of Contributors   ix

1 **Rejecting the dull hypothesis: the relation between
   method and theory in cognitive aging research**
   TIMOTHY J. PERFECT AND ELIZABETH A. MAYLOR   1
2 **Steps toward the explanation of adult age differences in cognition**
   TIMOTHY A. SALTHOUSE   19
3 **The parallels in beauty's brow: time–accuracy functions
   and their implications for cognitive aging theories**
   PAUL VERHAEGHEN   50
4 **Cognitive slowing among older adults: what kind and how much?**
   DONALD L. FISHER, SUSAN A. DUFFY,
   AND KONSTANTINOS V. KATSIKOPOULOS   87
5 **New directions for research into aging and intelligence:
   the development of expertise**
   JOHN L. HORN AND HIROMI MASUNAGA   125
6 **Measurement indices, functional characteristics, and
   psychometric constructs in cognitive aging**
   PATRICK M. A. RABBITT   160
7 **Determinants of age-related memory loss**
   ALAN J. PARKIN AND ROSALIND I. JAVA   188
8 **Theoretical approaches to language and aging**
   DEBORAH M. BURKE, DONALD G. MACKAY, AND LORI E. JAMES   204
9 **Dual-process theories of memory in old age**
   LEAH L. LIGHT, MATTHEW W. PRULL, DONNA J. LA VOIE,
   AND MICHAEL R. HEALY   238

Index   301

Contributors

Deborah M. Burke Department of Psychology, 550 Harvard Avenue, Pomona College, Claremont, CA 91711, USA

Susan A. Duffy Department of Psychology, University of Massachusetts, Amherst, MA 01003, USA

Donald L. Fisher Department of Mechanical and Industrial Engineering, University of Massachusetts, Amherst, MA 01003, USA

Michael R. Healy Department of Psychology, Claremont Graduate University, Claremont, CA 91711, USA

John L. Horn Department of Psychology, University of Southern California, Los Angeles, CA 90089-1061, USA

Lori E. James Department of Psychology, University of California, Los Angeles, 405 Hilgard Avenue, Los Angeles, CA 90095–1563, USA

Rosalind I. Java Laboratory of Experimental Psychology, University of Sussex, Falmer, Brighton, BN1 9QG, UK

Konstantinos V. Katsikopoulos Department of Mechanical and Industrial Engineering, University of Massachusetts, Amherst, MA 01003, USA

Donna J. La Voie Department of Psycholgy, St. Louis University, St. Louis, MO 63103, USA

Leah L. Light Department of Psychology, Pitzer College, 1050 N. Mills Avenue, Claremont, CA 91711, USA

Donald G. MacKay Department of Psychology, University of California, Los Angeles, 405 Hilgard Avenue, Los Angeles, CA 90095-1563, USA

Hiromi Masunaga Department of Psychology, University of Southern California, Los Angeles, CA 90089-1061, USA

Elizabeth A. Maylor Department of Psychology, University of Warwick, Coventry, CV4 7AL, UK

Alan J. Parkin Laboratory of Experimental Psychology, University of Sussex, Falmer, Brighton, BN1 9QG, UK

Timothy J. Perfect Department of Psychology, University of Plymouth, Plymouth, PL4 8AA, UK

Matthew W. Prull Department of Psychology, Stanford University, Stanford, CA 94305, USA

Patrick M. A. Rabbitt Age and Cognitive Performance Research Centre, University of Manchester, Oxford Road, Manchester, M13 9PL, UK

Timothy A. Salthouse School of Psychology, Georgia Institute of Technology, Atlanta, GA 30332-0170, USA

Paul Verhaeghen Department of Psychology, 430 Huntington Hall, Syracuse University, Syracuse, NY 13244-2340, USA

ONE

Rejecting the dull hypothesis: the relation between method and theory in cognitive aging research

TIMOTHY J. PERFECT AND ELIZABETH A. MAYLOR

INTRODUCTION

In this chapter, we begin by outlining a basic problem in cognitive aging research, namely that the statistical approach based on rejection of the null hypothesis is not appropriate for theory building. We then discuss two broad approaches that have been used in an attempt to overcome this shortcoming. We end with a discussion of potential ways forward, as outlined in the chapters that follow.

THE DULL HYPOTHESIS

Psychologists spend considerable time and effort attempting to establish the reliability of basic effects. Over the past century psychologists have utilized many sophisticated statistical techniques to determine whether the variability in performance they are measuring is likely to represent a real phenomenon to be explained, or whether it is just chance variation about the population mean. We inculcate this approach upon our students, against considerable resistance. Students' intellectual opposition to this idea is entirely understandable: if one stops to consider, it is odd that we base our science on setting up, and then rejecting the hypothesis that there will be no effect in our studies. Nonetheless, after a few years' formal teaching most students learn to accept the principle that the first aim of an experiment in psychology is to reject the null hypothesis.

However, when one turns to the study of aging it is not easy to see the utility of the null hypothesis. If one were to ask members of the public whether the average 80 year old and the average 25 year old are the same, then it is doubtful whether many would believe so, whatever the measure chosen (e.g. memory, speed, strength, health, visual acuity). However, that is what the null hypothesis requires us to assume. The standard approach would be to conduct a study comparing older and younger adults on a certain test and to use our statistical techniques to determine whether the two populations are reliably different. What would the public make of this? They would probably think that testing this null hypothesis was a somewhat pointless exercise, that our ability to reject the null hypothesis was extremely unimpressive, and they may start to ask questions about how taxpayers' money was being spent.

Clearly, the null hypothesis is not an appropriate starting point for studies in aging. In fact, if the measures were reliable and valid, it would be more interesting to accept the null hypothesis than to reject it. That is, it would be more unexpected, more counter-intuitive and more unusual in the normative sense to find something at which older and younger adults are equally good (see the chapter by Burke et al. for examples of exactly this). In this context the uninteresting finding is that there is a difference, that is, that younger people in general can remember more, are quicker, stronger, healthier, have better vision, and so on. If the psychology of aging is going to have anything to offer, it must go beyond merely demonstrating that younger adults outperform older adults, that is, we must be able to reject the *dull* hypothesis.

GOING BEYOND THE DULL HYPOTHESIS

Nearly a century of research has allowed us to accumulate a reasonably comprehensive picture of the cognitive change that accompanies increased age. Setting aside caveats about methodology, it is clear that there are reasonably ubiquitous age differences in cognition across the lifespan, across most domains of cognitive activity. However, at the behavioural level it is clear that the magnitude of age-related changes is different across different domains. We do not wish to discuss which domains of intellectual activity show the most age related change in this chapter (but see the chapters by Burke et al., and Light et al. for examples), but rather to focus on the relationship between the methods used to support different theoretical positions in cognitive aging.

One approach to the rejection of the dull hypothesis has been to contrast the magnitude of age-related differences in different domains of cognition, or in different processing steps within a cognitive domain. The dull hypothesis is rejected if it can be shown that older adults are particularly poor at some classes of tasks compared to other tasks, or compared to their performance in general. Such an approach is based on analysis of age-group differences between behavioural measures. Utilizing the cognitive–neuropsychological model, the aim has been to detect dissociations, or better, double dissociations, between age and domain of cognition. Researchers adopting this approach have tended to use the ANOVA approach, with the aim of not merely finding a main effect of age (the dull hypothesis), but of finding an age × task or age × condition interaction. Researchers using this approach are essentially testing a localist model of cognitive aging, that carries the assumption that aging consists of a series of local (or modular) deficits that can be isolated with the appropriate experimentation. We discuss the use of this method in greater detail below (see also the chapter by Verhaeghen).

The second approach has been to study associations in age-related change across different domains of cognition. The logic of this approach is that it is possible to reject the dull hypothesis if it can be shown that age-related change in one domain of cognition is independent of age-related change in another domain. Thus, the focus here is not on the magnitude of age-related change, but whether different changes are independent of one another. Thus, under this approach, two different domains of cognition may show the same average change, but if they are independent the degree of age-related change on one test will tell you nothing about the age-related change on the other test. Researchers using this approach generally hold a global (or general) view of cognitive decline with age. The purpose of their analyses is to determine the extent to which cognitive change across many domains can be explained by change in a single (or relatively few) 'primitive' measure, designed to tap a general aspect of cognition, such as neural speed, or working memory capacity (see the chapter by Salthouse for a full discussion of this approach). Thus, this approach restates the dull hypothesis in terms of whether age-related sensitivity on a task is greater, or less, than that expected from a general decline based upon age-related change in the 'primitive'. This is assessed by means of correlational techniques such as partial correlation, multiple regression, and path analysis to control for the effects of age-related change in the primitive on the age–task association. This approach is discussed further below.

THE USE OF DISSOCIATIONS TO REJECT THE DULL HYPOTHESIS

The idea behind this approach is simple: one measures age differences across two (or more) measures, and attempts to determine whether the age differences are the same magnitude across these tasks. If not, then one expects to find an age × task interaction in an analysis of variance (ANOVA). There are numerous examples that could be used to illustrate the ANOVA based approach to cognitive aging, but only one will be used here. In 1982, Salthouse and Somberg examined age-related change in performance at encoding, storage, and output in a Sternberg search paradigm, with the stated aim of determining which stages of processing are most age-sensitive. They manipulated encoding by having participants study intact or visually degraded stimuli. Storage was manipulated by varying the set size for comparison (one vs four items) and response was manipulated by varying the difficulty of the manual response required (simple button press vs complex use of two keyboards).

In the study participants were presented with digits to be remembered (1 vs 4) for 1.5 seconds, followed after a further 1.5 seconds by a target digit (intact vs degraded). The task was to indicate as quickly as possible whether the target digit had been present in the initial set, and responses were made via button press (simple vs complex). Using response time as the dependent variable, there were main effects of age for all stages of processing (encoding, storage, response) and there were also age × complexity interactions. That is, older adults were particularly slowed by having four items to search rather than one, by the use of degraded stimuli, and by the use of a complex response.

The presence of age × complexity interactions appear to offer a clear rejection of the dull hypothesis. This is not what Salthouse and Somberg (1982) conclude, however. They argue that the data are entirely consistent with the idea that there is a single monolithic change with increased age. Their argument is based on two facts: firstly, that the age × complexity interactions were ubiquitous rather than specific to one processing stage. Secondly, that in proportionate terms, the complexity effect is equivalent for young and old. The essence of this argument is captured in Fig. 1.1.

Figure 1.1 illustrates the classic age × task interaction often reported in the literature. There are several important features to these data. First there is not only a main effect of age overall, but there is an effect of age in the baseline task. Second, there is a complexity effect for both groups. In terms of mean performance, these two facts mean that in absolute terms, the age difference is greater in the more complex task, and hence there is a significant age × task interaction. However, if one takes differences in baseline response time into account (by using logarithms, or proportionate change) then the age × task interactions disappear.

The issue of taking baseline differences into account is central for cognitive aging research, because baseline differences are almost inevitably found. However, there is not a clear agreement as to how baselines should be used, and none of the methods currently used is entirely satisfactory. One common solution is to control for baseline task reaction time by calculating proportional increase

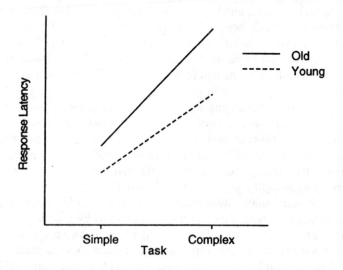

Fig. 1.1   Typical age × task interaction plot showing a larger age difference in response latencies between young and old for a complex task than for a simple task.

due to the complex task. (In the area of dual tasks, this is known as divided attention costs – see Somberg and Salthouse 1982; Perfect and Rabbitt 1993 for examples.)

However, dividing the increase in response time due to the complex task by the baseline measure carries with it several assumptions which may not be warranted. Foremost of these is that response time is a linear scale such that a change in RT from 200 ms to 300 ms is equivalent to a change in RT from 2 to 3 s. Verhaeghen discusses this issue in Chapter 3, and makes clear that such an assumption is unjustified. Speed–accuracy trade-off functions are non-linear, and so division by baselines may produce data that are difficult to interpret.

The second problem is that division by baseline does not produce a pure measure of costs if the behavioural index (response time) is not determined solely by the process under manipulation. This is probably a ubiquitous problem. Consider the visual degradation factor in Salthouse and Somberg's (1982) experiment, which was assumed to be a manipulation of encoding factors (rather than storage or response factors). In the visually intact condition, response time will be a combination of motor speed and central processing time. If we assume, for the sake of simplicity, that the motor and central processes are independent and additive, then the response time (RT) for younger adults on the baseline task can be described as:

$$RT_{base} = RT_{Motor} + RT_{Central(base)} \qquad (1\text{-}1)$$

In a complex version of the task (e.g. visually degraded stimuli, which are assumed not to produce slower motor responses) then response time will be:

$$RT_{complex} = RT_{Motor} + RT_{Central(complex)} \qquad (1\text{-}2)$$

Taking the proportionate costs gives us:

$$Pcosts = (RT_{Central(complex)} - RT_{Central(base)}) / (RT_{Motor} + RT_{Central(base)}) \qquad (1\text{-}3)$$

Equation 1-3 tells us that proportionate costs due to a change in visual degradation are in part a function of the motor response latency, a factor which is assumed not to vary across conditions, and so should not influence costs due to an increase in visual complexity. It also tells us that the extent to which true costs are under-estimated for changes in task complexity will be greater where motor speed becomes a larger proportion of the total response time.

Now let us consider the effects of aging, to see what effect this will have on our ability to draw conclusions about proportional costs with increased age. If we assume that the effect of aging on motor speed is a slowing factor of m, whilst for central processes it is a factor of c, substitution of the slowing factors into Equation 3 to get the costs for older adults gives us

$$Pcosts_{old} = c\,(RT_{Central(complex)} - RT_{Central(base)}) / (m\,RT_{Motor} + c\,RT_{Central(base)})$$

$$Pcosts_{old} = (RT_{Central(complex)} - RT_{Central(base)}) / ((m/c)\,RT_{Motor} + RT_{Central(base)}) \qquad (1\text{-}4)$$

Equation 1-4 tells us that if the only effects of age are multiplicative on the underlying processes then the proportional costs for older adults will approach the proportional costs for younger adults as the ratio m/c approaches unity. As m/c decreases from 1, so we would expect proportional costs for older adults to exceed those of the young, whilst increases in m/c over 1 would produce reduced estimates of proportional costs in older adults. As a first step towards estimating the ratio m/c, we can use the estimates of central and peripheral slowing from the meta-analysis by Cerella (1985). His estimates were that peripheral (motor) slowing (m) is less marked than central slowing (c), with a ratio of approximately 1.1:1.4, or 0.79. Thus, according to this analysis one might expect to find greater estimates of age-related costs in the elderly, *even when the 'true' costs are matched across age groups*. However, the magnitude of this differential effect on the estimate of change due to complexity will itself be proportional to the relative influence of the motor speed element. If motor speed is a larger proportion of total baseline response time, one would expect greater age differences in proportional costs. If the motor speed element is a relatively small proportion of total baseline response time, one might expect the age differences in proportional costs to be negligible.

The foregoing argument rests upon the assumption that the age differences can be expressed as simple linear multiplicative effects. However, this may not be true. If the effects of age are non-linear (e.g. Hale *et al.* 1987), then proportional costs become harder to interpret. Likewise, if older adults solve more complex tasks in fundamentally different ways from younger adults, then the assumption of multiplicative effects would be false. Thus, if one then wishes to compare younger and older adults on this measure in any sensible way, one needs to ensure that the proportionate measure means the same thing for both groups. This is an assumption that is rarely tested.

A development of the proportionate costs idea is the plotting of older adults' response latencies against the response latencies of younger adults. Under this technique, the proportionate costs emerge as the slope of the function which relates younger and older response times across experimental conditions. However, in addition to the slope there is an intercept term in a linear function, or other parameters in more complex functions (see Hale *et al.* 1991 for a summary of a range of functions that have been proposed). Such functions – known as Brinley plots after their originator (Brinley 1965) – have become very influential in cognitive aging, although their use has not gone unchallenged (Perfect 1994; Fisk *et al.* 1992). We return to the issue of Brinley plots in the section on regression analysis below, since Brinley plots are correlational in nature.

Salthouse (e.g. 1991) has argued in favour of converting older adults' performance into z-scores based on the distribution of scores in the younger population, in order to compare across different tasks. This escapes the assumption of linearity inherent in using proportionate measures. However, it involves another assumption that is not justified; it assumes that all variation about a mean is systematic, that is, that the standard deviation measure for a task is a measure of true variance in that process (Chapman and Chapman 1973). Since no measure has perfect reliability, this assumption is false, and variance in a test is always in part due to error. Thus, if the average older adult is one standard deviation below the average younger adult on a simple task and on a complex task, this does not mean that the age effect is necessarily equivalent across the two tasks. If a large proportion of the variance in a task is random (i.e. the reliability is low) it is harder to obtain a group difference. Thus 1 SD of age-related change on a task of low reliability is indicative of greater age-sensitivity in the underlying process than 1 SD of age-related change on a task of high reliability. This is problematic in aging research when comparing the magnitude of age effects in tasks that vary widely in their complexity. Simple speeded measures are highly reliable, and so estimates of the magnitude of age effects on such tests are likely to be accurate. However, more complex tasks, such as memory tasks or tests of executive function, have either lower, or unknown, reliability, and hence are probably less likely to show age sensitivity. For example, Salthouse (1996b) reported that a battery of speed measures had estimated reliabilities ranging from 0.56 to 0.96 with an unweighted mean of 0.85, whilst tests of short- and long-term memory had estimated reliabilities of between 0.37 and 0.89, with an unweighted mean of 0.62.

Another difficulty with the interpretation of interactions comes with the realization that no task is process pure. No behavioural measure tests only what it purports to and nothing else. Thus the reason that tests may or may not be age sensitive might not be because of what they are supposed to measure, but because of something else that is being tested at the same time. For example, fluency tasks requiring written responses may show age effects, not because of the generational aspect of fluency, but because of the effect of writing speed on performance. Likewise, the Wisconsin Card Sort Test is not merely tapping the ability to change rule-based behaviour, but also comprehension of the instructions, memory for prior responses, and many other factors. Thus comparing two tasks which are chosen to differ on a specified construct may produce interactions with age for reasons that have nothing to do with the construct itself. Alternatively, two tasks that do tap the same construct may give age interactions either because of what else they tap, or because they differentially load on the construct itself. In the latter case, it is possible that an interaction may still emerge because of a single factor. Salthouse discusses this issue in greater detail in Chapter 2.

THE USE OF CORRELATIONAL DATA TO REJECT THE DULL HYPOTHESIS

The idea behind the correlational approach is as simple as the ANOVA-based approach. If one measures age change in a range of cognitive abilities, then one can reject the dull hypothesis if correlations between age and cognitive ability in one domain are independent of correlations between age and ability in another domain. The logic of this approach is illustrated in Fig. 1.2, which uses the conventional Venn diagram notation to indicate the shared variance between variables. (For a fuller account, see Salthouse 1994.) In this example, age (A), and cognitive abilities B and C are all interrelated. The question of interest is the extent to which the A–B association, shown as the region (a + b) in Fig. 1.2, is independent of the A–C association, shown as the region (b + c). The correlational technique used is to measure the A-B association, and then to see how much variance in this association is reduced by controlling for C. Salthouse (1994, 1996a) has promoted the use of proportional reduction in age-associated variance, calculated as the proportion b / (a + b), and use of this technique has repeatedly shown that controlling for speed measures in this way markedly reduces the age association with measures of higher order cognitive function, such as learning and memory (Dunlosky and Salthouse 1996), intelligence (Hertzog 1989) and executive function (Salthouse *et al.* 1996).

As with the ANOVA approach, we begin with an example before discussing difficulties of interpretation. Baltes and Lindenberger (1997) collected 14 separate psychometric assessments of cognitive ability, from a total of 687 individuals aged between 25 and 103 years of age. These 14 assessments were combined to provide estimates of five intellectual factors – perceptual speed, reasoning, memory, knowledge, and fluency. In addition they collected data on visual and auditory acuity. As expected there were age-related declines across all the measures. The question of interest for Baltes and Lindenberger was whether the cognitive change could be predicted by the sensory change. That is,

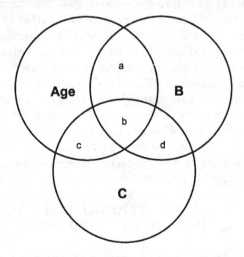

Fig 1.2   Venn diagram illustrating shared and unique variance associated with Age, and cognitive abilities B and C.

if one controls for age change in sensory acuity, does this result in the age-change in cognition being reduced, or even removed altogether? Rather than discuss each cognitive ability separately, we will illustrate the approach with their data based upon a composite of all five factors.

There was an age correlation with the composite measure of $r = -0.79$. In addition, there was a non-linear (quadratic) association, such that the rate of intellectual decline increased at the latter end of the age span. This quadratic effect correlated with age at $r = -0.23$, bringing the total age-related variance in the composite measure to 67.4%. However, if age-related change in hearing was controlled (by partialling out scores on the auditory acuity test) then the age-related variance in the cognitive measure was reduced to 7.0%. The equivalent figure for visual acuity was 16.7%, and the effect of controlling for both vision and hearing was to reduce the age-related variance in the composite cognitive score to a mere 3.0%. On the basis of such evidence, Baltes and Lindenberger (1997, p. 20) conclude that:

a large portion of the mechanisms that drive negative age differences in sensory performance also bring about the aging of complex cognition. This finding has implications regarding the search for 'psychological primitives' of negative age differences in cognition ... The very high degree of commonality between the age-related variance of the two domains is consistent with the notion that at least a major portion of these primitives is operating at a relatively global, rather than modular or domain-specific, level.

Thus these authors are clear in indicating that they subscribe to the view that a single factor can explain the majority of age-related variance. That is, that age-related change in one domain is not independent of age-related change in another domain, and so one must conclude that the age-related change observed across domains does not represent modular, independent change, but is probably the result of a single process operating throughout the central nervous system. Baltes and Lindenberger (1997) do not specify what they believe this 'primitive' to be, but clearly the implication is that age-related change in hearing loss and reasoning (for example) are highly interrelated; thus the most plausible conclusion is that some single biological process underpins them both.

Other authors have gone further and proposed specific primitives that might explain age-related change. Salthouse (1996*a* and this volume) is most associated with the view that age-related differences in neural speed can explain most of the age-related variance in cognition. Others have proposed alternative primitives, such as processing resources (e.g. Fastenau *et al.* 1996), working memory capacity (Kirasic *et al.* 1996), loss of connections in a network (Cerella 1990), or information loss in transmission through a network (Myerson *et al.* 1990). It is not within the scope of the present chapter to review the relative merits of these different theoretical claims. Rather, we will focus on the method-ologies used to support these positions. The accounts founded on speed, atten-tional resources and working memory capacity have all been based on the regression technique as used by Baltes and Lindenberger, described above. The theoretical accounts founded upon properties of networks (cell loss and information loss) are principally based upon analyses of Brinley functions. We discuss each of these in turn.

PROBLEMS WITH REGRESSION ANALYSES

It may sound trite, but one should not forget the old chestnut that correlation does not imply causation. The regression-based techniques, including hierarchical regression and path analytic techniques, used to support single-factor accounts of aging are based on correlations in cross-sectional data. Finding an association between age-related variance in a 'primitive' and in a more complex cognitive task does not mean that the former causes the latter, but merely that they are associated in the data set analysed. There may be many intervening variables that can account for the association between the two measures. This issue is discussed fully in the chapter by Salthouse, and we will not explore it further here. It is worth noting, however, that a convincing demonstration that changes in a primitive cause changes in more complex cognitive measures can only come with longitudinal designs, that is, demonstrations that the degree to which an individual slows down is predictive of how much cognitive change they show in other domains.

Related to the point about causation is the issue of task purity. As was discussed in relation to ANOVA-based analyses, no task is process pure, and this has important consequences for interpretation of correlational designs. Regression techniques are based upon individual differences, and the relation between individual differences and cognitive structure is by no means always obvious. This point was made in an analysis of the properties of motor cars by Lykken (1971). He asked the question of whether correlational analysis of the performance measures of cars would tell us something about how cars worked. Based on manufacturers' specifications, he found, for instance, that heavier cars tend to be able to accelerate faster and have a higher top speed than lighter cars. If we believed that correlation told us about structure, then we would be forced to argue that massive objects accelerate more easily than lighter ones, which is contrary to the laws of physics. (In the motoring world, large cars have disproportionately large engines.)

The difficulty in interpretation of behavioural data reflects the fact that none of the measures used directly taps the putative primitive that is used to explain age-related change in performance (see the chapter by Rabbitt for a fuller articulation of this view). Neural speed is not measured directly, but instead is inferred from behavioural indices of speed in simple tasks. Likewise, working memory capacity is not measured directly, but is inferred from performance measures using specific memory tests. One might quibble that pure measures can never be obtained, but the point remains that individual differences in the behavioural measure cannot uniquely be attributed to individual differences in the primitive assumed to underlie performance.

A consequence of the fact that tasks do not uniquely measure what they purport to measure, and the fact that regression analyses are conducted in cross-sectional aging designs means that the potential for overestimating the effect of change in one variable on change in the other variable is high. In cross-sectional designs – of the kind used by Baltes and Lindenberger (1997) – the measures are not just indications of domain specific ability, but also markers of the aging process and cohort differences. The older the individual the more likely they are to be either chronically or acutely ill, to be less well educated, to be less familiar with testing, to be further away from formal education, and so forth. It is also likely that they will bring different attitudes and motivations into the test session. All of these factors will mean that any measures of cognitive ability collected across a large age range will intercorrelate to some degree, whether the underlying constructs are related or not. For instance, memory performance on a recognition task and accuracy of responding in an inspection time task may be theoretically distinct, but education may affect both, and since older adults are in general less well educated than younger ones, the measures will intercorrelate. More specifically, the age-related variance in both may be highly related.

More recently, there has been a more direct criticism of the logic that underpins the regression approach, including path analysis. Lindenberger and Pötter (1998) conducted a systematic analysis of the statistical properties of this approach. Their argument is best illustrated by reference to Fig. 1.2. They were interested in whether controlling the strength of the age-independent relation between cognitive abilities B and C had an effect on the estimate of age-related variance that they share. Strictly, the logic of the argument that underpins the use of regression analyses, of the kind used by Baltes and Lindenberger (1997), is that the effect of controlling for ability C on the age (A) association with B (i.e. A–B) should be independent of the effect of the age-independent relation between B and C. However, this was not the case. It was found that the influence that C had on the A–B relation was proportionate to the quadratic of the partial correlation between B and C. Thus, it is not possible to conclude that a particular primitive explains the age-related association between age and a dependent variable, because the estimate of the influence is confounded by the partial correlation between the dependent and the primitive *that is age-independent* which corresponds to the area labelled 'd' in Fig. 1.2. Because the nature of the effect is quadratic, this can lead to unpredictable outcomes.

As an example, Lindenberger and Pötter (1998) show that path analyses which vary the partial correlation represented by 'd' from zero to $r = 0.572$, whilst holding constant the relation between Age and B, can lead to radically different path models, which are either consistent with the view that all age change is mediated by C, or are consistent with a positive effect of Age on B, independent of C, or a negative effect of Age on B, independent of C. That is, with regards to the independence of the Age–B association, all outcomes are possible, depending upon the partial correlation between B and C. Lindenberger and Pötter make clear that such analyses technically do not tell us about how much age-related change in B is related to age-related change in C, but rather tell us whether age-related change in B is related to individual differences in C, which will include differences that are not age-related. Given that simple age correlations with measures are often in the region of 0.3–0.5, this means that only 9–25% of individual differences in test performance are age-related. With regards to the general use of the technique, it is hard to disagree with Lindenberger and Pötter's (1998, p. 227, italics added) conclusion that:

the decision to entertain the hypothesis that a certain variable mediates the causal effect of another should be based on theoretical considerations, *and not on the outcome of hierachical linear regression analyses.*

THE USE OF BRINLEY PLOTS

'Brinley plots' refer to scattergrams, plotted in Young–Old co-ordinate space. Most conventionally, these are plotted using the mean response times from different experimental conditions (e.g. Cerella 1985), although mean errors have also been used (e.g. Brinley 1965). Sometimes the data represent pairs of individuals in a single experimental condition, with each point representing a younger and an older person in the same rank order in their respective population. Thus a point represents the response time for the fastest younger adult plotted against the response time for the fastest older adult. A second point represents the equivalent point for the second fastest individual in each population and so on (e.g. Maylor and Rabbitt 1994).

Brinley plots have been used to address the dull hypothesis in the following fashion. (We focus on the use of experimental means as the unit of analysis, but the argument also applies to individual-based analyses.) Data are collected across a range of experimental tasks, and plotted as a Brinley plot. Regression equations are then fitted to these points to determine the goodness of fit for simple functions. Age differences in such plots are revealed to the extent that points fall above the line $y = x$, that is, to the extent that older response times are slower than younger ones. It has been found that, using such an approach, most of the variance between experimental conditions can be explained by simple functions. However, there is some debate as to whether a linear function, or a non-linear function best captures the regularity seen in the data (Hale *et al.* 1991).

There has been considerable debate as to the interpretation of Brinley plots (e.g. Cerella 1994; Fisk and Fisher 1994; Myerson *et al.*, 1994; Perfect 1994), and it is not the intention to revisit those arguments here. In any case the technique is discussed in full later in the volume (see chapters by Verhaeghen, Horn and Masunaga, and Fisher *et al.*). However, we will note that the majority of Brinley plots are based on an analysis across experimental conditions, rather than across individuals. Thus estimates of the predictive power of these functions can be extremely misleading, because individual variance has been excluded. Such effects can be extremely powerful, and we illustrate with an example that is not age related, to avoid clouding the issue.

Fienberg (1971) examined the relation between the probability of being drawn in the US draft lottery, conducted in 1970, and when in the year a person's birthday fell. Across individuals, there was a correlation of *rho* = -0.226, which was moderately predictive, such that there was greater likelihood of being drawn for the draft if the person was born earlier in the year. However, Fienberg also collapsed the data by month, and conducted another correlational analysis. Now the probability of being selected correlated with birthday, as measured by month at a level of *rho* = -0.839. Thus, using group means greatly increases the regularity of the data, and greatly inflates the apparent predictive power of the analysis; the analysis based upon means for each month suggests that most of the variance in probability of draft selection can be accounted for by birthday, but clearly, at the individual level this is not the case. Theory-building based upon explanation of the regularity seen in the monthly figures would greatly over-estimate the predictability of data at the individual level, and would likely lead to the adoption of single factor explanatory models. However, whilst such models would explain impressively high levels of variance at the level of the group, they would tell us little at the individual level.

THE RELATION BETWEEN METHOD AND THEORY IN COGNITIVE AGING

The previous sections have taken a critical look at the two kinds of methodology used to reject the dull hypothesis. These two methodologies have been linked with two broad theoretical approaches to understanding cognitive aging – the ANOVA-based approach is associated with the modular or localist approach to aging, whilst the correlational approach is associated with the general or single-factor approach to aging. Given the problems associated with both methodologies, what can be done to improve the understanding of our data and hence our theories of cognitive aging?

The work reported in the chapters that follow show a number of approaches to this question, ranging from empirical studies to mathematical modelling. Interestingly, despite the different methods adopted by the authors in the present volume, there are consistent themes running through the book. One such theme is the relation between data interpretation and theory in aging. Too often in the past we have let the data, taken at face value, drive the theory. Now there is greater realization that in fact the same data may be compatible with many theoretical approaches. Rather than worry about how our data inform our theories, many authors argue that our theories should inform our understanding of our data, and our drive to collect new data that are informative with regard to theory.

In Chapter 2, Salthouse offers an overview of the methods used to answer theoretical questions in cognitive aging. He argues that dissociation-based approaches, which seek to localize age effects in specific task components, do not offer explanations of cognitive aging, but merely refine what needs to be explained. He favours instead the broader approach to age-related change, and describes three methods for determining the extent to which age-related change in cognition is unique, or shared across tasks. His conclusion – that a relatively small number of factors can explain the majority of age-related cognitive change – offers a challenge to the other authors in the volume. What Salthouse also makes clear in this chapter is the theoretical work that remains to be done: finding that age-related change is explained by a small number of cognitive primitives that can be called 'processing efficiency' does not in itself specify what those primitives are, nor what their explanatory status is. Are such primitives explanations in themselves, or are they merely markers of biological decline?

Chapter 3 (by Verhaeghen) makes the challenging statement that 'everything we thought we knew about cognitive aging may be wrong' (p. 80) because we have used inappropriate methods. The chapter begins with a discussion of the problems with existing analytic techniques before suggesting the addition of a new technique to the armoury of cognitive aging researchers, namely, time-accuracy methodology. The starting point for this technique is the examination of state traces, such as the time taken by younger and older adults to achieve the same level of accuracy, plotted across a range of accuracy levels. By manipulating response deadlines, functions describing the performance of younger and older adults can be constructed in terms of three underlying parameters, whose interpretation is theoretically driven. Verhaeghen draws two radical conclusions on the basis of the adoption of this approach. The first is captured in the quotation above – that interactions in behavioural data across tasks can arise even when the underlying parameters suggest no interaction, and conversely in some circumstances lack of interactions in behavioural data can mask interactions in the underlying parameters. Thus, Verhaeghen is making the very strong claim that behavioural data can only be understood in terms of an underlying theoretical model, and should not be taken at face value. The second radical conclusion is that dissociations with aging can be found, contrary to generalist accounts, and that such dissociations are caused by underlying quantum states of complexity rather than cognitive domain (e.g. lexical vs non-lexical, executive vs non-executive). Verhaeghen concludes by arguing that viewing age-related change in this way represents a middle way between those who believe that all aging is driven by a single underlying primitive, and those who believe in multiple independent or modular changes with age.

Fisher *et al.* (Chapter 4) offer a theoretical analysis of a very different kind. This chapter is a formal mathematical analysis of the concept of slowing as it is used in cognitive aging research. They begin by arguing that previous research has conflated two distinct forms of slowing: chronological and chronocentric. By chronological slowing they mean the extent to which age-related change is general, task-, or process-specific. By chronocentric slowing they mean the extent to which the speed of baseline performance has an impact on criterion task performance, in younger and older adults. They go on to explore the extent to which these two constructs are related, and examine the effects of two estimates of chronocentric slowing – a novel measure they call *P(speed)* which is the proportion of the age difference in response times on criterion tasks that is due to differences in baseline speed, and the more conventional measure of how much age-related variance is explained by speed, *P(shared)*. They argue that the former measure offers a more intuitive measure than the more commonly used technique, which can lead to misleading conclusions if there are task-specific age changes in slowing. Interestingly, although their methods are very different from the previous chapters, they end with a conclusion that would not be out of place in either of the preceding chapters. They argue that without a clear underlying theoretical model, data interpretation (in particular the estimate *P(shared)*) is problematic.

Horn and Masunaga (Chapter 5) bring a radically different theoretical perspective to the issue of human aging. They begin by reviewing the literature from the psychometric tradition that is supportive of the Gf–Gc theory of intelligence. They argue that the evidence favours the view that intelligence is multifactorial, and that a key part of the evidence for such a conclusion comes from the fact that across the adult lifespan some abilities decline whilst others either increase or are maintained. Since intelligence is not a single construct they further argue that it cannot be accounted for by a single construct such as 'g' or processing speed, and consequently, neither can age changes in this construct be so explained. Instead they propose a very different way of thinking about intelligence and aging: they argue that the highest intellectual achievements are those reached by experts in a domain; that is, they are the result of extensive practice and specialization. They further argue that the evidence suggests' that expertise takes years to achieve, and that older experts show maintenance of their skills. Thus, they argue, conclusions about intellectual change over the lifespan that are based on general tests may underestimate the abilities that older adults may reach in their areas of expertise.

Rabbit (Chapter 6) offers a theoretical critique of the notion of single-factor accounts of cognitive aging. He begins with a critique of the construct of speed as a causal explanation in cognitive aging. He argues that speed measures are merely a measure of the efficiency of the cognitive system, rather than being a fundamental property of it. This is particularly true in simple tasks where the only way in which individuals can differ is in the speed with which they reach asymptotic performance. In any case, argues Rabbitt, finding basic differences in speed merely begs the question of what causes the speed difference, since slower responses may stem from slower neurons, more impoverished neural networks, noisier systems, and so forth.

Having discussed speed as a putative primitive for cognitive aging, Rabbitt goes on to offer an empirical demonstration that simple speed is not sufficient to capture all age-related individual differences. He shows that trial-to-trial variability is another stable individual characteristic that can explain individual differences in performance which mean response time cannot explain. However, the purpose behind this line of argument is not to argue for another primitive, but to demonstrate that single primitives are insufficient. Rabbitt is very clear that he does not believe in the usefulness of such an approach; instead he favours a model-driven strategy.

Chapter 7, by Parkin and Java, also concentrates on the issue of general accounts of age-related decline. However, rather than discussing the issue of general versus local accounts, Parkin and Java instead focus on contrasting three of the most commonly proposed 'primitives' that have been advanced as explaining age-related decline (frontal functioning, processing speed, and fluid intelligence). Thus, their approach can be seen as an attempt to answer some of the questions raised by Salthouse's chapter, in terms of what (set of) putative primitives might best explain cognitive aging. They then report a small-scale study that directly contrasts the explanatory power of the three primitives to explain age-related memory loss. They report a series of regression analyses in which performance on the digit symbol substitution test (DSST) (a measure of perceptual speed) is the strongest predictor of memory, with no residual effects of IQ or executive function. Thus, their empirical findings are consistent with those reported previously by Salthouse as supporting the idea that perceptual speed is the best primitive for cognitive aging. However, these authors take a very different view of the DSST, and their chapter finishes with speculation as to what that test is measuring, and why it is so predictive of memory performance and general intelligence. They argue that the DSST should instead be considered to be a form of working-memory task, and that this may explain its success in predicting variance in memory performance.

Several of the chapters conclude with an appeal for clearer theoretical models within which to work: Chapter 8, by Burke *et al.* represents just such an approach. It focuses on one specific area of cognition – language functioning – as a test bed for theories of cognitive aging. The authors offer a clear theoretical model, and clear empirical dissociations with which to test their model against other theoretical accounts. The model – Node Structure Theory – in which aging is instantiated as a weakening of connections between units within the language-processing system, is tested with data from three domains of language production, namely tip-of-the-tongue experiences, retrieval of names, and spelling. Broadly, they report dissociations between language comprehension (input) and language production (output), with age insensitivity for the former and age decrements for the latter. They argue that whilst their model can account for such a pattern of findings, general accounts, such as generalized slowing or decreased inhibition with age, cannot.

The final chapter (9) by Light *et al.* also focuses on a particular theoretical model – the dual process model of memory – but uses a different analytic approach. These authors use meta-analysis to test whether effect sizes observed across many studies are compatible with a single-factor view of memory change across the lifespan. Thus, this approach tests the general model of aging across many studies, thereby overcoming the problems associated with any single study that may result from particular samples, particular materials, or particular sets of instructions. Three theoretical areas of memory functioning are examined: implicit memory, recollection versus familiarity-based recognition memory (using the Tulving 1985 technique), and intentional versus automatic processes (using Jacoby's 1991 process-dissociation procedure). As well as examining whether age-related change in each area is compatible with single or dual-process models, the authors also attempt to relate the different areas of research.

Light *et al.*'s chapter is a thorough and scholarly piece of research in which the authors rigorously test alternative conceptualizations of their data sets in order to test alternative theoretical models. We do not wish to recapitulate here the alternative classificatory schemes used in the meta-analysis. However, there are two clear themes that are noteworthy, and fit with the themes that emerge from the other chapters. First, it is clear that age differences are not equal in magnitude across the different data sets. Second, and more interesting, is the fact that how one understands or interprets these effects is by no means clear or straightforward. The conclusions about age sensitivity alter according to one's underlying theoretical model (e.g. should recollection and familiarity be seen as independent or redundant processes?). Thus, even in large meta-analytic data sets, the importance of a theoretical model emerges as paramount.

ACKNOWLEDGEMENTS

The writing of this chapter was partially supported by a Medical Research Council grant (G9503572) to the first author.

REFERENCES

Baltes, P. B. and Lindenberger, U. (1997). Emergence of a powerful connection between sensory and cognitive functions across the adult life span: a new window to the study of cognitive aging? *Psychology and Aging*, **12**, 12–21.

Brinley, J. F. (1965). Cognitive sets, speed and accuracy of performance in the elderly. In A. T. Welford and J. E. Birren (ed.), *Behavior, aging and the nervous system* (pp. 114–49). Springfield, IL: Thomas.

Cerella, J. (1985). Information processing rates in the elderly. *Psychological Bulletin*, **89**, 67–83.

Cerella, J. (1990). Aging and information processing rates. In J. Birren and K. W. Shaie (ed.) *Handbook of the Psychology of Aging* (3rd edn., pp. 201–21). San Diego: Academic Press.

Cerella, J. (1994). Generalized slowing in Brinley plots. *Journal of Gerontology: Psychological Sciences*, **49**, P65–71.

Chapman, L. J. and Chapman, J. P. (1973). Problems in the measurement of cognitive deficit. *Psychological Bulletin*, **79**, 380–85.

Dunlosky, J. and Salthouse, T. A. (1996). A decomposition of age-related differences in multitrial free recall. *Aging, Neuropsychology, and Cognition*, **3**, 2–14.

Fastenau, P. S., Denburg, N. L., and Abeles, N. (1996). Age differences in retrieval: further support for the resource-reduction hypothesis. *Psychology and Aging*, **11**, 140–6.

Fienberg, S. E. (1971). Randomization and social affairs: the 1970 draft lottery. *Science*, 171, 255–61.

Fisk, A. D. and Fisher, D. L. (1994). Brinley plots and theories of aging: the explicit, muddled and implicit debates. *Journal of Gerontology: Psychological Sciences*, 49, P81–9.

Fisk, A. D., Fisher, D. L., and Rogers, W. A. (1992). General slowing cannot explain age-related search effects: reply to Cerella (1991). *Journal of Experimental Psychology: General*, 121, 73–8.

Hale, S., Lima, S. D., and Myerson, J. (1991). General cognitive slowing in the nonlexical domain: an experimental validation. *Psychology and Aging*, 6, 512–21.

Hale, S., Myerson, J., and Wagstaff, D. (1987). General slowing of nonverbal information processing: evidence for a power law. *Journal of Gerontology*, 42, 131–6.

Hertzog, C. (1989). Influences of cognitive slowing on age differences in intelligence. *Developmental Psychology*, 25, 636–51.

Jacoby, L. L. (1991). A process dissociation framework: separating automatic from intentional uses of memory. *Journal of Memory and Language*, 30, 513–41.

Kirasic, K. C., Allen, G. L., Dobson, S. H., and Binder, K. S. (1996). Aging, cognitive resources and declarative learning. *Psychology and Aging*, 11, 658–70.

Lindenberger, U. and Pötter, U. (1998). The complex nature of unique and shared effects in hierarchical linear regression: implications for developmental psychology. *Psychological Methods*, 3, 218–30.

Lykken, D. T. (1971). Multiple factor analysis and personality research. *Journal of Experimental Research in Personality*, 5, 161–70

Maylor, E. A. and Rabbitt, P. M. A. (1994). Applying Brinley plots to individuals: effects of aging on performance distributions in two speeded tasks. *Psychology and Aging*, 9, 224–30.

Myerson, J., Hale, S., Wagstaff, D., Poon, L., and Smith, G. A. (1990). The information-loss model: a mathematical model of age-related cognitive slowing. *Psychological Review*, 97, 475–87.

Myerson, J., Wagstaff, D., and Hale, S. (1994). Brinley plots, explained variance and the analysis of age differences in response latencies. *Journal of Gerontology: Psychological Sciences*, 49, P72–80.

Perfect, T. J. (1994). What can Brinley plots tell us about cognitive aging? *Journal of Gerontology: Psychological Sciences*, 49, P60–4.

Perfect, T. J. and Rabbitt, P. M. A. (1993). Age and the divided attention costs of category exemplar generation. *British Journal of Developmental Psychology*, 11, 131–42.

Salthouse, T. A. (1991). *Theoretical perspectives on cognitive aging*. Hillsdale, NJ: Lawrence Erlbaum.

Salthouse, T. A. (1994). How many causes are there of aging-related decrements in cognitive function? *Developmental Review*, 14, 413–37.

Salthouse, T. A. (1996a). The processing-speed theory of adult age differences in cognition. *Psychological Review*, 103, 403–28.

Salthouse, T. A. (1996b). General and specific mediation of adult age differences in memory. *Journal of Gerontology: Psychological Sciences*, 51, P30–42.

Salthouse, T. A., Fristoe, N., and Rhee, S. H. (1996). How localized are age-related effects on neuropsychological measures? *Neuropsychology*, 10, 272–85.

Salthouse, T. A. and Somberg, B. L. (1982). Isolating the age deficit in speeded performance. *Journal of Gerontology*, 37, 59–63.

Tulving, E. (1985). Memory and consciousness. *Canadian Psychology*, 26, 1–12.

TWO

Steps toward the explanation of adult age differences in cognition

TIMOTHY A. SALTHOUSE

Age-related differences have been documented in a wide variety of cognitive variables. Typical results are illustrated in Fig. 2.1 with data from a recent study involving 259 adults between 18 and 94 years of age (Salthouse, et al. 1996a). Note that roughly comparable age-related declines of about 1 to 1.5 standard deviation units are evident in variables representing perceptual speed (letter comparison and pattern comparison), episodic memory (paired associates and free recall), inductive reasoning (series completion and Wisconsin Card Sorting Test number of categories), and spatial visualization (object assembly and block design) abilities. Similar patterns are apparent in many different data sets (e.g. Baltes and Lindenberger 1997; Horn 1982; Horn et al. 1981; Salthouse 1992b, 1993a, 1994a, 1996d; 1998; Salthouse et al. 1998; Schaie and Willis 1993), and thus these negative age relations can be viewed as the principal phenomenon in need of explanation by theories of cognitive aging. That is, any satisfactory theory in this area will ultimately need to account for the negative relations of age on a range of different cognitive variables. In order to be comprehensive, the theory should probably also explain why there are few or no age relations on other cognitive variables (e.g. those reflecting crystallized or product aspects of cognition largely reflecting knowledge acquired in the past), but at minimum it will need to provide an explanation for the age-related declines that have been reported across several kinds of cognitive variables.

The discovery that age differences exist on many cognitive variables leads to the question of whether the age-related differences on separate variables are independent of one another. This question is important because if the age-related effects were discovered to be independent, then the effects on individual variables could be interpreted as reflecting the operation of multiple specific (i.e., discrete) influences associated with increased age. In other words, if age-related effects on one variable were known to be unrelated to the age-related effects on other variables, the various influences might be assumed to correspond to factors that were functionally distinct. However, if many of the age-related effects on different variables were shared with other variables, a quite different conclusion might be reached. That is, if only a small proportion of the age-related influences across different cognitive variables were discovered to be

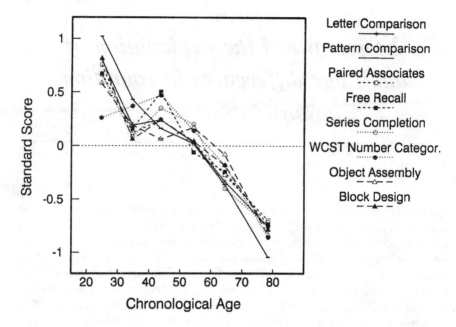

Fig. 2.1 Age relations in standard score units for eight different variables representing perpetual speed, episodic memory, inductive reasoning, and spatial visualization. Data from Salthouse *et al.* (1996*a*).

independent, then it might be inferred that there is a relatively small number of distinct age-related influences, or that at least some of the separate influences converge on a common mechanism that contributes to the age-related differences on many variables (Salthouse 1994*c*, 1996*d*).

The preceding considerations suggest that a fundamental issue in interpreting the nature or cause of adult age differences in cognition is whether the age-related difference on a particular observed variable is a novel finding, or is merely another manifestation of a broader or more general phenomenon. Unfortunately these two possibilities are not easily distinguished unless the new result is examined in the context of age-related differences on a variety of other variables.

One of the first researchers to plead for a broader perspective in interpreting age-related differences in cognition was Anderson (1956, p. 77), who posed the question: 'Is there an overall commonality in decline which can be used as a base from which to analyze the decline of particular parts or structures or is it the summation of a host of specific declines?' Similar queries have been made by others, including several by the present author (Salthouse 1982, 1985*b*, 1992*b*, 1994*c*, 1996*d*; 1998; Salthouse *et al.* 1996*a*).

It is important to emphasize that the proposal under consideration is not whether all age-related cognitive differences are general rather than specific, or whether there is only a single cause of all age-related differences in measures of cognitive functioning. Indeed, although some authors tend to use all-or-none terms in characterizing theoretical positions (especially the positions being criticized by those authors), monolithic interpretations of age-related phenomena are almost certainly much too simplistic because it is unrealistic to expect all age-related influences on many different types of cognitive variables to be exclusively determined by a single factor. Instead the current suggestion is that analytical methods need to be identified and employed to allow the relative contributions of different types of influences to be evaluated on empirical, rather than a priori, grounds. Only after the relative degree of independence of the age-related influences has been determined will it be possible to specify the type of theoretical interpretation – highly specific to a few particular tasks, or broad and affecting many different types of tasks – that is most likely to be viable in accounting for cognitive aging phenomena.

MICRO AND MACRO APPROACHES

Two major approaches to interpreting age-related differences in cognition can be distinguished. I will use the term **micro** to refer to the approach in which explanations are sought in terms of processes or components hypothesized to be required to perform the task of primary interest. These processes or components are often based on a task analysis, or a model of how the task is performed, and thus the micro approach is both theoretical and analytical in nature. The goal in this approach is to determine which of the hypothesized components is, or are, responsible for the observed age-related effects on the task.

I will refer to the second approach as the **macro** approach because in this case explanations of the age-related differences in one cognitive task are sought in terms of broader influences that are not restricted to particular types of tasks. That is, a major focus in the macro approach is the relations among the age-related influences on variables from different tasks.

The micro–macro distinction is loosely analogous to the difference between experimental and psychometric perspectives, but although the micro approach shares an analytical focus with the experimental perspective, macro is not the same as psychometric and does not merely refer to the identification of distinct abilities and determination of the interrelations among them. The distinction is somewhat related to the contrast between the emphasis on cognitive components versus cognitive correlates that was discussed in the field of cognitive psychology in the 1980s (e.g. Hunt 1985; Sternberg 1985), but once again the analogy is incomplete because the macro approach does not simply consist of examining correlations of the criterion variable with other cognitive abilities as in the cognitive correlates approach. Perhaps the closest parallel is the distinction between an internal (within-task) and an external (outside of task) focus, but the terms micro and macro still seem the most descriptive for the intended distinction.

Variations on the micro approach have been used extensively in developmental research over the past 25 years, and it is currently represented in the field of cognitive aging by research focusing on distinctions between implicit and explicit memory, between automatic and controlled processing, and virtually all research attempting to localize age-related cognitive differences, or to identify patterns of age dissociations. A key feature of the micro perspective is the emphasis on specific or discrete deficits in the sense that one or more critical processes are postulated to be impaired with increasing age, and are presumed to be responsible for most of the age-related differences observed in a particular type of cognitive task.

The principal contribution of the micro approach is that it attempts to indicate which aspect or component of task performance is most sensitive to effects associated with increasing age. Research of this type can be quite valuable if it is supplemented by three additional pieces of information: (1) evidence that each of the hypothesized processes or components is relevant to overall performance (because there would be little interest in the absence of age relations on components that are unrelated to the criterion task); (2) evidence that the measures of the various components are of comparable sensitivity and reliability (because it would not be very interesting if the weaker age relations in some measures were an artefact of low discriminating power or reliability); and (3) an interpretation is offered about how the components are different from one another (because it is important to have some ideas about why the age relations vary across the components).

If these conditions are satisfied then the micro approach can be extremely useful in more precisely indicating exactly what needs to be explained to account for the observed age-related differences in measures of cognitive functioning. However, questions can be raised as to whether this type of 'conceptual localization' is really an explanation, or is more appropriately considered a form of refined description. Clearly, when the micro approach is successful it provides more detailed information about the specific nature of the observed age differences than that which existed prior to the research, but ultimately we would like to know *why* those differences occur. This is not a simple issue because from some perspectives description can be considered equivalent to explanation at a proximal level. For example, if the age-related differences were found to be confined to one of several possible parameters in a theoretical model, then in terms of that model the differences could be considered to be 'explained' as alterations in the processes associated with the critical parameter. Nevertheless, eventually we would like to identify and understand the distal determinants of the proximal characteristics associated with low levels of functioning on cognitive tasks (i.e., what is responsible for the age-related differences observed on the critical parameters?), and in this respect the micro approach can be considered incomplete.

Another limitation of the micro perspective is that it does not provide any means of examining the impact of broader sets of influences. That is, because the focus is exclusively on one particular task, this approach makes it difficult, if not impossible, to investigate age-related influences that might be shared with other tasks. Indeed, because most researchers operating within the micro perspective have tended to study their tasks in isolation of other tasks, there seems to be an implicit assumption that the tasks are independent, at least with respect to the age-related influences acting upon them. This assumption of independence is often related to views about modularity and information-ally encapsulated processes in which components are postulated to have limited communication with one another, and to interact only when the processing within the relevant component has been completed (e.g. see Farah 1994).

In the macro approach the age-related differences in one task are examined in the context of age-related differences in other tasks. That is, while the micro approach focuses on which specific components of a particular task are respon-sible for the age differences in that task, the focus in the macro approach is on whether the age-related differences evident in the target task are independent of the age-related differences apparent on other tasks. As noted earlier, the macro perspective is important because if it were eventually discovered that only a small proportion of the age-related effects on a particular task were distinct, and independent of the age-related effects on other tasks, then task-specific influences could be inferred to have relatively minor effects on the age-related differences observed in that task. In other words, mechanisms specific to a particular task could not be responsible for many of the age-related differences in that task if almost all of the age-related effects on the task were found to be shared with the age-related effects present on other tasks.

A prominent theme of macro approaches is the role of broad or general factors presumed to affect many types of variables. These are sometimes referred to as processing resources, and although they are seldom precisely defined, concepts such as attention, working memory, and processing speed are often mentioned in this connection. Some advocates of the macro approach occa-sionally claim that general mechanisms are sufficient to account for most, or possibly even all, of the age-related differences observed in many different cognitive measures. However, it is more prudent to suggest that the relative contributions of general and specific age-related influences is an empirical question, and that results from a variety of different analytical methods are needed to provide a convincing answer to this question.

MACRO ANALYTICAL PROCEDURES

What analytical procedures could be used to investigate the macro perspective, and yield estimates of the relative contributions of both common (or shared) and unique (or specific) age-related influences? First, several methods will be considered that either are not currently practical, or are otherwise inadequate, for this purpose.

When the groups of interest represent points along a continuum, such as developmental comparisons, one possibility is to examine longitudinal changes within the same individuals. That is, a researcher could determine whether the change in variable X is related to the change in variable Y, and he or she may also be able to examine whether there is structure in the pattern of age-related changes across a collection of variables. Unfortunately, very few developmental data sets are available with moderately long intervals between observations (which may be necessary to provide an opportunity for appreciable change to have occurred), and data on a wide range of variables (which is needed to allow analyses of interrelations of the change scores). Until longitudinal studies with these characteristics are completed and the data analysed in this manner, it does not appear possible to reach strong conclusions regarding the relative contributions of general and specific age-related influences from longitudinal comparisons.

Although some authors have suggested that age-by-treatment interactions in an ANOVA model can be used to separate general and specific influences, this is not as simple as sometimes assumed. Many complications with the interpretation of interactions have been pointed out (e.g. Chapman and Chapman 1973; Loftus 1978; Salthouse 1991a; Verhaeghen, this volume), and for a variety of reasons the mere presence of a statistical interaction is not sufficient to infer the existence of a selective or specific deficit. To illustrate, one problem with this procedure is that an interaction reflects whether there is a difference in the absolute magnitude of the age-related effects across two or more variables, and not whether the age-related effects on those variables are independent of one another. That is, the age difference could be much larger on variable X than on variable Y and result in a significant age-by-variable interaction, and yet the age-related effects on variable X may not be independent of those on variable Y. In recognition of this issue, Salthouse and Coon (1994) proposed that conventional ANOVA interaction tests should be supplemented with tests of the independence of age-related effects with procedures such as hierarchical regression analysis.

A primary goal of macro analyses is to determine the extent to which the age-related differences on particular cognitive variables are unique, and independent or distinct from the age-related differences on other variables. One way to think of lack of independence in the present context is that this condition exists whenever knowledge of the magnitude of the age-related effects on some variables is informative about the magnitude of the age-related effects on other variables.

Two quite different conceptualizations of independence could be proposed. One is based on a criterion of less than perfect prediction, in the sense that there is some variance in the criterion variable that is not accounted for by a combination of all available predictor variables. For example, a variable could be considered to be independent of other variables when the squared multiple R in the prediction of that variable is less than its reliable variance. An alternative conceptualization of independence is based on a criterion of greater than zero prediction in the sense that the squared multiple R in the prediction of the variable is significantly different from zero. These two definitions are obviously endpoints along a continuum, and therefore it may be more meaningful to attempt to estimate the relative degrees of shared and unique variance instead of considering only these extreme positions. Stated somewhat differently, it will likely be more productive to attempt to evaluate the relative contribution of each type of influence rather than merely to try to demonstrate that one type (e.g. independent or specific) is necessary, or that another type (e.g. shared or general) is not sufficient.

Three analytical procedures will be described that have been used to examine age-related differences in particular cognitive variables in the context of age differences in other variables. However, it is important to preface the descriptions by noting that no single method should be considered definitive, because each analytical procedure involves a number of assumptions that have not been fully examined, and each has characteristics that limit its applicability in at least some circumstances. Nevertheless, we will see that the results from the different procedures tend to converge on the same general conclusion that large proportions of the age-related effects on many different cognitive variables are shared, and are not independent.

METHOD OF SYSTEMATIC RELATIONS

If the variables of interest are all in the same metric then the researcher can determine whether some regularity exists among the age differences in the variables. To the extent that there is regularity, then the systematic relation might be used to provide an estimate of the shared age-related effects (Salthouse 1992b). Furthermore, if a quantitative function accurately describes a substantial portion of the data, then the researcher can determine whether the age difference in the target variable deviates significantly from the overall pattern of differences between the age groups.

Many examples of systematic relations with timed variables have been reported in comparisons of adults of different ages. Most of the analyses were conducted at the level of group means, but several studies have reported analyses based on functions computed for individual participants (e.g. Charness and Campbell 1988; Salthouse 1993a). Systematic relations with variables representing accuracy or quality of performance have also been reported with variables from tasks assessing reasoning (e.g., Salthouse 1987; 1992b), memory (e.g. Verhaeghen and Marcoen 1993), mental arithmetic (Campbell and Charness 1990), and miscellaneous comparisons (e.g. Brinley 1965). As suggested above, if the empirical functions allow relatively accurate prediction of the age-related differences in performance in a particular task from information about performance in other tasks, then it seems reasonable to conclude that the measures of performance in the various tasks are not independent (see Salthouse 1993a).

Limitations

Applications of this analytical method have been controversial, and some of the following issues have been discussed in more detail in a variety of articles (e.g. Cerella 1994; Fisher and Glaser 1996; Fisk and Fisher 1994; Myerson, *et al.* 1994; Perfect 1994; Rabbitt 1996; Salthouse 1988*a*, 1992*b*, 1996*a,c*). One limitation of the method of systematic relations is that the variables must be in the same units or else the quantitative relation cannot be determined. Moreover, for the analyses to be meaningful there should also be some basis for assuming that the variables are assessing the same constructs in people of different ages, and that there are not major differences in strategies or other factors that might contribute to measurement inequivalence.

A second limitation is that the method may not be sensitive for detecting specific or independent age-related influences. This is particularly true if the specific effects are small relative to the shared or general effects (Fisk and Fisher 1994; Fisher and Glaser 1996), or if the quantitative relation is not defined very precisely because only a limited set of variables is available (in which case there would be low power to detect deviations from the function presumed to reflect shared influences).

Another problem with the method of systematic relations from the current perspective is that estimates of the relative contributions of shared and unique age-related influences are seldom reported when analyses of systematic relations are conducted. Instead most researchers have focused on all-or-none conclusions, with little attention to the issue of the extent to which each type of influence might contribute to the observed age-related differences. Madden and colleagues (e.g. Madden *et al.* 1992) proposed using the empirically determined quantitative function to adjust for global effects, but that procedure has seldom been used and consequently there have been few reports attempting to quantify the relative influence of shared (or global) and unique (or local) effects with the method of systematic relations.

Three additional issues are related to how the quantitative functions corresponding to the systematic relations should be interpreted. One issue is that a finding of significant outliers from the overall function, or of subsets of variables with different quantitative relations (Salthouse 1992*b*), may not necessarily signify the existence of independent age-related influences, but instead may simply reflect the operation of one or more additional influences beyond that involved in the other variables. As an example, one set of variables might be influenced by factor A and another set of variables might be influenced by both factor A and factor B. If this were the case then the absolute differences between groups would probably be expected to be larger for the second set of variables than for the first set because of the additional age-related influence. Moreover, one way in which the larger age-related effects might be manifested is in the form of different quantitative relations between the performance levels of adults of different ages across the two sets of variables. However, it would still be an open question whether the age-related effects on variables affected by both factors A and B were independent of the effects on variables affected by only factor A. That is, the existence of distinct functions, or of deviations from a systematic relation, can be interpreted as suggesting that more than one factor is involved in contributing to the observed levels of performance, but it does not necessarily imply that the relevant factors are independent of one another with respect to age-related influences. In fact, analyses reported in Salthouse (1996a) of data from comparisons of hierarchical versus sequential arithmetic, and data from comparisons of performance with and without a concurrent task, revealed that, although in both cases measures from the two sets of tasks led to quantitatively distinct functions, they still shared large proportions of their age-related influences with each other, and with measures of speeded performance from other types of tasks.

A second issue related to the interpretation of systematic functions concerns the role of parameters from this quantitative relation on the relations between age and other aspects of cognition. That is, if the systematic relation reflects the existence of some type of general factor, then parameters of that function should be expected to have an important mediational role on the relations between age and measures of cognitive functioning. In fact, however, evidence suggests that parameters of the systematic relation functions have only a weak mediational influence. For example, if the slope of the function relating the times of the individual on a set of variables to times on a reference group is considered an index of the general slowing factor for that individual, then statistical control of this slope parameter might be expected to result in a large attenuation of the age-related differences on other cognitive variables. In contrast to the expectation, the actual amount of attenuation has been found to be much less than that associated with a variety of other speed variables (Salthouse 1993a).

Finally, a third issue related to the interpretation of systematic relations is that without additional information the nature of the hypothesized general or common factor cannot be determined. This point was made several years ago in the following passage:

the fact that a systematic relation may exist between age differences on measures of speed of performance does not imply that the common factor is an age-related speed reduction, for the same reason that the existence of a systematic relation between age differences on measures of accuracy would not necessarily imply that the common factor is an age-related accuracy reduction.

(Salthouse 1992b, p. 334.)

In other words, a systematic relation implies that there is regularity, and presumably non-independence, of the age-related effects on the variables under consideration, but it is not by itself informative about the reasons for the systematicity or regularity.

MEDIATIONAL MODELS

The mediational approach is based on the idea that one or more factors intervene between age and measures of cognitive performance. A fundamental assumption of this approach is that chronological age is best conceptualized as a continuum along which changes occur, and not as a direct influence in and of itself. The reasoning has therefore been that if some aspects of what is changing with advancing age can be measured, it should be possible to determine whether, and if so to what extent, those aspects contribute to the observed age-related effects on the cognitive variables of interest.

The selection of mediators in this approach is based on theoretical assumptions about causal sequences between age and the target or criterion variables. Because the mediators are typically assumed to reflect basic aspects of processing, they are usually considered to be simpler or more elementary than the criterion variables they are postulated to mediate. After a candidate mediator, or set of mediators, has been identified, the plausibility of the postulated relations can be examined with a variety of statistical methods such as hierarchical regression, analysis of covariance, partial correlation, or path analyses on either observed (manifest) or hypothesized (latent) variables.

Statistical control procedures typically involve comparing the magnitude of the age-related effects before and after control of a variable postulated to be involved in the mediation of the relations of age on the target variable. If the age-related effects are substantially reduced after control of that variable, then it is typically assumed that the data are consistent with the intervening variable functioning as a mediator of the relations between age and the target variable. This approach is relevant in the current context because evidence suggesting that a variable may be functioning as a mediator also means that the age-related influences on the hypothesized mediator and criterion variables are not independent of one another. Non-independence can also be inferred from structural or path models whenever the paths or relations among variables are found to be significantly different from zero. In other words, if age is related to some variables in a structural model, then it can be concluded that the age-related effects on all other variables to which they are linked are not independent of the age-related effects on the initial variables.

Many analyses with different combinations of mediator and criterion cognitive variables have been reported, frequently with measures of attention, working memory, or processing speed assumed to function as mediators of age differences in other variables. To illustrate, numerous studies have been reported with various speed variables serving as the hypothesized mediator of the relations between age and different measures of cognitive functioning (e.g., Baltes and Lindenberger 1997; Bors and Forin 1995; Bryan and Luszcz 1996; Graf and Uttl 1995; Hertzog 1989; Hultsch et al. 1990; Lindenberger et al. 1993; Nettelbeck and Rabbitt 1992; Nettelbeck et al. 1996; Park et al. 1996; Salthouse 1991b, 1992a, 1993a, 1994a, 1995a, 1996a,c; Salthouse and Babcock

1991; Salthouse and Coon 1993; Salthouse *et al.* 1996*a*; Schaie 1989, 1990; Verhaeghen and Salthouse 1997). The typical result in these analyses is that if measures of speed are used as a mediator they often account for a large proportion of the age-related effects on variables reflecting many types of cognitive functioning. Fewer studies have been reported with other variables serving as the hypothesized mediator, but qualitatively similar results have been obtained when measures of working memory (e.g. Salthouse 1991*b*) and attention (e.g. Stankov 1988) served as the mediator.

Other variance partitioning procedures, such as commonality analysis (Baltes and Lindenberger 1997; Hertzog 1989; Lindenberger and Baltes 1994; Lindenberger *et al.* 1993; Salthouse 1993*a*, 1994*a*, 1994*c*, 1996*c*,*d*), and hierarchical regression and part correlation analysis (e.g. Horn 1982; Horn *et al.* 1981; Salthouse 1991*b*, 1993*a*, 1994*a*, 1996*a*; Stankov 1988), are also related to mediational techniques because they can be used to estimate how much of the age-related variance in the target variable is shared with various potential mediator variables. A frequent finding from these types of analyses is that 50% or more of the age-related variance in the target variable is shared with variables that might be assumed to function as mediators.

The mediational method is quite useful for examining the plausibility of different hypothesized mechanisms, although considerable caution is needed in making any causal inferences. That is, because all of the observed relations are concurrent, and because random assignment to ensure equivalence of the individuals on all dimensions except age is impossible, one cannot conclude that the inferred relations are necessarily causal in nature. Moreover, without replication and confirmation with longitudinal data it is impossible to examine the validity of the assumption that what are hypothesized to be mediators of age-related differences in cross-sectional comparisons actually function to mediate the age-related changes that might be observed if longitudinal comparisons were available. Nevertheless, various types of mediational procedures can be valuable for evaluating the plausibility of causal hypotheses because an absence of a relation involving a postulated mediator would clearly be inconsistent with hypotheses postulating that that variable contributes to the relation between age and other variables.

Limitations

One weakness of many mediational analyses is that alternative structural models with different patterns of relationships are seldom evaluated to determine whether the hypothesized model provides a better fit to the data than plausible rivals (e.g. MacCallum *et al.* 1993). Furthermore, most analyses have examined only a small number of potential 'mediators', and there is still considerable controversy about which constructs are the most meaningful as 'cognitive primitives', and the best method by which each should be operationalized. These characteristics mean that the results from the analyses should not be considered definitive, but merely consistent (or inconsistent) with the observed results.

A second limitation of mediational approaches is that information about the relative contribution of shared and distinct age-related effects on the target criterion variable is seldom reported. Quantitative estimates of direct and indirect effects related to age can be derived from structural models, but the calculations can become quite complicated when there are many paths in the model. Lindenberger and Pötter (1998) have also recently demonstrated that estimates of the unique effects derived by many multivariate analytical procedures are influenced by the relations among other variables included in the analyses. Their results do not invalidate the usefulness of mediational analyses, but they do serve to reiterate the importance of exerting caution when interpreting outcomes of mediational, and other variance partitioning, procedures.

Finally, moderately large samples are needed to provide powerful tests of the significance of residual age-related effects after control of the hypothesized mediator. Particularly if the variable representing the mediator is closely related to the target or criterion variable, control of that variable may result in a large reduction in age-related variance in the criterion variable, but when small samples are used there would be low power to detect whether the residual age-related effects differ significantly from zero. This is a potentially serious problem if a researcher were then to conclude that there are few or no specific (i.e., independent) age-related effects, because those effects merely may not have been detectable because of limited power associated with small sample sizes.

SHARED INFLUENCE ANALYSIS

The shared influences approach is based on the idea of identifying what many variables have in common, and then statistically controlling an estimate of the influence of age on that shared or common factor before examining the relations of age to particular variables. This approach is conceptually analogous to a combination of principal components analysis and hierarchical regression analysis. That is, initially the first principal component is computed from a set of variables to represent what is shared among all variables. Next that component score is entered in the first step of a hierarchical regression analysis predicting a particular target variable, with age entered as a second predictor. If there is significant variance in the target variable associated with age in the second step of the analysis, then one can conclude that there is an influence of age on the target variable independent of the influence of age on what is shared among all variables. On the other hand, if there is no residual age effect then there would be no evidence for a distinct or independent influence of age on that variable.

A more efficient and elegant analytical method to accomplish this same goal is with structural equation models (Kliegl and Mayr 1992; McArdle and Prescott 1992). The first step in this approach consists of postulating a common factor with loadings from all variables, and a relation of age to the common factor. Next, relations of age to each variable are examined to determine which of the direct relations are significantly different from zero.

Although the analyses are performed with structural equation models, global fit statistics are not directly relevant for the current purposes because they reflect the extent to which the entire covariance matrix is approximated by the model, and in this application the primary focus is on covariances involving age. In other words, because there is no attempt to account for relations among variables that are not related to age, the overall fit statistics may be only of secondary interest in this application of structural equation models. The shared influences method might therefore be best viewed as a method of partitioning age-related effects on a set of variables into shared (common) and unique (specific) portions, and not as an attempt to reproduce the entire pattern of relations among variables.

It is important to emphasize that, although this analytical method is based on the idea of a shared or common factor, it does not assume that there is a single monolithic age-related influence on all variables. Indeed, a major advantage of this particular procedure is that it allows quantitative estimates of each type of contribution, both general and specific, to be determined for every variable of interest. That is, because the common factor in this type of analysis represents what is shared among all the variables, an estimate of the shared age-related influences on the individual variables can be derived from the product of the standardized coefficients corresponding to the age–common and common–variable relations. Estimates of the unique age-related effects in these models correspond to the direct relations of age to the variable because they represent effects that are independent of the age-related effects shared with other variables.

A primary assumption underlying the shared influences analytical procedure is that there are many simultaneous effects associated with increasing age, and that it may be premature to assign causal priority to certain variables until a better understanding is achieved of the nature and scope of the age-related differences across a wide range of variables. (In fact, Baltes and Lindenberger (1997; Lindenberger and Baltes 1994) have referred to this type of model as a 'common cause' model to acknowledge that a variety of different variables might share a similar set of age-related influences.) Nevertheless, the loadings of variables on the common factor can be examined to help identify which variables might be most central to what is shared among variables. For example, variables with the highest loadings (assuming equal sensitivities and reliabilities) might be assumed to be the most fundamental with respect to what is shared, and therefore they might be the best candidates for cognitive primitives that could ultimately function as mediators.

Figure 2.2 illustrates three informative outcomes of the shared influences analytical procedure. One possible outcome (a) is that there is no common factor, and that all age-related effects on individual variables are direct. A finding that there was no evidence for a common factor would indicate that the variables, and the age-related influences on them, are largely independent, and have no shared variance. An outcome of this type would be consistent with the strongest version of the multiple specific influences perspective. That is, if the age-related effects on the variables were found to be independent of one another, the results would be consistent with an inference that discrete and specific effects are responsible for the relation of age on the variables.

It may be unrealistic to expect complete independence because it is likely that there is always at least some commonality among the variables. However even if there was some shared variance, it is possible that there could be very weak, or non-existent, relations between age and the common factor, which would suggest that the bulk of the age-related influences on individual variables were independent of one another.

A second possible outcome (b) of shared influences analyses is that all age-related effects are channelled through the common factor, with no (statistically significant) direct relations of age to any variables. A finding of this type would

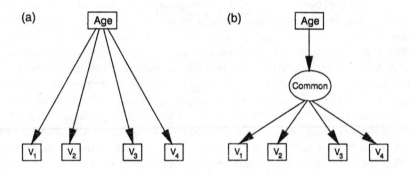

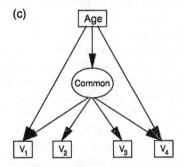

Fig. 2.2   Three possible outcomes of a single common factor analysis.

indicate that there was no evidence of unique or independent age-related effects on the variables because all of the age-related influences were shared across variables. This would not necessarily mean that there is a single cause of the age differences on all variables, but the absence of evidence of unique or specific age-related effects would suggest that there is probably a shared mechanism at some level. That is, there could be numerous determinants of the common or general factor, but if there are no independent age-related effects on the individual variables then all of the age-related influences can be presumed to be somehow funnelled through the factor representing the variance shared among all variables.

It is important to recognize that a discovery that a single common factor contributes to the age differences on all variables does not mean that the age-related effects on all variables should be uniform in magnitude. As noted earlier, it is sometimes claimed that differential magnitude of effects, as reflected in a significant age-by-variable interaction, is evidence for the existence of specific influences. However, this is not necessarily the case because interactions in the present context could arise due to differential loadings on the common factor (see Salthouse 1996a; Salthouse and Coon 1994). That is, the overall age-related effect on a variable in this type of structural model is equal to the product of the age–common and the common–variable relations, and thus variables could differ in the magnitude of the age effects if they differ in the strength of the common–variable relation even though only a single, shared, influence may be operating.[1]

A third possible outcome (c) of shared influences analyses is a pattern in which age-related effects are evident on both the common factor and on one or more individual variables. An outcome such as this would imply the existence of at least two distinct types of age-related influences; one shared with other variables, and one independent of the other variables. Even if the independent effects are

---

1 There are at least three reasons why the loadings of a variable on the common factor might differ. First, reliability or sensitivity may vary across variables. That is, if one variable has less systematic variance than another, it will tend to have weaker relations to other variables because it does not have as much variance available to be shared. Second, the loadings could vary because of variation in the nature of other influences on the variables. It is possible (and even likely) that multiple factors are operating on many variables, and to the extent that this is the case those other factors can affect the magnitude of the relations between the individual variables and what is common to all variables. And third, the loadings on the common factor could vary because they reflect the extent to which the variables are dependent on whatever is common among the variables. In fact, it is probably unrealistic to expect all variables to have equivalent relations to whatever is shared among them because some variables might be 'purer', or more direct, reflections of the shared aspects than other variables.

In addition to variations in the strength of the common-variable relations, variables could also differ with respect to presence or absence of a common-variable relation and the presence or absence of an independent (i.e., direct) relation from age. That is, if a variable is not related to what other variables have in common then it may reflect a qualitatively different type of processing, and direct age relations in addition to the relations mediated through the common factor could either enhance, or compensate for, the age-related effects on the variable. The important point to be noted from this discussion is that there are several ways in which patterns of differential age relations could easily be accommodated within the shared influences framework.

small in absolute magnitude, they could be theoretically very important because with this analytical procedure they would have been established to be distinct from the shared influence common to most other variables. Of course theoretical importance would need to be established on the basis of other considerations, but an advantage of the shared influences analytical technique is that the age-related effects on a variable can be established to be unique to that variable, and not shared with the effects on other variables.

If several variables are found with independent age-related effects the researcher can then determine whether there is structure among those variables. That is, the question can be asked whether the specific or independent age-related effects are independent of one another, as well as of the shared age-related effects channelled through the common factor. To the extent that several variables have similar types of secondary age-related influences, it might be possible to postulate second-order structure among variables with direct effects related to age. The nature of this secondary influence could then be investigated by examining the nature of the variables, or by considering the effect of various manipulations on the pattern of relations involving those variables.

Although only a relatively small number of shared influences analyses have been reported, most of them have resembled outcome (c) from Fig. 2.2 (e.g., Lindenberger and Baltes 1994; Lindenberger et al. 1993; Salthouse 1996d; 1998; Salthouse et al. 1997; Salthouse et al. 1998; Verhaeghen and Salthouse 1997). Moreover, this is even true with variables often hypothesized to reflect functioning in different neuroanatomical regions (see figure 5 in Salthouse 1996d), and when non-cognitive variables such as visual acuity are included in the analyses (Salthouse et al. 1996b; Salthouse et al. 1998).

Figure 2.3 illustrates the results of a shared influences analysis conducted on both cognitive and non-cognitive variables from a study involving 380 adults reported in Salthouse et al. (1998). Notice that all of the variables have moderately large loadings on the common factor, with the highest loadings for perceptual speed variables and for a variable representing performance on a matrix reasoning test. It is also noteworthy that the non-cognitive variables (i.e. measures of visual acuity, grip strength, and systolic and diastolic blood pressure) load on the same common factor with the cognitive variables, although two of them also have independent (direct) age-related effects. These findings are consistent with several recent reports that non-cognitive variables such as lower limb strength (e.g. Anstey et al. 1993, 1997) or measures of vision, hearing, and balance (e.g. Baltes and Lindenberger 1997; Lindenberger and Baltes 1994; Salthouse et al. 1996b), and even measures of tactile sensitivity (e.g. Li et al. 1998), share moderate amounts of age-related variance with many cognitive variables.

The discovery that a variety of non-cognitive variables have moderate to high loadings on the same common factor involved in many cognitive variables also raises questions about the meaningfulness of mediational approaches to explaining cognitive aging phenomenon. To illustrate, while visual acuity or

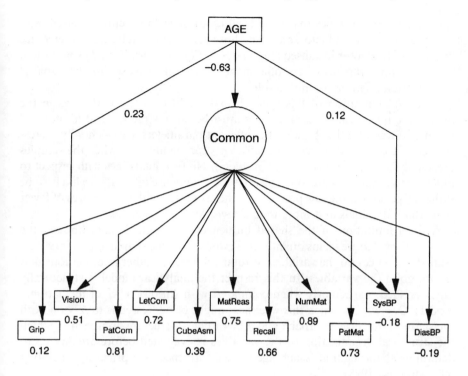

Fig. 2.3   Results of shared influences analyses in a sample of 380 adults from a study by Salthouse *et al.* (1998).

other sensory measures might be plausible as contributing to the age-related declines on higher-order cognitive tasks, it is difficult to conceive of how grip strength might be thought to mediate age-related declines on a task such as matrix reasoning. Instead, a more plausible interpretation seems to be that the common factor may represent broad aspects of central nervous system functioning, and that at least some non-cognitive variables reflect this system efficiency as well as cognitive variables (e.g. Anstey *et al.* 1997; Baltes and Lindenberger 1997; Li, *et al.* 1998; Lindenberger and Baltes 1994).

Limitations

One limitation of the shared influences analytical procedure is that estimates of shared and unique age-related influences are dependent on the particular combination of variables included in the analysis. For example, if the variables included in the analysis are all quite similar, then it may be unlikely that evidence of a unique age-related influence would be found. While this limitation is real, it does not appear insurmountable because it should eventually be possible to specify a set of variables that have been established to function as good indicators of the common factor, and then those variables could be used as reference markers of the factor in subsequent analyses. For example, in studies of normal aging certain measures of episodic memory, inductive reasoning, and spatial visualization might serve in this role.

A second limitation of this type of analytical procedure is that, as in the mediation approach, the sample sizes must be fairly large to yield meaningful results. In this case it is because the relevant parameters are essentially regression coefficients, and regression coefficients can be unstable when the samples are small (i.e. the 'bouncing beta' problem). No firm guidelines with respect to minimum sample sizes are available, but the confidence intervals are likely to be rather large, indicating low precision of the estimates, with sample sizes of fewer than 100 individuals and more than a few predictor variables.

A third limitation of the shared influences approach is that although the analytical procedure yields quantitative estimates of the shared and unique age-related influences on the variables, it totally ignores all other interrelations that exist among the variables. In this respect the analytical model is structurally impoverished, particularly when compared with various types of mediational models. One way in which this weakness might be addressed is to rely on both the shared influences approach and a hierarchical structure approach in which the structural organization of the variables is evaluated before attempting to determine the level(s) at which age-related influences are primarily operating (cf. Salthouse 1998).

SUMMARY OF RESULTS FROM MACRO ANALYSES

The macro approach focuses on evaluating the relative magnitude of shared and unique age-related influences on variables found to exhibit age-related differences. Several different macro analytical methods have been used, and all have been consistent in indicating that a relatively small proportion of the age-related effects on a given variable are independent of the age-related effects on other variables. The estimates of the amount of shared age-related variance vary according to the number and type of other variables included in the analysis, and the particular analytical method employed, but some of the estimates approach 100%, indicating that under certain circumstances there may be no age-related effects on the variables that remain to be explained by task-specific processes.

It is worth noting that the concept of independence with respect to age-related influences is not necessarily identical to the notion of functional independence inferred from lack of interference in concurrent task situations, or from selective deficits associated with focal brain damage (but see Farah 1994, for a critical discussion of the meaning of independence in the latter situation). In other words, the results of these macro analyses do not imply that distinct functional systems do not exist, or that distinct cognitive abilities cannot be identified. Rather, the empirical evidence seems to suggest that only a relatively small proportion of the age-related influences on some neuroanatomical systems or cognitive abilities are independent of the age-related influences on other systems or abilities.

There are at least two major implications of the discovery that much of the age-related variance in different cognitive variables appears to be shared. The first is that task-specific interpretations of cognitive aging phenomena may be misleading unless the contributions of broader or more general factors are also considered. As an illustration, a researcher could attempt to 'explain' age-related differences in memory in terms of deficits in specific processes such as elaborative encoding or spontaneous organization, or to 'explain' age-related differences in reasoning in terms of deficits in integration or abstraction. However, if most of the age-related influences on the target cognitive variables are shared with other cognitive variables, then these interpretations may simply be describing different manifestations of the same underlying common factor. That is, under circumstances such as these the task-specific interpretations could be viewed as merely detailed specifications of the manner in which the common factor exerts its influence in particular tasks, and not as explanations of the primary cause of the age-related differences on any of the variables. This does not mean that task-specific interpretations are meaningless or without value. However, it does imply that a broader and more encompassing perspective will be needed to take into account the age-related influences that are shared with other variables.

A second implication of the discovery that large proportions of age-related variance are shared is that at least some attempts to investigate mediational or structural models of the directional relations among variables may turn out to be unproductive. The reason is that if many variables share substantial amounts of age-related variance, then a large number of models with different hypothesized mediators (e.g. working memory, processing speed, or other cognitive primitives) might be able to provide equally good fits to the data. Moreover, if there really are many variables with similar relations to the common factor, then any one of them could presumably be selected to serve as the 'critical' mediator, and the results of the structural analyses would likely be very similar.

WHAT IS RESPONSIBLE FOR SHARED AGE-RELATED INFLUENCES?

Aging-related effects on cognition almost certainly have many different sources. Indeed, many of the analyses referred to above have revealed evidence for independent or unique age-related influences in addition to shared influences (e.g. Salthouse 1993a, 1994c, 1995b; 1998; Salthouse and Coon 1993; Salthouse et al. 1996a; Salthouse et al. 1998; Verhaeghen and Salthouse 1997). Nevertheless, there is considerable evidence that a small number of factors with wide-ranging consequences are also contributing to the observed age-related differences in measures of cognitive functioning. These shared or common factors are not responsible for all age-related differences in cognitive variables, but they do seem to be involved in a large proportion of the age-related effects on many variables. An important next question, therefore, is what is responsible for the shared or common age-related influences that appear to operate on a variety of cognitive variables?

Although no definitive answer can yet be provided, some hints are available from several different types of evidence. For example, analyses have revealed that most of the independent age-related effects occur at the earliest stages of practice, at short presentation times (perhaps as soon as the stimuli can be registered), and on the simplest versions of cognitive tasks (e.g. Salthouse 1992c, 1996b; Salthouse and Coon 1994; Salthouse et al. 1995). Findings such as these suggest that higher-order factors probably contribute relatively little to the age-related differences found on many cognitive tasks. Instead, it appears that something operating at a more basic or fundamental level is likely to be involved in the shared age-related influences.

A number of researchers have speculated that one or more critical cognitive primitives might be responsible for many of the shared age-related influences on different cognitive variables. As an example, one candidate for a critical cognitive primitive is the speed of executing many cognitive operations (Salthouse 1996c). The following evidence has been cited as support for the processing speed interpretation (see Salthouse 1996c, for additional details). First, even though different types of speed can be distinguished (e.g. Earles and Salthouse 1995; Hertzog 1989; Salthouse 1995b, 1996a,c), coherent speed constructs can be identified with measures derived from paper-and-pencil, manual reaction time, and vocal reaction time procedures. Second, measures of speed have been found to share large proportions of age-related variance with other cognitive variables (Salthouse 1994c, 1996a,c; Salthouse et al. 1996a). Third, structural models with measures of speed as the primary mediator provide good fits to the data, and the age-related variance on many cognitive variables has been found to be substantially reduced after measures of speed are statistically controlled (e.g. Salthouse 1991b, 1993a, 1994a,b). And fourth, speed variables have been found to have among the highest loadings on the common factor in shared influences analyses (e.g. Salthouse 1994c, 1996d; Salthouse et al. 1998).

Evidence such as this has led to the hypothesis that 'a major factor contributing to age-related differences in memory and other aspects of cognitive functioning is a reduction with increased age in the speed with which many cognitive operations can be executed' (Salthouse 1996c, p. 403). However, it is important to emphasize that the hypothesis was not based on a monolithic explanatory factor because it was also stated that: 'A slower speed of executing many cognitive operations is not assumed to be the exclusive source of age-related differences, because other age-related influences are also postulated to exist' (p. 404).

While it is remarkable that what appear to be very simple and brief (i.e. reliable assessments can be obtained in 30 seconds) measures have been found to share a large proportion of the age-related variance in so many different cognitive variables, there is still little consensus on what these speed variables actually represent. It is therefore useful to consider the nature of these simple tasks, and to attempt to specify exactly what might be involved in their successful performance.

Perceptual speed tasks usually involve substitution, matching, or comparison of simple elements, and performance is almost always measured in terms of quickness of performance. The tasks are typically designed to have minimal involvement of knowledge, and of other cognitive abilities. Because the tasks are so simple, such that virtually everyone performs without errors if allowed enough time, the primary way individual differences can be manifested in these tasks is in terms of time or speed. However, this does not necessarily mean that speed factors are responsible for the individual differences observed on these types of tasks (Salthouse 1993*a*; 1996*c,d*). It is thus important to distinguish the concept of processing efficiency as a description of an empirical phenomenon (i.e. reflected in the speed and accuracy of performance in very simple tasks) from a variety of possible explanatory factors that might be responsible for the observed age-related differences in processing efficiency. Stated somewhat differently, processing efficiency might be viewed as the final common pathway in the relation between age and various measures of cognitive performance, but there are a number of different routes by which processing efficiency could be altered with increasing age.

Some of the potential primitives that might function as determinants of individual differences in processing efficiency are listed in Fig. 2.4. Note that within this framework processing speed is viewed as only one of many possible factors that could contribute to individual differences in processing efficiency. Motivation refers to interest in, or effort expended on, the task because one factor that could affect performance on tasks postulated to assess perceptual speed is how seriously they are viewed by the participants. Strategy factors are also potentially important because performance could vary according to the particular method or approach to the task, such as the relative emphasis on accuracy or quality as opposed to speed. Input and output factors could also contribute to individual differences in simple processing efficiency because performance could be impaired due to low levels of sensory abilities (reducing sensitivity to environmental stimulation) or motor abilities (affecting the quickness or precision of simple overt responses).

The remaining factors included in Fig. 2.4 are more cognitive in nature. Perceptual grouping or unitization refers to the ability to integrate, or possibly segregate, stimuli such that subsequent processing is facilitated. Working memory refers to the ability to maintain information about the task requirements, such as goals, assignment of decisions to responses, etc., while also performing the relevant operations without time-consuming pauses to re-orient

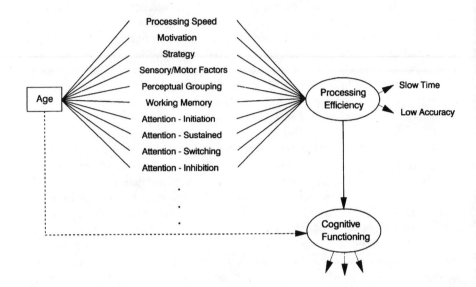

Fig. 2.4 Illustration of the mediational framework in which alternative cognitive primitives are postulated to function as mediators of the age-related influences on processing efficiency and cognitive functioning.

oneself and reinstate the task goal or the appropriate response assignment rule. Several aspects of attention could also function as cognitive primitives. For example, initiation may correspond to the ability to allocate or focus attention on relevant aspects of the task, sustainment to the ability to maintain attention on important aspects of the task as it is repeatedly performed, switching to the ability to withdraw or redirect attention across different task components (such as input and output, or between one item and the next), and inhibition to the ability to avoid distraction from irrelevant aspects of the task, or from characteristics external to the task.

The factors listed in Fig. 2.4 are unlikely to be exhaustive and are almost certainly not mutually exclusive, but reasonable arguments could probably be generated for how each of them might function as a cognitive primitive underlying individual differences in more complex cognitive tasks. A meaningful next question, therefore, is how can we determine which of these (or other) alternatives is the most fundamental with respect to age-related influences on cognition?

One approach to answering this question involves examining the relations among age, measures of cognitive performance, and the theoretical constructs of interest. The rationale is that the construct with the greatest involvement in mediating age-related influences on cognition should be the one with the strongest relations to both age and cognition (see Salthouse 1996c; Salthouse *et al.* 1994). Figure 2.5 illustrates this argument, where Construct 1 is postulated to be more important in mediating the age–cognition relations than Construct 2. The direct path from age to cognition (B) in this diagram is represented as a weak relation to signify that many of the age-related influences on cognition are mediated through Constructs 1 and 2. Note that there are strong indirect age-related effects on Construct 2 mediated through Construct 1 (via paths A and D), in addition to the possibility of smaller direct effects (via path C). In addition, Construct 1 has a stronger relation to cognition (via path E) than does Construct 2 (via path F). By examining these patterns when the two variables under consideration alternate in the role of Construct 1 and Construct 2 it should be possible to determine which variable contributes more to the age-related effects on measures of cognitive functioning. That is, the variable with the strongest contribution to the overall age effects will be associated with a greater reduction of the direct relation from age to the other variable when it functions in the role of mediator (e.g., Construct 1 might be inferred to be more fundamental than Construct 2 if statistical control of Construct 1 reduces the age-related variance by 90% but statistical control of Construct 2 reduces the age-related variance of Construct 1 by only 20%).

However, it is important to note that the purpose of this analytical procedure is not necessarily to determine which construct is the most elementary or fundamental in the sense that it may be a component of the other construct. Indeed, circumstances could easily be imagined in which Construct 1 might be a component of Construct 2 and hence be considered more elementary, but if Construct 2 had strong independent relations from age and to measures of cognition it would inferred to be more important as a mediator of the age–cognition relations.

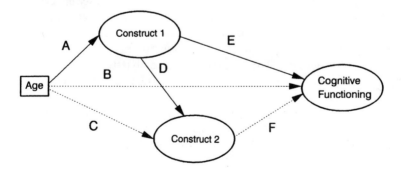

Fig. 2.5   Hypothesized relations among age, measures of cognitive functioning, and two possible mediators of the age-cognition relations.

There are several prerequisites for analyses of this type. For example, it is essential that the constructs be assessed reliably, and ideally with multiple measures to minimize the influence of specific methods or materials. Moderately large samples are also needed to provide narrow confidence intervals around the estimates of the relations. Some data meeting these criteria have been reported in comparisons of perceptual speed with a variety of other candidate cognitive primitives. For example, statistical control of measures of perceptual speed has been found to substantially reduce the age-related variance in working memory as assessed with computation span, reading span, and other tasks requiring simultaneous processing and storage (Salthouse 1991b, 1992a, 1995a; Salthouse and Babcock 1991; Salthouse and Coon 1994; Salthouse and Kersten 1993; Salthouse and Meinz 1995; Salthouse et al. 1996). Similar patterns of attenuation have been found with constructs of inhibition, as estimated from Stroop interference measures (Salthouse and Meinz 1995), and divided attention ability, as estimated from measures of dual task performance (Salthouse et al. 1995). Furthermore, in most of these analyses the measures of perceptual speed have been reported to have larger independent effects on various measures of cognitive functioning than have the measures of alternative cognitive primitives.

The analytical procedure can also be applied when relevant data are reported in the form of a correlation matrix. To illustrate, Noll and Horn (1998) recently suggested that many of the age-related differences in certain cognitive variables might be mediated by declines in concentration ability. They further proposed that one possible measure of concentration ability might be obtained from the time taken to trace a line as slowly as possible because slowness in these circumstances can be considered a reflection of concentration. This measure, along with a measure of perceptual speed based on a letter comparison task and a measure of reasoning based on a letter series task, were obtained from a sample of 577 adults between 22 and 92 years of age. Because a complete correlation matrix was reported (table 13.1B in Noll and Horn 1998), it is possible to compare the mediational effectiveness of the concentration and perceptual speed constructs in accounting for the relations between age and letter series performance according to the procedures described above. (Ideally this type of analysis would be based on constructs defined with multiple variables and either the raw data or a covariance matrix instead of a correlation matrix, but the results are nevertheless informative.) The analyses revealed that the two variables were largely independent of one another (i.e., the coefficients for path D in Fig. 2.4 were 0.08 when the speed variable served as construct 1 and 0.06 when the concentration variable served as construct 1), and the two variables had similar relations to age (i.e., -0.63 and -0.65 for the speed variable and -0.45 and -0.50 for the concentration variable in the two analyses) and to the letter series variable (i.e. 0.21 for concentration and 0.27 for speed). This pattern suggests that the variables did not function as mediators of one another but instead were nearly independent with respect to their mediation of age-related influences on letter series performance. However, it is interesting that the three variables (i.e., speed, concentration, and letter series) all had strong relations to a common factor with no direct relations from age in a shared influences analysis, implying that they might all be reflections of a common age-related determinant.

Although the results just summarized are interesting, there are a number of reasons why they should merely be considered suggestive rather than conclusive. First, only a limited number of alternative constructs have been examined, and it is possible that those that have been examined were not operationalized in the most effective manner. Second, interpretations of these types of results can become quite complicated when, as was frequently the case, the variables differ in their reliability, or in the magnitude of their relations with age. Finally, in order to have convincing evidence of causal priority longitudinal data are needed to determine the exact sequence in which the changes in variables occur.

AN ALTERNATIVE PERSPECTIVE

In this final section the question is raised as to whether processing efficiency is best conceptualized as a consequence, or as a cause, of age-related differences in one or more cognitive primitives. That is, in contrast to the view represented by Fig. 2.4, it is conceivable that various age-related biological changes directly affect the time and accuracy in simple behavioural tasks (i.e., processing efficiency), and that age-related differences in what have been considered cognitive primitives are actually symptoms or manifestations of more basic alterations in processing efficiency (see Fig. 2.6). According to this perspective, the slower and less accurate performance associated with increasing age in a variety of simple cognitive tasks is the most fundamental or direct consequence of age-related biological changes, and the interpretation of these effects in terms of cognitive primitives depends on which particular aspects of elementary performance are emphasized. Factors such as a slower processing speed, impaired working memory, deficiencies in various types of attention, variations in the efficiency of specific cognitive operations, and differences in strategy effectiveness or even in level of motivation, could be postulated, but in virtually every case the inferences about age-related differences in the cognitive primitive are based on age-related differences in measures of either time or accuracy in elementary tasks (i.e., processing efficiency).

A variety of biological changes could lead to age differences in the time and/or accuracy of very simple aspects of behaviour. For example, reductions in processing efficiency could result from decreases in the number of functional neurons, in the extent of dendritic branching or myelin sheathing for the surviving neurons, in the quantity of particular types of neurotransmitters, etc. However, the key distinction between the perspectives portrayed in Figs 2.4 and 2.6 is not whether variations in processing efficiency can eventually be related to differences at the neuroanatomical level, because neither position would deny that there is a relation between brain and behaviour. Instead, the perspectives appear to differ primarily in terms of whether the age-related

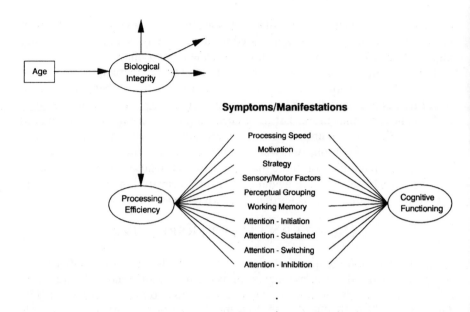

Fig. 2.6   Possible framework for interpreting age-cognition relations in which processing efficiency is a cause rather than a consequence of age-related differences in other variables.

neuroanatomical changes are discrete and specific, and thus might selectively affect some cognitive primitives more than others, or are diffuse and distributed, and are thus likely to affect the efficiency of many types of processing.

Although there is some evidence that age-related effects are greater in some regions of the brain than in others (e.g. Kemper 1994), it is still too early to reach strong conclusions about whether age-related impairments in processing efficiency (i.e., the immediate behavioural consequences of the brain changes) are discrete or diffuse. Nevertheless, it is worth noting that the perspective represented in Fig. 2.6 appears better able than the alternative represented in Fig. 2.4 to account for the finding that large proportions of the age-related effects in a variety of cognitive variables are shared with the age-related effects in non-cognitive variables such as sensory acuity, grip strength, and blood pressure (cf. Fig. 2.3). Moreover, the framework portrayed in Fig. 2.6 may help explain the success of shared influences models if the common factor corresponds to a construct such as processing efficiency or biological integrity.

SUMMARY

Although progress has clearly been made in accounting for age-related effects in cognition, we are still quite far from a complete explanation. A major focus in this chapter has been an attempt to identify some of the steps that have led to particular classes of explanation of cognitive aging phenomena. At this point it is useful to consider steps that seem likely to lead to further progress in explaining adult age differences in cognitive functioning.

One desirable goal for future research is the development of new and more powerful methods to investigate macro approaches to explaining cognitive aging phenomena, and to quantify the degree of independence of different types of age-related influences. A few methods are currently available, but each has limitations, and it is always preferable to have converging evidence for major conclusions.

A second goal is to consider and investigate alternative types of cognitive primitives that might account for the shared age-related influences that seem to exist. The key to accomplishing this goal may be in devising useful operationalizations of the various constructs, and then investigating both the convergent and discriminant validity of those constructs. As it currently stands, there are many speculations about how age-related cognitive differences might emerge, but very few of the proposals have been specified in sufficient detail to allow them to be empirically evaluated.

Finally, future research should consider and evaluate models in which the various cognitive constructs are postulated to be consequences of more fundamental age-related changes. This will probably require that the set of variables examined in a given study be broadened to include various non-cognitive variables, but only by incorporating them into the analyses will it be possible to examine the degree to which they share age-related variance with the cognitive variables of primary interest.

REFERENCES

Anderson, J. E. (1956). The assessment of aging: background in theory and experiment. In J. E. Anderson (ed.), *Psychological aspects of aging* (pp. 75–80). Washington: American Psychological Association.

Anstey, K. J., Lord, S. R., and Williams, P. (1997). Strength in the lower limbs, visual contrast sensitivity, and simple reaction time predict cognition in older women. *Psychology and Aging*, **12**, 137–44.

Anstey, K. J., Stankov, L., and Lord, S. R. (1993). Primary aging, secondary aging and intelligence. *Psychology and Aging*, **8**, 562–70.

Baltes, P. B. and Lindenberger, U. (1997). Emergence of a powerful connection between sensory and cognitive functions across the adult life span: a new window to the study of cognitive aging? *Psychology and Aging*, **12**, 12–21.

Bors, D. A. and Forrin, B. (1995). Age, speed of information processing, recall, and fluid intelligence. *Intelligence*, **20**, 229–48.

Brinley, J. F. (1965). Cognitive sets, speed and accuracy of performance in the elderly. In A. T. Welford and J. E. Birren (ed.), *Behavior, aging and the nervous system* (pp. 114–49). Springfield, IL: Thomas.

Bryan, J. and Luszcz, M. A. (1996). Speed of information processing as a mediator between age and free recall performance. *Psychology and Aging*, **11**, 3–9.

Campbell, J. I. D. and Charness, N. (1990). Age-related declines in working memory skills: evidence from a complex calculation task. *Developmental Psychology*, **26**, 879–88.

Cerella, J. (1994). Generalized slowing in Brinley plots. *Journal of Gerontology: Psychological Sciences*, **49**, P65–71.

Chapman, L. J. and Chapman, J. P. (1973). Problems in the measurement of cognitive deficit. *Psychological Bulletin*, **79**, 380–5.

Charness, N. and Campbell, J. I .D. (1988). Acquiring skill at mental calculation in adulthood: a task decomposition. *Journal of Experimental Psychology: General*, **117**, 115–29.

Earles, J. L. and Salthouse, T. A. (1995). Interrelations of age, health, and speed. *Journal of Gerontology: Psychological Sciences*, **50B**, P33–41.

Farah, M. J. (1994). Neuropsychological inference with an interactive brain: a critique of the 'locality' assumption. *Behavioral and Brain Sciences*, **17**, 43–104.

Fisk, A. D. and Fisher, D.L. (1994). Brinley plots and theories of aging: the explicit, muddled, and implicit debates. *Journal of Gerontology: Psychological Sciences*, **49**, P81–9.

Fisher, D. L. and Glaser, R. A. (1996). Molar and latent models of cognitive slowing: implications for aging, dementia, depression, development, and intelligence. *Psychonomic Bulletin and Review*, **3**, 458–80.

Graf, P. and Uttl, B. (1995). Component processes of memory: changes across the adult lifespan. *Swiss Journal of Psychology*, **54**, 113–38.

Hertzog, C. (1989). Influences of cognitive slowing on age differences in intelligence. *Developmental Psychology*, **25**, 636–51. .

Horn, J. L. (1982). The theory of fluid and crystallized intelligence in relation to concepts of cognitive psychology and aging in adulthood. In F. I. M. Craik and S. Trehub (ed.), *Aging and cognitive processes* (pp. 237–78). New York: Plenum.

Horn, J. L., Donaldson, G., and Engstrom, R. (1981). Apprehension, memory and fluid intelligence decline in adulthood. *Research on Aging*, **3**, 33–84.

Hultsch, D. F., Hertzog, C., and Dixon, R. A. (1990). Ability correlates of memory performance in adulthood and aging. *Psychology and Aging*, **5**, 356–68.

Hunt, E. (1985). The correlates of intelligence. In D. K. Detterman (ed.), *Current topics in human intelligence*, (Vol. 1 pp. 157–78). Norwood, NJ: Ablex.

Kail, R. and Salthouse, T. A. (1994). Processing speed as a mental capacity. *Acta Psychologica*, **86**, 199–225.

Kemper, T. L. (1994). Neuroanatomical and neuropathological changes during aging and dementia. In M. L. Albert and J. E. Knoefel (ed.), *Clinical neurology of aging* (2nd ed.), (pp. 3–67). New York: Oxford University Press.

Kliegl, R. and Mayr, U. (1992). Commentary on Salthouse (1992) 'Shifting levels of analysis in the investigation of cognitive aging'. *Human Development*, **35**, 343–9.

Li, S-C., Jordanova, M., and Lindenberger, U. (1998). From good senses to good sense: a link between tactile information processing and intelligence. *Intelligence*, **26**, 99–122.

Lindenberger, U. and Baltes, P. B. (1994). Sensory functioning and intelligence in old age: A strong connection. *Psychology and Aging*, **9**, 339–55.

Lindenberger, U. and Baltes, P. B. (1997). Intellectual functioning in old and very old age: Cross-sectional results from the Berlin Aging Study. *Psychology and Aging*, **12**, 410–32.

Lindenberger, U. and Pötter, U. (1998). The complex nature of unique and shared effects in hierarchical linear regression: implications for developmental psychology. *Psychological Methods*, **3**, 218–30.

Lindenberger, U., Mayr, U., and Kliegl, R. (1993). Speed and intelligence in old age. *Psychology and Aging*, **8**, 207–20.

Loftus, G. R. (1978). On the interpretation of interactions. *Memory and Cognition*, **6**, 312–19.

McArdle, J. J. and Prescott, C. A. (1992). Age-based construct validation using structural equation modeling. *Experimental Aging Research*, **18**, 87–115.

MacCallum, R. C., Wegenere, D. T., Uchino, B.N., and Fabrigar, L. R. (1993). The problem of equivalent models in applications of covariance structure analysis. *Psychological Bulletin*, **114**, 185–99.

Madden, D. J., Pierce, T. W., and Allen, P. A. (1992). Adult age differences in attentional allocation during memory search. *Psychology and Aging*, **7**, 594–601.

Myerson, J., Wagstaff, D., and Hale, S. (1994). Brinley plots, explained variance, and the analysis of age differences in response latencies. *Journal of Gerontology: Psychological Sciences*, **49**, P72–80.

Nettelbeck, T. and Rabbitt, P. M. A. (1992). Aging, cognitive performance, and mental speed. *Intelligence*, **16**, 189–205.

Nettelbeck, T., Rabbitt, P., Wilson, C., and Batt, R. (1996). Uncoupling learning from initial recall: the relationship between speed and memory deficits in old age. *British Journal of Psychology*, **87**, 593–607.

Noll, J. G. and Horn, J. (1998). Age differences in processes of fluid and crystallized intelligence. In J. J. McArdle and R. W. Woodcock (ed.), *Human Cognitive Abilities in Theory and Practice* (pp. 263–81). Mahwah, NJ: Lawrence Erlbaum Associates.

Park, D. C., Smith, A. D., Lautenschlarger, G., Earles, J. L., Frieske, D., Zwahr, M., and Gaines, C. L. (1996). Mediators of long-term memory performance across the life span. *Psychology and Aging*, **11**, 621–37.

Perfect, T. J. (1994). What can Brinley plots tell us about cognitive aging? *Journal of Gerontology: Psychological Sciences*, **49**, P60–4.

Rabbitt, P. (1996). Do individual differences in speed reflect 'global' or 'local' differences in mental abilities? *Intelligence*, **22**, 69–88.

Salthouse, T. A. (1982). *Adult Cognition: an experimental psychology of human aging*. New York: Springer-Verlag.

Salthouse, T. A. (1985a). Speed of behavior and its implications for cognition. In J. E. Birren and K.W. Schaie (ed.), *Handbook of the psychology of aging* (2nd Edn) (pp. 400–26). New York: Reinhold.

Salthouse, T. A. (1985b). *A theory of cognitive aging*. Amsterdam: North-Holland.

Salthouse, T. A. (1987). The role of representations in analogical reasoning. *Psychology and Aging*, **2**, 357–62.

Salthouse, T. A. (1988a). The complexity of age × complexity functions: Comment on Charness and Campbell. *Journal of Experimental Psychology: General*, **117**, 425–8.

Salthouse, T. A. (1988b). Initializing the formalization of theories of cognitive aging. *Psychology and Aging*, **3**, 3–16.

Salthouse, T. A. (1991a). *Theoretical perspectives on cognitive aging*. Hillsdale, NJ: Lawrence Erlbaum Associates.

Salthouse, T. A. (1991b). Mediation of adult age differences in cognition by reductions in working memory and speed of processing. *Psychological Science*, **2**, 179–83.

Salthouse, T. A. (1992a). Influence of processing speed on adult age differences in working memory. *Acta Psychologica*, **79**, 155–70.

Salthouse, T. A. (1992b). Shifting levels of analysis in the investigation of cognitive aging. *Human Development*, **35**, 321–42.

Salthouse, T. A. (1992c). Why do adult age differences increase with task complexity? *Developmental Psychology*, **28**, 905–18.

Salthouse, T. A. (1993a). Speed mediation of adult age differences in cognition. *Developmental Psychology*, **29**, 722–38.

Salthouse, T. A. (1993b). Attentional blocks are not responsible for age-related slowing. *Journal of Gerontology: Psychological Sciences*, **48**, P263–70.

Salthouse, T. A. (1994a). The nature of the influence of speed on adult age differences in cognition. *Developmental Psychology*, **30**, 240–59.

Salthouse, T. A. (1994b). Aging associations: influence of speed on adult age differences in associative learning. *Journal of Experimental Psychology: Learning, Memory and Cognition*, **20**, 1486–503.

Salthouse, T. A. (1994c). How many causes are there of aging-related decrements in cognitive functioning? *Developmental Review*, **14**, 413–37.

Salthouse, T. A. (1995a). Influence of processing speed on adult age differences in learning. *Swiss Journal of Psychology*, **54**, 102–12.

Salthouse, T. A. (1995b). Differential age-related influences on memory for verbal-symbolic information and visual-spatial information. *Journal of Gerontology: Psychological Sciences*, **50B**, P193–201.

Salthouse, T. A. (1996a). General and specific speed mediation of adult age differences in memory. *Journal of Gerontology: Psychological Sciences*, **51B**, P30–42.

Salthouse, T. A. (1996b). Where in an ordered sequence do independent age-related effects occur? *Journal of Gerontology: Psychological Sciences*, **51B**, P166–78.

Salthouse, T. A. (1996c). The processing-speed theory of adult age differences in cognition. *Psychological Review*, **103**, 403–28.

Salthouse, T. A. (1996d). Constraints on theories of cognitive aging. *Psychonomic Bulletin & Review*, **3**, 287–99.

Salthouse, T. A. (1998). Independence of age-related influences on cognitive abilities across the life span. *Developmental Psychology*, **34**, 851–64.

Salthouse, T. A. and Babcock, R. L. (1991). Decomposing adult age differences in working memory. *Developmental Psychology*, **27**, 763–76.

Salthouse, T. A. and Coon, V. E. (1993). Influence of task-specific processing speed on age differences in memory. *Journal of Gerontology: Psychological Sciences*, **48**, P245–55.

Salthouse, T. A. and Coon, V. E. (1994). Interpretation of differential deficits: The case of aging and mental arithmetic. *Journal of Experimental Psychology: Learning, Memory, and Cognition*, **20**, 1172–82.

Salthouse, T. A. and Kersten, A. W. (1993). Decomposing adult age differences in symbol arithmetic. *Memory & Cognition*, **21**, 699–710.

Salthouse, T. A. and Meinz, E. J. (1995). Aging, inhibition, working memory, and speed. *Journal of Gerontology: Psychological Sciences*, **50B**, P297–306.

Salthouse, T. A. and Mitchell, D. R. D. (1990). Effects of age and naturally occurring experience on spatial visualization performance. *Developmental Psychology*, **26**, 845–54.

Salthouse, T. A., Letz, R., and Hooisma, J. (1994). Causes and consequences of age-related slowing in speeded substitution performance. *Developmental Neuropsychology*, **10**, 203–14.

Salthouse, T. A., Fristoe, N. M., Lineweaver, T. T., and Coon, V. E. (1995). Aging of attention: Does the ability to divide decline? *Memory & Cognition*, **23**, 59–71.

Salthouse, T. A., Fristoe, N., and Rhee, S. H. (1996*a*). How localized are age-related effects on neuropsychological measures? *Neuropsychology*, **10**, 272–85.

Salthouse, T. A., Hancock, H. E., Meinz, E. J., and Hambrick, D. Z. (1996*b*). Inter-relations of age, visual acuity, and cognitive functioning. *Journal of Gerontology: Psychological Sciences*, **51B**, P317–30.

Salthouse, T. A., Toth, J. P., Hancock, H. E., and Woodard, J. L. (1997). Controlled and automatic forms of memory and attention: process purity and the uniqueness of age-related influences. *Journal of Gerontology: Psychological Sciences*, **52B**, P216–28.

Salthouse, T. A., Hambrick, D. Z., and McGuthry, K. (1998). Shared age-related influences on cognitive and noncognitive variables. *Psychology and Aging*, **13**, 486–500.

Schaie, K. W. (1989). Perceptual speed in adulthood: Cross-sectional and longitudinal analyses. *Psychology and Aging*, **4**, 443–53.

Schaie, K. W. (1990). Correction to Schaie (1989). *Psychology and Aging*, **5**, 171.

Schaie, K. W. and Willis, S. L. (1993). Age difference patterns of psychometric intelligence in adulthood: generalizability within and across ability domains. *Psychology and Aging*, **8**, 371–83.

Stankov, L. (1988). Aging, attention, and intelligence. *Psychology and Aging*, **3**, 59–74.

Sternberg, R. J. (1985). Componential analysis: A recipe. In D. K. Detterman (ed.), *Current topics in human intelligence* (Vol. 1. pp. 179–201). Norwood, NJ: Ablex.

Verhaeghen, P. and Marcoen, A. (1993). More or less the same? A memorability analysis on episodic memory tasks in young and older adults. *Journal of Gerontology: Psychological Sciences*, **48**, P172–8.

Verhaeghen, P. and Salthouse, T. A. (1997). Meta-analyses of age-cognition relations in adulthood: Estimates of linear and non-linear age effects and structural models. *Psychological Bulletin*, **122**, 231–49.

THREE

The parallels in beauty's brow: time–accuracy functions and their implications for cognitive aging theories

PAUL VERHAEGHEN

Nativity, once in the main of light,
Crawls to maturity, wherewith being crowned,
Crooked eclipses 'gainst his glory fight,
And Time, that gave, doth now his gift confound.
Time doth transfix the flourish set on youth,
And delves the parallels in beauty's brow.

William Shakespeare, 'Sonnet LX'

Cognitive aging is not a field lacking in theoretical efforts. On the contrary, we may be suffering from too many theories. In his 1992 review of the field, Salthouse concluded, in what perhaps was a slight overstatement, that 'there appear to be nearly as many explanations or interpretations of [age-related] deficits as there are published articles' (p. 323). Most of these theories operate on a micro-level, that is, they pertain to only a small range of phenomena. It seems that what we need is not more theories, but a more integrated theory, that is, a set of propositions that explains more than a narrow collection of data through a limited set of mechanisms. Some such grand theories of aging have been proposed in the past (e.g. Cerella *et al.* 1980; Hasher and Zacks 1988; Myerson *et al.* 1990; Salthouse 1996), but these remain largely controversial (see, for instance, recent controversies in the Journals of Gerontology regarding generalized-slowing theories of aging; Cerella 1994; Fisk and Fisher 1994; Myerson *et al.* 1994; Perfect 1994; or regarding the inhibition account of aging; Burke 1997; McDowd 1997; Zacks and Hasher 1997).

In this chapter, I will not provide yet another well worked-out, global scheme, a grand unified theory of cognitive aging. Rather, I will take a step back by pointing at some obstructions to the generation of such a theory (first section: Cognitive aging as a not-so-integrative enterprise), namely, the problems of issue isolationism, lack of a common metric across different types of research, and the peculiarities of the psychometrics of between-group comparisons. I will argue that a solution to the latter two problems might be found in adopting techniques that measure the dynamics of processing by examining time–accuracy functions. The time–accuracy methodology will be outlined in the second section (Time–accuracy functions in an age-comparative perspective). Then, I will demonstrate that time–accuracy functions provide a common metric across tasks, and I will show that results obtained with the technique highlight some of the problems associated with between-group comparisons, and offer some suggestions to remediate those problems (third section: State traces). In a final section, I will argue that time–accuracy research can indeed be beneficial to the enterprise of constructing integrative theories of aging, and may thus be helpful in the development of potentially exciting Middle Way theories about aging. Along the way, I will provide many illustrations of applications of the techniques advocated, drawn from diverse fields within cognitive aging.

COGNITIVE AGING AS A NOT-SO-INTEGRATIVE ENTERPRISE

In his 60th sonnet, as in a number of others, Shakespeare seems mostly preoccupied with the outwardly visible signs of aging. Indeed, developing and growing older has a powerful impact on the way a person looks in the sense that one of the first things one seems to notice about a person (besides gender) is approximate age. I never have trouble spotting my older volunteers in the lobby of the psychology building that is usually teeming with undergraduate life. Physical aging is a powerful characteristic that our visual system just picks up – the 'parallels on beauty's brow' that Shakespeare finds so cruel being just one of its many tell-tale signs.

This sheer visibility of the aging process may be part of the reason why so many theoreticians in the field of cognitive aging opt to present their results in ways that catch the eye. The technique of Brinley plotting (Salthouse 1978) is one such eye-catcher. In a Brinley plot (named after the researcher who was presumably the first to use this method; Brinley 1965), data of older adults are presented as a function of data of young adults. Many varieties exist: one can plot mean latencies (e.g. Cerella *et al.* 1980) or mean accuracies (e.g. Verhaeghen and Marcoen 1993*a*) of a number of studies, or mean latencies of a number of tasks or conditions with the same group of participants (e.g. Hale and Myerson 1996). The resulting graphs and accompanying statistics usually show not only that older adults are slower or less accurate than young adults, but also that performance of the two age groups is highly correlated. This means that within broad classes of tasks one can predict performance of a group of older subjects quite well simply from knowing the performance of a group of young subjects. This strongly suggests that processing differences between young and older adults are quantitative rather than qualitative in nature. The suggestion is that the nature of processing (the type of processes involved and their sequencing) is well preserved with age, but that there are general efficiency problems. Shakespeare's image of 'parallels in beauty's brow' can thus be taken at a more metaphorical level, as denoting parallelism in cognitive processes between young and older adults.

Of course, as pointed out by Cerella (1990, p. 215), this parallelism 'probably cannot be tested rigorously', which is the reason why this researcher labels it an axiom (the 'correspondence axiom', p. 215), rather than a hypothesis – some element of belief is involved. Consequently, the conclusion of parallelism is not the conclusion that everyone derives from the literature (e.g. Smith 1996). Also, the technique of Brinley plotting itself has recently come under close scrutiny (e.g. Fisk and Fisher 1994; Perfect 1994). Nevertheless, the model of a generalized, quantitative decline in performance with advancing age seems to provide a good null-hypothesis (Cerella 1991; Myerson and Hale 1993). One challenge cognitive aging researchers could set for themselves is to prove Cerella and the Bard wrong and denounce the parallelism axiom as an oversimplification. One then has to show evidence for non-parallelism, that is, either demonstrate the existence of qualitative differences between performances of young and older adults or demonstrate the existence of different kinds or levels of parallelism, that is, show that performance of young and older adults is different in nature or that age differences are meaningfully larger on some subset of tasks than on others.

One particular type of research aimed at proving the parallelism assumption wrong can be labeled interactionism, after the favoured method of analysis for this endeavour. Interactionist studies are designed to locate age differences in specific well-circumscribed processes. The minimal design of an interactionist study is this: a group of young adults and a group of older adults are confronted with some baseline task and with a manipulated version of that task. If an interaction is found between age and condition, meaning that age differences are not identical across the two conditions, this interaction is interpreted as evidence for the age-sensitivity of particular postulated processes that make the difference between the two conditions. For instance, assume one presents young and older adults with a list of words and asks them in a baseline condition to count the number of letters in each word (a 'shallow' condition), and in a critical condition to generate an associate for each word (a 'deep' condition). After some time the research participants are asked to recall as many words from the list as they can rememember. Typically, one will observe that participants recall more words in the deep condition (this is the well-known levels-of-processing effect, Craik and Lockhart 1972). When it is found that the age difference is smaller in the shallow condition, one infers that older adults have a particular deficit in the types of processes involved in deep processing of information. Further theoretical meaning might then be attached to that inference. For instance, if one supposes that such processes require more attentional resources, then the conclusion would be that older adults have less of these resources available. When the age difference is smaller in the deep condition, one might infer, for instance, that older adults suffer from a production deficit, that is, that they are capable of encoding material in an effective way if guided towards that way of encoding, but do not spontaneously engage in effective operations. Finding no age by condition interaction could be taken as evidence for a general age-related deficit across conditions.

In theory, an interactionist approach should lead to clear-cut conclusions about the age-relatedness of particular processes – and in many research articles one can indeed find at least one locus of age differences pinned down with confidence. However, faced with the task of having to integrate results across several studies, certainty stops. Reviewers arrive at quite different conclusions from what is largely the same corpus of data. For instance, Verhaeghen *et al.* (1993, p. 167) concluded from their meta-analysis on age differences in episodic memory performance that 'rather than factors that covary with tasks..., a general factor may be responsible for a large part of adult age differences in memory proficiency'. Smith (1996, p. 237), on the other hand, concludes that in many memory studies with seemingly conflicting results 'the two-way interaction between age and conditions assumed to vary along some memory dimension was simply modified by another condition or variable that produced a triple interaction'. Salthouse (1991, p. 248), discussing evidence about the levels-of-processing effect and aging, opts for a prudent way out: 'It is obviously difficult to draw conclusions ... in the face of these conflicting results'.

What, then, is the problem when painting the broader picture? In my opinion, at least three circumstances seem to work against constructing solid theoretical integration of research findings in the field. First, as cognitive aging researchers, we have been quite industrious indeed. The literature is growing rapidly (Hultsch and Dixon 1990, estimated that between 1985 and 1990 about 80 articles were published yearly on the topic of aging in learning and memory alone), and it now seems as if every effect ever found in the general cognitive literature has been replicated at least once in an age-comparative design. The inherent danger is what Salthouse (1985) calls issue isolationism, and what MacKay (1988, p. 562) refers to as empirical epistemology: 'Even the best psychologists sometimes seem to assume not just that experiments can proceed in the absence of theory but that potential experiments are finite in number and that our job as psychologists is to do them all.' Unfortunately, while cognitive aging researchers are working hard, they seem hardly concerned to tie in their results with those of other researchers (see also the Salthouse 1992, quotation in the introduction to this chapter). We each carefully plant our trees, but we hardly care for the forest.

A second problem is that there is a large gap dividing dependent measures in different domains. For instance, recall from episodic memory and reasoning ability are typically measured as number-of-items-correct, whereas lexical processes or mental arithmetic (almost error-free tasks) are typically measured as latencies. Consequently, there is no common metric to express age differences across these different domains. Meta-analyses have been conducted on age differences or differential age differences within measurement domains (e.g. Cerella 1990, and Cerella *et al.* 1980, on reaction times; Laver and Burke 1993, and LaVoie and Light 1994, on priming; Lima *et al.* 1991, on lexical processing; Spencer and Raz 1995, on context memory; Verhaeghen and De Meersman 1998*b*, on the Stroop effect; Verhaeghen and De Meersman 1998*a*, on negative priming; Verhaeghen *et al.* 1993, on episodic memory; Zelinski and Gilewski 1988 on prose memory), but, to my knowledge, meta-analytic integration has not been attempted across the accuracy and time domains. Indeed, one might question the validity of such an approach. For instance, Verhaeghen and De Meersman (1998*a*) found that the age difference in naming the colour of colour patches, as expressed in a mean standardized difference, is about 2; Verhaeghen *et al.* (1993) found that the mean standardized difference in episodic memory functioning is about 1. Does this imply that the age difference in colour naming (which might largely reflect a semantic retrieval process) is really twice as large as the age difference in memory functioning – or is it simply not a good idea to compare data from latencies with data from episodic memory on this type of metric?

Third, there are problems associated with the psychometrics of group-comparison research, and cognitive aging researchers are only beginning to address some of the more pressing ones. For one, in all our industriousness, we often seem less concerned with issues such as sampling differences, sample size and even reliability and validity of measures than we should be. Results may differ between studies for reasons other than the design or procedure of the experiment itself. Error, noise and randomness are out there – and not just in other people's data. And there are other, even more basic psychometric problems. To illustrate, cognitive aging researchers have long treated latency measures as if they were located on a true interval scale, that is, it was assumed that whenever some manipulation influences the latency of young adults as compared with some baseline, it should produce exactly the same change in latency in older adults. However, there is now ample evidence that young and older adults live on their own processing time scale, so that an x ms change in one age group is not equal to an x ms change in the other group. This is reflected in the fact that the relation between young and older adults' mean latencies is best expressed as a linear equation with a negative intercept and a slope larger than 1 (Cerella 1990; for an alternative model, see Myerson *et al.* 1990). One explanation for this finding is that the slope reflects age-related slowing in central processes, as opposed to peripheral, input/output processes (Cerella 1990). In non-lexical tasks, this slope typically equals about 1.8 to 2.0 (Cerella 1990). This means that, whatever time it takes a young adult to complete a certain central process, an older adult will need about 1.9 times longer. In other words, the age difference in response time is not expected to be constant across conditions, but will typically grow larger with increasing latency of the task, by virtue of this general 90% slowing of central processes. Consequently, before it can be stated with some confidence that there is true age-sensitivity in some process tapped by a critical condition, one needs to demonstrate that the shift in the age difference from the baseline to the critical condition is reliably larger than the age effect predicted from general slowing alone. Failure to take the general effect into account may result in erroneous conclusions. One striking example of this is the Stroop interference effect. Authors of primary studies regarding age differences in this effect (for an overview, see Verhaeghen and De Meersman 1998*b*) have consistently concluded that older adults are more susceptible to the Stroop effect than young adults. This has been taken as evidence for a breakdown in inhibition (Hasher and Zacks 1988) or in control processes (Monsell 1996) in old age, and has been linked to deficient functioning of the frontal lobes (West 1996). However, these conclusions are largely based on difference scores, and fail to take slowing in the baseline condition into account. A meta-analysis (Verhaeghen and De Meersman 1998*b*) has clearly shown that the larger interference effect in older adults is a mere artifact of the general slowing effect: in both colour naming and naming the colour of an incongruent word, older adults are about 1.9 times slower than young adults.

This problem with the interpretation of interactions has been demonstrated repeatedly in the latency domain. There are indications that, much as in the latency domain, a more or less general effect may also be present in accuracy data, such as recall from episodic memory (Verhaeghen and Marcoen 1993*b*). This general effect sometimes appears to be non-linear and non-additive, that is, the general data pattern is clearly not that performance of older adults equals performance of younger adults minus a constant. The implication is that, just as it is necessary to concede that absolute changes in the latencies of young and older adults cannot be compared directly, identical absolute changes in accuracy measures may well not have the same meaning in young as in older subjects. If we assume that this general pattern indeed reflects a general and meaningful age trend, the same reservations about interaction analysis that apply to latency research also apply to accuracy data.

While little can be done about the first problem, except warning for the dangers of issue isolationism, it is my belief that relatively painless remedies exist for the two other problems. To that extent, I wish to propagate the use of a comparatively new tool for the study of cognitive aging, namely the study of the relation between processing time and accuracy in young and older adults. Time–accuracy research is not meant to supplant existing methodologies in the field; rather, I wish to present it as an additional tool in the growing toolbox used by cognitive aging researchers.

Time–accuracy research seems ideally suited for countering the second problem, that is, one important advantage of the time–accuracy methodology is that it provides a joint time–accuracy platform for the data, so that research results from domains that are traditionally latency domains (e.g. arithmetic) can now be directly integrated with research results from domains that have traditionally been accuracy domains (e.g. recall from episodic memory).

Time–accuracy research also speaks to the third problem. If the idea of time–accuracy functions and their mathematical expression is taken seriously, then it follows that the relation between mean accuracy data of young and older adults will be governed by a particular mathematical relation. We shall see that this relation captures the type of relation found by Verhaeghen and Marcoen (1993a) quite nicely.

TIME–ACCURACY FUNCTIONS IN AN
AGE-COMPARATIVE PERSPECTIVE

When assigning the responsibility for the less pleasant aspects of aging to the capitalized persona 'Time', Shakespeare was thinking of 'Time' as a developmental variable – the advancing adult years. At another level of analysis, recent theories attribute cognitive aging to another type of 'Time', namely the speed at which the cognitive system processes information (for an overview, see Salthouse 1996). Above, I already mentioned the general slowing view in the latency domain, based on the analysis of Brinley plots. Other evidence comes from correlational research showing that basic processing speed is a very important mediating factor between adult age and complex forms of cognition such as primary memory, spatial ability, reasoning ability, and episodic memory performance. In a meta-analysis using linear structural modelling, Verhaeghen and Salthouse (1997) found that effects of age on these different aspects of cognition mediated through perceptual speed were typically larger than the direct effects, showing that even if speed-of-processing is not the whole story of cognitive aging, it is certainly a major part of the narrative.

If processing time is such an important variable, one obvious other way to investigate its influence is by manipulating the time available to the subject – time as an external resource for processing. Interestingly, only a limited number of studies exist in which the systematic relation between presentation or processing time and performance have been examined in an age-comparative context (Kliegl 1995; Kliegl et al. 1993; Kliegl et al. 1994; Mayr et al. 1996; Verhaeghen et al. 1997; Verhaeghen et al. 1998).

Researchers studying the relationship between presentation or processing time and cognitive performance in young adults have demonstrated that time and accuracy are related in a non-linear way, usually modelled by a delayed exponential equation (e.g. Dosher 1976; Lohman 1989; McClelland 1979; McElree and Griffith 1995; Wickelgren 1977):

$$p = c\,(1 - \exp[(a - t)/b]) \text{ for } t > a; \text{ and } p = 0 \text{ for } t \leqslant a \qquad (3.1)$$

In this equation, p stands for performance, usually expressed in terms of percentage of items correct, t stands for presentation or processing time, and a, b, and c are the parameters describing the function. (We assume here, for the sake of simplicity, that the prior probability of a correct response is zero. Readers interested in models including a guessing parameter may wish to consult Kliegl et al. 1994, or Verhaeghen et al. 1997.) The basic procedure involves presenting a series of stimuli at different presentation times, and measuring mean accuracy at each point in time. Equation 3.1 is then fitted to these data using a curve-fitting program. An example of such a curve for recall from episodic memory, for a single individual, along with the series of 12 data points from which it is derived is presented in Fig. 3.1 (data from Verhaeghen et al. 1998, Exp. 1).

The curve described by eqn 3.1 is negatively accelerating, that is, it remains at zero up to a certain point in time (viz., the point *a*), where it starts to rise steeply, and it becomes less and less steep with advancing presentation time, flattening towards a horizontal asymptote. The *a* parameter (the onset time) represents the point on the time axis where performance starts to rise above zero. The *c* parameter (the asymptote) represents the level of performance a participant would reach if an unlimited amount of time were available. Otherwise stated, it represents the maximum level of performance that the individual participant can reach, given the specific task at hand. The *b* parameter (the rate of approach) represents the rate at which performance goes from zero to the asymptotic level from the onset time on. Higher values of *b* indicate that the time–accuracy function is less steep, that is, participants with higher *b* values are slower in reaching the asymptotic level of performance than participants with lower *b* values. Note that the *b* parameter is conditional on the asymptote, that is, if one has two curves with different asymptotes but equal rate and onset parameters, each curves reaches a given proportion of its asymptotic level at the same point in time. This implies that the absolute growth is smaller in the curve with a lower *c* value. Such curves differ in asymptotic level, but are said to have equivalent dynamics (McClelland 1979).

One of the advantages of the time–accuracy methodology is that an individual's performance is now captured in three distinct parameters. Depending on the task, each parameter can be assigned a specific meaning. To take list recall as an illustration, a simple time–accuracy function could relate the percentage of words recalled correctly during a retrieval phase to the time that each word has been shown on the screen during a study phase. The onset time then reflects

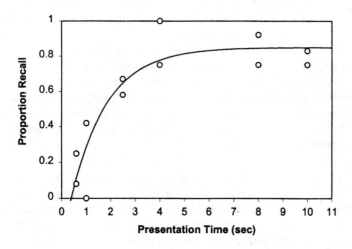

Fig. 3.1 Time–accuracy function as derived for one participant in Verhaeghen *et al.* (1998).

the time needed for the word to stand a minimal chance of being remembered. If we assume that a memory trace is formed as soon as a word has been identified, the onset time presumably would mainly capture perceptual and early semantic processes. Consistent with this interpretation is the finding that presenting cue–word pairs leads to longer onset times than presenting single words (Verhaeghen *et al.* 1998, Exp. 1), as does presenting two words, one of which has to be ignored (ibid. Exp. 2). If we assume that the main process driving the level of recall is elaboration during the encoding stage, then the rate of approach parameter can be taken to reflect the speed of deployment of the elaboration process, that is, the rate at which associations can be generated to the stimulus (Kliegl 1995). The asymptote can be taken to reflect the strength of activation of the items in episodic memory (McClelland 1979), or as the carrying capacity of the system (van Geert 1993). In research on memory in my laboratory (Verhaeghen *et al.* 1998), the parameters of the time–accuracy functions were found to covary with conditions in unsurprising ways, demonstrating that the parameters have validity (and hence reliability). That is, research participants are faster in cued than in free recall (encoding when cues are presented already provides a form of elaboration and hence should be faster), and slower under conditions of articulatory suppression and when distractors are present (these conditions do not allow the full capacity of working memory to be deployed in the elaboration process, and hence would presumably slow subjects down). Likewise, asymptotic accuracy is lower for less deep conditions (encoding and recall cued with rhymes versus cued with semantic associates) and lower when distractors are present or when the subject engages in articulatory suppression.

The interpretation of the parameters can vary according to the task at hand. For instance, Verhaeghen *et al.* (1997) had subjects perform chains of either 5 or 10 simple additions and subtractions. The solutions (both partial and final) were always larger than 0 and smaller than 10. In one condition, subjects were presented with just a string of such additions/subtractions (e.g. 8 - 3 - 2 + 4 - 5 + 3); in another condition, brackets were inserted (e.g. [6 + (2 + 1)] - [9 - (4 + 2)]). In order for performance to rise above the measurement floor in this task, subjects obviously have to compute up till the next-to-last operation and encode the last operation and operand. The onset parameter will thus reflect the time needed for this computation and encoding. The rate of approach parameter then indicates the speed with which the last operation is carried out. Because this type of operation is usually not really counting, but rather retrieval from semantic memory (e.g. LeFevre *et al.* 1996), the rate of approach captures the speed of access to semantic memory. The asymptote in this simple arithmetic task probably does not reflect the effectiveness of the last computation (every adult should be expected to be ultimately perfect on a single simple addition or subtraction operation), but rather taps control processes or self-monitoring ability, that is, the asymptote reflects the extent to which errors earlier in the chain are detected and corrected. Note that because the time measure used was presentation time, and not presentation time plus time to respond, output processes are not included in this time–accuracy function. Inasmuch as reaction time differences between young and older adults also partially reflect slowing in output processes, our time–accuracy functions for mental arithmetic provide a more pure measure of central processes.

The decomposition of processing into dynamic and asymptotic effects is potentially important for cognitive aging theories. One rather trivial interpretation of age-related slowing could be that older adults simply need more time to complete a task or to attain the same level of accuracy as younger persons. In this case, age differences would be situated solely in dynamic aspects of processing (i.e. onset time and/or rate of approach). Salthouse (1996) calls this the limited-time mechanism of cognitive aging. This model seems to hold for a large number of tasks. For instance, if it is found that performance is virtually errorless for both older and younger adults, but older adults take longer to complete the task, the most parsimonious conclusion is that only the dynamics of processing are different. This is for instance the case in reaction time studies of single-operation mental arithmetic (e.g. Birren and Botwinick 1951; Charness and Campbell 1988; Geary *et al.* 1993; Geary and Wiley 1991; Rogers and Fisk 1991; Salthouse and Coon 1994; Salthouse and Kersten 1993; Sliwinski *et al.* 1994) or in studies on lexical processing (for an overview, see Myerson and Hale 1993). Direct measurements of time–accuracy functions show that in the domains of figural scanning, word scanning, figural reasoning, and cued recognition, the asymptote for young and old is at 100%, and older adults are merely slower in reaching that asymptote (Kliegl *et al.* 1994; Mayr *et al.* 1996).

On the other hand, slowing may have more dire consequences, in that it might affect the end product of processing either by bringing down the asymptotic level of performance or by altering the quality of the outcome. For instance, Salthouse (1996) has argued for a simultaneity mechanism of age-related slowing, claiming that one consequence of slowing might be that the products of earlier information processing are more readily displaced from working memory or are decaying more rapidly. The consequence would be that there is a lower probability that these products are available for subsequent processing, and this will affect the ultimate performance of the system. This simultaneity mechanism depends solely on the internal speed of executing operations, and not on external factors such as time limits. Whatever the mechanism, asymptotic age differences have indeed been observed in time–accuracy research for some tasks, namely recall and recognition from episodic memory (Kliegl *et al.* 1993; Verhaeghen *et al.* 1998), and in arithmetic tasks containing brackets as described above (Verhaeghen *et al.* 1997).

STATE TRACES

So far, we have dealt with age differences in time–accuracy parameters for a single task. One of the more interesting aspects of the time–accuracy method is that it allows for a unique way of investigating age by task interactions by reverting to state trace analysis. A state trace graph is a graph in which the covariation of two (or more) variables in the system under study is displayed (the term stems from physics; see e.g. Bamber 1979, Mayr *et al.* 1996, or van Geert 1993, for applications in psychology). In other words, in such a graph empirically derived states of the system are depicted; the variables defining the system are used as the axes.

Time–accuracy analysis makes it possible to investigate processing in terms of both time and accuracy. Correspondingly, time–accuracy data can yield two types of state traces: one in which the times needed by young and older adults for a given level of accuracy are plotted against each other, and one in which the accuracy levels reached by young and older adults for a given amount of processing time are plotted against each other. The former graph can be labeled an iso-accuracy trace; the latter an iso-temporal trace. In this section, I will derive the mathematical form of these two types of traces from the delayed exponential time–accuracy function, and explore some of the implications of these equations. More specifically, I will demonstrate that under certain circumstances the young–old traces are independent of the parameters of the original functions, and rely solely on the age differences in the parameters, thus opening the possibility of meta-analysis of state traces and of integration of results across different domains.

Iso-accuracy state traces

The Brinley plots mentioned in the introduction are an example of state trace graphs in which mean performance of young and older adults is used to define the space (Kliegl *et al.* 1994). When complete time–accuracy functions are available, an analogous graph can be constructed by plotting the time needed by older participants to reach a given level of accuracy against the time needed by the young to reach the same level of accuracy. This graph can be labeled an iso-accuracy trace, since it contains points derived from equal levels of accuracy in the two age groups. In the next two subsections, I will first derive a model for iso-accuracy traces, and then illustrate the usefulness of this model with some data pertaining to Kliegl *et al.*'s levels-of-dissociation framework.

The model

Verhaeghen *et al.* (1997) demonstrated that the time t needed to reach a given level of accuracy p (also called the time demand for p) can be expressed as a function of the parameters of the time–accuracy function in the following way:

$$t = a + b \ln[c/(c - p)] \tag{3.2}$$

When depicting iso-accuracy points in a Brinley plot, it sometimes makes more sense to revert from total time needed to processing time demand, that is, total time needed minus the onset time, or:

$$t' = t - a = b \ln[c/(c - p)] \qquad (3.3)$$

This transformation is useful in contexts in which the onset parameter is assumed to mainly capture peripheral (input) aspects of processing. In that case, processing time demand gives a clearer picture of age differences in central aspects of processing. For instance, in memory research we are probably more interested in the effects of age on elaboration and carrying capacity than on the time needed to pick up information from the visual display. In the context of mental arithmetic, t' would give us the time needed for semantic retrieval of a single arithmetic fact.

What do iso-accuracy traces actually look like? In Fig. 3.2, effects of aging are depicted on each of the parameters of delayed exponential time–accuracy functions (left-hand panels), along with the corresponding iso-accuracy traces for processing time demands (middle panels). A more formal exploration of the relation between young and older adults' processing time demands can be found in Table 3.1. The table gives the equations governing iso-accuracy traces (and iso-temporal traces, see below) under selected types of age-related differences. The second column describes the time–accuracy equation under the age-related differences as outlined in the first column (i.e., no age difference, an age difference in onset time, an age difference in rate of approach, an age difference in asymptote, age differences in both rate of approach and asymptote, and age differences in all three parameters). The third column shows the corresponding equations for iso-accuracy traces, that is, processing time demand t' of older adults as a function of processing time demand t' of the young for a number of models. In these models, the effects of aging are described by three parameters α, with subscripts a, b, and c referring to the time–accuracy parameter where the effect is located. In these models, I assume that the effects of aging are multiplicative, that is, proportional. (Note that proportional age differences have consistently been found to fit rate differences better than additive, or absolute age differences; e.g. Cerella 1990; Cerella *et al.* 1980; Hale and Myerson 1996. In the present model, I assume that this proportional relation also holds for asymptotic differences.) Thus, if young subjects have a mean rate of approach equal to b, I assume older subjects will have a mean rate equal to $\alpha_b b$, and the α_b parameter denotes age-related slowing in the rate of approach to the asymptote. Likewise, α_a will denote the age-related slowing factor in the onset time, and α_c will denote the age-related effect on the asymptote. Presumably, α_a and α_b will be equal to or larger than 1, and α_c will be equal to or smaller than 1. All the iso-accuracy equations in the third column are formulated in terms of the parameters a, b, c, and t' of the young, plus the effects of aging.

As can be seen, age differences in the onset time and in rate of processing will result in a linear iso-accuracy trace. The iso-accuracy trace for an onset time difference is equal to the first diagonal. The iso-accuracy state trace for a rate of approach difference is a line starting at the origin and diverging from the diagonal; the slope of this line is equal to the age-related slowing factor b. If the

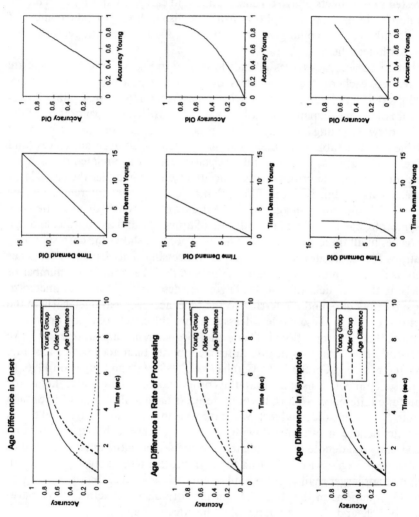

Fig. 3.2 Three models for age differences in exponential time–accuracy functions.

Table 3.1 Equations for time–accuracy functions of older adults and performance of young adults under selected age-effect models

Age difference	p_o as a function of presentation time t	t_o as a function of t_y	p_o as a function of p_y	p_o as a function of p_y if $c = 1$
None	$c[1 - \exp(\frac{a-t}{b})]$	t_y	p_y	p_y
Onset	$c[1 - \exp(\frac{\alpha_a a - t}{b})]$	t_y	$c[1 + \frac{(p_y-c)\exp(\frac{a(\alpha_a-1)}{b})}{c}]$	$1 + (p_y - 1)\exp(\frac{a(\alpha_a-1)}{b})$
Rate of approach	$c[1 - \exp(\frac{a-t}{\alpha_b b})]$	$\alpha_b t_y$	$c[1 - (\frac{c-p_y}{c})^{1/\alpha_b}]$	$1 - (1 - p_y)^{1/\alpha_b}$
Asymptote	$\alpha_c c[1 - \exp(\frac{a-t}{b})]$	$b\ln[1 + \frac{\alpha_c \exp(t_y'/b)}{1+(\alpha_c-1)\exp(t_y'/b)}]$	$\alpha_c p_y$	$\alpha_c p_y$
Rate and asymptote	$\alpha_c c[1 - \exp(\frac{a-t}{\alpha_b b})]$	$\alpha_b b\ln[1 + \frac{\alpha_c \exp(t_y'/b)}{1+(\alpha_c-1)\exp(t_y'/b)}]$	$\alpha_c c[1 - (\frac{c-p_y}{c})^{1/\alpha_b}]$	$\alpha_c[1 - (1 - p_y)^{1/\alpha_b}]$
All three	$\alpha_c c[1 - \exp(\frac{\alpha_a a - t}{\alpha_b b})]$	$\alpha_b b\ln[1 + \frac{\alpha_c \exp(t_y'/b)}{1+(\alpha_c-1)\exp(t_y'/b)}]$	$\alpha_c c[1 - \exp(\frac{\alpha_a - a + b\log[(c-p_y)/c]}{\alpha_b b})]$	$\alpha_c[1 - \exp(\frac{\alpha_a - a + b\log(1-p_y)}{\alpha_b b})]$

Subscripts o and y refer to old and young adults, respectively. See text for the meaning of the parameters.

data for two or more conditions are governed by the same slowing factor, a single trace should emerge, regardless of what the precise parameters of the underlying time–accuracy functions are. A statistical test for the equality of the different slopes can be conducted by reverting the data to proportional measurement space. This is done by conducting standard repeated-measures analysis of variance on the log-transformed rate parameters b; a significant age by condition interaction will indicate that the young–old slopes of the different conditions are reliably different (see Kliegl *et al.* 1994, for more details).

The reader may note that the situation is more complicated when an asymptotic difference is present, for two reasons. First, the iso-accuracy trace for an asymptotic difference is not linear, precluding obvious transformations of the dependent variable to make the trace additive. Second, unlike the traces discussed in the previous section, the iso-accuracy state trace for an asymptotic age difference does not continue ad infinitum. This is because when an asymptotic age difference is present, at some point in processing time performance of the young will become larger than the asymptotic level of performance of the old. The iso-accuracy trace necessarily ceases to exist beyond this point – the old simply cannot reach the level of performance that young adults attain from that point on. I refer the interested reader to Verhaeghen *et al.* (1997) for ways of dealing with this problem.

Illustration: the levels-of-dissociation framework

The time–accuracy methodology has been used extensively within the levels-of-process-dissociation framework advanced by Kliegl, Mayr, and colleagues (Kliegl 1996; Kliegl *et al.* 1994; Kliegl *et al.* 1995; Mayr *et al.* 1996; Verhaeghen *et al.* 1997). This framework tries to provide an account of cognitive aging in terms of processing modules (Kliegl 1996), that is, it is claimed (a) that the effects of aging on the cognitive system are organized in an orderly fashion, with smaller effects for less complex tasks, and (b) that the transition from one level of complexity to the next is discontinuous. An analogy would be state transitions in physics, where a system jumps from one state to another as a function of some underlying variable – for instance, ice turning into water turning into vapour with increasing energy levels. How many levels need to be distinguished and where the boundaries are situated is a matter of empirical investigation. Note that this framework considers complexity of processes as the dividing agent between levels. This makes this framework quite different from the task-domain-oriented theoretical underpinning that Hale, Myerson and colleagues provide for lexical versus non-lexical dissociations (e.g. Hale and Myerson 1996). At present, complexity level seems a more powerful construct for dissociations than task domain. That is, contrary to predictions made by the task-domain framework, dissociations can be present within a single task domain, such as simple mental arithmetic (maybe a lexical process) or figural reasoning (presumably a non-lexical process). Note also that complexity is defined in a way different from the sheer latency definition that was sometimes used in the 1980s (Cerella *et al.* 1980).

To illustrate the power of this levels-of-dissociation framework, Fig. 3.3 provides iso-accuracy traces for four types of tasks reported in two recent articles, namely the simple addition-and-subtraction mental arithmetic tasks (5 and 10 operations) with and without brackets used by Verhaeghen *et al.* (1997) and outlined above, and recognition and recall from episodic memory under a number of different encoding conditions as studied by Verhaeghen *et al.* (1998). The traces suggest that at least three levels of age differences exist. (The one dissident condition was a standard recognition task; the age difference there was almost exclusively restricted to the asymptote.) Note that this figure combines data from traditional latency domains and traditional accuracy domains, now integrated through the time–accuracy methodology.

A theoretical framework to capture these different levels has been offered by Kliegl (1996). The first transition illustrated in Fig. 3.3, the jump from arithmetic without to arithmetic with brackets, has been labelled a transition from the level of sequential to the level of coordinative complexity by Mayr and Kliegl (1993). Sequential complexity refers to task manipulations which alter the mere number of independent processing components. Efficiency in terms of basic speed of operations is presumably the main source of age differences in

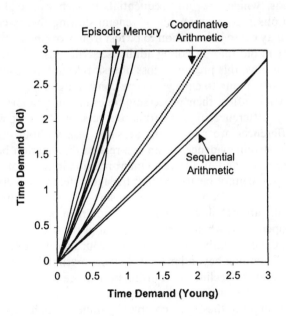

Fig. 3.3 Combined iso-accuracy traces for different conditions of sequential and coordinative arithmetic (Verhaeghen *et al.* 1997) and recall and recognition from episodic memory (Verhaeghen *et al.* 1998).

tasks requiring sequential complexity. Coordinative complexity on the other hand refers to manipulations which affect the need for organizing the transfer of information between processing steps, thus forcing the system to store intermediate results while concurrently processing other information. This makes coordinative manipulations sensitive to potential age differences in working memory functions (Baddeley 1986; Just and Carpenter 1992; Salthouse 1992). In our arithmetic task (Verhaeghen et al. 1997), sequential complexity was manipulated simply by increasing the number of operations. When subjects are working through a simple chain of additions/subtractions, one operation is carried out after another in a serial chain of processes. When brackets are present, however, subjects have to retain intermediate solutions in working memory while performing the task. Thus, on the one hand, one should expect age differences to be larger in the bracket condition than in the no bracket condition; on the other hand, one should expect equality of age differences in processing time demand within the bracket and no bracket conditions when the number of operations is increased from 5 to 10. This was exactly what was found.

Interestingly, in the study just described we found no age differences in any of the parameters in the no bracket condition. Consequently, it cannot be claimed that the age difference in the bracket conditions, which require coordination, is simply an indirect effect of a basic age-related slowing observed in the no bracket conditions, which are only sequential. If such age-related slowing would have been observed, proponents of general slowing theory could argue that this slowing may cause information to be lost from working memory with a higher probability in old than in young adults (see Salthouse, this volume). In coordinative conditions, this presumed loss of task-relevant information could then force older participants to engage in time-consuming reiterations of steps, and this in turn would affect their processing times in a disproportionate way. The finding of age differences in a coordinative version of a task when absolutely no age differences are present in the same task without coordinative demands provides strong evidence for an age-related dissociation between the two levels of complexity, and disallows an interpretation in terms of basic speed differences. That is, it cannot be argued that the age differences in coordinative arithmetic are an indirect consequence of a slower basic arithmetic speed, because older adults are not slower than young adults in performing the exact same arithmetic operations when carried out without the task-generated working memory load. Consequently, the deficit in the coordinative conditions needs to be ascribed to something beyond mental slowing–presumably an age-related but slowing-independent decline in coordination processing within working memory.

Other studies examining these two complexity dimensions have consistently revealed larger age differences in coordinative than in sequential complexity conditions. Whereas in sequentially complex figural transformation tasks, old adults were about twice as slow as young adults, the slowing factor was between three and four in coordinatively complex tasks (Kliegl *et al.* 1994; Mayr and Kliegl 1993; Mayr *et al.* 1996). Likewise, dissociations have been found between word scanning and word recognition (Kliegl *et al.* 1994). With respect to the boundaries of the coordinative level, it has been demonstrated that there is no jump to a different level when the working memory load increases from 1 to 2, suggesting that in old age the distinction between sequential and coordinative complexity is all-or-none (Mayr *et al.* 1996). Interestingly, the dissociation boundary is different for children, who do not suffer disproportionately from a working memory load of 1, but do suffer when the load is increased to 2 (Mayr *et al.* 1996). This indicates a clear asymmetry between development and aging of coordinative functions.

As illustrated in Fig. 3.3, a different level of complexity is clearly attained with episodic memory tasks. Older adults are much slower when encoding words for either recognition or recall from episodic memory, as can be seen in the elevated iso-accuracy traces. Thus, at least a third level of complexity needs to be distinguished, that goes beyond coordinative processing.

On the basis of this and other evidence, Kliegl (1996) has proposed the existence of at least four levels of dissociations. The results point at age invariance in access of semantic memory (e.g. simple arithmetic), relatively slight age differences in information intake from the environment (e.g. figural scanning), larger age differences in coordination and integration of information (e.g. figural reasoning), and very large age differences (probably involving asympotic differences) in building new high-quality representations (e.g. recognition and recall from episodic memory).

Iso-temporal state traces

Iso-accuracy traces appear to be the preferred mode of constructing state traces. As demonstrated above, all information regarding age by condition interactions can be derived from such iso-accuracy traces. Also, the tradition of Brinley plotting in cognitive aging research has probably predisposed researchers to think of age effects in terms of slopes of young–old functions in some form of time space. Moreover, latency data usually result in neat plots, as they tend to be much less noisy than accuracy data, if only because they are measured with more precision. In the few articles that have actually plotted both latency and error data from the same set of tasks, scatter in the young–old latency function was consistently lower than scatter in the young–old error function. For instance, Brinley (1965) found a linear R^2 of 0.99 for latency compared with 0.79 for error rate; Salthouse (1991, p. 315) reports R^2s of 0.96 and 0.99 for latency in two of his studies compared with R^2s of 0.80 and 0.84 for error rate.

Very few studies have been conducted that describe the accuracy of older adults as a function of accuracy of young adults, given equal processing times (i.e., iso-temporal traces). It is, then, not surprising that no serious effort has been made to model young–old iso-temporal traces or a series of iso-temporal data points. However, such models are as badly needed as models relating reaction time of older adults to reaction time of young adults, if only to check whether the assumption of a common accuracy scale for young and older adults is correct or not.

The model

Just as iso-accuracy traces can be derived from time–accuracy functions, equations for iso-temporal traces can be constructed. These traces indicate what level of accuracy old and young adults will obtain, given that they process the same stimulus for the same amount of time. In Fig. 3.2 (right hand panels), iso-temporal traces for age differences in each of the three parameters of the time–accuracy function have been depicted. In Table 3.1 (next-to-last column), equations for iso-temporal traces are described for each of the types of age-differences for which the iso-accuracy traces were derived. In the last column of the table, equations are given for the simplified case in which the asymptote of the young equals 1.

Looking at the equations, one interesting conclusion is that for the asymptotic difference model, the young–old relation is adequately described without any reference to the actual parameters of the underlying time–accuracy function (i.e., none of the parameters a, b, or c figure in the equation). The same is true for the rate difference model and the rate plus asymptotic difference model if it is assumed that c equals 1. An interesting aspect of this mathematical derivation is that young–old accuracy plots can now be treated much the same way as Brinley plots, that is, under these models accuracy plots provide direct estimates of age differences in the underlying time–accuracy functions, even when the actual functions are unknown. In other words, iso-temporal traces or a series of iso-temporal points provide sufficient information to determine whether age differences are situated in dynamic or asymptotic effects, or both. This is true regardless of the actual presentation times used in the studies and regardless of the actual underlying time–accuracy functions. Thus, this method of mapping points in young–old accuracy space and looking for the best fitting curve offers an advantage over traditional, effect-size based, meta-analytic techniques, in that it allows for an investigation of the locus of the deficit in dynamic versus asymptotic aspects of processing. Fitting the equations from Table 3.1 to a set of data (e.g. a series of meta-analytically derived data-points) provides a direct estimate of the age-related slowing factor, the age-related asymptotic effect and, if one wishes, the average asymptote of the young adult samples. By way of illustration, in the next three subsections (Illustrations 1, 2, and 3), iso-temporal traces will be fitted to three data sets, two of which are meta-analytical, and one of which concerns multiple conditions within a single study.

Illustration 1: a meta-analysis of recall from episodic memory

As a first illustration of these models, iso-temporal curves were fitted to the meta-analytic database compiled by Verhaeghen and Marcoen (1993a). These authors found that when proportion of items recalled by older adults in a number of studies was plotted against proportion of items recalled by young adults, linear or non-linear curves fitted the data quite nicely. Separate non-linear traces in accuracy Brinley space had to be distinguished for list recall, prose recall, and paired-associate recall. Thus, separate iso-temporal analyses were conducted for each of these three episodic memory task types for the present analysis. The data-base consisted of 81 data points for list recall, 54 data points for prose recall, and 19 data points for paired-associate recall. It should be noted here that the degree of dependency among data points was kept to a minimum by averaging data from within-subject comparisons, so that no two data points within each task type were obtained from the same groups of subjects. Analyses were conducted using the non-linear regression module of SPSS, weighting data points for the number of subjects from which they were derived.

Because no data were available on the parameters of the underlying time–accuracy functions, it was decided to estimate models in which these parameters do not figure. Consequently, aging parameters were estimated under: (a) the model of rate differences, assuming that asymptotic performance of the young was perfect; (b) the model of asymptotic differences; and (c) the model of both rate and asymptotic differences, assuming that asymptotic performance of the young was perfect. Note that the assumption of perfect asymptotes of the young in the first and the third model is possibly incorrect and may lead to an underestimation of the true proportion of variance in the mean performance of older adults explained by the mean performance of young adults.

Results of the meta-analysis are presented in Table 3.2. Scatter graphs, along with the best fitting curves for each of the task types, are represented in Fig. 3.4. A number of results are noteworthy. First, a sizeable proportion of the variance (from 0.68 to 0.91) is explained in all three tasks. Given that recall performance

Table 3.2 Goodness-of-fit and parameter values for four alternative models fitted to episodic memory data from Verhaeghen and Marcoen (1993*a*)

	List recall ($k = 81$)	Prose recall ($k = 54$)	Paired-associate recall ($k = 19$)
Rate of processing difference			
R^2	0.77	0.91	0.79
α_b	1.68	1.47	1.84
Asymptotic difference			
R^2	0.79	0.87	0.68
α_c	0.73	0.79	0.69
Rate of processing and asymptotic difference			
R^2	0.79	0.91	0.79
α_b	1.09	1.47	1.84
α_c	0.77	1.00	1.00

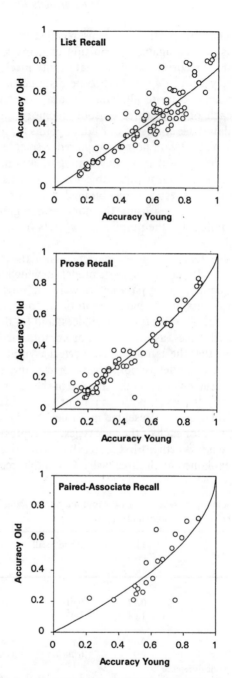

Fig. 3.4 Proportion recalled from list recall tasks (81 subject groups), prose recall tasks (54 subject groups) and paired-associate recall tasks (19 subject groups) by older adults as a function of proportion recalled by young adults, along with best fitting curves.

of the old will typically be lower than recall performance of the young, some spurious correlation between the recall performance of young and older adults may be predicted due to the fact that the data points can be expected to be mostly situated below the diagonal in accuracy Brinley space. Using simulated data, Verhaeghen and Marcoen (1993b) estimated the mean spurious correlation for 20 data-points to be .51, with 95% of the correlations for the simulated data points falling below 0.74 (the values for mean spurious correlation and percentile 95 were lower when more than 20 data-points were generated). Thus, each of the models estimated here appears to explain more of the variance than would be expected if the correlation were merely due to the fact that the elderly consistently perform less well than the young.

Second, the best fitting model differs across type of task. For list recall, the asymptotic difference model and the rate plus asymptotic difference model fit the data about equally well. This suggests that, in list recall, age has an important effect on the asymptote of recall performance (bringing the asymptote down by a factor of about 0.77), and a slight effect of slowing in the rate of approach to that asymptote (slowing factor of about 1.1). The existence of an asymptotic difference in list recall is consistent with recent primary research using the time–accuracy paradigm (Verhaeghen *et al.* 1998, Exp. 1; average α_c in this study was 0.70). For prose recall, the best fitting model is the rate of processing difference model, suggesting that in prose recall the age difference is located solely in the slowing of the rate of approach to the asymptote (slowing factor of about 1.5). For paired-associate recall, the best-fitting model was again the rate of processing difference model (slowing factor of about 1.8; note that for the rate plus asymptote model $\alpha_c = 1$, meaning there are no age differences in the asymptote, and thus the rate plus asymptote model in this task reduces to the rate only model). Thus, the proposed method of analysing data points in accuracy Brinley space suggests that different loci of age effects may exist for different tasks.

Illustration 2: a meta-analysis for recall for frequency-of-occurrence

In a second illustration, meta-analytic data on a measure of so-called automatic (as opposed to effortful; Hasher and Zacks 1979) processing in episodic memory are presented. Initially, Hasher and Zacks argued that no age differences should be found for such automatic processes. In the 1980s, a number of studies were conducted to examine this hypothesis. One of the tasks most frequently used to tap presumably automatic processes is the frequency-of-occurrence task. In this task, the research participant is presented with a list of to-be-remembered stimuli, at least some of which occur more than once. The participant is not told to pay attention to the number of times each stimulus appears in the list. Afterwards, the participant is required to indicate the number of occurrences for each stimulus. In Fig. 3.5, 18 different data points on frequency-of-occurrence performance are represented, along with the best fitting three-parameter iso-temporal trace curve. The data are derived from 16 studies on frequency-of-occurrence performance reported in 12 articles (Attig and Hasher 1980; Ellis *et al.* 1988; Freund and Witte 1986; Hasher and Zacks 1979; Kausler and Hakami 1982; Kausler *et al.* 1982; Kausler *et al.* 1984; Kausler and Puckett 1980; Kellogg 1983; Salthouse *et al.* 1988; Sanders *et al.* 1990; Warren and Mitchell 1980).

The asymptotic difference model fits the data quite well ($R^2 = 0.85$, $\alpha_c = 0.93$). The rate of processing difference model ($R^2 = 0.84$, $\alpha_b = 1.22$) fits slightly less well. The best fit (although the difference in R^2 from the second best fitting model is an admittedly very modest 0.008) is obtained under the rate and asymptotic difference model ($R^2 = 0.86$, $\alpha_b = 1.09$, $\alpha_c = 0.96$). Interestingly, this latter curve is qualitatively similar to the one observed for list recall: age differences are apparent in both the asymptote and rate of processing, with the age-related slowing parameter for frequency-of-occurrence recall nearly identical to the slowing parameter for standard list recall episodic memory data. Thus, the data suggest that recall of frequency of occurrence is simply a less difficult version of a standard list recall task, resulting in smaller age differences in the asymptote, but with an identical slowing factor.

Illustration 3: the role of expertise in recall under the method of loci

The third illustration concerns data from a single study (Lindenberger 1990), in which 48 different lists of words were administered to three different groups, namely one group of young subjects and two groups of older participants: a group of randomly selected older persons ('non-experts') and a group of older graphic designers ('experts'). Subjects studied the lists using the method of loci.

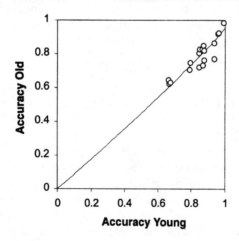

Fig. 3.5 Proportion recalled from frequency-of-occurrence information (18 subject groups) by older adults as a function of proportion recalled by young adults, along with best fitting curve.

This mnemonic technique consists of building visual associations between each to-be-remembered word and a place taken from a route that the subject has learned by heart. In the original study, it was assumed that expertise in forming mental images would lead to smaller age differences when study and recall were guided by a visual mnemonic. The different points plotted in Fig. 3.6 represent these 48 different lists, administered at different points in time after training, and using different presentation times. Data of the older non-experts and older experts are plotted against the data of the younger subjects.

When fitted to the rate and asymptotic difference model, fit was 0.83 for the expert group and 0.66 for the non-experts. Constraining the rate of approach to be equal across groups did not significantly alter fit of the functions. In the final model, R^2 was 0.83 and 0.65, respectively, with α_b being 2.04 for the two groups, and α_c equalling 0.80 and 0.44, respectively.

When compared to the recall data described above, the present results suggest that performance under the method of loci leads to larger age differences than performance in standard list recall. This conclusion is consistent with a meta-analysis (Verhaeghen and Marcoen 1996) demonstrating an exacerbation of age differences from pretest to posttest using this mnemonic device. (Note that pre- to posttest data represent a qualitative shift in strategy use, and hence these results are not in contradiction with reports of diminishing age differences across the course of practice with a single mental algorithm [Baron and Cerella 1993;

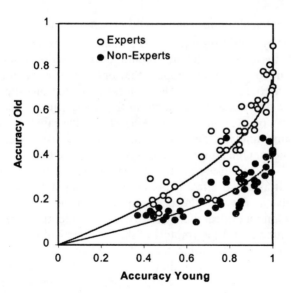

Fig. 3.6 Proportion recalled from 48 lists, studied under the method of loci, by older experts and non experts as a function of proportion recalled by a group of younger subjects (data from Lindenberger 1990), along with best fitting curves.

Salthouse, this volume].) Moreover, the results suggest that the locus of expertise is situated solely in the asymptote and that experts showed the same amount of slowing as non experts. This suggests that the carrying capacity of the episodic memory system may be influenced through life-long experience, whereas the slowing factor seems to be less immune to the effects of aging.

Iso-temporal traces and the psychometrics of age comparisons in accuracy data

The third problem mentioned in the first section of this chapter relates to psychometric problems with accuracy data. In the three illustrations provided above, I have demonstrated that age differences in accuracy data are indeed not typically well-described by an additive model (i.e., performance of the old is not simply performance of the young minus a constant), but are better described by curves that can take quite complicated forms. Moreover, the form of these curves is meaningful, that is, they can be derived from relatively simple models that assume that there may be age differences in the dynamics of processing, in asymptotic accuracy, or both. This has implications for the way we should analyse young–old data when age by condition interactions are the focus of our analysis. In the next two subsections, I wish to expand on this point, first by providing some calculated examples, and then by providing some possible remedies to the problem.

The psychometric problems of age comparisons in accuracy data

Testing for an age by condition interaction amounts to testing for changes in age differences between the different conditions. Interaction analysis using ANOVA on untransformed scores implies that one tests for absolute equality of age differences across conditions. The implication is that one supposes that performance of the old equals performance of the young minus some constant. In the introduction I pointed out that this is clearly not the case for latency data and that interaction analysis on untransformed latency scores can lead to erroneous conclusions. One important conclusion from the theoretical analysis of the expected form of iso-temporal trace analyses, illustrated in Figs 3.4 through 3.6, is that a similar effect is present in accuracy data.

Let me first give a few calculated examples. Assume two conditions (a baseline condition and a critical condition) yielding an identical age difference of $\alpha_c = 0.80$ (meaning that the asymptote of the old is 80% of the asymptote of the young), and no age difference in any of the other parameters. This is a realistic scenario for list recall studies. Table 3.1 shows that under such circumstances performance of the old can be predicted from performance of the young by multiplying the latter performance by the asymptotic age effect. Let performance of the young be 0.80 in a baseline condition and 0.40 in a more difficult critical condition. Consequently, corresponding performance of the old will be 0.64 (i.e., 0.80×0.80) and 0.32 (i.e., 0.80×0.40), respectively. The age difference thus equals 0.16 in the baseline condition, and .08 in the critical condition – the age difference in the critical condition is half the age difference in the baseline condition. This constitutes a false positive: even though the age difference in the parameters of the underlying time–accuracy function does not change across conditions, the observed scores show an ordinal interaction. False negatives are also possible. Let there be an asymptotic age effect of 0.80 in the baseline condition and 0.60 in the critical condition, and let performance of young adults be 0.80 and 0.40, respectively. Performance of older adults will then equal 0.64 in the baseline condition (i.e., 0.80 × 0.80) and 0.24 in the critical condition (i.e. 0.60 × 0.40). In this case, the age difference (0.16) is identical across conditions, but there is a clear age difference in the parameters of the underlying time-accuracy function.

The situation is even more precarious when an age difference is present in the rate of processing, as is probably the case in prose recall and paired-associate recall. If one looks at performance when accuracy is generally low, one might obtain spurious subadditive interactions, that is, making the task more difficult will hurt the young relatively more than the old, resulting in smaller age differences. On the other hand, if accuracy is high, the opposite pattern might be observed, namely a spurious superadditive interaction. Only in the middle range of performance is the constant age difference assumption approximated, and will young and older adults be affected about equally by complexity manipulations.

These are merely mathematical examples. The different illustrations on meta-analytic and primary data above demonstrate that the theoretical iso-temporal traces derived from age differences in different parameters of the time–accuracy function fit the available data quite well. Consequently, the danger of mis-interpreting interactions or the absence of interactions is rather real. As an index of the extent of the problem, the three meta-analytic data sets on recall from episodic memory (Verhaeghen and Marcoen 1993*a*) were fitted to the traditional null-model of ANOVA, namely a model that states that perfor-mance of the old equals performance of the young minus a constant for all conditions. That is, I forced a regression line parallel to the diagonal and calculated R^2, and then compared this percentage of variance explained with the percentages explained by the models as outlined in Table 3.2. For list recall, the best fitting model derived from time–accuracy functions (see Table 3.2), ex-plained a non-trivial 11% of the observed across-subject-group variance over and above the variance explained by the constant difference model. This is an important finding, because list recall is by far the most often used task in episodic memory research. The implication is that a large part of the assertions made in the literature about the nature of episodic memory aging are based on a method of data analysis that is potentially flawed. In particular, theories that predict smaller age differences when tasks are less difficult (such as the compensation theory, Bäckman 1989; or the environmental/cognitive support theory, Craik 1986) will have problems being confirmed with list recall data if no correction for the general aging effect is applied.

For prose recall and paired-associate recall, the extra proportion of variance explained by the best fitting time–accuracy derived model over and above the variance explained by the constant difference model is much smaller or non-existent, namely 3% and 0%, respectively. Thus, the problems with ANOVA seem less outspoken for prose recall and paired-associate recall than for list recall. Previous debate on reaction time Brinley plots, however, has shown that even extremely small proportions of the variance accounted for above a certain baseline model (in the present case, the constant difference model) can be quite meaningful (Fisk and Fisher 1994; Perfect 1994).

Some remedies for the psychometric problems with age comparisons in accuracy data

Given the psychometric problems with accuracy data, what can be done? There seem to be primarily two alternatives to the traditional age by condition approach in ANOVA. The first alternative is to adopt the average age effect as the null hypothesis rather than using the traditional additive null hypothesis of equal age differences across conditions. The new null hypothesis then tests whether the data exhibit more than this average age effect. The second alternative is to abandon the age by condition approach altogether, and examine the age-relatedness of cognitive processes in a more direct way, for instance by looking at age differences in time–accuracy functions.

Adapting the null hypothesis is the solution that has been advocated for the psychometric scaling problem associated with general slowing in latency data (e.g. Cerella 1991). In the latency domain, two ways for adopting the average age effect as the null hypothesis have been advanced. The first is to apply a meaningful transformation to the raw data so that the transformed data are brought in line with the assumption of equal age differences across conditions. For instance, data characterized by a multiplicative relation can be log-transformed, which results in constant absolute differences in log–log space, so that interactions can now be interpreted correctly. In the context of young–old reaction time data, which are characterized by a near-multiplicative relation, the application of the log transformation has been argued for since the early 1980s (Cerella *et al.* 1980). For list recall, a multiplicative model (the asymptotic difference model) fits the available data as well as the rate and asymptotic difference model does, and much better than the constant difference model. A problem, however, is that it is not certain whether the model derived from the meta-analysis is applicable to age differences in all list recall data. The only firm conclusion that can be reached from the meta-analysis is that, on average, age differences in list recall data are well described by a multiplicative model. It is not clear whether this average (around which a lot of variation is present, as can be seen in Fig. 3.4), presents the average of a number of proportional Brinley traces, or whether it is the average from a number of iso-temporal traces, which are not necessarily all proportional.

A second way to arrive at an acceptable null hypothesis is to partial out the average age effect that is present in the experiment itself. One quite elegant technique for dealing with the average age effect when examining ordinal interactions is the three-step approach proposed by Madden *et al.* (1992). First, the average age effect in the experiment is determined by computing the curve describing the young–old relation in mean performance for each of the conditions. This curve is described in a single equation in which performance of the old is described as a function of performance of the young (the equations from Table 3.1 can be used to that effect). Second, the data of the young participants are transformed according to this equation. In this way, the average age effect in the data is mimicked in the data of the young. Third, ANOVA is conducted on the transformed data of the young and the untrans-formed data of the old. A significant age by condition interaction then signals a condition-specific departure from the average age effect. The drawback of this method is that one needs multiple conditions (instead of the usual two) for a good estimate of the average effect.

The second alternative consists in looking directly at age sensitivity in processes, rather than looking at age by condition interactions. One might, for instance, estimate the parameters of the time–accuracy curve directly and apply the statistical methods described in 'The Model' section (see pp. 60–4).

A third, but suboptimal, alternative that deserves some attention because it may be tempting for some is experimental elimination of the age effect in the baseline condition. Recently, a number of researchers have applied a method of individually engineering presentation times so that all subjects reach a preset level of accuracy in a baseline condition. Next, stimuli are presented in a critical condition, using the individually engineered presentation times from the base-line condition. The reasoning is that if age differences emerge in the critical condition, there is age sensitivity in the processes that make up the difference between the two conditions. For instance, Kliegl and Lindenberger (1993) equated episodic recall performance across age groups and measured age differences in interference proneness. Thompson and Kliegl (1991) equated episodic recall performance and measured age differences in the plausibility effect. Schacter *et al.* (1994) equated fact recall and measured age differences in source recall. Unfortunately, logical as it seems, this method is not flawless. Table 3.3 provides a number of calculated examples illustrating this. In the table, I started from the parameters of hypothetical time–accuracy functions for a group of young and older subjects in a baseline condition. In the upper part of the table, the age difference is situated solely in the rate of processing, with the older adults being slowed by a factor of 2. In the lower part, this rate of processing difference is accompanied by an asymptotic age difference of 90%. From these time–accuracy functions, the time needed for a given accuracy level can be calculated. Here, the time needed to reach a level of 50% accuracy was used. Next, a number of hypothetical time–accuracy functions for the critical condition were generated. These time–accuracy functions are different from the

Table 3.3　Performance as a function of age in a critical condition when presentation time in a baseline condition is engineered to yield 50% accuracy for each group; age differences for parameters in the baseline and critical conditions are identical.

Age group	Baseline condition Parameters			Presentation time	Critical condition Parameters			Performance
	a	b	c		a	b	c	
Young	0.2	4	0.90	3.45	1	4	0.90	0.41
Old	0.2	8	0.90	6.69	1	8	0.90	0.46
Young	0.2	4	0.90	3.45	0.2	1.5	0.90	0.80
Old	0.2	8	0.90	6.69	0.2	3	0.90	0.80
Young	0.2	4	0.90	3.45	0.2	4	0.70	0.39
Old	0.2	8	0.90	6.69	0.2	8	0.70	0.39
Young	0.2	4	0.90	3.45	0.2	1.5	0.70	0.62
Old	0.2	8	0.90	6.69	0.2	3	0.70	0.62
Young	0.2	4	0.90	3.45	1	1.5	0.70	0.56
Old	0.2	8	0.90	6.69	1	3	0.70	0.59
Rate and asymptotic difference								
Young	0.2	4	0.90	3.45	1	4	0.90	0.41
Old	0.2	8	0.81	7.89	1	8	0.81	0.47
Young	0.2	4	0.90	3.45	0.2	1.5	0.90	0.80
Old	0.2	8	0.81	7.89	0.2	3	0.81	0.75
Young	0.2	4	0.90	3.45	0.2	4	0.80	0.45
Old	0.2	8	0.81	7.89	0.2	8	0.72	0.45
Young	0.2	4	0.90	3.45	0.2	1.5	0.80	0.71
Old	0.2	8	0.81	7.89	0.2	3	0.72	0.66
Young	0.2	4	0.90	3.45	1	1.5	0.80	0.64
Old	0.2	8	0.81	7.89	1	3	0.72	0.65

baseline time–accuracy functions, but they preserve the age difference. That is, for the upper part of the table, the sole difference in the critical condition time–accuracy functions is that the rate of processing is twice as slow in older adults; in the lower part of the table, rate of processing is twice as slow for older adults, and asymptotes are 90% of those of the young adults. If the presentation time needed for 50% accuracy in the baseline condition is applied to the equations for the critical conditions, we obtain the performance as reported in the last column of the table. If the logic of equating accuracy of the participants in the baseline condition and then examining age differences in the critical condition is correct, we should expect no age differences in the critical conditions, because nothing changes from the baseline to the critical condition in terms of age differences in the underlying time–accuracy functions. However, it can be seen that in quite a number of cases age differences are present in performance in the critical condition. Thus, even when performance is equated in the baseline condition, and nothing changes with respect to the underlying parameters of the time–accuracy functions, age differences may occur in the critical condition, (mis)leading the naive observer to conclude that there is differential age sensitivity in the processes involved in the two conditions.

CONCLUSION: TIME–ACCURACY FUNCTIONS AND THEIR IMPLICATIONS FOR COGNITIVE AGING THEORIES

I started this chapter by referring to the lack of integration of research findings in the field of cognitive aging. I have presented the case that examining age differences and age by condition interactions in the parameters of time–accuracy functions may be an interesting tool for such integrative efforts. I pointed at the possibilities of a joint time–accuracy platform, and at methods of data analysis that are psychometrically more sound than the raw score approach usually applied. I did not promise an integrative theory, and I am far from offering one right now. However, the journey through this chapter has provided us with some interesting points that a well-grounded theory of cognitive aging should take into account.

At the risk of oversimplifying, it seems that theories in the field come in two kinds. A few are generalist theories, claiming a global depressing effect of age on performance; many are interactionist theories, claiming that aging is responsible for differential effects in myriads of processes. To be parallel or not to be parallel – that is the question. It seems to me that the mathematical musings and illustrative data gathered here have something to say to occupants of both positions.

First, the available data show that a general model assuming a single level of parallelism (i.e., general slowing theory) is probably wrong. Rather, as posited by Kliegl *et al.* (1995) and Kliegl (1996), there appear to be a number of levels of parallelism, driven by an underlying continuum of complexity that causes age differences to jump from one level or state to another. Mental arithmetic data clearly demonstrate that there are circumstances in which the age differences in one level cannot be reduced to age differences at a lower level. Many questions remain – to name but one: how exactly the underlying continuum should be defined and described – and at present this view is clearly more a framework than a consistent theory. However, examining levels of dissociation seems a promising way to look at cognitive aging, if only because it provides a unique Middle Way between the general and interactionist beliefs.

The levels-of-dissociation framework also avoids one of the embarrassing problems of one-factor theories, namely how to distinguish the effects of aging from effects the same factor has on other group differences. For instance, it has been demonstrated that 7-year-old children are as slow as 75-year-old persons (Cerella and Hale 1994), and it has been claimed that speed-of-processing is the major causative variable in cognitive aging (e.g. Salthouse 1996) and development (e.g. Anderson 1992); still there is a huge difference in everyday and laboratory cognitive behaviour between the average 75-year-old and the average

7-year-old. Likewise, schizophrenics are known to suffer from a breakdown in inhibition (McDowd *et al.* 1993), a mechanism that has been cited as the main cause of cognitive aging (Hasher and Zacks 1988); yet aging individuals typically do not exhibit psychotic behaviour. Some data gathered within the level-of-dissociation framework (Mayr *et al.* 1996) point at asymmetries between development and aging in the points along the complexity continuum that are associated with the jumps from one level of age differences to another. Such breaks in symmetry (for other such instances within two-factor theories, see Cerella 1995, and Hale and Myerson 1996) are important to define what makes aging aging – what makes it different from reverse development or from other forms of more or less global challenges to the central nervous system.

With regard to the interactionist position, the data, both meta-analytic and primary, do point at regularities and show that performance of older adults can be predicted quite well from performance of young adults. There are clear commonalities between the two groups, both in latency and accuracy data, that seem hard to explain but by large parallels in the way young and older systems process information.

Another aspect of the data that has theoretical consequences is the presence, probably only at a high level of complexity, of asymptotic age differences. Age sometimes imposes limits on the system that cannot be remediated in a superficial way by giving subjects more time for the task. Clearly, we need theories that make sense of these asymptotic differences, and we have only begun to develop and explore those. These theories can be task-specific (such as the self-monitoring explanation advanced by Verhaeghen *et al.* 1997) or general (such as the simultaneity mechanism advanced by Salthouse 1996), or may present a mixture of both.

The reflections on the psychometrics of age-comparative (in fact, all group-comparative) research have clear implications for interactionist studies. The tacit assumption of equal accuracy scales for young and older adults may well be mistaken. Meta-analytic data to that effect have been available for some years (Verhaeghen and Marcoen 1993*a*); the present chapter provides a model-derived and interpretable confirmation of the form of the curves found earlier. The implication is that the classic null hypothesis for interactions, namely the hypothesis of equal age differences across conditions, is untenable for at least some types of tasks (such as recall of lists from episodic memory). Overstating the point (or maybe not, that is a matter of empirical verification), this implies that everything we thought we knew about cognitive aging may be wrong, because our knowledge is based on a method of data analysis that is suboptimal. Fortunately, alternative methods of data analysis are available, and some were pointed out here.

In sum, I tried to advance time–accuracy research as a new and exciting tool for cognitive aging research. Data glimpsed along the way seem to indicate that the parallels on beauty's brow are multiple, opening theoretical perspectives towards a Middle Way in theorizing about how Time doth his gift confound.

ACKNOWLEDGEMENTS

This research was conducted in part while I was a Research Assistant and a Post-Doctoral Fellow at the Fund for Scientific Research – Flanders (Belgium). Funding was provided by a grant of the Fund for Scientific Research – Flanders (Belgium) and the Prof. Dr. Jan Hellemans Fonds to Alfons Marcoen, Chair of the Center for Developmental Psychology at the Katholieke Universiteit Leuven, where I worked from 1989 to 1997. I gratefully acknowledge discussions with John Cerella, Paul De Boeck, Vicky Dierckx, William Hoyer, Ulman Lindenberger, Joel Myerson, Timothy Salthouse, and Anneloes Vandenbroucke on some the topics covered here. The ReCALL lab group at Syracuse University offered many helpful comments. Special thanks go to Reinhold Kliegl, who introduced me to time–accuracy research and helped shape my thoughts on the matter during my stay at the University of Potsdam in spring 1995. Portions of this research have been presented at the IIIrd European Congress of Gerontology, Amsterdam, September 1995, at the 1996 Cognitive Aging Conference, Atlanta, GA, April 1996; the 2nd International Conference On Memory, Padua, Italy, July 1996; and the VIièmes Journées d'Etude du Vieillissement Cognitif, Louvain-La-Neuve, Belgium, November 1996. Sonnet LX (four different lines) was first cited in the context of cognitive aging by Cerella (1990).

Address correspondence to Paul Verhaeghen, Psychology Department, 430 Huntington Hall, Syracuse University, Syracuse, NY 13244–2340, USA.

REFERENCES

Anderson, M. (1992). *Intelligence and development: a cognitive theory*. Oxford: Blackwell.

Attig, M. and Hasher, L. (1980). The processing of frequency occurrence information by adults. *Journal of Gerontology*, **35**, 66–9.

Bäckman, L. (1989). Varieties of memory compensation by older adults in episodic remembering. In L. W. Poon, D. C. Rubin, and B. A. Wilson (ed.), *Everyday cognition in adulthood and late life* (pp. 509–44). Cambridge: Cambridge University Press.

Baddeley, A. D. (1986). *Working memory*. Oxford: Clarendon Press.

Bamber, D. (1979). State-trace analysis: a method of testing simple theories of causation. *Journal of Mathematical Psychology*, **19**, 137–81.

Baron, A. and Cerella, J. (1993). Laboratory tests of the disuse account of cognitive decline. In J. Cerella, W. Hoyer, J. Rybash and M. Commons (ed.), *Adult information processing: Limits on loss* (pp. 175–203). San Diego: Academic Press.

Birren, J. E. and Botwinick, J. (1951). Rate of addition as a function of difficulty and age. *Psychometrika*, **16**, 219–32.

Brinley, J. F. (1965). Cognitive sets, speed and accuracy of performance in the elderly. In A. T. Welford and J. E. Birren (ed.), *Behavior, aging and the nervous system* (pp. 114–49). Springfield, IL: Thomas.

Burke, D. M. (1997). Language, aging, and inhibitory deficits: evaluation of a theory. *Journal of Gerontology: Psychological Sciences*, **52B**, P254–64.

Cerella, J. (1990). Aging and information processing rate. In J. E. Birren and K. W. Schaie (ed.), *Handbook of the psychology of aging* (3rd. edn, pp. 201–21). San Diego: Academic Press.

Cerella, J. (1991). Age effects may be global, not local: comment on Fisk and Rogers (1991). *Journal of Experimental Psychology: General*, **120**, 215–23.

Cerella, J. (1994). Generalized slowing in Brinley plots. *Journal of Gerontology*, **49**, P65–71.

Cerella, J. (1995). Reaction time. In G. L. Maddox (ed.), *The encyclopedia of aging: a comprehensive resource in gerontology and geriatrics* (pp. 792–5). New York: Springer.

Cerella, J. and Hale, S. (1994). The rise and fall in information-processing rates over the life span. *Acta Psychologica*, **86**, 109–97.

Cerella, J., Poon, L. W., and Williams, D. M. (1980). Age and the complexity hypothesis. In L. W. Poon (ed.), *Aging in the 1980s* (pp. 332–40). Washington: American Psychological Association.

Charness, N. and Campbell, J. I. D. (1988). Acquiring skill at mental calculation in adulthood: a task decomposition. *Journal of Experimental Psychology: General*, **117**, 115–29.

Craik, F. I. M. (1986). A functional account of age differences in memory. In F. Klix and H. Hagendorf (ed.), *Human memory and cognitive capabilities* (pp. 409–22). Amsterdam: North-Holland.

Craik, F. I. M. and Lockhart, R. S. (1972). Levels of processing: a framework for memory research. *Journal of Verbal Learning and Verbal Behavior*, **11**, 671–84.

Dosher, B. A. (1976). The retrieval of sentences from memory: a speed-accuracy study. *Cognitive Psychology*, **8**, 291–310.

Ekstrom, R. B., French, J. W., Harman, H. H., and Derman, D. (1976). *Manual for kit of factor-referenced cognitive tests*. Princeton: Educational Testing Service.

Ellis, N. R., Palmer, R. L., and Reeves, C. L. (1988). Developmental and intellectual differences in frequency processing. *Developmental Psychology*, **24**, 38–45.

Fisk, A. D. and Fisher, D. L. (1994). Brinley plots and theories of aging: the explicit, muddled, and implicit debates. *Journal of Gerontology: Psychological Sciences*, **49**, P81–9.

Freund, J. L. and Witte, K. L. (1986). Recognition and frequency judgments in young and elderly adults. *American Journal of Psychology*, **99**, 81–102.

Geary, D. C. and Wiley, J. G. (1991). Cognitive addition: strategy choice and speed-of-processing differences in young and elderly adults. *Psychology and Aging*, **6**, 474–83.

Geary, D. C., Frensch, P. A., and Wiley, J. G. (1993). Simple and complex subtraction: strategy choice and speed-of-processing differences in younger and older adults. *Psychology and Aging*, **8**, 242–56.

Hale, S. and Myerson, J. (1996). Experimental evidence for differential slowing in the lexical and nonlexical domains. *Aging, Neuropsychology, and Cognition*, **3**, 154–65.

Hasher, L. and Zacks, R. T. (1979). Automatic and effortful processes in memory. *Journal of Experimental Psychology: General*, **108**, 356–88.

Hasher, L. and Zacks, R. T. (1988). Working memory, comprehension, and aging: a review and a new view. In G. H. Bower (ed.), *The psychology of learning and motivation* (Vol. 22, pp. 193–225). San Diego: Academic Press.

Hultsch, D. F. and Dixon, R. A. (1990). Learning and memory in aging. In J. E. Birren and K. W. Schaie (ed.), *Handbook of the psychology of aging* (3rd. ed., pp. 258–74). San Diego: Academic Press.

Just, M. A. and Carpenter, P. A. (1992). A capacity theory of comprehension: Individual differences in working memory. *Psychological Review*, **99**, 122–49.

Kausler, D. H. and Hakami, M. K. (1982). Frequency judgments by young and elderly adults for relevant stimuli with simultaneously present irrelevant stimuli. *Journal of Gerontology*, **37**, 438–42.

Kausler, D. H., Hakami, M. K., and Wright, R. (1982). Adult age differences in frequency judgments of categorical representations. *Journal of Gerontology*, **37**, 365–71.

Kausler, D. H., Lichty, W., and Hakami, M. K. (1984). Frequency judgments for distractor items in a short-term memory task: instructional variation and adult age differences. *Journal of Verbal Learning and Verbal Behavior*, **23**, 660–8.

Kausler, D. H. and Puckett, J. M. (1980). Frequency judgments and correlated cognitive abilities in young and elderly adults. *Journal of Gerontology*, **35**, 376–82.

Kellogg, R. T. (1983). Age differences in hypothesis testing and frequency processing in concept learning. *Bulletin of the Psychonomic Society*, **21**, 101–4.

Kliegl, R. (1995). From presentation time to processing time: a psychophysics approach to episodic memory. In W. Schneider and F. E. Weinert (ed.), *Memory performance and competencies: issues in growth and development* (pp. 89–110). Mahwah, NJ: Lawrence Erlbaum.

Kliegl, R. and Lindenberger, U. (1993). Modeling intrusions and correct recall in episodic memory: Adult age differences in encoding of list context. *Journal of Experimental Psychology: Learning, Memory, and Cognition*, **19**, 617–37.

Kliegl, R. (1996, July). *Cognitive development and cognitive complexity: a psychophysics approach.* Paper presented at the Max Planck Institute for Psychological Research, Munich.

Kliegl, R., Krampe, R. T., and Mayr, U. (1993, July). Time–accuracy relations for two episodic memory functions. In M. Storandt and B. Winblad (Chairs), *Changes in memory.* Symposium conducted at the XVth Congress of the International Association of Gerontology, Budapest, Hungary.

Kliegl, R., Mayr, U., and Krampe, R. T. (1994). Time–accuracy functions for determining process and person differences: an application to cognitive aging. *Cognitive Psychology*, **26**, 134–64.

Kliegl, R., Mayr, U., and Krampe, R. T. (1995). Process dissociations in cognitive aging. In M. Bergener, J. C. Brocklehurst, and S. I. Finkel (ed.), *Aging, health, and healing.* New York: Springer.

Laver, G. D. and Burke, D. M. (1993) Why do semantic priming effects increase in old age? A meta-analysis. *Psychology and Aging*, **8**, 34–43.

LaVoie, D. and Light, L. L. (1994) Adult age differences in repetition priming: a meta-analysis. *Psychology and Aging*, **9**, 539–53.

LeFevre, J. A., Sadesky, G. S., and Bisanz, J. (1996). Selection of procedures in mental addition: reassessing the problem size effect in adults. *Journal of Experimental Psychology: Learning, Memory, and Cognition*, **22**, 216–30.

Lima, S. D., Hale, S. and Myerson, J. (1991). How general is general slowing? Evidence from the lexical domain. *Psychology and Aging*, **6**, 416–25.

Lindenberger, U. (1990). The effects of professional expertise and cognitive aging on skilled memory performance. Unpublished doctoral dissertation, Free University Berlin.

Lohman, D. F. (1989). Estimating individual differences in information processing using speed-accuracy models. In R. Kanfer, P. L. Ackerman, and R. Cudeck (ed.), *Abilities, motivation, and methodology: the Minnesota symposium on learning and individual differences* (pp. 119–63). Hillsdale, NJ: Lawrence Erlbaum.

McClelland, J. L. (1979). On the time relations of mental processes: An examination of systems of processes in cascade. *Psychological Review*, 86, 287–330.

McDowd, J. M. (1997). Inhibition in attention and aging. *Journal of Gerontology: Psychological Sciences*, 52B, P265–73.

McDowd, J. M., Filion, D. L., Harris, M. J., and Braff, D. L. (1993). Sensory gating and inhibitory function in late-life schizophrenia. *Schizophrenia Bulletin*, 19, 733–46.

McElree, B. and Griffith, T. (1995). Syntactic and thematic processing in sentence comprehension: evidence for a temporal dissociation. *Journal of Experimental Psychology: Learning, Memory, and Cognition*, 21, 134–57.

MacKay, D. G. (1988). Under what conditions can theoretical psychology survive and prosper? Integrating the rational and empirical epistemologies. *Psychological Review*, 95, 559–65.

Madden, D. J., Pierce, T. W., and Allen, P. A. (1992). Adult age differences in attentional allocation during memory search. *Psychology and Aging*, 7, 594–601.

Mayr, U. and Kliegl, R. (1993). Sequential and coordinative complexity: age-based processing limitations in figural transformations. *Journal of Experimental Psychology: Learning, Memory, and Cognition*, 19, 1297–320.

Mayr, U., Kliegl, R., and Krampe, R. (1996). Sequential and coordinative processing dynamics in figural transformation across the life span. *Cognition*, 59, 61–90.

Monsell, S. (1996). Control of mental processes. In V. Bruce (ed.), *Unsolved mysteries of the mind: tutorial essays in cognition* (pp. 93–148). Hove, UK: Lawrence Erlbaum.

Myerson, J. and Hale, S. (1993). General slowing and age invariance in cognitive processing: the other side of the coin. In J. Cerella, J. Rybash, W. Hoyer, and M. L. Commons (ed.), *Adult information processing: limits on loss* (pp. 115–41). San Diego: Academic Press.

Myerson, J., Hale, S., Wagstaff, D., Poon, L. W., and Smith, G. A. (1990). The information-loss model: A mathematical theory of age-related cognitive slowing. *Psychological Review*, 97, 475–87.

Myerson, J., Wagstaff, D., and Hale, S. (1994). Brinley plots, explained variance, and the analysis of age differences in response latencies. *Journal of Gerontology: Psychological Sciences*, 49, P72–80.

Perfect, T. J. (1994). What can Brinley plots tell us about cognitive aging? *Journal of Gerontology: Psychological Sciences*, 49, P60–4.

Rogers, W. A. and Fisk, A. D. (1991). Age-related differences in the maintenance and modification of automatic processes: arithmetic Stroop interference. *Human Factors*, 33, 45–56.

Salthouse, T. A. (1978). Age and speed: the nature of the relationship. Unpublished manuscript.

Salthouse, T. A. (1985). *A theory of cognitive aging*. Amsterdam: North-Holland.

Salthouse, T. A. (1991). *Theoretical perspectives on cognitive aging.* Hillsdale, NJ: Lawrence Erlbaum Associates.

Salthouse, T. A. (1992). Shifting levels of analysis in the investigation of cognitive aging. *Human Development*, **35**, 321–42.

Salthouse, T. A. (1996). The processing-speed theory of adult age differences in cognition. *Psychological Review*, **103**, 403–28.

Salthouse, T. A. and Coon, V. E. (1994). Interpretation of differential deficits: The case of aging and mental arithmetic. *Journal of Experimental Psychology: Learning, Memory, and Cognition*, **20**, 1172–82.

Salthouse, T. A., Kausler, D., and Saults, J. S. (1988). Investigation of student status, background variables, and feasibility of standard tasks in cognitive aging research. *Psychology and Aging*, **3**, 29–37.

Salthouse, T. A. and Kersten, A. W. (1993). Decomposing adult age differences in symbol arithmetic. *Memory & Cognition*, **21**, 699–710.

Sanders, R. E., Wise, J. L., Liddle, C. L., and Murphy, M. D. (1990). Adult age comparisons in the processing of event frequency information. *Psychology and Aging*, **5**, 172–7.

Schacter, D. L., Osowiecki, D., Kaszniak, A. W., Kihlstrom, J. E., and Valdiserri, M. (1994). Source memory: Extending the boundaries of age-related deficits. *Psychology and Aging*, **9**, 81–9.

Sliwinski, M., Buschke, H., Kuslansky, G., Senior, G., and Scarisbrick, D. (1994). Proportional slowing and addition speed in old and young adults. *Psychology and Aging*, **9**, 72–80.

Smith, A. D. (1996). Memory. In J. E. Birren, K. W. Schaie, R. P. Abeles, M. Gatz, and T. A. Salthouse (ed.), *Handbook of the psychology of aging* (4th. edn, pp. 236–50). San Diego: Academic Press.

Spencer, W. D. and Raz, N. (1995). Differential effects of aging on memory for content and context: a meta-analysis. *Psychology and Aging*, **10**, 527–39.

Thompson, L. A. and Kliegl, R. (1991). Adult age effects of plausibility on memory: the role of time constraints during encoding. *Journal of Experimental Psychology: Learning, Memory, and Cognition*, **17**, 542–55.

van Geert, P. (1993). A dynamic systems model of cognitive growth: competition and support under limited resource conditions. In L. B. Smith and E. Thelen (ed.), *A dynamic systems approach to development: Applications* (pp. 265–331). Cambridge, MA: Bradford.

Verhaeghen, P. and De Meersman, L. (1998a). Aging and the negative priming effect: A meta-analysis. *Psychology and Aging*, **13**, 435–444.

Verhaeghen, P. and De Meersman, L. (1998b). Aging and the Stroop effect: a meta-analysis. *Psychology and Aging*, **13**, 120–6.

Verhaeghen, P., Kliegl, R., and Mayr, U. (1997). Sequential and coordinative complexity in time–accuracy functions for mental arithmetic. *Psychology and Aging*, **12**, 555–64.

Verhaeghen, P. and Marcoen, A. (1993a). Memory aging as a general phenomenon: episodic recall of older adults is a function of episodic recall of the young. *Psychology and Aging*, **8**, 380–8.

Verhaeghen, P. and Marcoen, A. (1993b). More or less the same? A memorability analysis on episodic memory tasks in young and older adults. *Journal of Gerontology: Psychological Sciences*, **48**, P172–8.

Verhaeghen, P. and Marcoen, A. (1996). On the mechanisms of plasticity in young and older adults after instruction in the method of loci: evidence for an amplification model. *Psychology and Aging*, **11**, 164–78.

Verhaeghen, P. and Salthouse, T. A. (1997). Meta-analyses of age-cognition relations in adulthood: estimates of linear and non-linear age effects and structural models. *Psychological Bulletin*, **122**, 231–49.

Verhaeghen, P., Marcoen, A., and Goossens, L. (1993). Facts and fiction about memory aging: a quantitative integration of research findings. *Journal of Gerontology: Psychological Sciences*, **48**, P157–71.

Verhaeghen, P., Vandenbroucke, A., and Dierckx, V. (1998). Growing slower and less accurate: the effects of age on time–accuracy functions for recall from episodic memory. *Experimental Aging Research*, **24**, 3–19.

Warren, L. R. and Mitchell, S. A. (1980). Age differences in judging the frequency of events. *Developmental Psychology*, **16**, 432–42.

West, R. L. (1996). An application of prefrontal cortex function theory to cognitive aging. *Psychological Bulletin*, **120**, 272–92.

Wickelgren, W. A. (1977). Speed-accuracy tradeoff and information processing dynamics. *Acta Psychologica*, **41**, 67–85.

Zacks, R. and Hasher, L. (1997). Cognitive gerontology and attentional inhibition: a reply to Burke and McDowd. *Journal of Gerontology: Psychological Sciences*, **52B**, P274–83.

Zelinski, E. M. and Gilewski, M. J. (1988). Memory for prose and aging: a meta-analysis. In M. L. Howe and C. J. Brainerd (ed.), *Cognitive development in adulthood: progress in cognitive development research* (pp. 133–58). New York: Springer-Verlag.

FOUR

Cognitive slowing among older adults: what kind and how much?

DONALD L. FISHER, SUSAN A. DUFFY, AND KONSTANTINOS V. KATSIKOPOULOS

INTRODUCTION

Older adults generally perform more poorly than younger adults on a variety of different measures of performance. These measures include the large range of reaction time tasks so prevalent today (e.g. Sternberg 1969), as well as the many different tests of memory, reasoning and spatial abilities first administered back in the 1940s (e.g. Hebb 1942; Cattell 1943). The argument has been made that much of the decline in performance among older adults can be traced to a single factor, cognitive slowing. Birren (e.g. 1965, 1974) was the first to propose this general line of argument, an argument which has since been vigorously pursued by a number of different investigators (e.g. Cerella 1985; Salthouse 1980, 1985). Although cognitive slowing is not the only factor that has been put forward as an explanation for the differences between younger and older adults, it has remained the dominant one and is the one upon which we will focus (for a review of the alternative potential mediators, see Salthouse 1991).

Two related questions have been of central concern to investigators interested in understanding the role of cognitive slowing in the aging process. Historically, the first question to be addressed is focused on the type of age-related slowing. In particular, this question is focused on a determination of why older adults are slower than younger adults at the level of individual processes. For example, the slowing among older adults could be the same across all processes and all tasks (Cerella 1985), in which case we will refer to it as *general slowing*. It could be the same across all processes in a given task, but vary from task to task or domain to domain (Hale *et al.* 1987; Lima *et al.* 1991), in which case we will refer to it as *task-specific slowing*. It could be the same for a given process across all tasks, but vary from one process to the next (Fisk and Rogers 1991; Fisk *et al.* 1992), in which case we will refer to it as *process-specific slowing*. Or, it could vary across both tasks and processes. Today, it is generally acknowledged that there do exist differences both in the extent to which particular processes are slowed within tasks and in the extent to which overall performance is slowed across tasks (e.g. Salthouse 1996c).

The second question to be addressed is focused on the relative influence of age-invariant (*common*) as opposed to age-specific factors on the slowing observed in older adults. In particular, this question is focused on a determination of how much of the slowing among older adults, as tasks become more complex, is due to common factors (i.e., factors that influence younger and older adults equally) and how much is due to factors that affect only older adults. In order to answer this question we will need to differentiate between *control* and *criterion* tasks. In a control task, we will assume that the behaviour required is a relatively simple one and the latent processes are at their baseline duration. Thus, the control task provides a measure of each subject's baseline processing speed. (We will also refer occasionally to a control task as a *baseline* task.) In a criterion task, we will assume that the behaviour required is a more complex one and therefore the latent processes have a somewhat longer duration. We can now rephrase the second question more precisely. In particular, we want to know whether the slowing we observe in the younger adults in the criterion task (compared to their performance on the control task) is the same as the slowing we observe in the older adults in the criterion task (compared again to their performance on the control task). If it is, then we can attribute all of the slowing to differences in an individual's baseline speed. We speak of the baseline speed as a common factor because we imagine that the time that it takes a younger or older adult in a criterion task is a function of their baseline speed (the common factor) and, possibly for older adults, additional age-related factors.

As the reader may already suspect the above two questions are related. Their relation is displayed graphically in the two panels in Fig. 4.1. When we ask the first question, we are in effect asking whether the function f_1 that maps younger adults' response times in Task 1 to older adults' response times in this task is the same as the function that maps younger adults' response times in Task 2 to older adults' response times in this task (top panel). When we ask the second question, we are in effect asking how closely related the function g_Y, which maps younger adults' response times in the control task to their response times in the criterion task, is to the function g_O, which maps older adults' response times in the control task to their response times in the criterion task (bottom panel). If the functions were truly age invariant, they would be identical.

It is important to note that a shift from the first question to the second question has changed significantly the nature of the debate about the role of general slowing. When one is concerned with the first, and only the first, question (with what we will call *chronological* slowing, that is, the type of slowing–general, task specific or process specific–that occurs with age), evidence from just one study that older adults are slowed differentially across tasks is sufficient to reject the hypothesis that there exists a general chronological slowing. That is, we can reject the hypothesis of general chronological slowing if we can find any two tasks such that f_1 does not equal f_2. However, when one turns one's attention to the second question (to the impact of what we will call *chronocentric* slowing, that is, the impact of the speed of both younger and older adults in control tasks

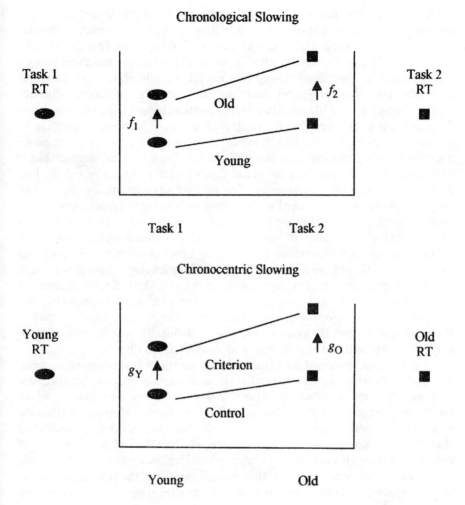

Fig. 4.1 The chronological (f_1 and f_2) and chronocentric (g_Y and g_O) slowing functions.

on their performance in criterion tasks), evidence that younger and older adults are slowed differentially in criterion tasks is not considered sufficient to reject the hypothesis that there exists a common chronocentric slowing factor which can explain most (but not necessarily all) of the slowing in the performance of older adults on criterion tasks (Salthouse 1996c). That is, we are not interested here solely in the identity of the functions g_Y and g_O. Instead we are interested in how well we can predict older adults' response times in the criterion task, given that we know their baseline speed and the common function which maps control task response times to criterion task response times.

Our focus in this chapter is on the second question. In particular, we want to understand how we might measure the relative influence of a common chrono-centric slowing on the criterion response times of older adults. In order to make sense of a measure of common slowing, we need to consider the underlying or latent model of processing. Using this model, we will show that when the chronological slowing is general, then the existing measures of common chrono-centric slowing are readily interpretable. When the chronological slowing varies from one task to another, then the existing measures of common slowing can be misleading. And when the chronological slowing varies from one process to another, then the existing measures of common slowing are uninterpretable.

In order to make good on the claim that the interpretation of the existing measures of common chronocentric slowing depends critically on the type of chronological slowing, we need at the outset to develop the machinery (mathematical tools) for constructing a model of chronological slowing for each of the different types of such slowing. By a model of chronological slowing we mean an equation which relates the response times of older adults in a given task j to a function of the durations of the latent psychological processes which govern the performance of younger adults in this same task. So, for example, if the processes in some task j are arranged in series with mean durations of, say, 100, 200 and 300 ms for the younger adults, then the expected response time of the older adults when all processes are slowed identically by some factor, say β, can be written as the sum $\beta \times 100 + \beta \times 200 + \beta \times 300$.

Once we have developed the three different models of chronological slowing, we need to develop the machinery for constructing a model of chronocentric slowing. By a model of chronocentric slowing we mean an equation which relates the response times of younger and older adults performing a criterion task to their response times in a control task. We need to develop a model of chronocentric slowing so that we can predict the effect of a given type of chronological slowing on the type of chronocentric slowing that we will observe, that is, on the functions g_y and g_o that map, respectively, the younger and older adults' response times on the control task into their response times on the criterion task.

Finally, given that we know the type of chronological slowing (f_1 and f_2) and can therefore predict the type of chronocentric slowing (g_o and g_y), we need to evaluate the information provided by the measures of common chronocentric slowing about the role that such a slowing plays in the determination of older adults' response times. In particular, we need to determine whether what we can infer from the measure of common slowing about the type of chronocentric slowing agrees with what we know to be the case. The reader should note the critical relation that we believe exists between a macroscopic measure (such as the degree of common chronocentric slowing) and a more detailed microscopic measure (such as the degree of chronological slowing in a particular process or task). The reader may want to refer back to Chapter 2 to obtain an additional perspective on this relation.

TYPES AND AMOUNT OF COGNITIVE SLOWING

In this first section, we want to prepare the way for a discussion of the interpretability of the measures of common chronocentric slowing under the three different types of chronological slowing. This preparation requires first that we develop a model of chronological slowing, second that we develop a model of chronocentric slowing, and finally that we describe various measures of common chronocentric slowing.

Type of chronological slowing

As noted at the outset, there are at least three different types of chronological slowing one might observe: general, task-specific and process-specific slowing. What we want to do in this section is develop a generic model of chronological slowing from which each of the three more specific models can be derived. In the generic model, we will relate older adults' response times in a given task to younger adults' response times in the same task when the response times in the task are themselves a function of the durations of the latent processes that govern performance.

In order to construct a generic model of slowing from which the more specific models of chronological slowing can be derived, we need to introduce some notation at this point. In the most general case, at least the most general case we will consider, the slowing could vary as a function of the process i, the task j, and the age or cohort k of individuals whose response time is being measured.[1] Let X_{ijk} represent the duration of process i in task j averaged over all individuals in cohort k. And let the number of processes in task j range from 1 to I_j, the number of tasks from 1 to J, and the number of cohorts from 1 to K.

We can now derive a general expression for the expected time $E[T_{jk}]$ that it takes a cohort k performing a particular task j to respond as a function of the arrangement and durations of the latent processes in that task. The processes can potentially be represented in simple serial networks, more complicated parallel networks, or still more complex PERT networks (Schweickert 1978; Schweickert and Townsend 1989). To keep things simple, we will assume that the processes are arranged in series. Thus, the time on average, T_{jk}, that it takes individuals in cohort k to execute all of the processes in task j can be written as the sum of the average durations of the processes in this task:

$$T_{jk} = \sum_{i=1}^{I_j} X_{ijk} \tag{4.1}$$

1 Readers may find it helpful to think of the index k as representing the relative ages of the cohorts, in which case $k = 0$ represents the youngest cohort. Similarly, readers can think of the index j as representing the relative complexity of the tasks, in which case $j = 0$ represents the least complex task, or what we are calling the control task.

We now want to compute the expected value of the sample mean T_{jk} in eqn 4.1. We can simplify the notation by letting $\mu_{ijk} = E[X_{ijk}]$. Taking expectations and then noting that the expectation of a sum is the sum of the expectations, one obtains:

$$E[T_{jk}] = \sum_{i=1}^{Ij} E[X_{ijk}] = \sum_{i=1}^{Ij} \mu_{ijk} \tag{4.2}$$

In summary, the expected time $E[T_{jk}]$ that it takes cohort k to respond in task j can be written more simply as the sum of the expected durations μ_{ijk} of the I_j processes in task j.

We are not done quite yet with the construction of a formal model of chronological slowing. In eqn 4.2 above we relate the response times of an older cohort k to the durations of *this* cohort's latent processes. By itself, this tells us nothing about the relation between the response times of the older cohort k and the durations of a younger cohort's latent processes. Thus, in order to complete the development of a formal model of chronological slowing, we need to replace the durations of the cohort k's latent processes in eqn 4.2 with some function of the duration of the younger cohort's latent processes. In particular, if we set the cohort index k on a constant or variable equal to 0 (zero) when the index represents a younger cohort, then for each different type of chronological slowing we can write the expected response time $E[T_{jk}]$ as follows:

$$E[T_{jk}] = \sum_{i=1}^{Ij} \mu_{ijk} = \sum_{i=1}^{Ij} f_{ijk}(\mu_{ij0}) \tag{4.3}$$

The exact restrictions on the functions determine whether the slowing is general, task specific or process specific. For example, if the function $f_{ijk}(\bullet)$ is equal to β_k for all processes i and tasks j in cohort k, then this represents what is commonly referred to as the multiplicative model of general slowing.

Before turning to the next section, it may help readers if they have a more visual sense of the generic model of chronological slowing and, in particular, the relation of eqns 4.2 and 4.3 to the underlying architecture and associated assumptions. In Fig. 4.2 we attempt to do just this for two tasks, each with three processes. Task 1 is diagrammed in the top panel. The processes are represented by the solid arrows heading diagonally up the figure. The networks for both younger (left side of top panel) and older (right side) adults appear side by side. Equation 4.2 is simply a statement that the time on average it takes older adults to complete the task graphed in the upper right is equal to the sum of the average times it takes them to complete each of the latent processes. A horizontally positioned arrow connects each process in the younger adults' network to the corresponding process in the older adults' network. These arrows are labelled by a function which is indexed by the process i ($i = 1,2,3$

in our example) and task ($j = 1$ in our example in the top panel). We drop the cohort index here for clarity. The function maps the duration of a process in the younger adults' network to its corresponding duration in the older adults' network. Equation 4.3 is simply a statement that the time on average it takes older adults to complete the processes in a task (right side of panels) can also be written as a sum of functions of the times it takes younger adults to complete each of the identical processes in the same task (left side).

In the following sections, we will describe in detail how to rewrite the generic formulation of a model of chronological slowing as given in eqn 4.3 for each of

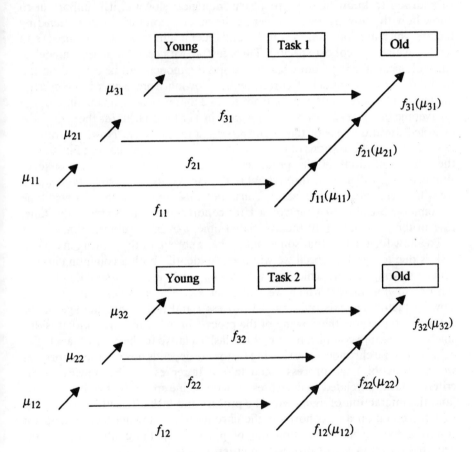

Fig. 4.2 Visual representation of the mapping of younger to older adults' response times in Tasks 1 (top) and 2 (bottom). (The arrows heading diagonally up the figure represent the latent processes – three processes in Tasks 1 and 2 for both younger and older adults. The arrows heading across the figure represent the chronological slowing functions which map the duration of the processes when younger adults are performing a given task to the duration of these same processes when older adults are performing the task.)

the three different types of slowing. And we will refer back to Fig. 4.2 in order better to understand these different types of models. Now, however, the generic formulation is sufficient for our needs. In particular, using eqn 4.3 it is clear how we can write the expected response time of the older cohort k performing task j as a function of the expected durations μ_{ij0} of the latent processes of the younger cohort performing this same task.

Type of chronocentric slowing

In addition to knowing the type of chronological slowing, it is important to know how the slowing among older adults on criterion tasks is determined by factors which are common to younger and older adults (e.g. baseline speed) and factors which are cohort specific. Thus, just as we needed a generic model of chronological slowing from which more specific models can be derived, so too we need a generic model of chronocentric slowing from which more specific models can be derived. We know from eqn 4.2 that we can write the time $E[T_{jk}]$ on average that it takes cohort k to respond in a criterion task j as the sum of the expected durations μ_{ijk} of the latent processes in that task. Now, we want to rewrite the latent durations of the processes in the criterion task as a function of the latent durations of the processes in the control task. For the sake of simplicity, we will assume throughout that there is only one control task, which we will label control task 0 (zero). Thus, we let μ_{i0k} represent the expected time to complete process i in a control task for cohort k. We want to relate this time, μ_{i0k}, in the control task to the associated time, μ_{ijk}, in the criterion task.

To allow for the fact that some, but perhaps not all, of the slowing in a given task is due to baseline speed we will need to identify both a common chronocentric slowing factor, which we will label γ_{ij}, and a cohort-specific chronocentric slowing factor, which we will label δ_{ijk}. The common chronocentric slowing factor depends only on the process i and task j, not the age of the cohort. It represents the slowing of the process in the criterion task that is due solely to the more complex nature of the task (relative to the control task). The cohort-specific chronocentric slowing factor δ_{ijk} depends now on the cohort k as well as (possibly) the process i and task j. It represents the slowing in the criterion task, unrelated to decreases in the baseline speed, that is due to aging (and the interaction of aging with the process and task). Together, we assume that the common and cohort-specific chronocentric slowing factors map for cohort k the expected duration μ_{i0k} of process i in the control task to the expected duration μ_{ijk} of process i in criterion task j:

$$E[T_{jk}] = \sum_{i=1}^{Ij} \mu_{ijk} = \sum_{i=1}^{Ij} \gamma_{ij}\, \delta_{ijk}\, \mu_{i0k} \tag{4.4}$$

Very little attention has actually been paid to the form of the aforementioned factors, γ_{ij} and δ_{ijk}. We will talk more about these factors later in the chapter.

As with the discussion of chronological slowing, it may help readers if they have a more visual sense of the generic model of chronocentric slowing and, in particular, the relation of eqn 4.4 to the underlying architecture and associated assumptions. In Fig. 4.3 we attempt to do just this both for older adults in control and criterion tasks (top panel) and younger adults in control and criterion tasks. To keep things simple, we assume that the control and criterion tasks each consist of the same three processes (this assumption can easily be relaxed; see below). Consider just the top panel. The middle sum in eqn 4.4 is simply a statement that the time on average it takes older adults to complete a criterion task is equal to the sum of the average times it takes them to complete each of the three latent processes. A long, horizontal arrow connects each process in the network governing the performance of older adults in the control task to the corresponding process in the network governing the performance of these same older adults in the criterion task. These arrows are labelled by the function (the product of the common chronocentric and cohort-specific chronocentric slowing factor) that is used to produce the slowing of each control process that is observed in the criterion task. The second sum in eqn 4.4 is simply a statement that the time on average it takes older adults to complete the processes in the criterion task can also be written as a sum of functions of the times it takes the older adults to complete each of the processes in the control task.

We should note that in many situations the processes in a particular criterion task will not map so neatly onto the processes in a particular control task. In this case, one may be able to partition the processes in both tasks into identical subsets, say encoding, control and output subsets. The process index i could then refer to these subsets. Or, alternatively, one could, as we do below, lump all processes in the control and criterion tasks into a single subset, in which cases the process index i can be dropped altogether.

Influence of chronocentric slowing

We observe that older adults are slowed absolutely in criterion tasks when compared to younger adults. We would like to know the influence of differences in the baseline speed of the older and younger adults on differences in criterion task response times. There are two ways we might go about answering this question, using measures that we will refer to as *P*(*speed*) and *P*(*shared*).

P(speed) We want first to motivate the choice of a method for identifying the fraction of the difference in the response times of the older and younger adults on criterion tasks that is due to differences in baseline speed. We will label this fraction or proportion as *P*(*speed*). An understanding of this proportion depends critically on a distinction we will draw between common (age-variant) and cohort-specific chronocentric slowing. For the sake of simplicity, we will assume that the common chronocentric slowing factor is a function only of the task (and can therefore be written as γ_j) and that the cohort-specific chronocentric slowing factor is a function only of the cohort (and can therefore be

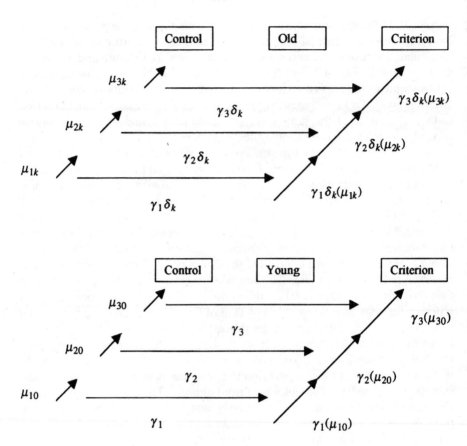

Fig. 4.3 Visual representation of the mapping of control to criterion task response time for both older (top) and younger (bottom) adults. (The arrows heading diagonally up the figure represent the latent processes – three in the control and criterion task for both younger and older adults. The arrows heading across the figure represent the chronocentric slowing functions which map the duration of control processes to the duration of the corresponding criterion processes for a given cohort.)

written as δ_k). To begin, we want to rewrite the general model of chronocentric slowing [eqn 4.4] with our new coefficients:

$$E[T_{jk}] = \sum_{i=1}^{Ij} \gamma_j\, \delta_k\, \mu_{i0k} = \gamma_j\, \delta_k\, E[T_{0k}] \tag{4.5}$$

In words, the time $E[T_{jk}]$ on average that it takes cohort k to complete criterion task j is a multiple of the time on average $E[T_{0k}]$ that it takes this cohort to complete the control task 0. This multiple consists of a factor γ_j representing the common chronocentric slowing across cohorts and a factor δ_k representing an age-specific slowing across tasks. If $\delta_k = 1$ for all cohorts k, then we will refer to the chronocentric slowing as *common* since there is no separate contribution of age beyond the baseline, that is,

$$E[T_{jk}] = \sum_{i=1}^{Ij} \gamma_j \, \mu_{i0k} = \gamma_j E[T_{0k}] \tag{4.6}$$

for all cohorts k. If $\delta_k > 1$ for at least one cohort k, then we will say that the chronocentric slowing is *cohort specific*. Obtaining unique solutions for γ_j in eqn 4.6 is straightforward. Obtaining unique solutions for γ_j and δ_k in eqn 4.5 is only slightly more complex (Appendix A).

We now want to determine just how much of the chronocentric slowing is common. In order to do this, we need to predict the older cohort k's response time $\hat{T}_{jk}$ on task j based on the assumption that the chronocentric slowing is a common one, that is, based on the assumption that the function used to derive the response times of the older cohort in the criterion task from the response times of this cohort in the control task is the same as the function used to derive the response times of the younger adults in the criterion task from the response times of this cohort in the control task. If our assumption is correct, then we can estimate the chronocentric slowing factor γ_j from the younger adults' performance in the criterion and control tasks. Let this estimate equal g_{j0}. Then, if the slowing in the criterion tasks is solely a function of the baseline speed of the subjects, the predicted older cohort k's response time $\hat{T}_{jk}$ on criterion task j is equal to the estimated chronocentric slowing factor g_{j0} times this cohort's observed response time T_{0k} on the control task:

$$\hat{T}_{jk} = g_{j0} T_{0k} \tag{4.7}$$

Thus, the proportion $P(speed)$ of the increase that can be explained by changes in speed alone is equal to the difference between the predicted older adults' response time in the criterion task and their observed response time in the control task normalized by the difference between their observed response times in the criterion and control task:

$$\begin{aligned} P(speed) &= \frac{\hat{T}_{jk} - T_{0k}}{T_{jk} - T_{0k}} \\ &= \frac{g_{j0} T_{0k} - T_{0k}}{T_{jk} - T_{0k}} \end{aligned} \tag{4.8}$$

The approach taken here to the identification of the influence of an age-invariant slowing is very similar to other approaches that have been proposed (e.g. Madden *et al.* 1992, 1993; Salthouse and Kersten 1993).

As a simple example, assume that the younger adults take on average 1 s to respond in the control task ($T_{00} = 1$) and 2 s to respond in the criterion task (T_{j0}

= 2). Then g_{j0} = 2. And suppose that older adults take on average 1.5 s to respond in the control task (T_{0k} = 1.5) and 4.5 s to respond in the criterion task (T_{jk} = 4.5). Then $\hat{T}_{jk}$ = $g_{j0}T_{0k}$ = 2 × 1.5 = 3.0. And $P(speed)$ = 0.5.

P(shared) The above is one answer to the question of how much of an influence differences in the observed response times of the older and younger adults in the control task have on differences in criterion task response times. We can answer this question in a different way. Specifically, we can ask how much of the age-related variability in the criterion task response times is shared with the variability in baseline speed. We want now to describe briefly how this latter question has been answered using correlational techniques (e.g. Salthouse 1992*a*, 1992*b*, 1994, 1996*a*, 1996*b*, 1996*c*).

To understand the correlational techniques, we first need to partition the total variability in the criterion measure as indicated in Fig. 4.4 (note $a + b + c + d$ = 1). Specifically, the proportion of the total variability in the criterion measure shared with age is represented by the sum $b + c$. The proportion of the total variability in the criterion measure shared with speed (the control measure) is represented by the sum $a + b$. Then, the proportion $P(shared)$ of the total *age-related* variability in the criterion variable that is shared with speed is equal to the ratio $b/(b + c)$. This is the proportion that investigators have used to determine the relative impact of a common chronocentric slowing factor on performance.

The statistical procedures required to separate out the desired fraction are straightforward to implement. To begin then, we first need to compute the square of the correlation $R^2_{crit, age}$ between the criterion measure and age. This yields the sum $b + c$ (Fig. 4.4). We next need to compute the square of the semipartial correlation $R^2_{crit, (age|speed)}$ between the criterion measure and age, holding speed constant. This can be done by regressing age on speed, computing

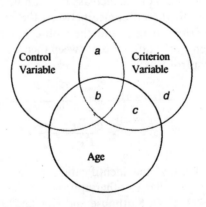

Fig. 4.4 Partitioning the variance among a control measure, a criterion measure and age. (Note that $a + b + c + d$ = 1.)

the difference between the predicted and observed age, and then correlating the performance on the criterion measure with these differences or errors. Thus, one obtains the identity $R^2_{crit, (age|speed)} = R^2_{crit, errors}$ (Myers and Well 1991, p. 486). Either correlation then yields the quantity c by itself. Finally, subtracting the second quantity from the first and dividing by the first yields the fraction, $b/(b + c)$, that we want:

$$P(shared) = \frac{R^2_{crit,age} - R^2_{crit,(age/speed)}}{R^2_{crit,age}}$$

$$= \frac{R^2_{crit, age} - R^2_{crit, errors}}{R^2_{crit,age}} \qquad (4.9)$$

We see immediately that if age is predicted perfectly by speed, then there is no relation between criterion performance and age after speed is partialled out (i.e., $R^2_{crit, (age|speed)} = 0$). Thus, all of the age-related variability in performance on the criterion task is due to changes in speed. Conversely, if age is unrelated to speed, then the relation between criterion performance and age after speed is partialled out (i.e., $R^2_{crit, (age|speed)} = r$) will be the same as the relation between criterion performance and age when speed is not partialled out (i.e., $R^2_{crit, age} = r$). Thus, none of the age-related variability in performance in the criterion task will be due to changes in speed. We now turn to a more detailed discussion of *P(speed)* and *P(shared)* in the context of models of general, task-specific, and process-specific chronological slowing.

GENERAL CHRONOLOGICAL SLOWING

Perhaps the most ubiquitous model of chronological slowing is one in which the slowing of any one latent process is identical to the slowing of any other latent process for both those processes which appear in the same task and those which appear in different tasks. As noted above, we will refer to this as the model of general chronological slowing (or, more specifically when necessary, as the multiplicative model of general chronological slowing). The evidence that older adults' response times are systematically related to younger adults' response times came first from Brinley (1965) who cross plotted within various tasks the two sets of times in what now has come to be known as a Brinley plot. Cerella *et al.* (1980) extended Brinley's analysis, now across many different tasks. When they regressed older adults' response times on younger adults' response times they found that the regression explained almost 90% of the variability in the older adults' response times.

To keep things simple, we will assume that the actual nature of the slowing is a proportional one equal to β_k for any given cohort k, an assumption that is not unreasonable when the tasks take on the order of 2000 ms or less to complete (Cerella 1985; Cerella and Hale 1994). After developing the model of general chronological slowing, we will describe the logical relation between this model and the model of chronocentric slowing that was described above. Next, using techniques developed here, we will estimate how much of the difference between the response times of the older and younger adults in the criterion task is a function of the differences in their baseline speed when the model of general chronological slowing governs behaviour. And, using existing correlational techniques, we will estimate the amount of age-related variability in criterion task response times that is shared with variability in the baseline speed, again when the model of general chronological slowing governs behaviour. Finally, we will undertake a principled comparison of these two measures of the influence of common slowing.

Model of general chronological slowing

We now want to give formal expression to the multiplicative model of general slowing and to show how we can predict an older cohort's expected response time in a criterion task based on the observation of younger adults' response time in the same task. As the reader will recall, we will set the index k on a variable equal to 0 when the cohort to which we are referring is made up of younger adults. We assume that the expected duration μ_{ijk} of process i in task j when being executed by cohort k is equal to a constant β_k times the expected duration μ_{ij0} of process i in task j when being executed by the younger cohort. Thus, setting f_{ijk} ($\bullet$) in eqn 4.3 equal to β_k yields:

$$E[T_{jk}] = \sum_{i=1}^{I_j} \beta_k \mu_{ij0} = \beta_k E[T_{j0}] \tag{4.10}$$

In words, the time on average that it takes older adults in cohort k to complete all processes in task j is a multiple β_k of the time it takes younger adults to complete the same set of processes in task j.

We can now use a simple procedure to predict the older cohort k's response time $\hat{T}_{jk}$ on criterion task j based on the assumption that the slowing in this task is the same as the slowing in the control task. Specifically, we can estimate the slowing factor β_k in the control task by regressing the speed of the older adults in this task on the speed of the younger adults (and setting the intercept equal to 0). Let this estimate equal b_{0k}. Then, if the chronological slowing is general, the predicted older cohort k's response time on criterion task j is equal to the estimated slowing factor b_{0k} times the younger cohort's average response time on criterion task j:

$$\hat{T}_{jk} = b_{0k} T_{j0} \tag{4.11}$$

for all tasks j.

Model of chronocentric slowing

One of the fundamental goals of this chapter is to understand better the formal relations between the different types of models of chronological slowing and the model of chronocentric slowing. What we want to do here is determine whether it is the case that if the underlying model of general chronological slowing governs behaviour then so too does the model of common chronocentric slowing. As the reader may have suspected, these two models are not identifiably different. Formally, this is stated in the following theorem:

Theorem 1.   At the level of the means, the models of common chronocentric slowing and general chronological slowing are indistinguishable.

Proof.   Consider some criterion tasks u and v. To begin, assume that the model of chronocentric slowing is common. From eqn 4.6 it follows that the ratio of the younger adults' criterion response time in task u to their control response time must equal the ratio of the older adults' criterion response time in task u to their control response time. A similar identity must hold in criterion task v:

$$\frac{E[T_{u0}]}{E[T_{00}]} = \frac{E[T_{uk}]}{E[T_{0k}]} = \gamma_u$$

$$\frac{E[T_{v0}]}{E[T_{00}]} = \frac{E[T_{vk}]}{E[T_{0k}]} = \gamma_v \tag{4.12}$$

Rearranging the above equations, we get:

$$\frac{E[T_{0k}]}{E[T_{00}]} = \frac{E[T_{uk}]}{E[T_{u0}]}$$

$$\frac{E[T_{0k}]}{E[T_{00}]} = \frac{E[T_{vk}]}{E[T_{v0}]} \tag{4.13}$$

It follows immediately that the ratios on the right hand sides of eqn 4.13 are equal to one another since the ratios on the left hand sides are identical. But, the statement that the two right hand sides of eqn 4.13 are identical is just another way of defining the model of general chronological slowing in eqn 4.10. Similarly, it can be shown that if the chronological slowing is general, then the chronocentric slowing is common.

Influence of chronocentric slowing

We now want to determine what proportion $P(speed)$ of the difference in the response times of the younger and older adults in the criterion task can be explained by differences in the baseline speed when the model of general chronological slowing governs the performance of older adults. And we want to compare this proportion, P(*speed*), with the proportion, P(*shared*), of the age-related variability in criterion performance shared with variability in the baseline speed. We will construct examples when the sample size is both very small and moderately large. Although both lead to the same conclusion, it is easier to follow the argument with the small sample size.

Small sample size

To begin, consider the information in Table 4.1 on the left hand side. Suppose that we have two cohorts, a younger and older cohort, with three individuals in each cohort. The time it takes individuals in each cohort to perform the control and criterion tasks is listed in the third and fourth columns, respectively. These times are consistent with the assumptions of a model of general chronological slowing: the mean response time $T_{0k} = 8$ of the older adults in the control task is twice the mean response time $T_{00} = 4$ of the younger adults in this task; and the mean response time $T_{jk} = 16$ of the older adults in the criterion task is twice the mean response time $T_{j0} = 8$ of the younger adults in this task. The slowing factor β_k is equal to 2. These times are also consistent with a model of common chronocentric slowing: the mean response time $T_{j0} = 8$ of the younger adults performing criterion task j is equal to $\gamma_j = 2$ times their mean response time $T_{00} = 4$ performing the control task and the mean response time $T_{jk} = 16$ of the older cohort k in criterion task j is also equal to $\gamma_j = 2$ times their mean response time $T_{0k} = 8$ in the control task.

We now want to compute both P(*speed*) and P(*shared*) when, as in the example above, the chronological slowing is general. To begin, consider P(*speed*). We want to predict the older adults' response time $\hat{T}_{jk}$ on the criterion task if the speed of an individual on the control task determined entirely his or her performance on the criterion task. To do this, we need to know how much the younger adults are slowed in the criterion task. The common chronocentric

Table 4.1   General and task-specific chronological slowing: small sample

General chronological slowing[a]				Task-specific chronological slowing[b]			
Cohort	Age	Control task 0 RT	Criterion task j RT	Cohort	Age	Control task 0 RT	Criterion task j RT
0	20	2	4	0	21	2.0	2.0
0	20	4	8	0	22	2.2	2.2
0	20	6	12	0	23	2.4	2.4
k	60	6	12	k	61	6.0	60.0
k	60	8	16	k	60	8.0	80.0
k	60	10	20	k	99	10.0	100.0

[a] $\beta_k = 2$; $\gamma_j = 2$; $\delta_0 = 1$; $\delta_k = 1$.
[b] $\beta_{0k} = 8.0/2.2$; $\beta_{jk} = 80.0/2.2$; $\gamma_j = 1$; $\delta_0 = 1$; $\delta_k = 10$.

slowing factor, g_{j0}, is equal to 2 in this example. We also need to know how long it takes older adults to perform the control task. This time, T_{0k}, is equal to 8. Substituting into eqn 4.7, we predict that it will take older adults 16 s to perform the criterion task:

$$\hat{T}_{jk} = g_{j0}T_{0k} = 2 \times 8 \qquad (4.14)$$

And substituting the expression for $\hat{T}_{jk}$ in eqn 4.14 into eqn 4.8 and then computing the percentage of the increase in the response times of the older adults that is due to speed, we find that the difference in the baseline speed of the older and younger adults is responsible for all of the decline in performance of the older adults on the criterion variable, that is, $P(speed) = 1.0$.

Similarly, using eqn 4.9 and the data in the left hand side of Table 4.1 to compute $P(shared)$ we find that all of the age-related variability in the criterion measure is shared with the variability in the baseline speed measure. Specifically, although age explains only 60% of the variability in the criterion variable ($R^2_{crit.age} = 0.60$), there is no relation between performance on the criterion variable and age after partialling out the effects of the control variable from age ($R^2_{crit, (age|speed)} = 0$). Thus, all of the age-related variability is shared with speed. This is exactly what one would like to see happen given Theorem 1.

Large sample size

Readers may have some concern that the above examples may be too specialized and although true in theory, unlikely in practice. Thus, we set out to construct a more elaborate example, one where we simulated a random sample of 500 observations from younger, and 500 observations from older, adults. In particular, we assumed that the response times on the control and criterion tasks for both the younger (all age 20) and older (all age 60) adults were independent, identically distributed normal random variables. In response time tasks, the standard deviation is often about 1/3 of the mean, so we assumed that this was the case in our simulation, that is, $\sigma = \mu/3$. We assumed that the younger adults had a mean response time of 300 ms on the control task and that the older adults had a mean response time twice as long (600 ms) on the control task (the means and standard deviations are displayed in Table 4.2 at the top). And we assumed that the younger adults had a mean response time of 450 ms on the criterion task and that the older adults again had a mean response time twice as long (900 ms) on the criterion task. The sample means and variances were very close to the population means and variances (see numbers in parentheses in Table 4.2). Since older and younger adults are each slowed by a factor of 2 on the criterion tasks, it should be and was the case that the difference in the criterion task response times of the older and younger adults were due entirely to differences in their baseline speed, as determined by computing the quantities in eqn 4.8. Similarly, it should be and was the case that all of the variance was shared, as determined by computing the quantities in eqn 4.9.

Table 4.2   General and task-specific chronological slowing: large sample

	Control distributions		Criterion distributions	
	μ	σ	μ	σ
General chronological slowing				
Younger	300	100	450	150
	(298.1)[a]	(101.1)	(447.2)	(151.6)
Older	600	200	900	300
	(608.3)	(203.6)	(912.4)	(305.4)
Task-specific chronological slowing				
Younger	300	100	450	150
	(229.5)	(99.2)	(449.2)	(148.8)
Older	600	200	1350	450
	(600.7)	(197.8)	(1351.5)	(445.0)

[a] Numbers in parentheses are sample means and standard deviations for samples based on 500 observations from a normal distribution with given population mean and standard deviation.

In summary, if the chronological slowing is general, then the two measures of the influence of common slowing lead to the same conclusion, at least in our examples. In particular, we conclude that differences in the criterion task response times of the older and younger adults are determined entirely by differences in the baseline speed. Though we have not proven that, if the model of chronological slowing is a general one, the measure $P(shared)$ will always equal one (or a quantity very near one), we conjecture that this is the case based on the above examples. If this is true, then the measure $P(shared)$ has the above straightforward interpretation: the common chronocentric slowing function is age-invariant.

TASK-SPECIFIC CHRONOLOGICAL SLOWING

As noted above, some of the earliest research suggested that the chronological slowing was general across processes and tasks. However, more recent work suggests that the slowing may be constant across processes within a task, but vary from one set of tasks (or domains) to another. For example, Mayr and Kliegl (1993) find that one slowing factor, constant across processes, governs older adults' response times when the activity in working memory that is needed to coordinate inputs at different points in time is relatively small, whereas another slowing factor, again constant across processes, governs their response times when the coordinative operations required are more complex. Other investigators find that one slowing factor governs performance when the tasks require lexical operations (Hale *et al.* 1987; Lima *et al.* 1991), whereas a second slowing factor governs performance when the tasks require non-lexical operations (Hale *et al.* 1995). Thus, there is some reason to believe that slowing may vary across tasks, but be constant for the processes associated with any given task.[2] As in the previous section, after developing the relevant model of chronological slowing, we go on to describe the logical relation between it and the model of chronocentric slowing. And finally, we use both existing and alternative techniques to identify the influence of differences in the baseline speed of younger and older adults on differences in their criterion speeds when the model governing behaviour is one which assumes that the chronological slowing is task specific.

Model of task-specific chronological slowing

The task-specific model of chronological slowing can now be given more formal expression. Specifically, given the above assumptions about the nature of task-specific chronological slowing, we can write the expected duration μ_{ijk} of process i in task j for individuals in cohort k as a constant β_{jk} times the expected duration μ_{ij0} of the younger adults in the task. Then, substituting β_{jk} for $f_{ijk}(\bullet)$ in eqn 4.3 we can write:

$$E[T_{jk}] = \sum_{i=1}^{Ij} \beta_{jk}\,\mu_{ij0} = \beta_{jk}E[T_{j0}] \tag{4.15}$$

Readers who find Fig. 4.2 helpful will note that eqn 4.15 leads to a straightforward simplification of that figure. In particular, we can replace the three functions f_{11}, f_{21}, and f_{31} in Task 1 with β_1 (top panel) and similarly, we can replace the three functions f_{12}, f_{22}, and f_{32} in Task 2 with β_2 (bottom panel).

Note that it may be the case that not every task j has its own slowing coefficient. Thus, for example, if one coefficient (say β_{1k}) determines the slowing within the lexical domain and a second coefficient (say β_{2k}) determines the slowing coefficient within the non-lexical domain (Hale *et al.* 1995; Lima *et al.* 1991), then we can create two index sets, J_1 and J_2, where J_1 is the set of indices of all tasks that are classified as lexical and J_2 is the set of indices of all tasks that are classified as non-lexical. The expression for the expected time it takes individuals in cohort k to complete process i in task j can now be written as:

2   The equations used by both Mayr and Kleigl (1993) and Hale *et al.* (1987, 1995) relate the molar response times of older adults to the molar response times of younger adults. These equations have important implications for the slowing of the latent processes (Fisher and Glaser 1996). In particular, they imply that all of the latent processes are slowed by the same proportion in older adults in one task domain (lexical or non-lexical, sequential or coordinative). However, if the latent processes were explicitly represented, it is likely that the above authors would have argued that only some of the processes were slowed differentially across task domains (e.g. the working memory processes in coordinative tasks). Thus, whereas the quantitative models imply a proportional slowing of all processes in a given task domain, a closer reading of the articles suggests that the slowing may well be localized in particular processes.

$$E[X_{ijk}] = \beta_{1k}\,\mu_{ij0} \text{ for } j\epsilon J_1 \tag{4.16}$$
$$= \beta_{2k}\,\mu_{ij0} \text{ for } j\epsilon J_2$$

We can substitute for the task-specific slowing factor β_{jk} in eqn 4.15 either β_{1k} or β_{2k} as appropriate.

Model of chronocentric slowing

We now want to ask about the formal relation between a model of chronological slowing which is a task-specific one and a model of chronocentric slowing which is a common one. Here we show that the models of task-specific chronological slowing and common chronocentric slowing cannot logically describe the same set of data.

Theorem 2.   At the level of the means, the models of task-specific chronological slowing and common chronocentric slowing are logically distinct.

Proof.   To begin, assume that the model of task-specific chronological slowing governs performance. Assume for the sake of simplicity that there are two different criterion tasks, u and v, with different chronological slowing coefficients, β_{uk} and β_{vk}, that is, $\beta_{uk} \neq \beta_{vk}$. And assume that the slowing coefficient is the same in the control task as it is in task u, that is, $\beta_{0k} = \beta_{uk}$. Equation 4.10 implies that for both criterion tasks and the control task:

$$\frac{E[T_{uk}]}{E[T_{u0}]} = \frac{E[T_{0k}]}{E[T_{00}]} \neq \frac{E[T_{vk}]}{E[T_{v0}]} \tag{4.17}$$

Assume that the model of common chronocentric slowing governs performance. Then Equation 4.6 implies:

$$E[T_{v0}] = \gamma_v E[T_{00}]$$

$$E[T_{vk}] = \gamma_v E[T_{0k}] \tag{4.18}$$

Rearranging Equation 4.18 yields:

$$\frac{E[T_{vk}]}{E[T_{v0}]} = \frac{E[T_{0k}]}{E[T_{00}]} \tag{4.19}$$

Clearly, eqn 4.17 and eqn 4.19 contradict one another. (We should note that Theorem 2 follows in a straightforward fashion from Theorem 1. However, we included the detail above so that the reader could see explicitly why the two models, the models of task-specific chronological slowing and common chronocentric slowing, were not identical at the level of the means.)

Influence of chronocentric slowing

We now want to compare the two measures of the influence of baseline speed on criterion task performance, P(*speed*) and P(*shared*), when the chronological model governing the performance of behaviour is a task-specific one. As before, we will look both at small and large samples.

Small sample size

Suppose that younger adults take on average 2.2 s to perform a simple control task, as they do in the example listed on the right hand side of Table 4.1, that is, $T_{00} = 2.2$. Suppose that older adults take approximately four times as long on average to perform this same control task, that is, $T_{0k} = 8$. Suppose that younger adults take again 2.2 sec to perform the criterion task. Now suppose that older adults take approximately 36 times as long to perform this same criterion task, that is, $T_{jk} = 80.0$. These changes can be realized by setting $\beta_{0k} = 8.0/2.2$ and $\beta_{jk} = 80.0/2.2$. Similarly, one can determine the parameters of the model of cohort-specific chronocentric slowing. These changes can be realized by setting $\gamma_j = 1$, $\delta_0 = 1$ and $\delta_k = 10$ in the model of cohort-specific chronocentric slowing, eqn 4.5. If we estimated the chronocentric slowing factor using just the younger cohort, we would find $g_{j0} = 1$.

We now want to compute P(*speed*) and P(*shared*) when the chronological slowing is task specific. To begin, consider computing P(*speed*). Using eqns 4.7 and 4.8, we find that differences in baseline speed are responsible for only 7.5% of the difference between the performance of older and younger adults on the criterion variable:

$$P(speed) = \frac{8.0 - 2.2}{80.0 - 2.2} \tag{4.20}$$

But note what happens when we compute P(*shared*) using eqn 4.9. Specifically, when we correlate the criterion variable with age, we find that age accounts for 99.44% of the variance in the criterion measure ($R^2_{crit,age} = 0.9944$). When we correlate the criterion variable with age after speed has been factored out, we find that age accounts for 0.75% of the variance ($R^2_{crit,(age|speed)} = 0.0075$). Plugging these values into eqn 4.5 yields P(*shared*) = 0.992.

We are now faced with what appears to be something of a contradiction. We find that P(*speed*) is under 10% whereas P(*shared*) is close to 100%. Since the younger adults are not slowed at all in the criterion task, it is difficult to see how one can argue that differences in the baseline speed of younger and older adults explain why older adults are slower in the criterion task than they are in the control task. Thus, at least in this case, the measure P(*shared*) does not appear to have a direct relation to the extent to which a common chronocentric slowing is operating. Why the measure leads to such a high estimate of the extent to which the age-related variability in the criterion measure is shared with the baseline measure, even though there is very little common slowing, can easily be determined from the quantities used in the computation of this measure (i.e., the quantities in eqn 4.9).

The explanation is as follows. First, note that if the relation between age and speed is linear and age is predicted well by speed, then the semipartial correlation $R^2_{crit.(age|speed)}$ between criterion response times and age, controlling for speed, will be close to zero. Second, note that if the relation between criterion response times and age without controlling for speed is linear and the criterion response times are well predicted by age, then the correlation $R^2_{crit,age}$ between the two will be near perfect. (Or, relaxing this restriction somewhat, we need assume merely that the correlation between response times and age without controlling for speed is much larger than the semipartial correlation between the criterion response times and age when controlling for speed.) Third, note that the above two conditions imply that the percentage of the age-related variability in the criterion response times shared with baseline speed will be close to 100%. Finally, note that the above two conditions do not require that the chronocentric slowing be a common one. In particular, the proportion $P(shared)$ of age-related variability in the criterion response times shared with baseline speed does not change when one chronocentric slowing factor applies to the younger adults and a second, very different chronocentric slowing factor applies to the older adults. In fact, we just saw this happen in the second example drawn from Table 4.1, where the age-specific slowing factor $\delta_k = 10$ was ten times larger than the common slowing factor $\delta_0 = 1$. We prove in Appendix B that the proportion $P(shared)$ of age-related variability in the criterion task response times does not depend on the identity of the cohort-specific chronocentric slowing factor across cohorts.

Large sample size

The same problems occur when the sample is a larger one. Specifically, we will assume that the older adults are slowed by a factor of 2 on the control task and a factor of 3 on the criterion task (bottom of Table 4.2). This translates into a slowing of younger adults in the criterion task by a factor of 1.5 and a slowing of older adults in the criterion task by a factor of 2.25. Thus, using eqn 4.8 we find that 40% of the increase in the response times of the older adults on the criterion task is due to increases in response times on the control task and the remaining 60% of the increase in the response times of the older adults on the criterion task is due to factors unrelated to the control task, that is, $P(speed) = 0.4$. Using eqn 4.9 to compute the percentage of age-related variability in the criterion task that is shared with speed, we find that fully 95% of that variability can be attributed to changes in speed, that is, $P(shared) = 0.95$. Again, we need to ask ourselves whether this captures our sense of the contribution of a common (age-invariant) speed factor to changes in performance among older adults on the criterion measure that are due to decreases in speed.

In summary, if the chronological slowing is task specific, then the measure $P(speed)$ may indicate very little common slowing whereas the measure

P(*shared*) may indicate that almost all of the slowing is common. In this case the measure P(*shared*) can easily be misinterpreted as indicating a preponderance of age-invariant slowing across tasks. In fact, as we show in Appendix B, one cannot infer anything about the level of cohort-specific chronocentric slowing from the measure of P(*shared*) since it is independent of the size of the cohort-specific slowing.

PROCESS-SPECIFIC CHRONOLOGICAL SLOWING

There exists one additional type of cognitive slowing to which we will want to pay close attention. In particular, recently some investigators have found it is the case that even when the type of task is held constant (e.g. the lexicality or coordinative complexity), there exists evidence for a differential slowing of the processes. For example, when estimates are made of the encoding and comparison times in simple visual search tasks, it appears that older adults take somewhat longer than younger adults to encode and compare each stimulus in the visual display with the target when they are well practised (50%, Gorman and Fisher 1998) and much longer than younger adults when they are less well practised (150%, Hale *et al.* 1995). In either case, slowing is observed in the encoding and comparison times among older adults. However, estimates of the duration of a different process such as the length of the retrieval process suggest that there is no slowing as a function of age. For example, when older and younger adults are asked to multiply two numbers it is found that the response times of both groups of adults increase with problem size, but there is no interaction between problem size and age (Allen *et al.* 1992). This suggests that the time it takes older and younger adults to retrieve arithmetic facts from long-term memory does not vary as a function of age. A failure to find retrieval time differences between younger and older adults is also reported when participants are asked to perform either simple addition (Geary and Wiley 1991) or subtraction (Geary *et al.* 1993) problems. In short, there is evidence for a variation in the slowing factor from one category of processes to the next (cf. Cerella 1985, peripheral vs central slowing).

Model of process-specific chronological slowing

Again, we will want to express this model of chronological slowing more formally. Given the above assumptions about the nature of process-specific chronological slowing, we can write the expected duration μ_{ijk} of process i in task j when being executed by individuals in cohort k as a constant $\beta_{i\bullet k}$ times the expected duration μ_{ij0} of process i in task j when being executed by the younger cohort:

$$E[T_{jk}] = \sum_{i=1}^{I_j} \beta_{i\bullet k}\, \mu_{ij0} \tag{4.21}$$

[Note that a dot (•) is inserted in place of the task index j on the process-specific slowing factor because this factor is not assumed to vary with the task and because we need a place marker between the indices i and k.]

Of course, we do not expect that across tasks every process i will have its own slowing factor. Rather, we expect that there will exist some finite number of different categories of processes and that all processes from the same category, regardless of the task, are slowed by a single factor. So, for example, suppose that there were three different categories of processes, categories 1, 2, and 3. Assume that one or more processes from these categories were present in each task. Then we can create three different index sets, IJ_1, IJ_2, and IJ_3. Index set IJ_1 consists of the set of pairs of sequences of process and task indices (i, j) for which it is the case that process i in task j is of type 1. Index sets IJ_2 and IJ_3 can be defined similarly. Suppose that processes in categories 1, 2, and 3 for individuals in cohort k are slowed, respectively, by amounts $\beta_{1 \bullet k}$, $\beta_{2 \bullet k}$, and $\beta_{3 \bullet k}$. Then, the expression for the expected time it takes individuals in cohort k to complete process i in task j can be written as:

$$E[X_{ijk}] = \beta_{1 \bullet k}\, \mu_{ij0} \text{ for } (i, j) \epsilon I J_1$$

$$= \beta_{2 \bullet k}\, \mu_{ij0} \text{ for } (i, j) \epsilon I J_2$$

$$= \beta_{3 \bullet k}\, \mu_{ij0} \text{ for } (i, j) \epsilon I J_3 \tag{4.22}$$

And these durations can be substituted back into eqn 4.2 in order to obtain the expected time that it takes cohort k to complete task j.

Model of chronocentric slowing

We want now to consider what relations, if any, obtain between the models of process-specific chronological slowing and common chronocentric slowing. To begin, we will need to distinguish between two types of tasks, what we will call *iterative* tasks and *non-iterative* tasks. By an iterative task, we mean one in which the expected duration of each criterion task latent process is one and the same multiple of the expected duration of the associated control task latent process. So, for example, if there were two processes 1 and 2 in the control task with expected durations μ_1 and μ_2 for the younger adults, then an iterative criterion task j would be one in which the expected durations of these two processes were each multiplied by a constant, say π. Thus, the expected time $E[T_{j0}]$ that it takes the younger cohort to complete the criterion task j can be written as a simple multiple of their expected control task response time:

$$E[T_{00}] = \mu_1 + \mu_2$$
$$E[T_{j0}] = \pi \mu_1 + \pi \mu_2 = \pi E[T_{00}] \tag{4.23}$$

Additionally, if we assume that the chronological slowing is process-specific and that process 1 is slowed by a constant β_1 and process 2 is slowed by a constant β_2, then the expected times $E[T_{0k}]$ and $E[T_{jk}]$ that it takes older adults to complete, respectively, the control task and the criterion task j have the following form:

$$E[T_{0k}] = \beta_1\,\mu_1 + \beta_2\,\mu_2$$
$$E[T_{jk}] = \beta_1\,\pi\,\mu_1 + \beta_2\,\pi\,\mu_2 \tag{4.24}$$

This leads directly to the following theorem.

Theorem 3. *If the criterion tasks are iterative, then at the level of the means the models of process-specific chronological slowing and common chronocentric slowing are logically indistinguishable.*

Proof. We assume that the tasks are iterative. Form the ratio of the expected time that it takes younger adults to complete the criterion task to the expected time that it takes younger adults to complete the control task. This yields:

$$\frac{E[T_{j0}]}{E[T_{00}]} = \frac{\pi(\mu_1 + \mu_1)}{(\mu_1 + \mu_2)} \tag{4.25}$$

Similarly, form the ratio of the expected time that it takes older adults to complete the criterion task to the expected time that it takes older adults to complete the control task. This yields:

$$\frac{E[T_{jk}]}{E[T_{0k}]} = \frac{\pi(\beta_1\mu_1 + \beta_2\mu_2)}{(\beta_1\mu_1 + \beta_2\mu_2)} \tag{4.26}$$

It is clear that the right hand sides of eqns 4.25 and 4.26 both reduce to π. This is exactly what is predicted if the slowing were a common chronocentric one. It follows immediately that $\pi = \gamma_j$. Readers who find Figure 4.3 helpful will note that this implies that the cohort-specific chronocentric slowing factor δ_k that appears in the top panel should everywhere be set equal to one. Note that a common chronocentric slowing governs performance in this case even though the latent processes 1 and 2 are slowed differentially in the older cohort.

If the criterion task were not an iterative one, then the more general expressions for the expected times, $E[T_{00}]$ and $E[T_{j0}]$, that it takes the younger cohort to complete, respectively, the control task and criterion task j have the following form:

$$E[T_{00}] = \mu_1 + \mu_2$$
$$E[T_{j0}] = \pi_1\,\mu_1 + \pi_2\mu_2 \tag{4.27}$$

And, given that the model of chronological slowing is a process-specific one, the expected times $E[T_{0k}]$ and $E[T_{jk}]$ that it takes the older cohort to complete, respectively, the control task and criterion task j can be written as follows:

$$E[T_{0k}] = \beta_1 \mu_1 + \beta_2 \mu_2$$
$$E[T_{jk}] = \beta_1 \pi_1 \mu_1 + \beta_2 \pi_2 \mu_2 \tag{4.28}$$

Given these formulations of the latent models, we have the following corollary.

Corollary 1.   If the criterion tasks are not iterative, then at the level of the means the models of process-specific chronological slowing and common chronocentric slowing are logically distinguishable.

Proof.   The proof is similar to that for Theorem 3 and is left as an exercise for the reader.

Influence of chronocentric slowing

We now want to compute the influence of chronocentric slowing on performance in the criterion tasks when the latent model of chronological slowing is process specific and the criterion tasks either are or are not iterative. To begin, let's consider the case where the criterion tasks are iterative. An example set of data is contained in Table 4.3. It is assumed that there are two latent processes in the control and criterion tasks (a and b). Moreover, we assume that each of the control processes is repeated twice in the criterion task, for both the younger and older adults. Thus, younger adults are slowed by a factor of 2 in the criterion task, as are the older adults ($\pi = 2$). Additionally, it is assumed that the model of chronological slowing is a process-specific one. Specifically, in both the control and criterion tasks we assume that among older adults the first process is slowed by a factor of 2 ($\beta_1 = 2$) and the second process is slowed by a factor of 3 ($\beta_2 = 3$). The control and criterion response times are simply the sum of the two latent process durations (i.e., the sum of the durations of processes a and b).

We now want to compute *P(speed)* and *P(shared)*. We will begin with *P(speed)*. Note that we need to generalize eqn 4.8 since this eqn does not apply when the latent processes are slowed differentially in the control and criterion tasks. We will now imagine that the influence of speed is age invariant when the chronological slowing is process specific if the slowing of each process in the control task is age invariant (we do not require that the same slowing apply to each control process). This generalization requires that we estimate the slowing of each process i in task j for a younger cohort (represented here as g_{ij0}). We then obtain the following as an estimate of the proportion of the difference in the criterion task response times of the older and younger adults that is due to differences in the baseline speed:

$$P(speed) = \frac{\sum_{i=1}^{I_j} g_{ij0} X_{i0k} - T_{0k}}{T_{jk} - T_{0k}} \tag{4.29}$$

Using this eqn, we find that *P(speed)* in our current example is equal to 1.0.

Next, consider computation of *P(shared)*. This measure is by construction a macroscopic one and so is not a function of the type of chronological slowing. Thus, the measure can be applied as is. Doing such, we find that the correlation between criterion performance and age is 0.902. And the correlation between criterion performance and age after partialling out speed is 0. Thus, all of the age-related variability in criterion performance is shared with speed, exactly as one would expect.

It is important to note that the above estimates of the dominance of common chronocentric slowing do not imply that the chronological slowing is general. In fact, as Theorem 3 makes clear formally, and this example makes clear concretely, a common chronocentric slowing can coexist with process-specific chronological slowing when the tasks are iterative (much as previous work has made clear that general chronological slowing can mimic process-specific chronological slowing; e.g. see Fisher and Glaser 1996).

Now let us consider tasks where the chronological slowing is process specific, but which are not iterative (Table 4.4). In particular, we will assume that the first process is not slowed at all in the criterion task ($\pi_1 = 1$) and the second process is slowed by a factor of 1.5 ($\pi_2 = 1.5$, in which case the task is not an iterative one). For example, note that for the first simulated subject the duration of process *a* in both the control and criterion tasks is 100 ms. However, for this subject the duration of process *b* is 200 ms in the control task whereas it is 300 ms in the criterion task. As noted above, we assume that the chronological slowing is process specific. Thus, for the older adults process *a* in both the control and criterion tasks is slowed by a factor of 2 ($\beta_1 = 2$) and process *b* in both the control and criterion tasks is slowed by a factor of 3 ($\beta_2 = 3$). Now, using eqn 4.29 we determine that *P(speed)* equals 1. And, using eqn 4.9 to compute the amount of the age-related variability in the criterion measure shared with speed, we find that it is very high, in this case equal to 0.999. Again, large differences in the slowing of individual processes can exist at the same time as the amount of age-related variability that can be attributed to speed approaches 100%.

Table 4.3 Process-specific chronological slowing: iterative tasks

Age	Control task		Criterion task	
	Process *a*	Process *b*	Process *a*	Process *b*
20	100	200	200[c]	400[c]
20	120	240	240	480
20	140	280	280	560
60	200[a]	600[b]	400	1200
60	240	720	480	1440
60	280	840	560	1680

[a] $\beta_1 = 2$
[b] $\beta_2 = 3$
[c] $\pi = 2$

Table 4.4   Process-specific chronological slowing: noniterative tasks

Age	Control task		Criterion task	
	Process a	Process b	Process a	Process b
20	100	200	100[c]	300[d]
20	120	240	120	360
20	140	280	140	420
60	200[a]	600[b]	200	900
60	240	720	240	1080
60	280	840	280	1260

[a] $\beta_1 = 2$
[b] $\beta_2 = 3$
[c] $\pi_1 = 1$
[d] $\pi_2 = 1.5$

In summary, if the chronological slowing is process specific, then the measure *P(shared)* indicates that the slowing is exclusively a common chronocentric one. However, this is clearly not the interpretation we want since by assumption there is not a *single* age-invariant chronocentric slowing function. Thus, if the chronological slowing is process specific, the measure *P(shared)* cannot be interpreted as defined.

DISCUSSION

Knowledge of the influence of baseline speed on the slowing of older adults in criterion tasks has broad implications for theories of cognitive aging, implications which have been discussed at length by others (e.g. Salthouse 1996*a*, 1996*c*). However, this information, which can essentially be reduced to one number, is not all that is of interest. In particular, knowledge of the differences which still remain after the effects of chronocentric slowing have been removed also has important implications for theories of cognitive aging, especially if we can partition the space of processes or tasks into psychologically meaningful subsets (e.g. lexical and non-lexical tasks, central or peripheral processes) each of which is governed by its own, subset-specific slowing coefficient. Knowledge of these differences also has important implications for theories of neuronal aging, especially if the different cognitive processes can be mapped onto identifiable and separate neural generators (Bashore 1993; Cerella and Hale 1994). Finally, knowledge of which individual processes are slowed the most has clear implications for practice. This knowledge can be used to target the development of interfaces (broadly conceived) which overcome as best as possible the processes which are compromised the most. In summary, a better understanding of procedures which can be used to identify both the type of chronological slowing and the influence of chronocentric slowing in criterion tasks can serve a number of different goals.

We have spent some time in this chapter trying to understand what two of the measures designed to identify the influence of baseline speed on the slowing of older adults in criterion tasks are telling us. We have also spent some time trying to understand the relation between the type of chronological slowing and the model of chronocentric slowing. We now want to speak to this and other issues in more detail.

Influence of common slowing

We want to know the influence that differences in younger and older adults' speeds on a control task have on differences in their speeds on a criterion task. And, in particular, we are interested in knowing how much of the difference in the speeds of the younger and older adults in a criterion task can be attributed to a slowing that is common to younger and older adults. We have defined slowing as common if the same function maps younger adults' baseline speeds to criterion task speeds as maps older adults' baseline speeds to criterion task speeds. We developed an estimate of the proportion $P(speed)$ of the difference in the criterion task response times of younger and older adults that could be traced to differences in their baseline speed if the slowing were a common one. We argued that this estimate agreed with our intuitions of what should be happening. In particular, if the chronological slowing were general, then the chronocentric slowing was common and the measure $P(speed)$ was equal to one. If the chronological slowing were task specific, then the chronocentric slowing was cohort specific and the measure $P(speed)$ was considerably less than one. Finally, if the chronological slowing were process specific, then the chronocentric slowing was common at the level of individual processes and again the measure $P(speed)$ was equal to one. The measure $P(speed)$ is consistent with our intuitions because it is equal to one when the chronocentric slowing is age invariant and is equal to some fraction less than one when the chronocentric slowing is cohort specific.

Another estimate has been used to identify the influence of differences in baseline speed on differences in criterion task speeds. This estimate, $P(shared)$, makes use of correlational techniques to determine the age-related variability in the criterion task response times that is shared with baseline speed. If the chronological slowing was general, then this measure reflected well the fact that an age-invariant function mapped control task response times onto criterion task response times. However, this measure did not always yield results which were necessarily in agreement with our intuition of the influence of common slowing. In particular, if the chronological slowing was task specific and therefore the chronocentric slowing was cohort specific, the estimate $P(shared)$ could be close to one even though almost none of the chronocentric slowing was common (as defined above). This apparent problem arises because the measure $P(shared)$ requires only that age and speed be very highly correlated (on the one hand) and that the criterion task response times and age be moderately correlated (on the other hand). The measure does not require that the older and younger adults be slowed in the criterion task by the same factor (Appendix B). Thus, we saw an example where $P(shared)$ was close to one even though the older adults were slowed ten times as much in the criterion task as the younger adults. Similarly, if the chronological slowing was process specific, the estimate $P(shared)$ was equal to one even though there was most definitely not a single age-invariant function which mapped the control task response times onto the criterion task response times. Thus, we could construct examples where $P(shared)$ was equal to one even though one control process was slowed by a factor of two and another control process was slowed by a factor of three.

Type of chronological slowing

We have also considered the formal relation between the models of chronocentric and chronological slowing. We have done so, in part, because in the past there has been a tendency to assume that if the model of general chronological slowing explained most of the variability, then the models of task- or process-specific chronological slowing were left with little if any variability to explain. However, it has been argued recently that this is not the case (Fisher and Glaser 1996; Fisher *et al.* 1995; Fisk and Fisher 1994; Perfect 1994). In this context, we want to make sure that it is clear to the reader that even if the estimate $P(shared)$ of the influence of common slowing is close to one, there is still room for models of task-specific and process-specific chronological slowing.

We made the argument by way of example. To begin, consider the case where the chronological slowing was task specific. We constructed an estimate of $P(shared)$ which was close to one for this case. However, the older adults were slowed by a factor of 3.6 (8.0/2.2) in the control task but by a factor of 36.4 (80/2.2) in the criterion task. Thus, the fact that most of the age-related variability in criterion task response times is shared with baseline speed is irrelevant to a determination of the influence of task-specific chronological slowing. Next, consider the case where the chronological slowing was process specific. Here, we saw that the models of common chronocentric and process-specific chronological slowing were formally identical to one another. Thus, the measure $P(shared)$ will equal one even when there is a large difference in the amount by which older adults are slowed in each of the latent processes.

Latent models

In summary, we appear to have two related problems. First, we cannot use the correlational method to determine clearly the influence of a common chronocentric slowing across all types of chronological slowing. Specifically, we cannot use the estimate $P(shared)$ to determine the influence of a common chronocentric slowing when the chronological slowing is task or process specific. This leads directly to our second problem. In particular, the measure $P(speed)$, which can be used meaningfully in many tasks, cannot be used to determine the influence of common slowing if the latent model is other than a simple serial one.

We believe that these two problems can be overcome if we look more closely at the underlying or latent models of processing. In order to understand the approach, it is first necessary to differentiate between *molar* and *latent* models. In a molar model, the expected response time of the older adults is written as a function of the expected response time of the younger adults. The left and right hand sides of eqn 4.10 represent such a relation. In a latent model, the expected response time of the older adults is written as a function of the durations of the latent (hidden) cognitive processes. The expressions on the left hand side and in the middle of eqn 4.10 represent this relation. The latent models can now yield an interpretable measure of the contribution of baseline speed to the slowing of older adults in criterion tasks. And, at the same time, these models can make it possible to identify the type of chronological slowing that is governing performance.

First, consider the use of latent models in the measure of the contribution of speed defined in eqn 4.8 and elaborated in eqn 4.29. We will assume that this measure captures what we mean when we are asking about the role that common slowing plays in criterion task performance. The question we now want to address is the extent to which latent models are needed in order to apply this measure. The equation was developed (and in particular the predicted response time of the older adults in the criterion task) based on the assumption that the processes were arranged in a simple serial network. This assumption may well not be true. More complex arrangements are frequently observed in standard laboratory tasks (Schweickert *et al.* submitted). The latent architecture can readily be checked with existing techniques (Schweickert 1978; Schweickert and Townsend 1989). The formula for the predicted response times would then need to be changed. In short, it is clear that one cannot get along without knowledge of the latent network if one is going to use correctly a measure of the extent to which speed controls the performance of older adults in criterion tasks and if one is going to formulate alternative measures when the simplifying assumptions are not satisfied, as is frequently the case.

Second, consider the use of latent models in the identification of the type of chronological slowing. Neither measure, *P(speed)* or *P(shared)*, was designed to yield the information we would like in order to determine the nature of the chronological slowing. However, the identification of the latent model can solve this problem immediately. In particular, assuming that estimates of the coefficients in the model of chronological slowing are stable, we can infer from these estimates whether the slowing is task or process specific and, if process specific, whether iterative or non-iterative. For example, suppose that the slowing were task specific. Then, if there were two tasks and two processes in each task, we would predict that the slowing coefficients for processes 1 and 2 in task *j* were identical ($\beta_{1jk} = \beta_{2jk}$) and that the slowing coefficients for processes 1 and 2 in task j' were identical ($\beta_{1j'k} = \beta_{2j'k}$), but that these coefficients were not equal across tasks.

SUMMARY

Two questions have been at the centre of the debate about the role that cognitive slowing plays in the declines in performance observed as individuals age. The first question has focused on the type of slowing. It is now believed that the slowing is not a general one, but instead varies from task to task and possibly process to process. The second question has focused on the influence of common slowing on differences in criterion task response times. This question has only recently been addressed in a rigorous fashion. We explored two methods for answering the second question in this chapter. One method relied on the representation of processing as a latent model. We argued for the more general development of latent models. Latent models not only make possible a more direct measure of the extent to which speed played a role in the criterion performance of older adults; they also make it possible to identify the type of chronological slowing. Therefore, the latent models have important implications for both theory and practice, implications which are hard to derive when just their molar equivalents are used.

The second method relied on correlational techniques. We argued that it was difficult to interpret the measure unless one knew the underlying or latent model of processing. Other measures of common slowing have been developed as well. These include Brinley plots (Brinley 1965) and path analyses (Lindenberger *et al.* 1993; Salthouse and Babcock 1991; Salthouse 1994). We believe that the interpretation of the degree of common slowing that these measures can yield will also depend on the latent models. However, at this point our belief is just a conjecture. More work needs to be done.

ACKNOWLEDGEMENTS

This research was supported in part by grant AG12461 from the National Institute of Aging to Donald L. Fisher. Address correspondence to Donald L. Fisher, Department of Mechanical and Industrial Engineering, University of Massachusetts, Amherst, MA 01003.

REFERENCES

Allen, P. A., Ashcraft, M. H., and Weber, T. A. (1992). On mental multiplication and age. *Psychology and Aging*, 7, 536–45.

Bashore, T. R. (1993). Differential effects of aging on the neurocognitive functions subserving speeded mental processing. In J. Cerella, J. Rybash, W. Hoyer, and M. L. Commons (ed.), *Adult information processing: limits on loss* (pp. 37–76). San Diego: Academic Press.

Birren, J. E. (1965). Age-changes in speed of behavior: its central nature and physiological correlates. In A. T. Welford and J. E. Birren (ed.), *Behavior, aging and the nervous system* (pp. 191–216). Springfield, IL: Thomas.

Birren, J. E. (1974). Translations in gerontology: from lab to life: psychophysiology and speed of response. *American Psychologist*, **29**, 808–15.

Brinley, J. F. (1965). Cognitive sets, speed and accuracy of performance in the elderly. In A. T. Welford and J. E. Birren (ed.), *Behavior, aging and the nervous system* (pp. 114–49). Springfield, IL: Thomas.

Cattell, R. B. (1943). The measurement of adult intelligence. *Psychological Bulletin*, **40**, 153–93.

Cerella, J. (1985). Information processing rates in the elderly. *Psychological Bulletin*, **98**, 67–83.

Cerella, J. and Hale, S. (1994). The rise and fall of information-processing rates over the life span. *Acta Psychologica*, **86**, 109–97.

Cerella, J., Poon, L. W., and Williams, D. M. (1980). Age and the complexity hypothesis. In L. W. Poon (ed.), *Aging in the 1980s* (pp. 332–40). Washington: American Psychological Association.

Fisher, D. L. and Glaser, R. (1996). Molar and latent models of cognitive slowing: implications for aging, dementia, depression, development and intelligence. *Psychonomic Bulletin and Review*, **3**, 458–80.

Fisher, D. L., Fisk, A. D., and Duffy, S. A. (1995). Why latent models are needed to test hypotheses about the slowing of word and language processes in older adults? In P. Allen and T. Bashore, *Advances in psychology: age differences in word and language processing* (pp. 1–29). New York: Elsevier North-Holland.

Fisk, A. D. and Fisher, D. L. (1994). Brinley plots and theories of aging: the explicit, implicit and muddled debates. *Journal of Gerontology: Psychological Sciences*, **49**, P81–9.

Fisk, A. D. and Rogers, W. A. (1991). Towards an understanding of age-related visual search effects. *Journal of Experimental Psychology: General*, **121**, 131–49.

Fisk, A. D., Fisher, D. L., and Rogers, W. A. (1992). General slowing alone cannot explain age-related search effects: a reply to Cerella. *Journal of Experimental Psychology: General*, **121**, 73–8.

Geary, D. C. and Wiley, J. G. (1991). Cognitive addition: strategy choice and speed-of-processing differences in young and elderly adults. *Psychology and Aging*, **6**, 474–83.

Geary, D. C., Frensch, P., and Wiley, J. G. (1993). Simple and complex mental subtraction: strategy choice and speed-of-processing differences in younger and older adults. *Psychology and Aging*, **8**, 242–56.

Gorman, M. and Fisher, D. L. (1998). Visual search: the slowing of strategic and non-strategic processes. *Journal of Gerontology: Psychological Sciences*, **53B**, P189–200.

Hale, S., Myerson, J., and Wagstaff, D. (1987). General slowing of nonverbal information processing: evidence for a power law. *Journal of Gerontology*, **34**, 553–60.

Hale, S., Myerson, J., Faust, M., and Fristoe, N. (1995). Converging evidence for domain-specific slowing from multiple nonlexical tasks and multiple analytic methods. *Journal of Gerontology: Psychological Sciences*, **50B**, P202–12.

Hebb, D. O. (1942). The effect of early and late brain injury upon test scores and the nature of normal adult intelligence. *Proceedings of the American Philosophical Society*, **85**, 275–92.

Lima, S. D., Hale, S., and Myerson, J. (1991). How general is general slowing? Evidence from the lexical domain. *Psychology and Aging*, **6**, 416–25.

Lindenberger, U., Mayr, U., and Kliegl, R. (1993). Speed and intelligence in old age. *Psychology and Aging*, **8**, 207–20.

Madden, D. J., Pierce, T. W. Y., and Allen, P. A. (1992). Adult age differences in attentional allocation during memory search. *Psychology and Aging*, **7**, 594–601.

Madden, D. J., Pierce, T. W. Y., and Allen, P. A. (1993). Age-related slowing and the time course of semantic priming in visual word identification. *Psychology and Aging*, **8**, 490–507.

Mayr, U. and Kliegl, R. (1993). Sequential and coordinative complexity: age-based processing limitations in figural transformation. *Journal of Experimental Psychology: Learning, Memory and Cognition*, **19**, 1297–320.

Myers, J. L. and Well, A. D. (1991). *Research design & statistical analysis*. New York: HarperCollins.

Perfect, T. J. (1994). What can Brinley plots tell us about cognitive aging? *Journal of Gerontology: Psychological Sciences*, **49**, P60–4.

Salthouse, T. A. (1980). Age and memory: strategies for localizing the loss. In L. W. Poon, J. L. Fozard, L. Cermak, D. Arenberg, and L. W. Thompson (ed.), *New directions in memory and aging* (pp. 47–65). Hillsdale, NJ: Lawrence Erlbaum.

Salthouse, T. A. (1985). *A theory of cognitive aging*. Amsterdam: North-Holland.

Salthouse, T. A. (1991). *Theoretical perspectives on cognitive aging*. Hillsdale, NJ: Lawrence Erlbaum.

Salthouse, T. A. (1992a). *Mechanisms of age-cognition relations in adulthood*. Hillsdale, NJ: Lawrence Erlbaum.

Salthouse, T. A. (1992b). Shifting levels of analysis in the investigation of cognitive aging. *Human Development*, **35**, 321–42.

Salthouse, T. A. (1994). How many causes are there of aging-related decrements in cognitive functioning. *Developmental Review*, **14**, 413–37.

Salthouse, T. A. (1996a). Constraints on theories of cognitive aging. *Psychonomic Bulletin & Review*, **3**, 287–99.

Salthouse, T. A. (1996b). General and specific speed mediation of adult age differences in memory. *Journal of Gerontology: Psychological Sciences*, **51B**, P30–42.

Salthouse, T. A. (1996c). The processing-speed theory of adult age differences in cognition. *Psychological Review*, **103**, 403–28.

Salthouse, T. A. and Babcock, R. L. (1991). Decomposing adult age differences in working memory. *Developmental Psychology*, **27**, 763–76.

Salthouse, T. A. and Kersten, A. W. (1993). Decomposing adult age differences in symbol arithmetic. *Memory & Cognition*, **21**, 699–710.

Schweickert, R. (1978). A critical path generalization of the additive factor method: analysis of a Stroop task. *Journal of Mathematical Psychology*, **18**, 105–39.

Schweickert, R. and Townsend, J. T. (1989). A trichotomy: interactions of factors prolonging sequential and concurrent mental processes in stochastic discrete mental (PERT) networks. *Journal of Mathematical Psychology*, **33**, 328–47.

Schweickert, R., Fisher, D. L., and Goldstein, W. M. (submitted). *General latent network theory: structural and quantitative analysis of networks of cognitive processes*.

Sternberg, S. (1969). The discovery of processing stages: extensions of Donder's method. *Acta Psychologica*, **30**, 276–315.

APPENDIX A
CHRONOCENTRIC SLOWING COEFFICIENTS

The reader may have noticed at this point that eqn 4.5 actually defines a system of $J \times K$ equations in $J + K$ unknowns (the J common chronocentric slowing factors γ_j and the K cohort-specific slowing factors δ_k). We assume that the system of equations is consistent (has at least one solution). However, unfortunately, as formulated the system of equations is indeterminate, that is, has more than one solution. The source of this indeterminacy is apparent immediately if we consider a control task ($j = 0$), two criterion tasks ($j = 1,2$) and two cohorts ($k = 0,1$). In that case, we have the system of equations:

$$E[T_{10}] = \gamma_1 \, \delta_0 \, E[T_{00}]$$

$$E[T_{11}] = \gamma_1 \, \delta_1 \, E[T_{01}]$$

$$E[T_{20}] = \gamma_2 \, \delta_0 \, E[T_{00}]$$

$$E[T_{21}] = \gamma_2 \, \delta_1 \, E[T_{01}] \tag{4.30}$$

The first and second equations define, respectively, the expected response times of the younger ($E[T_{10}]$) and older ($E[T_{11}]$) cohort in the first task. The third and fourth equations define, respectively, the expected response times of the younger ($E[T_{20}]$) and older cohort ($E[T_{21}]$) in the second task. It is clear that we are not confined to a single choice of the parameters γ_1, γ_2, δ_0 and δ_1.

For example, assume that the younger adults in the control task take 1 s, $E[T_{00}] = 1.0$, and the older adults in the control task take 2 s, $E[T_{01}] = 2.0$. Assume that the younger adults in the first criterion task take twice as long as they do in the control task, $E[T_{10}] = 2.0 \times E[T_{00}] = 2.0$, whereas the older adults in the first criterion task take 2.5 times longer $E[T_{11}] = 2.5 \times E[T_{01}] = 5.0$. And assume that the younger adults take three times as long to complete the second criterion task as they do the control task, $E[T_{20}] = 3.0 \times E[T_{00}] = 3.0$, whereas the older adults take 3.75 times as long to complete the second criterion task as they do the control task, $E[T_{21}] = 3.75 \times E[T_{01}] = 7.5$. Then the following two solutions are both consistent with eqn 4.30: $\gamma_1 = 2.0, \gamma_2 = 3.0, \delta_0 = 1$, and $\delta_1 = 1.25$ or $\gamma_1 = 1.0, \gamma_2 = 1.5, \delta_0 = 2$, and $\delta_1 = 2.5$.

The solution to the problem of indeterminacy is to recognize that the cohort-specific slowing factor δ_0 is by assumption equal to one for some younger cohort. That is, we are assuming that there is some narrowly defined cohort among the broader set of younger adults for which speed is at a maximum. At this point, δ_0 is equal to one in the model. Thus, for this younger cohort we can solve directly for γ_j. And, once we have γ_j, we can solve directly for δ_k in any of the remaining equations in which it appears since we have assumed that the system of equations is consistent. In summary, the system of equations defined in eqn 4.5 has a unique solution.

APPENDIX B
P(*speed*) and P(*shared*)

We have defined the slowing as a common one if the younger adults are slowed on the criterion task by the same proportion as the older adults. We want to show that the percentage of age-related variability in the criterion tasks which is shared with baseline speed does not depend on the chronocentric slowing factor remaining invariant with age. To keep things simple, assume that there are two cohorts, a younger and older cohort where each individual within a cohort is of the same age as every other individual in that cohort. Let γ_{j0} be the chronocentric slowing factor for the younger adults and γ_{jk} be this factor for older adults in criterion task j. Specifically, we will assume:

$$E[T_{j0}] = \gamma_{j0} E[T_{00}], \ E[T_{jk}] = \gamma_{jk} E[T_{0k}] \tag{4.31}$$

And assume that we are working only with the means. Thus, the younger and older adults' baseline response times are labelled as, respectively, T_{00} and T_{0k}, and their criterion response times are labelled as, respectively, T_{j0} and T_{jk}.

We need to show that, for any choice of the cohort-specific chronocentric slowing coefficients, γ_{j0} and γ_{jk}, we can keep the relation between age and speed linear and the relation between the criterion response times and age linear. If this is the case, then it follows immediately that there can exist situations where P(*shared*) will be near one and P(*speed*) will be close to zero. To begin, we assume that the relation between the expected ages $E[A_0]$ and $E[A_k]$ of, respectively, the younger and older cohorts, and speed is a linear one:

$$E[A_0] = \alpha E[T_{00}], \ E[A_k] = \alpha E[T_{0k}] \tag{4.32}$$

If there is little variability, then $R^2_{age,speed}$ will be large and $R^2_{age,errors}$ will be small. Furthermore, we assume that the relation between the criterion response times and age is a linear one:

$$E[T_{j0}] = a + b \times E[A_0], \ E[T_{jk}] = a + b \times E[A_k] \tag{4.33}$$

Again, if there is little variability, then $R^2_{crit,age}$ will be large. Thus, P(*shared*) will be small.

The question now is whether our choice of eqns 4.32 and 4.33 are consistent only with $\gamma_{j0} = \gamma_{jk} = \gamma_j$, that is, only if there is a common chronocentric slowing. Substituting the terms on the right hand side of eqn 4.31 for those on the left hand side of eqn 4.33, and substituting the terms on the right hand side of eqn 4.31 for $E[A_0]$ and $E[A_k]$ in eqn 4.33 leads to the following two equations:

$$\gamma_{j0} \times E[T_{00}] = a + b \times \alpha \times E[T_{00}]$$

$$\gamma_{jk} \times E[T_{0k}] = a + b \times \alpha \times E[T_{0k}] \tag{4.34}$$

Solving both sides of the above equation for $b\,\alpha$, we get:

$$b\,\alpha = \gamma_{j0} - \frac{a}{E[T_{00}]} = \gamma_{jk} - \frac{a}{E[T_{0k}]} \tag{4.35}$$

Solving for a we find:

$$a = \frac{(\gamma_{j0} - \gamma_{jk})(E[T_{00}] \times E[T_{0k}])}{E[T_{0k}] - E[T_{00}]} \tag{4.36}$$

And solving for b we find:

$$b = \frac{\gamma_{j0} \times E[T_{00}] - \gamma_{jk} \times E[T_{0k}]}{\alpha(E[T_{00}] - E[T_{0k}])} \tag{4.37}$$

Thus, we can find values for a and b which are consistent with any choice of γ_{j0} and γ_{jk}. So, we conclude that *P(shared)* can remain large even when the chronocentric slowing of the younger and older adults differs greatly.

FIVE

New directions for research into aging and intelligence: the development of expertise

JOHN L. HORN AND HIROMI MASUNAGA

PURPOSE AND PERSPECTIVE

In this article we will review and critically evaluate what is believed, scientifically, about human cognitive capabilities and their development through adulthood. We will then discuss a major concern about this information – what appears to be wrong with it – and put forth some ideas about what is needed to fill in information that is more nearly correct. We will argue that the major thrust in research aimed at understanding the nature of human intelligence (viewed behaviourally) should be directed at understanding capabilities that emerge in adulthood. This argument stems from research findings that, for the most part, have been directed at describing cognitive declines that occur in adulthood. Yet this research has netted evidence of abilities that are maintained or that improve with advancing age. These findings have forced modifications in reductionistic assumptions that the maintenance of human intelligence is determined only by physiological (largely neurological) functions that inevitably decline in adulthood. The findings have led to questions about what, indeed, are the physiological/neurological functions that support expressions of different cognitive abilities: which of these functions are likely to deteriorate over adulthood and why. But most pertinent to the argument of this chapter, the findings have raised anew questions about what human intelligence is – in particular, what is intelligence at its highest level of expression. Here it is reasoned that development (through childhood into adulthood) is directed at realizing that highest level and that probably that apex is reached in adulthood. Thus, the question of what is intelligence becomes one of what is it that emerges in adulthood that is both different from what is called intelligence in childhood and that can be recognized as the sine qua non of human intelligence?

Two principal working hypotheses have been put forth. One builds on the connotations of the concept of wisdom (e.g. Baltes *et al.* 1992; Staudinger and Baltes 1996). The principal argument of this chapter is in support of the second hypothesis, namely, that the quintessence of human intelligence is found in expressions of expertise. We will mainly present the argument 'for', but to provide perspective we will review evidence that has led to current theory about the nature of human intelligence. In particular, we will review evidence on which extended Gf–Gc theory is based. In this, we will pay particular attention to the hypothesis that cognitive speed is the sine qua non of human intelligence (Eysenck 1987; Hertzog 1989; Horn *et al.* 1981; Jensen 1987; Nettelbeck 1994; Salthouse 1985, 1993). And we will look closely at hypotheses specifying that working memory, depth of processing, consolidation, and chunking are essential processes of intelligence (e.g. Baddeley 1994; Baddeley and Hitch 1994; Craik and Lockhart 1972; Mandler 1977). We will then review research on the development of expertise (Charness 1991; Ericsson 1997; Ericsson and Charness 1994; Ericsson and Kintsch 1995; Walsh and Hershey 1993). This will lead to the conclusion that Gf–Gc theory (including the processes of cognitive speed, working memory, etc.) does not adequately describe the capacities that can be said to indicate human intelligence. In particular, this theory does not adequately indicate what human intelligence can become. What is needed to describe the high levels of intelligence that emerge in adulthood is a description of abilities of expertise. From childhood and adolescence into adulthood the principal developmental task of humans shifts from one of becoming broadly aware of the facets of the intelligence of culture to one of maintaining and advancing that culture. This requires specialization, becoming expert at the limits of understanding the most advanced developments of particular features of the culture. There is societal pressure to do this: to become expert is required for optimal adjustment and adaptation in adulthood. And it is this development of expertise that exploits the full potential of the human for becoming intelligent. But such specialization pulls resources away from maintenance of abilities developed through the periods of childhood and adolescence. This loss of maintenance is seen as decline. Thus, there is decline in the intelligence of youth concomitant with increase in the intelligence of adulthood.

That, then, is the principal argument, and likely it is debatable. Let us now turn to review the knowledge that leads up to that argument.

EXTENDED Gf–Gc THEORY: CONSTRUCTS AND BASIS FOR MEASUREMENT

What we presently know about human cognitive abilities and their development in adulthood is embodied to a considerable extent in Gf–Gc theory. This is a descriptive–interpretative account of evidence obtained primarily from two kinds of research – (1) structural research: studies of the covariation patterns among tests designed to indicate basic features of human intelligence, and (2) developmental research: studies designed to indicate the ways in which cognitive capabilities develop over age, particularly in adulthood. To a lesser extent the theory incorporates findings from studies of physiological/neurological correlates of cognitive change, behavioral genetics, and the prediction of academic and occupational achievement. It will be sufficient for our purposes here to consider only the structural and developmental evidence.

Structural evidence: major capabilities of human intelligence

The accumulated results from nearly 100 years of research on covariations among tests, tasks, and paradigms designed to identify fundamental features of human intelligence indicate organization at what is referred to as primary mental abilities. At this level somewhat more than 60 kinds of concepts – dimensions indicated by common factors – are required to describe individual differences that putatively indicate the capacities of human intelligence (summarized by Carroll 1993; Eckstrom *et al.* 1979; Horn 1997).

The evidence of studies of structure also indicates that there is a broader, more general organization among the primary mental abilities. This general organization can be represented largely (although not fully, we will argue) by as few as nine common factors, indicating broad patterns of cognitive capabilities. These factors have been identified in samples that differ in respect to gender, level of education, ethnicity, nationality, language, and historical period in this century. The abilities these factors represent account for the reliable individual differences variability measured in IQ tests and neuropsychological batteries. The nine classes of abilities are briefly described as follows:

Acculturation knowledge (Gc, also referred to as crystallized intelligence), measured in tests indicating breadth and depth of knowledge of the language, concepts and information of the dominant culture.

Tertiary storage and retrieval (TSR, also referred to as fluency of retrieval from long-term storage and as long-term memory, Glm), measured in tasks that indicate consolidation and require retrieval through association of information stored minutes, hours, weeks, and years before.

Fluid reasoning (Gf, also referred to as fluid intelligence), measured in tasks requiring inductive reasoning (conjunctive and disjunctive), and capacities for identifying relationships, comprehending implications, and drawing inferences within content that is either novel or equally familiar to all.

Short-term apprehension and retrieval (SAR, also referred to as short-term memory, STM, and short-term working memory, STWM), measured in tasks that require one to maintain awareness of elements in the immediate situation – that is, events of the last minute or so.

Processing speed (Gs), although involved in almost all intellectual tasks, this factor is measured most purely in rapid scanning and comparisons in intellectually simple tasks in which almost all people would get the right answer if the task were not highly speeded.

Visual processing (Gv, also referred to as broad visualization), measured in tasks involving visual closure and constancy, and fluency in recognizing the way objects appear in space as they are rotated and flip-flopped in various ways.

Auditory processing (Ga, also referred to as g-auditory), measured in tasks that involve perception of sound patterns under distraction or distortion, maintaining awareness of order and rhythm among sounds, and comprehending elements of groups of sounds.

Correct decision speed (CDS), measured in quickness in providing answers in tasks that are not of trivial difficulty.

Quantitative knowledge (Gq, also referred to as g-quantitative), measured in tasks requiring understanding and application of the concepts and skills of mathematics.

These abilities are positively correlated, but independent. Independence is indicated initially by structural evidence: a best-weighted linear combination of any set of eight factors (representing eight of the classes of abilities) does not account for the reliable covariance among the elements of the ninth factor (representing a remaining class of abilities). More fundamentally, independence is indicated by evidence of distinct construct validities: measures representing the different factors have different, lawful relationships with other variables, particularly variables indicating development, neurological functioning and genetic determination. The factors are realized through learning influences operating in conjunction with biological and genetic influences that directly determine brain structure and physiology. The factors do not, however, define a clean distinction between genetic and environmental determinants.

More detailed and scholarly accounts of the structural evidence are provided in Carroll (1993), Cattell (1971), Horn (e.g. 1968, 1994), Horn and Hofer (1992), Horn and Noll (1997), and McGrew *et al.* (1991).

Developmental evidence: age differences and changes in adulthood

As indicated in our introduction, most of the research on the development of cognitive capabilities in adulthood has been directed at describing age-related declines in these capabilities. The findings clearly indicate declines in the abilities of Gf, Gs, and SAR. But some of this work has adduced evidence of improvements and maintenance of abilities, principally the abilities of Gc and TSR. The designs for the studies producing this evidence have been both cross-sectional and longitudinal. These two kinds of designs have different strengths and weaknesses; they control for, and reveal, different kinds of influences (Horn and Donaldson 1980). Yet in major respects, as concerns age-related differences and changes, the findings from the two kinds of studies are largely congruent (Botwinick 1977; Horn 1994, 1997; Horn and Donaldson 1980). The longitudinal findings suggest that the points in adulthood at which declines occur are later than is indicated by the cross-sectional findings, but the evidence of which abilities decline and which improve is essentially the same for cross-sectional and longitudinal studies (Horn and Donaldson 1980; Schaie 1996). To set the stage for later arguments, let us first consider the abilities that appear to be maintained throughout most of adulthood.

Capabilities for which there is little or no aging decline

The results indicating improvement and maintenance of abilities have come largely from the same studies in which evidence of aging decline was found. The kinds of abilities for which there is replicated evidence of improvement in adulthood are largely those of Gc, indicating breadth of knowledge of the dominant culture and those of TSR, indicating fluency in retrieval of information from this store of knowledge.

Gc: Knowledge

The abilities of Gc are indicative of the intelligence of the culture, inculcated into individuals through systematic influences of acculturation. The range of such abilities is very large. No particular battery of tests is known to sample over the entire range. The sum of the achievement tests of the Woodcock–Johnson Psycho-Educational Battery–Revised (WJ-R, Woodcock 1996) probably provides the most nearly representative measure available today. It takes about three hours of testing time to obtain this measure. The sum of the Armed Forces Qualification Tests (AFQT) is also a fairly broad indicator, and this, too, requires several hours of testing.[1] The verbal subscale of the WAIS (Wechsler Adult Intelligence Scales) is a commonly used estimate. Subscale and primary ability indicators are tests of vocabulary, esoteric analogies, listening comprehension, and knowledge in the sciences, social studies, and humanities. A combination of wide range knowledge, vocabulary, and esoteric analogy tests has been used to estimate the factor in much of our research. All of these different measures correlate substantially with social class, amount and quality of education, and other indicators of acculturation.

On average, through most of adulthood, there is increase with age in Gc knowledge (e.g. Botwinick 1977, 1978; Cattell 1971; Harwood and Naylor 1971; Horn 1968, 1972, 1982, 1997; Horn and Cattell 1967; Horn and Hofer 1992; Kaufman 1990; Rabbitt and Abson 1991; Schaie 1996; Stankov and Horn 1980; Woodcock 1995). Results from some studies suggest improvement into the 80s (e.g. Harwood and Naylor 1971 for WAIS Information, Comprehension, and Vocabulary). Such declines as are indicated show up in the averages late in adulthood – age 70 and beyond – and are small (Schaie 1996). If differences in years of formal education are statistically controlled, the increment of Gc with advancing age is increased (Horn 1968, 1972, 1994; Kaufman 1990).

TSR: Tertiary Storage Retrieval

Two different kinds of measures indicate this class of abilities. Both of the two kinds of indicators involve encoding and consolidation of information in long-term storage, which storage itself is mainly indicative of Gc, but both kinds of TSR measures involve fluency of association in retrieval from that storage. The

---

1 The battery used in the National Longitudinal Survey of Youth and the controversial studies of Herrnstein and Murray (1994).

first kind of test involves retrieval after periods of time that range from a few minutes to a few hours. This is not short-term memory as it is usually measured, in which there is little basis for relating the items of the to-be-remembered material and the time between presentation of this material and recall is a few seconds (up to a minute or so). Under such conditions virtually none of the presented material is consolidated for storage that can be retrieved with long-term memory. To be indicative of TSR some meaningful association between the items of the to-be-remembered material must occur and the time lapse must be sufficient to ensure that consolidation can occur. This is what distinguishes TSR measures from indicators of SAR. The second kind of test indicates associations among pieces of information that would have been consolidated and stored in a system of categories (as described by Broadbent 1966) many months and years before.

Retrieval over intermediate periods of time

An example of the first kind of measure is Memory for Names in the WJ-R. The subject is introduced to what are said to be space creatures by being shown a picture of each creature and being told the creature's name (e.g. here is a picture of Kiptron). After each introduction, the subject is shown a page of pictures of space creatures and asked to point to the creature just introduced and to previously introduced creatures as named by the examiner (McGrew *et al.*1991). The measure is the number of creatures correctly associated with their names. The creature just introduced is almost always correctly identified and those introduced most recently are remembered best, so the principal variance in the measure stems from differences in ability to identify creatures introduced some time before. People remember the names of the creatures hours and even days after they were first introduced.

This kind of measure involves consolidation through association learning (Bower 1972) over periods of several minutes. The consolidation in this case is different from that which is said to be indicated by the primacy effect in serial list recall (Atkinson and Shiffrin 1968; Waugh and Norman 1965), which is indicative of short-term memory. The retrieval of the primacy effect is over periods of seconds, not minutes or hours, and there is little basis for associating the elements of the list. Such short-term memory relates primarily to SAR (not TSR), which declines with age (Horn *et al.* 1981). In measures of TSR the time between presentation and recall needs to be several minutes and there is a semantic (meaningful) basis for association between elements.

A memory task to measure TSR should not measure, or be heavily dependent on, working memory, which here, for reasons that will become clear when we discuss expertise, will be referred to as short-term working memory (STWM). STWM relates mainly to SAR and Gf, both of which decline with age. For example, if a memory test requires holding nonsensical information in awareness while performing other tasks (as in competition measures of STWM), it will relate primarily to Gf and SAR, not TSR. Memory tests given under highly speeded conditions also place heavy demands on STWM and thus do not yield good measures of TSR.

Fluency measures

In the second kind of measure of TSR subjects retrieve (through association) information that would have been stored days, months, or years previously. In a word associations test, for example, subjects provide words similar in meaning to a given word; in an ideas test, subjects provide ideas similar to a given idea. The person accesses an association category of information and pulls information from that category into a response mode. It is important that the tests not be given under highly speeded conditions. Otherwise, the test will measure cognitive speed (Gs). To be a good measure of TSR the time limits for retrieval should be such that most people produce as many associations as they can. Most people should finish with each item of the test before time is called.

For most of the years of adulthood the slope for the curve by age for measures of TSR is positive, although negatively accelerating (Horn and Cattell 1967; Horn and Noll 1997; Horn *et al.* 1981). By about age 50 years the curve becomes practically flat. By about 70 years of age the slope may become slightly negative (Schaie 1996).

Thus, it appears that TSR is at least partly indicative of the size of store of associations that are built up through consolidation learning. Yet the factor is independent of (though positively correlated with) Gc, which indicates size of store of knowledge. It is independent primarily in the sense that the correlation between TSR and Gc is well below the respective internal consistencies, but also in the sense that the age differences in one factor do not fully account for the age differences in the other factor. The measures also have different patterns of correlations with a variety of other variables. For example, in studies of creativity (Getzels and Jackson 1962; Guilford 1967; Milgram 1990; Torrance 1972) fluency measures, compared with measures of Gc (often referred to as IQ in this research), have been found to have notably different correlations with self-report measures of personality (e.g. the 'outgoing', 'dominant', 'surgency', 'sensitivity', 'self-sufficient', 'self-sentiment' factors of the 16 PF, Cattell *et al.* 1970; Gruber 1988), although the findings from this line of research do not support an hypothesis that TSR is more indicative of genuine creativity than is Gc (Csikszentmihalyi 1992; Vernon 1972). In general, it appears that Gc (as distinct from TSR) more nearly indicates store of knowledge, as such, and TSR more nearly indicates facility in associating elements of knowledge.

Declining capacities

Item recall

The associational retrieval of TSR is different from item recall of a particular word or concept with which one is familiar (Schonfeld 1972). This latter is often described as episodic (in contrast to semantic) memory (Tulving 1972). It is the kind of memory involved when one can't recall a word or name that one knows perfectly well – what is referred to as 'tip-of-the-tongue' (TOT) memory failure. Evidence pertaining to adulthood age differences in this kind of memory is reviewed in detail by Burke *et al.* (Chapter 8, this volume). That review indicates that item-recall memory declines with age in adulthood (in contrast to TSR). Five kinds of findings lead to this conclusion.

First, relative to younger adults, older adults report more TOT memory failures. Second, they tend to be slower and less accurate in naming objects depicted in pictures. Third, in speech they evince more pauses, hesitations, dithering, looking for words. Fourth, also in speech, they produce more ambiguous references and pronouns. Fifth, despite higher vocabulary scores and little age difference in ability to detect spelling errors, older adults make more spelling errors in written production. These results are interpreted as indicating age-related increase in difficulty in retrieving the tags (nouns) for concepts of which one is aware – words available in one's knowledge store.

Item-recall inability in retrieval of words does not result simply from lack of vocabulary: in TOT the word that can't be retrieved is in one's vocabulary, and older adults who score lower (on average) than younger adults on item-recall indicators score higher on vocabulary tests (synonyms, antonyms). It is worth noting, however, that the vocabulary tests of the studies that indicate this outcome require only recognition (multiple-choice) memory, which is indicative of passive vocabulary, not recall memory, which measures active vocabulary. Recall is generally more difficult than recognition. Thus, it is possible that age-related decline in item recall indicates deterioration of active vocabulary. Bromley (1974) found age-related decrease in the ability to recognize subtle – more difficult – distinctions in the meanings of words and to employ these distinctions in very precise use of language.

Item-recall inability also does not seem to indicate merely lack of association for the to-be-remembered items. The word that can't be recalled in TOT is associated in a meaningful context with the stimulus concept the word represents – a person, place, or thing that one knows. The inability is one of retrieving a particular association. In TSR, by contrast, there is retrieval of many associations. Retrieval of precisely one association – the 'correct' association – is difficult in the sense that the measure of subtlety used in Bromley's study is difficult. In contrast, the associations in a word fluency measure of TSR are not difficult in this sense – the associations do not need to be logically highly similar. Thus, the item-recall retrieval that declines with age may indicate loss of facility in making precise associations, not loss in making associations.

As measured in fluency tasks, TSR is positively indicative of the size of the store of associations. Item recall and TOT, on the other hand, do not appear to be positively dependent on size of store associations and they may even be negatively related – that is, if associations similar to a stimulus word (concept) interfere in finding a particular association (Fozard 1980).

Burke *et al.* (Chapter 8, this volume) suggest that failures in item recall reflect inability to map a well defined idea or lexical concept into its phonological and orthographic forms. The reader is referred to that chapter for more detailed explanation of what this means.

Item recall has not been studied carefully in research on the structure of abilities. It appears to be mainly indicative of the reasoning of Gf (as indicated by analogies tests, for example), but may also involve the short-term memory of SAR. Both Gf and SAR decline with age in adulthood. These factors, together with Gs, are referred to as vulnerable abilities to contrast them with the maintained abilities, Gc and TSR.

Gf: Reasoning

The research findings are consistent in indicating steady decline of Gf over most of the period of adulthood. The decline is seen with measures of syllogisms and concept formation (McGrew *et al.* 1991), in reasoning with metaphors and analogies (Salthouse 1987, 1993; Salthouse *et al.* 1990*b*), with measures of comprehending series, as in letter series, figural series, and number series (Horn 1972, 1982, 1994; Noll and Horn 1997; Salthouse *et al.* 1990*a*), and with measures of mental rotation, figural relations, matrices, and topology (Cattell 1979). In each case the factor is most cleanly indicated – measures are most nearly uni-factorial – if the fundamentals of the test are novel or equally familiar to all, that is, give no advantage to those with greater knowledge of the culture. Although many of the tests that have indicated the aging decline of Gf have a speeded component, the decline is indicated very well by unspeeded tests that require resolution of high-level (difficult) complexities (Horn 1994; Horn *et al.* 1981; Noll and Horn 1997).

The reasoning of Gf is based on component abilities, termed processes, some of which have been identified in studies of aging. Prominent among these processes is one of maintaining awareness of the elements and relationships of a reasoning problem. This process is measured by tasks that have been interpreted as indicating a central executive function in working memory (Baddeley 1993, 1994). We shall return to a more detailed analysis of this and related processes in a section titled 'Analysis of interdependence among abilities', after first considering a major memory factor identified in studies of structure among abilities.

SAR: Short-term Apprehension and Retrieval

This factor indicates a persistent finding that tests that put demand on short-term memory correlate to the extent of this demand with tests in which the principal requirement is the apprehension of information, the retention of this information for short periods of time during which the information is used, and then virtually no retention of the information after it has been used. The factor has been most often identified with measures of the forward-span memory and the 'magical number seven plus or minus two' (Miller 1956), but the two major serial position memory functions – recency and primacy (Glanzer and Cunitz

1966) – also are prominently related to the factor. Recency memory dissipates very quickly indeed; if there is delay of even 30 seconds, it is practically absent. Primacy memory represents slightly longer retention, and it has been regarded as an early indication of long-term memory (LTM) (Atkinson and Shiffrin 1968; Waugh and Norman 1965), but primacy also practically disappears after delays of as little as a minute. The factor is indicated by measures of working memory, including memory-span backward, although to the extent that the processes measured are of the kind required in reasoning – that is, to the extent that they involve central executive function – they also indicate Gf.

The findings of many studies indicate aging decline of the memory abilities of SAR (Craik 1977; Craik and Byrd 1982; Craik and Trehub 1982; Horn *et al.* 1981; Salthouse 1991*a*; Schaie 1996). The decline is small in tasks that involve very short periods of retention, such as recency measures; there are virtually no age differences for the Sperling (1960) kind of task, in which the retention is for only a few milliseconds. But for measures in which retrieval is required after short periods of up to a minute or two, age-related declines generally have been found. This is true of memory for information the subject could regard as meaningful, as well as for nonsense material, although age differences appear to be smaller for memory of the meaningful kind of information (Cavanaugh 1997; Charness 1991; Craik and Trehub 1982; Ericsson and Delaney 1996; Gathercole 1994; Kaufman 1990; Salthouse 1991*b*; Schaie 1996). The more complex the memory task, the more the task measures the limits of apprehension and retention, the more the task requires that material be held in awareness while doing other things – as in definitions of working memory – the more the task will relate to Gf and the larger the negative relationship to age. More simply, the more difficult the short-term memory task is, the more it relates to Gf and to aging decline. For example, simple forward-span tests that do not measure very well at the upper limits of span have been found to have smaller (absolute value) negative relationships to age than backward-span tests, which typically do push subjects to the limits of their span capacities (Babcock and Salthouse 1990; Hayslip and Kennelly 1982; Horn *et al.* 1981), but if forward-span tests measure at the upper limits, then there is usually very little difference in the magnitude of the age differences for the forward-span and backward-span measures (Gregpore and Van der Linden 1997; Verhaeghen *et al.* 1993). Under these latter conditions, too, forward span and backward span are highly correlated and are substantially related to Gf as well as to SAR.

Gs: Cognitive speed

Most cognitive tests involve speed in one form or another – speed of reacting, speed in behaving, speed of thinking. Studies of chronometric measures, as such, and of their relationships with other cognitive capabilities (Eysenck 1987; Hertzog 1989; Jensen 1987; Nettelbeck 1994; Salthouse 1985, 1991*a, b*) indicate that the measures are positively intercorrelated in a range of upward from 0.50, and correlate significantly with a wide variety of cognitive abilities; the fallible correlations range between 0.15 and 0.65, depending on the measures, the measurement reliabilities, and the heterogeneity of the samples. Simple reaction time (SRT), in which one reacts as quickly as possible to a single stimulus, correlates at a low level ($r < 0.25$) with most measures regarded as indicative of human intelligence. The more a speeded measure involves complexity, the higher this correlation becomes. This is illustrated in Jensen's (1982, 1993) studies. He designed choice reaction time (CRT) tests that ranged in complexity from those in which the subject had to discriminate between only two stimuli to those in which subjects had to discriminate among eight stimuli. He found that as the logarithm to base 2 of the number of required discriminations increased, the correlation between reaction time measures and measures indicative of intelligence increased linearly: the more complex the speeded task, the larger the correlation (cf. Hick's 1952 'law').

Salthouse (1985, 1991a) has reviewed much of the evidence on how aging relates to various kinds of measures of speed. Most of the results he reports indicate that older adults perform more slowly than younger adults. This is true for tasks such as copying digits, crossing off letters, comparing numbers, picking up coins, zipping a garment, unwrapping Band-Aids, using a fork, dialling a telephone number, and sorting cards. It is true also for tests of perceptual speed, digit-symbol substitution, movement time, trail making, SRT, and CRT (Salthouse 1985). Comparisons of standard score measures of SRT and CRT suggest that the age differences are larger for CRT. In studies in which young and old subjects are provided opportunity to practise a CRT task, practice does not eliminate the age differences and no noteworthy Age × Practice interactions are found (Madden and Nebes 1980; Salthouse and Somberg 1982).

Such results have spawned theory that slowing with age in adulthood is a general feature of cognitive behavior (Birren 1974; Kausler 1990; Salthouse 1985, 1991a, 1992, 1993, 1994). Such theory has been closely linked to, and regarded as supportive of, the theory of general intelligence. Indeed, in Spearman's (1927) early, highly influential, theory of g (general intelligence) it was proposed that neural speed is the principal, underlying feature governing the eduction of relations and correlates – the central processes defining g. Building on Spearman's theory, Eysenck (1987), Jensen (1982, 1987, 1993) and Salthouse (1985, 1991a) have proposed that speed of information processing, reflecting speed of transmission in the neural system, is the essence of general intelligence; the level of ability manifested in any and all indicators of human intelligence is determined, they argued, by neural speed.

It is widely believed that the experimental evidence largely supports the theory of general intelligence and the theory of general slowing of cognitive processes with aging, and that neural transmission speed is probably the underlying correlate/determinant of both the slowing and the change in g. Yet serious doubts can be raised about both of these widely believed theories. Let us consider the evidence.

Speed in relation to cognition and aging

We need to consider two related but separate theories, one stipulating that speed is the sine qua non of general intelligence, as such – the Spearman, Eysenck, Jensen, Salthouse theory – the other stipulating that general slowing is the sine qua non of loss of cognitive capabilities (intelligence) with age in adulthood – the Birren, Kausler, Salthouse theory. We will consider the theories in the reverse of this order of identifying them, because there are two different meanings of the word 'general' as it is applied in theory of aging loss (Hertzog 1989; Hertzog *et al.* 1990; Hertzog *et al.* 1996), and distinguishing these two meanings helps provide a basis for evaluating the theory that speed is the sine qua non of general intelligence.

(a) Distinguishing slowing with age and a general factor of slowing

One meaning of the word 'general' in aging loss theory requires that there be slowing with age on all cognitive measures that in any sense require speed. Theory based on this meaning can be said to require support for an all-slow (ALS) hypothesis. A second meaning of the word 'general' in aging loss theory requires that all measures that involve speed in any sense indicate a single common factor that slows with age. This can be referred to as the common factor of speed (CFS) hypothesis.

Very high correlations based on what is called a Brinley (1965) plot have been presented as evidence in support of the (singular) general slowing hypothesis (Cerella 1985, 1990; Salthouse 1985). This evidence is relevant for evaluating the ALS hypothesis, but it is of no use for evaluating the CFS hypothesis.

In Cerella (1985, 1990) and Salthouse (1985) the average time a sample of young people took to perform a number of different speeded tasks was arrayed in a bivariate plot against the average time a sample of old people took to perform the same tasks – the Brinley plot. A regression line was fitted to this plot of averages, a correlation among these averages was calculated to indicate goodness of fit of the line, and this correlation was found to be large (> 0.90). The high correlation was said to support the general slowing hypothesis. Indeed, it is relevant for evaluating the ALS hypothesis: to the extent that the samples of subjects are representative of young and old people and the sample of tests is representative of the population of measures of cognitive speed, the findings support this hypothesis.

But results of this kind do not support the CFS hypothesis (although such results have been widely misinterpreted as providing such support). The problem is that one can have a very high – in fact perfect 1.00 – correlation between means when there is very low – in fact zero – correlation between the measures, as such. Thus, the correlation between means does not provide reliable evidence for evaluating the hypothesis that different measures all indicate a single common factor that slows with age (Perfect 1994; Walsh 1990). Walsh demonstrated this with examples of hypothetical data representing central processing and peripheral processing measures for which, in fact, he had found very low correlations.

The hypothetical data Walsh used in his demonstration are provided in Table 5.1. The numbers in the body of the table represent reaction times (RTs) of eight subjects – four young and four old – on six tasks. The mean RTs for groupings of young and old subjects are in the foot of the table. The Brinley plot for these means – the averages for the young plotted against the averages for old – is shown in Fig. 5.1.

Here it can be seen that a straight line fits the plot with no error: there is perfect linear correlation between the averages. But the correlations between the RTs, as such, for the first task and tasks 4, 5, and 6 are -0.04, 0.02, and .0.09 respectively – as near zero as one might get with a sample of only eight subjects. Similarly, the correlations of task 2 and task 3 with tasks 4, 5, and 6 are all small, not notably or significantly different from zero. These correlations represent Walsh's findings in an experiment in which backward-masking techniques were used to measure peripheral and central processing, which were found to be independent factors. The correlation between different estimates of these factors averaged 0.16 when corresponding correlations for Brinley-plot averages were upwards from 0.92.

In the averages of a Brinley plot the between-person variation in each variable is eliminated: individual differences are cancelled out. But the CFS hypothesis requires that the between-person variation on each speeded task

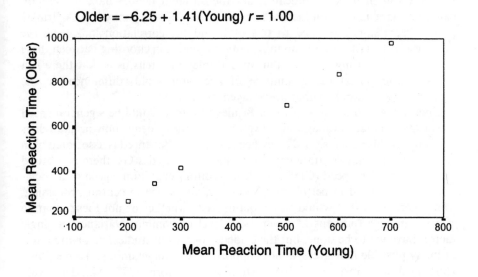

Older = –6.25 + 1.41(Young) *r* = 1.00

Fig. 5.1　Brinley plots of mean reaction times: old against young.

Table 5.1 Individual reaction time data for eight hypothetical subjects measured with three peripheral processing tasks and three central processing tasks.

	Task type					
	Peripheral			Central		
	1	2	3	4	5	6
YOUNG-1	155	205	255	600	700	800
YOUNG-2	175	225	275	450	550	650
YOUNG-3	225	275	325	550	650	750
YOUNG-4	245	295	345	400	500	600
OLDER-1	180	260	330	800	940	1080
OLDER-2	220	300	370	750	890	1030
OLDER-3	320	400	470	700	840	980
OLDER-4	360	440	510	550	690	830
Means young	200	250	300	550	600	700
Means older	270	350	420	700	840	980

covary with the between-person variation on every other such task. Because between-person variation is cancelled out in obtaining an average, covariation between averages provides no information about the between-person covariation. Quite separate factors may underlie each of the several measures for which there is high correlation in a Brinley plot. Indeed, age is associated with quite different factors. Plotting the means for samples of young and old subjects to illustrate this in no way indicates that the different factors have a common cause or share a common factor. They may, but also they may not. A Brinley plot, a regression line fitted to this plot, and the correlation indicating the goodness of this fit, provide no information of value in choosing between these 'mays'. All that a high correlation for a Brinley plot tells us is that there is a near-linear order in the magnitude of age (young–old) differences in the averages of the variables that are arrayed in the plot.

Underlying a straight-line fit to a Brinley plot there could be a general speed factor that changes with age. However, most of the evidence now in hand does not support this conclusion. The evidence suggests that speed is associated with several distinct and separate cognitive functions. Besides Gs, there is a broad factor of decision speed (CDS), speed in auditory cognition, speed of association in TSR, speed in peripheral processing, and speed in central processing. The experiments that would show, definitively, whether or not these separate systems involve (perhaps at a very low level of common variance) a single factor, have yet to be done, but the evidence of partial studies, involving a few of many possible indicators, is not supportive (Cunningham and Tomer 1990; Hertzog 1989; Horn *et al* 1981; Hundal and Horn 1977; Madden 1983; Salthouse 1991*a,b*; Walsh 1982). The intercorrelations among different measures involving speed do not satisfy the conditions of a Spearman (1927) model:

one, and only one, common factor (Horn and Noll 1997). Different measures indicating cognitive speed relate in different ways to primary abilities and to cognitive processing variables (Hertzog 1989; Horn *et al.* 1981; Madden 1983, 1985; Walsh 1982).

In sum, slowing with age has been indicated in many kinds of cognitive tasks, but it has yet to be shown that there is a single factor of speed underlying all of these manifestations of slowing. Rather, it appears that there are separate systems each of which involves a process, or processes, that slow with advancing age.

(b) Cognitive speed theory of general intelligence

Here again there are two separate hypotheses to consider: hypothesis g – that a unitary process, *g*, underlies all cognitive capabilities thought to be indicative of human intelligence; and hypothesis s – that cognitive speed (believed to indicate neural speed) is the essential element of *g*.

In respect to hypothesis g, two important lines of evidence suggest that cognitive abilities do not interrelate in a manner that would indicate a single unitary process. The evidence indicates several distinct organizations of cognitive capacities – several 'intelligences' – and so far, at least, no single unifying factor has been found to indicate organization among these capabilities.

The first line of evidence that threatens the g hypothesis is structural. Batteries of tests well selected to provide reliable measures of the various processes thought to be indicative of general intelligence do not fit the one common factor (i.e., Spearman *g*) model. This has been demonstrated time and time again (as reviewed by, for example, Horn,1968, 1982; Horn and Hofer 1992). The results from the analyses of Carroll (1993) indicate no fewer than eight general factors. That is, a general factor could be calculated in each of several batteries of tests. But the general factor of one battery was not the same as the general factor of other batteries.

The second line of evidence is that of construct validation. The relationships that putative indicators of general intelligence have with variables of development, neurological functioning, education, achievement, and genetic structure are varied. The relationships of some indicators are negative, others positive, for the same outside variable. For example, Gf correlates negatively with age in adulthood, Gc correlates positively. The curves relating Gf to age are monotonic decreasing, but the curve for Gv over the same period of aging first increases and then decreases. Such evidence suggests that different broad factors among abilities indicate different kinds of 'intelligence'. The many relationships defining the construct validities of the different broad factors do not indicate a single unitary principle. This evidence, too, has been reviewed recently and in some detail in Horn and Noll (1997).

As concerns hypothesis s, there are major problems with the studies, the results, and the interpretations of results that have been regarded (e.g. by Eysenck 1982, 1987; and Jensen 1982, 1987) as providing support. In these studies chronometric measures were correlated with cognitive capability measures regarded as indicating intelligence, corrections for unreliability were made and the resulting correlations were found to be close to unity. It was concluded that all the reliable variance in the indicators of intelligence was accounted for by cognitive speed. Major problems with drawing this conclusion include the following:

1. A central problem is that which was outlined in the previous section – the problem that there is no one factor, *g*, of general intelligence. The measures assumed to indicate *g* are mixtures of different cognitive capabilities – different mixtures in different studies, no one of them indicative of a unitary *g*. Evidence that a particular measure of cognitive speed accounts for the reliable variance in one such measure (of a mixture of abilities) thus is not evidence that it accounts for comparable variance in a measure of another mixture or for the variance of a *g*-factor if one were found.
2. The chronometric tests measured some of the same processes of attentiveness and dealing with complexities that are measured in the cognitive tests and, vice versa, the cognitive measures were speeded and thus measured the same thing as the chronometric tests. Thus the correlations between the chronometric and cognitive measures were inflated by overlap in measure of the same thing. In studies in which this confound was reduced by using power measures of Gf, only about one-third of the reliable variance of the cognitive measures was accounted for by chronometric measures (Horn *et al.* 1981; Horn and Noll 1997).
3. In the sampling of subjects, there was heavy sampling at the extremes. Sub-samples of retarded persons were included in some of the samples. Such sampling generates spuriously large correlations. Tests designed to distinguish between different cognitive capabilities do not do so in retarded people, for example, because these people fail the most elementary requirements for dealing with the measurement tasks – understanding what they are to do, getting started on time, sustaining attention to the task, remembering the test requirements. These elementary requirements are much the same for quite different tests, including chronometric tests. Thus the same lack of ability to do the tests is measured in all tests. This generates high correlations, high communality, and common factor covariance among tests that otherwise measure different factors.
4. Corrections for attenuation due to unreliability spuriously raised the estimated correlations. The reliability estimates used in the corrections were test–retest correlations, rather than at-the-time internal consistencies. They were thus underestimates relative to the at-the-time correlations between chronometric and cognitive measures. The estimates of the reliabilities were obtained in samples in which there was no sampling at the extremes. Thus, the reliabilities were not inflated to the extent that the correlations among the tests were inflated. The reliability estimates were small. Corrections for unreliability are obtained by dividing the obtained correlation by estimates of the reliabilities. If reliability estimates are unrealistically small, the 'corrected' correlation will be unrealistically large. These procedures thus generate spuriously large estimates of the amount of variance shared by chronometric and cognitive capability measures.

Together these conditions combine to produce substantial overestimates of the magnitude of the relationship between chronometric measures and estimates of different factors incorrectly regarded as indicating the same g factor. With appropriate corrections for unreliabilities in samples that are not loaded with extreme cases, the correlation between simple reaction time and any particular measure said to indicate g is no larger than about 0.3; the comparable correlation for complex reaction time may run as high as 0.65, but is well below 1.0 and even this represents, in part, the fact that CRT involves complexity resolution such as is measured under unspeeded conditions in Gf and Gc (Horn *et al.* 1981). The more reliable the measures, the larger the correlations, of course, but reasonable corrections for attenuation of correlation due to unreliability do not raise the correlations to unity. Indeed, in fairly homogeneous samples of people – people of approximately the same age and education level – highly speeded measures have been found to correlate near zero, or even negatively, with measures that emphasize resolution of high levels of complexity under unspeeded conditions (Guilford 1964).

To summarize: (1) The cognitive capabilities that have been regarded as indicating human intelligence do not appear to involve a single unitary process. They indicate separate kinds of intelligence. (2) Chronometric measures do not predict, or account for, all the reliable variance of conglomerates of separate intelligences (incorrectly interpreted as indicating g). There are separate speeded systems. They do not appear to form a single functional unity.

Having recognized that speed is not the sine qua non, or the only important feature, of cognitive capabilities, one still must recognize that speed is related to these capabilities and to their age differences. Speed is implicated in the aging decline of Gf, the factor that best represents Spearman's concept of g. And speed is related to the decline of SAR. This is seen clearly in results from studies of the interdependence among abilities, even as the results from these studies add to the evidence that speed is not the only process involved in the age differences of cognitive capabilities. More than this, the results suggest that it may not be speed itself that is central to the process of aging decline of Gf – the decline in speed may be due to other factors (cf. Salthouse, Chapter 2, this volume).

Analyses of interdependence among abilities

The cognitive behaviour displayed by a person is not, in itself, neatly partitioned into knowledge, reasoning, memory, speediness, etc. It is a whole in which all such aspects of capability are interwoven. Gc, TSR, Gf, Gs, and SAR are constructs isolated by analyses with tests, the requirements of which emphasize some aspects of capability relative to others. Such operational definitions never completely separate the different capabilities. This is seen in the positive intercorrelations among these factors. These intercorrelations indicate interdependence among capabilities. Gf, for example, is dependent on SAR: to reason effectively, as measured in Gf, one must apprehend the fundaments of a problem and hold them within the span of immediate awareness, processes emphasized in the measurements of SAR. Correlation between manifest indicators of Gf and SAR point to such latent interdependencies.

To describe the dependencies among different capabilities analytically, Horn (1982, 1989), Horn *et al.* (1981), Noll and Horn (1997), and Salthouse (1993) have used multiple-partialling procedures. These procedures have been directed mainly at describing aging decline of fluid reasoning in terms of elementary processes of memory, speed, concentration, attention, and incidental learning. Beginning with an observed age-related decline in Gf of approximately 0.25 standard deviation units (SDU) per 10 years of age (over a period from the early 20s through the mid-60s), Noll and Horn (1997) demonstrated that the decline of Gf is reduced by approximately 0.10 SDU per decade – to about 0.15 SDU – by controlling for processes of short-term memory (indicators of SAR). Gs speediness also accounted for about 0.10 SDU of the age decline of Gf (as in previous studies). Part of this relationship reflected an interdependence of Gs and SAR. When this was taken into account in multiple partialling, it was found that Gs, independently of SAR, accounted for about 0.055 of the Gf decline with age. This finding was replicated with different indicators of the basic constructs.

More fundamentally, further analyses of interdependence suggested that the basic process involved in both the Gs decline with age and the Gf decline may not be speed at all, but a capacity for maintaining attention. In the studies leading to this conclusion the measures of Gf were designed to, as much as possible, exclude speed of performance. Letter series and matrices tests were constructed to provide measures of the average level of difficulty of problems solved, not count of the number of problems solved. In such tests one person can score high by solving only a few problems, but problems of high difficulty, while another person who solves many problems scores lower because the problems solved are of only low difficulty. The measures obtained in this manner are referred to as power measures (Horn 1997; Noll and Horn 1997 for fuller descriptions).

Power test operations tend to ensure that any variance Gf may share with Gs is not simply speed in producing answers. Such operations do not ensure that the Gf measurements are devoid of speed of thinking, however. Indeed, Gs measures of simple speed of scanning and comparing relate to power measures of Gf and account for significant portions of Gf aging decline (Horn 1982, 1997; Horn *et al.* 1981; Horn and Noll 1993; Noll and Horn 1997). The simple measures appear to involve little memory or depth of processing or reasoning. For example, the task may be simply one of quickly marking all the letter 'd's' on a printed page, or determining whether sets of digits are the same or different.

The evidence suggesting that what is involved here is not speed, per se, but capacity for concentration, comes from partialling-out analyses with another very simple measure that involves no speediness. This measure is obtained with a slow tracing test first developed by Botwinick and Storandt (1974). High score on the measure is obtained by tracing very slowly – the slower the tracing, the higher the score. The test appears to measure focused attention concentration. It has now been established in studies based on five separate samples (Horn *et al.* 1981; Noll and Horn 1997) that this slowness/concentration measure accounts for most of the age-related variance that is associated with speediness. It accounts for all the reliable age-related variance that the speed measures have in common with measures of Gf.

Age-related declines have been found for other sustained attention tasks. For example, such declines have been found for measures of vigilance, in which subjects must detect a stimulus change imbedded in an otherwise invariant sequence of the stimuli (for review, see McDowd and Birren 1990; Kausler 1990). Declines have been found also in divided attention and selective attention tasks (Bors and Forrin 1995; Horn *et al.* 1981; Horn and Noll 1997; Madden 1983; McDowd and Birren 1990; McDowd and Craik 1988; Plude and Hoyer 1985; Rabbitt 1965; Salthouse 1991*b*; Wickens *et al.* 1987). Older adults perform more poorly than their younger counterparts on the Stroop, indicating interference effects (Cohn *et al.* 1984), and distracted visual search (Madden 1983; Plude and Hoyer 1985; Rabbitt 1965). Horn *et al.* (1981) found that concentration and divided attention separately and together account for much of the aging decline in measures of short-term and working memory.

These kinds of results are consistent with the Hasher and Zacks (1988) suggestion that aging decline in cognitive capability is due to distractibility and susceptibility to perceptual interference. These investigators found that manifest retrieval problems of older adults were attributable to inability to keep irrelevant information from obscuring relevant information. Horn *et al.* (1981) found that measures of eschewing irrelevancies in concept formation related to measures of short-term memory, working memory and Gf, and accounted for some of the age differences in these measures. Hasher and Zacks suggested that a basic process in working memory is one of maintaining attention. Baddeley (1993) suggested that working memory can be described as 'working attention'.

This kind of 'working attention', which is focused and deliberate and indicates concentration, is different from a kind of automatic attention, referred to as automaticity. With practice in developing skills, processing that is at first deliberate and slow becomes automatic and fast, and the amount of concentration effort needed in execution of the skill is reduced (see Smith 1996, for a recent comprehensive review). As measures become more and more indicative of automaticity, age differences disappear. As tasks require more and more of the kind of deliberate processing that calls for attention and close concentration, on the other hand, age differences appear. It is this kind of attention that relates to the abilities of Gf, Gs, and SAR and to their aging decline.

In sum, it appears that the aging declines of important reasoning capabilities that characterize human intelligence are due in part to loss of capacities for encoding and maintaining focused concentration. Inability to maintain focused concentration accounts for slowness in cognitive tasks and in particular the slowness that accompanies aging. The processes so far studied in partialling analyses account for only about one-half of the age-related decline in Gf reasoning. Other processes must be involved. Future research should be directed at identifying these processes.

EMERGING THEORY ABOUT ADULT INTELLIGENCE:
THE DEVELOPMENT OF EXPERTISE

Results indicating aging decline in cognitive abilities raise questions – and hopes – that the evidence is somehow incorrect or misleading. Indeed, the results present a paradox relative to common observation: they suggest that there are serious cognitive deficits of reasoning and memory in aged persons who, in the world of work, are leaders in politics, business, and academia, and who, in a variety of other real life pursuits, appear to function at a high level. Such observations suggest that the laboratory measures so far developed are not fully indicative of important features of human intelligence.

Inadequacies of current theory and measurement of adult intelligence

As we have seen, the Gc abilities of breadth of knowledge and the TSR abilities of association retrieval from the store of knowledge are maintained with age. They are in this sense indicative of adult intelligence. However, there are problems in assuming that the operational definitions of these variables truly can measure the peaks in expressions of intelligence in adults. These problems can be seen particularly in operational definitions of Gc.

We have noted that the concept of Gc pertains to an extremely broad and diverse range of knowledge – the knowledge of a culture – and that it is virtually impossible to representatively sample such a domain with objective tests. This is particularly true under the conditions of most research. The WJ-R achievement battery might well give a reasonable estimate of the 'intelligence of a culture', but the three hours of testing required to obtain this estimate is more time than can be given by volunteers and allocated by design in most research. The measures of Gc that can be obtained – composites of vocabulary, information, and analogy tests – can provide only very rough estimates. Such measures provide only a surface-like, dilettante estimate of an adult's grasp of the intelligence of the culture.

This is seen in esoteric analogies, the test most often used to estimate the reasoning aspect of Gc. The items of this test sample relationships across several areas of knowledge; for example, Marx is to Hegel as Aquinas is to __? Annual is to Perennial as Deciduous is to __? But the relationships are not particularly difficult if one has been introduced to the field of knowledge. The variance of the measure thus mainly indicates surface-like knowledge in diverse areas of scholarship, not ability in dealing with difficult abstractions in reasoning in any one such area. Yet it is effective reasoning with difficult problems that is seen as intelligence in much of the work of adults.

The items of vocabulary and information tests that measure the store of knowledge of Gc also sample only common knowledge in a number of fields, not the depth of knowledge in any field. Thus, the operational definition of Gc obtained with these measures, too, is a measure of only introductory understanding in several areas of knowledge.

A dilettante who flits over many areas will score higher on Gc measures than a person who neglects some areas in the process of developing truly profound understanding in a smaller segment of the domain of the knowledge of a culture. Yet is it not the latter who is most likely to make significant contributions to the culture and be judged, therefore, to be most intelligent? More to the point, does not the latter best exemplify the capabilities that indicate the nature and limits of human intelligence?

As people develop intelligence in adulthood they become able to comprehend some areas of knowledge in much more depth and intricacy than is sampled in any survey test. They come to know and understand a great deal about some things. They become specialized. They become experts. This development of expertise is accomplished somewhat to the detriment of becoming aware of, and retaining knowledge of, other things. The intelligence of an adult becomes a melange of deep knowledge in some areas and only shallow understanding in many others.

There are two important points suggested here: (1) the abilities that come to fruition in adulthood represent the quintessential expression of human intellectual capacity, and (2) the measures of current theory used to estimate intelligence probably do not measure the upper limits – the expertise – of the cognitive capabilities that most characterize intellectual development attained in adulthood.

Basis for defining intelligence in terms of expertise

Performance in some areas of expertise depends on effective application of a large amount of knowledge in reasoning to cope with novel problems. The abilities exemplified in these domains appear to be, or at least are similar to, abilities regarded as indicative of human intelligence. The levels of complexities in reasoning resolved in expressions of expertise are comparable to, and greater than, the levels of complexities resolved in expressions of Gf abilities, and the problems solved often appear to be novel. The difficulties of the problems solved in expert performance in chess, for example, appear to be at least as high as the difficulties of the items used to measure Gf. The complexities resolved in the game of GO appear to be even higher than those resolved in chess, and the problems are often clearly novel (Johnson 1997; Mechner 1998; Reitman 1976).

The reasoning involved in exercise of expertise is largely knowledge based and deductive, in contrast to the reasoning that characterizes Gf, which is inductive. This is seen in descriptions of the thinking in several areas of expertise – in particular, chess, financial planning, and medical diagnosis (Charness 1981*a*, 1991; de Groot 1978; Ericsson 1996; Walsh and Hershey 1993). For example, de Groot (1978) found that the highest-level experts in chess chose the next move by evaluating the current situation in terms of principles derived from vast prior experience, rather than by calculation and evaluation of move possibilities.

Other work (Charness 1981a, 1991; Ericsson 1996, 1997; Morrow *et al.* 1994; Walsh and Hershey 1993) demonstrated that the expert characteristically uses deductive reasoning under conditions where the novice uses inductive reasoning. The expert is able to construct a framework (e.g. possible diagnoses) with which to organize and effectively evaluate presented information, while novices, with no expertise basis for constructing a framework, search for patterns and do reasoning by trial-and-error evaluations. The expert apprehends large amounts of organized information, comprehends many relationships among elements of this information, infers possible continuations and extrapolations, and, as a result, is able to select the best from among many possibilities in deciding on the most likely outcome, consequence or extension of relationships. The expert goes from the general (comprehension of relations, knowledge of principles) to most likely specifics.

Expertise in problem solving appears to involve a form of long-term working memory (LTWM) that is different from the forms of memory that have been found to decline with age (Ericsson and Kintsch 1995). LTWM appears to emerge as expertise develops and to become a defining feature of advanced levels of expert skills (Ericsson and Delaney 1996). In theory, it is functionally independent of what heretofore has been described as short-term memory and working memory (Baddeley 1993), which here, for purposes of separation in language, will be referred to as short-term working memory (STWM). LTWM is described as a capacity for holding information in storage that can be quickly accessed over periods of minutes (perhaps even hours) while performing in ways that indicate the expertise. In the earliest research, de Groot (1946, 1978) described how, with increasing expertise, subjects became better able to rapidly access alternative chess moves of increasingly higher quality, and then base their play on these complex patterns rather than engage in extensive search. LTWM is different from STWM in respect to two major features: apprehension–retention limits and access in a sequence.

The apprehension–retention limits of STWM are small. The apprehension limits for the recency effect of the serial position function, which is often taken as an indicator of short-term memory, are only about three (plus or minus one), and this retention fades to zero in about thirty seconds (Glanzer and Cunitz 1966; Roediger and Crowder 1975). The apprehension limits for the primacy effect, which can endure longer, also are only about three (plus or minus one). In a classic article, Miller (1956) characterized the apprehension limits for forward-span memory as the 'magical number seven plus or minus two'; the retention limits for this memory are no more than a few seconds. These kinds of limits have been demonstrated also under conditions of competition for a limited resource, as in studies in which subjects are required to retain information while performing another task (Baddeley 1993; Carpenter and Just 1989; Stankov 1986). The limits seen in the Sperling (1960) effect are substantially larger than seven, but this span fades within milliseconds and is regarded as an indicator of apprehension alone, not a measure of short-term retention (memory).

The apprehension–retention limits for LTWM appear to be substantially larger than any of the limits accepted as indicating STWM – just how much larger is not clear, but chess experts, for example, appear to be able to hold many more than seven elements of separate games within the span of immediate awareness for as long as several minutes (Ericsson and Kintsch 1995; Gobet and Simon 1996). In playing blindfold chess (Ericsson and Staszewski 1989; Holding 1985; Koltanowski 1985) the expert is never able to literally see the board: all the outcomes of sequences of plays must be kept within a span of immediate apprehension. The number of elements the expert retains in such representations is more than the magical number seven plus two.

It has been argued that successive chunking in STWM is sufficient to account for the feats of memory displayed by experts and thus obviate any need for a concept of LTWM (Chase and Simon 1973; Gobet and Simon 1996). Chase and Simon (1973) reasoned that high-level chess memory was mediated by a large number (10 000 they estimated) of acquired patterns regarded as chunks, which could be hierarchically organized. The analyses of Richman *et al.* (1996) suggested that the number of such chunks would have to be in excess of 100 000, rather than 10 000.

To explain large span in blindfold chess in terms of chunking Chase and Simon (1973) suggested that the mechanism is one of direct retrieval of relevant moves cued by perceived patterns of chess positions that are stored in a form of short-term working memory (having a span of the order of seven plus two). But in expert retrievals in blindfold chess, the number of chunks appears to be larger than nine. If chunks are maintained in a hierarchy or other such template, the representation would be changed with successive moves, and the number of sequences of such changes is substantially larger than nine. Yet experts are able to go back through more than nine sequences to previous positions.

Similarly, in studies of experts playing multiple games of chess presented on a computer screen, Saariluoma (1991) found that a chess master could simultaneously play six different games each involving more than nine relationships. The expert appeared to retain representations of many more than nine chess positions in a flexibly accessible form while moving from one game to another.

STWM is characterized by sequencing in retention, but such sequencing seems to be unimportant in LTWM. In STWM maximum span is attained only if items are retained and retrieved in the temporal order of apprehension. If a task requires retrieval in a different order, the amount recalled is substantially reduced: memory-span backward, for example, is only about three to four, compared with the seven of forward span. In descriptions of chess experts displaying LTWM, on the other hand, information is almost as readily accessed from the middle or end of a sequence as from the front (Charness and Bosman 1990).

Using these observations, Ericsson and Kintsch (1995) made the case that while chunking helps to explain short-term memory that is somewhat larger than seven plus two, it is not fully able to account for the very large apprehension, long retention, and flexibility of access that experts display. In particular, if the different sequences experts access are regarded as chunks that must be maintained if the retrieval of experts is to be adequately described, the number of such chunks must be considerably larger than seven plus two, and they must be retained longer than a few seconds; thus, chunking cannot be the whole story (Ericsson and Kintsch 1995; Gobet and Simon 1996).

Chase and Simon (1973) rejected the suggestion (later proposed by Chase and Ericsson 1982) that storage of generated patterns in long-term memory is possible within periods as brief as the five-second presentations that were observed. But Cooke *et al.* (1993) and Gobet and Simon (1996) showed that this assumption is plausible. They found that highly skilled chess players could recall information from up to nine chess positions that had been presented one after the other as rapidly as one every five seconds without pauses.

How might LTWM work? Prior theory has not spelled this out. Our suggestion is that the development of expertise sensitizes the person to become more nearly aware of the large amount of information that is, for a very short period of time, available to all people (not just experts), but ordinarily is not accessed. Sperling's (1960) work indicates that for a split second the human is aware of substantially more information than is indicated by estimates of the limits of STWM, but most of this information fades from awareness very quickly. It fades partly because new information enters awareness to take the place of previous information and partly (relatedly) because meaningful systems are not immediately available in which to organize the incoming information. However, if meaningful systems for organizing information are built up through expertise development (the systems of LTWM), and such a system is available in the immediate situation, then very briefly seen information might be organized in accordance with this system in ways that would allow retention which is longer than is suggested by results from research on short-term memory. Information seen only briefly would be retained, and relatedly, new information might not take the place of (eradicate) briefly seen information. The briefly seen information would need to be that of a domain of expertise. Development of expertise would not, in general, improve memory. It would do so only in a limited domain.

Development of expertise

What we now know about expertise suggests that it is developed through intensive practice over extended periods of time and is maintained through regular practice and continued efforts (Anderson 1990; Ericsson 1996; Ericsson and Charness 1994; Ericsson and Lehmann 1996; Ericsson *et al.* 1993; Walsh and Hershey 1993). What is described as 'deliberate, well-structured practice' is essential for effective development of expertise. Such practice is not simply repetition and is not measured simply by number of practice trials. The practice must be designed to correct errors and move one to higher levels of performance. Practice must be well designed to identify errors. There should be goals and appropriate feedback. Practice should be directed at advancing to ever more difficult levels of performance. It was found that in developing expertise in chess, self-directed practice, using books and studying sequences of moves made by expert players, could be as effective as coach-directed practice (Charness 1981a, b, 1991; Ericsson 1996).

Just how long it takes to reach the highest levels of expertise – one's own asymptote – is not known with precision for any domain. A 'ten-year rule' has been given as an approximation for domains characterized by complex problem solving, but this has been much debated (Anderson 1990; Ericsson *et al.* 1993; Ericsson and Charness 1994). The upshot of the debate is that the time it takes to become expert varies with domain, the amount and quality of practice and coaching, the developmental level at which dedication to becoming an expert begins, health, stamina, and a host of other variables. Ten years is a very rough estimate for some domains, for example, chess, and medical diagnosis (Ericsson 1996).

Since it takes time (i.e., years) to reach high levels of expertise in complex problem solving, and expertise in such domains is developed, at least partially, through the period of adulthood, it follows that expertise can improve in adulthood. Indeed, the research literature is consistent in showing that across different domains of expertise, people beginning at different ages in adulthood advance from low to asymptotic high levels of expertise (Ericsson *et al.* 1993). Advanced levels of expertise in chess, GO, and financial planning have been attained and maintained by older adults (Charness and Bosman 1990; Charness *et al.* 1996; Ericsson and Charness 1994; Kasai 1986; Walsh and Hershey 1993). Rabbitt (1993) found that among novices, crossword-solving ability was positively correlated with test scores indicating Gf ($r = 0.72$) and negatively correlated with age ($r = -0.25$), just as Gf is so correlated, but among experts crossword-solving ability was positively associated with age ($r = 0.24$) and correlated near zero with Gf.

The results of Bahrick (1984), Bahrick and Hall (1991), Conway *et al.* (1991), Krampe and Ericsson (1996), and Walsh and Hershey (1993) indicate that continued practice is required to maintain a high level of expert performance – if the abilities of expertise are not used, they decline – but to the extent that practice is continued, expertise is maintained over periods of years and decades.

It appears, also, from the extant (albeit sparse) evidence that high levels of LTWM (as well as Gc/Gf-like expertise) can be maintained into advanced age. Baltes (1997) found that in domains of specialization, older adults can access information more rapidly than young adults. Charness (1981a, b, 1991) found no age decrement in the depth of search for the next move and the quality of the resulting moves in chess.[2] Such findings suggest that there may be little or no

---

2 Depth of search is described as a point at which a player can no longer retain accurate information about the projected changes to a presented chess position (Charness and Bosman 1990).

decline with age for complex thinking abilities if these abilities are developed within a domain of expertise.

Also suggesting that expertise abilities indicative of intelligence can be developed and maintained in adulthood are results showing that other kinds of abilities are so maintained. For example, Krampe and Ericsson (1996) found that, with continued practice, even highly speeded capabilities can be largely, although perhaps not entirely, maintained. They obtained seven operationally independent measures of speed in a sample of classical pianists who ranged from amateurs to concert performers with international reputations, and who ranged in age from the mid-20s to the mid-60s. Independently of age, experts performed better than amateurs on all music-related speeded tasks. Age-related decline was found at the highest level of expertise, but reliably only for one of the seven measures and the decline was notably smaller than for persons at lower levels of expertise. The single best predictor of performance on all music-related tasks was the amount of practice participants had maintained during the previous ten years.

In samples of practising typists of different ages, Salthouse (1985) found that while abilities of finger-tapping speed, choice-reaction time, and digit–symbol substitution that would seem to be closely related to typing ability declined systematically with age, typing ability, as such, did not: older typists attained the same typing speed as younger typists. The older typists had longer eye spans that enabled them to anticipate larger chunks of the material to be typed. Salthouse interpreted this as a compensatory mechanism. It can also be viewed as indicating a more advanced level of expertise, for, seemingly, it would relate to improving the skill of a typist of any age.

In a study of spatial visualization (Gv) in architects of different ages and levels of expertise, Salthouse *et al.* (1990*a*) found that high-level experts consistently scored above low-level experts at every age. Thus, in the abilities of expertise, elderly high-level experts scored higher than youthful low-level experts. This suggests, again, that with practice to increase and maintain expertise, cognitive abilities (of expertise) increase with advancing age.

Implications of emerging theory

Thus, there are suggestions that (1) expertise performance more nearly represents adult human intelligence than does performance on the tests that (so far) have been used to measure cognitive capabilities, and (2) advanced levels of expertise-intelligence are attained and maintained throughout adulthood. This implies that the aging declines seen in Gf, SAR, and Gs are not indicative of decline in the truly important features of intelligence. Practice related to these abilities is neglected as time and effort are devoted to the development of expertise. In consequence, there is decline of Gf, SAR, and Gs abilities. But expertise over adulthood develops in a form of deductive reasoning and long-term working memory. With intensive, well-structured practice, these abilities increase and thus may increase with age, at least among persons who work to become and remain experts. Within samples of people of approximately the same level of expertise there will be no aging decline of expertise-embedded measures. Expertise abilities of older high-level experts will exceed the abilities of younger persons at lower levels of expertise. The development of expertise may also result in a form of cognitive speed that is largely independent of the cognitive speed (Gs) measured with conventional tasks.

Such reasoning flows from sparse findings. The evidence of these findings is difficult to evaluate. Most of the results suggesting that adults maintain high levels of expertise into old age are based on case studies. The adults of these studies are exceptional people. There have been no longitudinal follow-up studies of substantial samples of adults to determine the extent to which people become expert in different domains and maintain that status. Indeed, there have been no cross-sectional studies of experts of different ages and levels of expertise. There have been no analyses of the component abilities of expertise. The theory laid down here is mainly a call for further study. There is need for much more research.

SUMMARY

Results from many studies of putative indicators of human intelligence indicate that there are distinct, independently determined systems of cognitive capability. Throughout adulthood there is decline with age in systems involved in retaining information in immediate awareness and reasoning with novel problems. In broad samples of children and adults the intercorrelations among most measures of human cognitive capability, including most chronometric measures, are positive.[3] Also, there is slowing with age in most chronometric measures and many measures of cognitive capability. There is positive correlation between a broad cognitive speed factor, Gs, and broad factors of reasoning, Gf, knowledge, Gc, facility in retrieving knowledge, TSR, and short-term apprehension and retrieval, SAR. This evidence is widely accepted as proof of the generality of cognitive capability and the generality of loss of speed of cognition with aging. But this evidence is not sufficient, and in fact the weight of evidence suggests that very likely neither intelligence nor loss of processing speed with cognitive aging is general.

The capabilities of Gf and SAR have been measured, by design, with materials that are either novel or equally familiar to most subjects, so that (by design) no advantage is given to a person with advanced, deep understanding in any particular domain of knowledge. Yet an important referent for the concept of intelligence is high-level ability to deal successfully with complex problems in

---

3   Although in restricted samples of people of approximately the same age, highly speeded measures correlate near zero or even negatively with measures that emphasize resolution of high levels of complexity under unspeeded conditions.

which the solutions require advanced, deep understanding of a knowledge domain.

Cognitive capability systems involved in retrieving information from the store of knowledge, TSR, and the store of knowledge itself, increase over much of the period of adulthood development. These increases indicate development of expertise, but the measures so far developed for these capabilities appear to be shallow. Tests measuring store of knowledge acquired throughout development tap only surface knowledge, not depth of knowledge. Neither these tests nor those indicating facility in retrieval from the store of knowledge measure the feats of reasoning and memory that characterize the most sublime expressions of adult intelligence. These capabilities have been adumbrated in studies of experts in chess, GO, medical diagnosis, and financial planning.

The superior performance of experts is characterized by a form of long-term working memory (LTWM). Within a circumscribed domain of knowledge, LTWM provides the expert with much more information in the immediate situation than is available in the system for short-term retention that has been found to decline with age in adulthood. LTWM appears to sublimate to a form of deductive reasoning that utilizes a complex store of information to effectively anticipate, predict, evaluate, check, analyse, and monitor in problem-solving within the knowledge domain. These abilities appear to characterize mature expressions of intelligence.

Years of intensive, well-structured learning, and regular practice are needed to develop and maintain a high level of expertise. To the extent that such developmental practice occurs through the years of adulthood, level of expertise is expected to increase with age in this period; to the extent that maintenance practice occurs, level of expertise intelligence should not decline with age.

ACKNOWLEDGEMENTS

We thank Richard Clark, Gretchen Guiton, Dennis Hocevar, Kayan Lewis, John Nesselroade, and David Walsh for the valuable suggestions and information we managed to incorporate in the final draft of this chapter. The writing of the chapter was supported in part by research grants (AG00156 and AG09936) of the National Institute on Aging.

REFERENCES

Anderson, J. R. (1990). *Cognitive psychology and its implications* (3rd edn.). New York: W. H. Freeman.

Atkinson, R. C. and Shiffrin, R. M. (1968). Human memory: a proposed system and its control processes. In K. W. Spence and J. T. Spence (ed.), *The psychology of learning and motivation* (Vol. 2, pp. 89–105). New York: Academic Press.

Babcock, R. L. and Salthouse, T. A. (1990). Effects of increased processing demands on age differences in working memory. *Psychology and Aging*, **5**, 421–8.

Baddeley, A. (1993). Working memory or working attention? In A. Baddeley and L. Weiskrantz (ed.), *Attention: selection, awareness, and control. A tribute to Donald Broadbent* (pp. 152–70). Oxford: Oxford University Press.

Baddeley, A. (1994). Memory. In A.M. Colman (ed.), *Companion encyclopedia of psychology* (Vol. 1, pp. 281–301). London: Routledge.

Baddeley, A. and Hitch, G. J. (1994). Developments in the concept of working memory. *Neuropsychology*, **8**, 485–93.

Bahrick, H. P. (1984). Semantic memory content in permastore: 50 years of memory for Spanish learned in school. *Journal of Experimental Psychology: General*, **113**, 1–29.

Bahrick, H. P. and Hall, L. K. (1991). Lifetime maintenance of high school mathematics content. *Journal of Experimental Psychology: General*, **120**, 20–33.

Baltes, P. B. (1997). On the incomplete architecture of human ontogeny: selection, optimization, and compensation as foundation of developmental theory. *American Psychologist*, **52**, 366–80.

Baltes, P. B. , Smith, J., and Staudinger, U. M. (1992). Wisdom and successful aging. In T. D. Sonderegger (ed.), Nebraska symposium on motivation (Vol. 39, pp. 123–67). Lincoln: University of Nebraska Press.

Birren, J. E. (1974). Translations in gerontology—from lab to life: psychology and speed of response. *American Psychologist*, **29**, 808–15.

Bors, D. A. and Forrin, B. (1995). Age, speed of information processing, recall, and fluid intelligence. *Intelligence*, **20**, 229–48.

Botwinick, J. (1977). Aging and intelligence. In J. E. Birren and K. W. Schaie (ed.), *Handbook of the psychology of aging* (pp. 580–605). New York: Reinhold.

Botwinick, J. (1978). *Aging and behavior: a comprehensive integration of research findings.* New York: Springer.

Botwinick, J. and Storandt, M. (1974). *Memory related functions and age.* Springfield, IL: Thomas.

Bower, G. H. (1972). Mental imagery and associative learning. In L. W. Gregg (ed.), *Cognition in learning and memory* (pp. 213–28). New York: Wiley.

Brinley, J. F. (1965). Cognitive sets, speed and accuracy of performance in the elderly. In A. T. Welford and J. E. Birren (ed.) *Behavior, aging and the nervous system* (pp. 114–49). Springfield, IL: Thomas.

Broadbent, D. E. (1966). The well-ordered mind. *American Educational Research Journal*, **3**, 281–95.

Bromley, D. B. (1974). *The psychology of human aging* (2nd edn.). London: Penguin.

Carpenter, P. A. and Just, M. A. (1989). The role of working memory in language comprehension. In D. Clahr and K. Kotovski (ed.), *Complex information processing: the impact of Herbert A. Simon* (pp. 31–68). Hillsdale, NJ: Lawrence Erlbaum.

Carroll, J. B. (1993*). Human cognitive abilities: a survey of factor-analytic studies.* New York: Cambridge University Press.

Cattell, R. B. (1971). *Abilities: their structure, growth and action.* Boston: Houghton-Mifflin.

Cattell, R. B. (1979). Are culture-fair intelligence tests possible and necessary? *Journal of Research and Development in Education*, **12**, 1–13.

Cattell, R. B., Eber, H. W., and Tatsuoka, M. M. (1970*). Handbook for the 16 personality factor questionnaire (16PF).* Champaign, IL: Institute for Personality and Ability Testing.

Cavanaugh, J. C. (1997). *Adult development and aging* (3rd edn). New York: ITP.

Cerella, J. (1985). Information processing rates in the elderly. *Psychological Bulletin*, **98**, 67–83.

Cerella, J. (1990). *The aging of information processes*. Cognitive Aging Conference. Atlanta, GA.

Charness, N. (1981*a*). Search in chess: age and skill differences. *Journal of Experimental Psychology: Human Perception and Performance*, **7**, 467–76.

Charness, N. (1981*b*). Visual short-term memory and aging in chess players. *Journal of Gerontology*, **36**, 615–19.

Charness, N. (1991). Expertise in chess: the balance between knowledge and search. In K. A. Ericsson and J. Smith (ed.), *Toward a general theory of expertise* (pp. 39–63). New York: Cambridge University Press.

Charness, N. and Bosman, E. A. (1990). Expertise and aging: life in the lab. In T. M. Hess (ed.), *Aging and cognition: knowledge organization and utilization* (pp. 343–86). New York: Elsevier.

Charness, N., Krampe, R., and Mayr, U. (1996). The role of practice and coaching in entrepreneurial skill domains: an international comparison of life-span chess skill acquisition. In K.A. Ericsson (ed.), *The road to excellence* (pp. 51–80). Mahwah, NJ: Lawrence Erlbaum.

Chase, W. G. and Ericsson, K. A. (1982). Skill and working memory. In G. H. Bower (ed.), *The psychology of learning and motivation* (Vol. 16, pp. 1–58). New York: Academic Press.

Chase, W. G. and Simon, H. A. (1973). Perception in chess. *Cognitive Psychology*, **4**, 55–81.

Cohn, N. B., Dustman, R. E., and Bradford, D. C. (1984). Age-related decrements in Stroop color test performance. *Journal of Clinical Psychology*, **40**, 1244–50.

Conway, M. A., Cohen, G., and Stanhope, N. (1991). On the very long-term retention of knowledge acquired through formal education: twelve years of cognitive psychology. *Journal of Experimental Psychology: General*, **120**, 395–409.

Cooke, N. J., Atlas, R. S., Lane, D. M., and Berger, R.C. (1993). Role of high-level knowledge in memory for chess positions. *American Journal of Psychology*, **106**, 321–51.

Craik, F. I. M. (1977). Age differences in human memory. In J. E. Birren and K. W. Schaie (ed.), *Handbook of the psychology of aging* (pp. 384–420). New York: Reinhold.

Craik, F. I. M. and Byrd, M. (1982). Aging and cognitive deficits: the role of attentional resources. In F. I. M. Craik and S. Trehub (ed.), *Aging and cognitive processes*. (pp. 191–211). New York: Plenum.

Craik, F. I. M. and Lockhart, R. S. (1972). Levels of processing: a framework for memory research. *Journal of Verbal Learning and Verbal Behavior*, **11**, 671–84.

Craik, F. I. M. and Trehub, S. (ed.). (1982). *Aging and cognitive processes*. New York: Plenum.

Cunningham, W. R. and Tomer, A. (1990). Intellectual abilities and age: concepts, theories and analyses. In A. E. Lovelace (ed.), *Aging and cognition: mental processes, self-awareness and interventions* (pp. 279–406). Amsterdam: Elsevier.

Csikszentmihalyi, M. (1992). Creativity. In R. J. Sternberg (ed.), *The encyclopedia of intelligence* (pp. 298–306). New York: Cambridge University Press.

de Groot, A. D. (1946*). Het denken vun den schaker [Thought and choice in chess]*. Amsterdam: North-Holland.

de Groot, A. D. (1978). *Thought and choice and chess*. The Hague: Mouton.

Eckstrom, R. B., French, J. W., and Harman, M. H. (1979). Cognitive factors: their identification and replication. *Multivariate Behavioral Research Monographs,* **79**.

Ericsson, K. A. (1996). The acquisition of expert performance. In K. A. Ericsson (ed.), *The road to excellence* (pp. 1–50). Mahwah, NJ: Lawrence Erlbaum.

Ericsson, K. A. (1997). Deliberate practice and the acquisition of expert performance: an overview. In H. Jorgensen and A. C. Lehmann (ed.), *Does practice make perfect? Current theory and research on instrumental music practice* (pp. 9–51). Norges, Sweden: NMH-publikasjoner.

Ericsson, K. A. and Charness, N. (1994). Expert performance. *American Psychologist,* **49**, 725–47.

Ericsson, K. A. and Delaney, P. F. (1996). Working memory and expert performance. In R. H. Logie and K. J. Gilhooly (ed.), *Working memory and thinking* (pp. 93–114). Hillsdale, NJ: Lawrence Erlbaum.

Ericsson, K. A. and Kintsch, W. (1995). Long-term working memory. *Psychological Review,* **105**, 211–245.

Ericsson, K. A. and Lehmann, A. C. (1996). Expert and exceptional performance: evidence of maximal adaptation to task constraints. *Annual Review of Psychology,* **47**, 273–305.

Ericsson, K. A. and Staszewski, J. (1989). Skilled memory and expertise: mechanisms of exceptional performance. In D. Klahr and K. Kotovsky (ed.), *Complex information processing* (pp. 235–68). Hillsdale, NJ: Lawrence Erlbaum.

Ericsson, K. A., Krampe, R. T., and Tesch-Romer, C. (1993). The role of deliberate practice in the acquisition of expert performance. *Psychological Review,* **100**, 363–406.

Eysenck, H. J. (ed.) (1982). *A model for intelligence.* Berlin: Springer-Verlag.

Eysenck, H. J. (1987). Speed of information processing, reaction time, and the theory of intelligence. In P. A. Vernon (ed.), *Speed of information processing and intelligence.* Norwood, NJ: Ablex.

Fozard, J. L. (1980). The time for remembering. In L. W. Poon (ed.): *Aging in the 1980s.* (pp. 273 – 90) Washington: American Psychological Association.

Gathercole, S. E. (1994). The nature and uses of working memory. In P. Morris and M. Gruneberg (ed.), *Theoretical aspects of memory* (pp. 50–78). London: Routledge.

Getzels, J. W. and Jackson, P. W. (1962). *Creativity and intelligence.* New York: Wiley.

Glanzer, M. and Cunitz, A. R. (1966). Two storage mechanisms in free recall. *Journal of Verbal Learning and Verbal Behavior,* **5**, 351–60.

Gobet, F. and Simon, H. A. (1996). Templates in chess memory: a mechanism for recalling several boards. *Cognitive Psychology,* **31**, 1–40.

Gregpore, J. and Van der Linden, M. (1997). Effect of age on forward and backward digit spans. *Aging, Neuropsychology, and Cognition,* **4**, 140–9.

Guilford, J. P. (1964). Zero intercorrelations among tests of intellectual abilities. *Psychological Bulletin,* **61**, 401–4.

Guilford, J. P. (1967). *The nature of human intelligence.* New York: McGraw-Hill.

Gruber, H. (1988). On the hypothesized relation between giftedness and creativity. In D. H. Feldman (ed.), *Developmental approaches to giftedness and creativity* (pp. 7–30). San Francisco: Josey-Bass.

Harwood, E. and Naylor, G.F.K. (1971). Changes in the constitution of the WAIS intelligence pattern with advancing age. *Australian Journal of Psychology,* **23**, 297–303.

Hasher, L. and Zacks, R.T. (1988). Working memory, comprehension, and aging: a review and a new view. In G.H. Bower (ed.), *The psychology of learning and motivation* (Vol. 22, pp. 193–225). San Diego: Academic Press.

Hayslip, B. and Kennelly, K. J. (1982). Short-term memory and crystallized-fluid intelligence in adulthood. *Research on Aging*, **4**, 314–32.

Herrnstein, R. and Murray, C. (1994). *The bell curve*. New York: Free Press.

Hertzog, C. (1989). Influences of cognitive slowing on age differences in intelligence. *Developmental Psychology*, **25**, 636–51.

Hertzog, C., Dixon, R. A., and Hultsch, D. F. (1990). Relationships between meta-memory, memory predictions, and memory task performance in adults. *Psychology and Aging*, **5**, 215–27.

Hertzog, C., Fisk, A. D., and Cooper, B. P. (1996). *Aging and individual differences in the development of skilled memory search performance*. Cognitive Aging Conference. Atlanta, GA.

Hick, W. (1952). On the rate of gain of information. *Quarterly Journal of Experimental Psychology*, **4**, 11–26.

Holding, D. H. (1985). *The psychology of chess skill*. Hillsdale, NJ: Lawrence Erlbaum.

Horn, J. L. (1968). Organization of abilities and the development of intelligence. *Psychological Review*, **75**, 242–59.

Horn, J. L. (1972). The structure of intellect: primary abilities. In R. M. Dreger (ed.), *Multivariate personality research* (pp. 451–511). Baton Rouge: Claitor's Publishing.

Horn, J. L. (1982). The aging of human abilities. In B. B. Wolman (ed.), *Handbook of developmental psychology* (pp. 847–70). Englewood Cliffs, NJ: Prentice Hall.

Horn, J. L. (1989). Models for intelligence. In R. Linn (ed.), *Intelligence: measurement, theory and public policy* (pp. 29–73). Urbana, IL: University of Illinois Press.

Horn, J. L. (1994). The theory of fluid and crystallized intelligence. In R. J. Sternberg (ed.), *The encyclopedia of intelligence* (pp. 443–51). New York: Cambridge University Press.

Horn, J. L. (1997). A basis for research on age differences in cognitive capabilities. In J. J. McArdle and R. Woodcock (ed.), *Human cognitive abilities in theory and practice* (pp. 57–91). Chicago: Riverside.

Horn, J. L. and Cattell, R. B. (1967). Age differences in fluid and crystallized intelligence. *Acta Psychologica*, **26**, 107–29.

Horn, J. L. and Donaldson, G. (1980). Cognitive development in adulthood. In O. G. Brim and J. Kagan (ed.), *Constancy and change in human development* (pp. 445–529). Cambridge, MA: Harvard University Press.

Horn, J. L. and Hofer, S. M. (1992). Major abilities and development in the adult period. In R. J. Sternberg and C. A. Berg (ed.), *Intellectual development* (pp. 44–99). New York: Cambridge University Press.

Horn, J. L. and Noll, J. (1993). A system for understanding cognitive capabilities. In D. K. Detterman (ed.), *Current topics in intelligence* (pp. 151–203). Norwood, NJ: Ablex.

Horn, J. L. and Noll, J. (1997). Human cognitive capabilities: Gf-Gc theory. In J. L. Flanagan, P. I. Genshaft and Harrison (ed.), *Contemporary intellectual assessment* (pp. 53–91). New York: Guilford Press.

Horn, J. L., Donaldson, G., and Engstrom, R. (1981). Apprehension, memory, and fluid intelligence decline in adulthood. *Research in Aging*, **3**, 33–84.

Hundal, P. S. and Horn, J. L. (1977). On the relationships between short-term learning and fluid and crystallized intelligence. *Applied Psychological Measurement*, **1**, 11–21.

Jensen, A. R. (1982). Reaction time and psychometric g. In H. J. Eysenck (ed.), *A new model for intelligence* (pp. 93–132). New York: Springer-Verlag.

Jensen, A. R. (1987). Psychometric g as a focus of concerted research effort. *Intelligence,* **11**, 193–8.

Jensen, A. R. (1993). Why is reaction time correlated with psychometric g? *Current Directions in Psychological Science,* **2**, 53–6.

Johnson, G. (1997). To test a powerful computer, play an ancient game. *The New Times, Science Times,* July 29, **B1**, B13–14.

Kasai, K. (1986). *Igo de atama ga yoku naru hon [Becoming smart with GO].* Tokyo, Japan: Shikai.

Kaufman, A. S. (1990). *Assessing adolescent and adult intelligence.* Boston: Allyn and Bacon.

Kausler, D. H. (1990). *Experimental psychology, cognition, and human aging.* New York: Springer.

Koltanowski, G. (1985). *In the dark.* Coraopolis, PA: Chess Enterprises.

Krampe, R.T. and Ericsson, K. A. (1996). Maintaining excellence: deliberate practice and elite performance in young and older pianists. *Journal of Experimental Psychology: General,* **125**, 331–59.

McDowd, J. M. and Birren, J. E. (1990). Aging and attentional processes. In J. E. Birren and K. W. Schaie (ed.), *Handbook of the psychology of aging* (3rd edn., pp. 222–33). New York: Academic Press.

McDowd, J. M. and Craik, F. I. M. (1988). Effects of aging and task difficulty on divided attention performance. *Journal of Experimental Psychology: Human Perception and Performance,* **14**, 267–80.

McGrew, K. S., Werder, J. K., and Woodcock, R.W. (1991). *Woodcock-Johnson technical manual.* Chicago: Riverside Press.

Madden, D. J. (1983). Aging and distraction by highly familiar stimuli during visual search. *Developmental Psychology,* **19**, 499–507.

Madden, D. J. (1985). Adult age differences in memory-driven selective attention. *Developmental Psychology,* **21**, 655–65.

Madden, D. J. and Nebes, R. D. (1980). Aging and the development of automaticity in visual search. *Developmental Psychology,* **16**, 277–96.

Mandler, G. (1977). Commentary on 'Organization and Memory'. In G. H. Bower (ed.), *Human memory: basic process* (pp. 12–65). New York: Academic Press.

Mechner, D. A. (January/February 1998). All systems go. *The Sciences,* **38**, 32–7.

Milgram, R. M. (1990). Creativity, an idea whose time has come and gone? In M. A. Runco and R. S. Albert (ed.), *Theories of creativity* (pp. 215–33). Newbury Park, CA: Sage.

Miller, G. A. (1956). The magical number seven, plus or minus two: some limits on our capacity for processing information. *Psychological Review,* **63**, 81–97.

Morrow, D., Leirer, V., Altieri, P., and Fitzsimmons, C. (1994). When expertise reduces age differences in performance. *Psychology and Aging,* **9**, 134–48.

Nettlebeck, T. (1994). Speediness. In R. Sternberg (ed.), *Encyclopedia of intelligence* (pp. 1014–19). New York: Macmillan.

Noll, J. and Horn, J. L. (1997). Age differences in processes of fluid and crystallized intelligence. In J. J. McArdle and W. Woodcock (ed.), *Human cognitive abilities in theory and practice* (pp. 263–81). Chicago: Riverside Press.

Perfect, T. J. (1994). What can Brinley plots tell us about cognitive aging? *Journal of Gerontology: Psychological Sciences,* **49**, P60–4.

Plude, D. J. and Hoyer, W. J. (1985). Attention and performance: identifying and localizing age deficits. In N. Charness (ed.), *Aging and human performance* (pp. 47–99). New York: Wiley.

Rabbitt, P. (1965). An age-decrement in the ability to ignore irrelevant information. *Journal of Gerontology*, **20**, 233–8.

Rabbitt, P. (1993). Crystal quest: a search for the basis of maintenance of practice skills into old age. In A. Baddeley and L. Weiskrantz (ed.), *Attention: selection, awareness, and control* (pp. 188–230). Oxford: Clarendon Press.

Rabbitt, P. and Abson, V. (1991). Do older people know how good they are? *British Journal of Psychology*, **82**, 137–51.

Reitman, J. (1976). Skilled perception in GO: deducing memory structures from inter-response times. *Cognitive Psychology*, **8**, 336–56.

Richman, H. B., Gobet, H., Staszewski, J. J., and Simon, H. A. (1996). Perceptual and memory processes in the acquisition of expert performance: the EPAM model. In K. A. Ericsson (ed.), *The road to excellence* (pp. 167–88). Hillsdale, NJ: Lawrence Erlbaum.

Roediger, H. L. and Crowder, R. G. (1975). Spacing of lists in free recall. *Journal of Verbal Learning and Verbal Behavior*, **14**, 590–602.

Saariluoma, P. (1991). Aspects of skilled imagery in blindfold chess. *Acta Psychologica*, **77**, 65–89.

Salthouse, T. A. (1985). Speed of behavior and its implications for cognition In J.E. Birren and K. W. Schaie (ed.), *Handbook of the psychology of aging* (2nd edn.) (pp. 400–26). New York: Reinhold.

Salthouse, T. A. (1987). The role of representations in age differences in analogical reasoning. *Psychology and Aging*, **2**, 357–62.

Salthouse, T. A. (1991a). Mediation of adult age differences in cognition by reductions in working memory and speed of processing. *Psychological Science*, **2**, 179–83.

Salthouse, T. A. (1991b). *Theoretical perspectives on cognitive aging*. Hillsdale, NJ: Lawrence Erlbaum.

Salthouse, T. A. (1992). *Mechanisms of age-cognition relations in adulthood*. Hillsdale, NJ: Lawrence Erlbaum.

Salthouse, T. A. (1993). Speed mediation of adult age differences in cognition. *Developmental Psychology*, **29**, 727–38.

Salthouse, T. A. (1994). The nature of the influence of speed on adult age differences in cognition. *Developmental Psychology*, **30**, 240–59.

Salthouse, T. A. and Somberg, B. L. (1982). Isolating the age deficit in speeded performance. *Journal of Gerontology*, **37**, 59–63.

Salthouse, T. A., Babcock, R. L., Skouronik, E., Mitchell, D. R., and Palmon, R. (1990a). Age and experience effects in spatial visualization. *Developmental Psychology*, **26**, 128–36.

Salthouse, T. A., Kausler, D. H., and Saults, J. S. (1990b). Age, self-assessed health status, and cognition. *Journal of Gerontology*, **45**, 156–60.

Schaie, K. W. (1996). *Intellectual development in adulthood: the Seattle longitudinal study*. Cambridge: Cambridge University Press.

Schonfeld, D. (1972). Theoretical nuances and practical old questions: the psychology of aging. *Canadian Psychologist*, **13**, 252–66.

Smith, A. D. (1996). Memory. In J.E. Birren and K. W. Schaie (ed.), *Handbook of the psychology of aging* (4th edn., pp. 236–50). San Diego: Academic Press.

Spearman, C. (1927). *The abilities of man: their nature and measurement.* London: Macmillan.

Sperling, G. (1960). The information available in brief visual presentations. *Psychological Monographs,* **74**, 498.

Stankov, L. (1986). Age-related changes in auditory abilities and in a competing task. *Multivariate Behavioral Research,* **21**, 65–71.

Stankov, L. and Horn, J. L. (1980). Human abilities revealed through auditory tests. *Journal of Educational Psychology,* **72**, 21–44.

Staudinger, U. M. and Baltes, P. B. (1996). Interactive minds: a facilitative setting for wisdom-related performance? *Journal of Personality and Social Psychology,* **71**, 746–62.

Torrance, E. P. (1972). Predictive validity of the Torrance tests of creative thinking. *The Journal of Creative Behavior,* **6**, 236–52.

Tulving, E. (1972). Episodic and semantic memory. In E. Tulving and W. Donaldson (ed.), *Organization of memory* (pp. 381–403). New York: Academic Press.

Verhaeghen, P., Marcoen, A., and Goossens, L. (1993). Facts and fiction about memory aging: a quantitative integration of research findings. *Journal of Gerontology: Psychological Sciences,* **48**, P157–71.

Vernon, P. E. (1972). The validity of divergent thinking tests. *The Alberta Journal of Educational Research,* **18**, 249–58.

Walsh, D. A. (1982). The development of visual information processes in adulthood and old age. In F. I. M. Craik and S. Trehub (ed.), *Aging and cognitive processes* (pp. 99–125). New York: Plenum.

Walsh, D. A. (1990). *Brinley plots: a window to view psychological laws or a mirror for distorting psychological phenomena?* Los Angeles, CA: Psychology Department, University of Southern California.

Walsh, D. A. and Hershey, D. A. (1993). Mental models and the maintenance of complex problem solving skills in old age. In J. Cerella, J. Rybash, W. Hoyer, and M. Commons (ed.), *Adult information processing: limits on loss* (pp. 553–84). San Diego: Academic Press.

Waugh, N. C. and Norman, D. A. (1965). Primary memory. *Psychological Review,* **72**, 89–104.

Wickens, C. D., Braune, R., and Stokes, A. (1987). Age differences in the speed and capacity of information processing: I. A dual-task approach. *Psychology and Aging,* **2**, 70–8.

Woodcock, R. W. (1995). Theoretical foundations of the WJ-R measures of cognitive ability. *Journal of Psychoeducational Assessment,* **8**, 231–58.

Woodcock, R. W. (1996). *The Woodcock–Johnson Psycho-Educational Battery – Revised.* Itaska, IL: Riverside Publishing.

SIX

Measurement indices, functional characteristics and psychometric constructs in cognitive aging

PATRICK M. A. RABBITT

This chapter addresses confusions about the nature of the performance indices that we measure in simple laboratory tasks and by means of which we test functional models for individual differences in performance. Measurements such as decision times, obtained from simple tasks, have been taken as irreducible 'primitives' which must correspond to objective, and primitive characteristics of the central nervous system (CNS). In fact while the process of measurement is objective, the indices derived from these measurements are not, since they are determined by the functional models that we use as frameworks to analyse our data.

People's efficiency on all laboratory tasks varies with their age and general intellectual ability and we need functional models to explain this. Such models have been developed in two different ways: as 'local' models for individual differences in particular, putatively separate, mental abilities such as 'memory', 'attention', 'imagery', or 'language', and as single factor 'global' models that interpret individual differences in all cognitive functions as consequences of levels of some single, 'master' performance characteristic that determines the efficiency of the entire brain and CNS.

Global models such as those proposed by Salthouse (1985, 1991, 1996) are widely and respectfully cited. They are very rarely used in empirical research because they account for overall impairments in all tasks but not for differential changes that occur in some mental abilities and not in others (although see Salthouse, Chapter 2, this volume, for an alternative interpretation) and so do not provide a useful framework within which to explore details of relationships between age-related changes in the brain and in behaviour. Nearly all investigations in cognitive gerontology describe comparisons that have been carried out in the context of local functional models borrowed from mainstream cognitive psychology and neuropsychology. Because these were initially developed to account for the ways in which the average performance of homogeneous groups of young adults was affected by particular changes of demands in particular experimental tasks, they describe implausible 'steady state' systems that offer no account of individual variability or change. The efforts of cognitive gerontologists to adapt them to account for age-related changes have greatly increased their intellectual plausibility and generality. Local models have proved especially interesting when they have been derived from neuropsychology and begin to allow insights into relationships between behavioural changes and brain aging (e.g. Hasher *et al.* 1991; Parkin and Walter 1991, 1992; Parkin *et al.* 1994; Robbins *et al.* 1994, 1997).

Even when adapted to account for individual differences and for change, local models remain intensely specific to the particular tasks from which they have been derived. Thus models for putatively different functional subsystems are not only articulated in terms of quite different hypothetical functional constructs, but are also based on measurements of quite different kinds of performance indices. When adapted to account for age-related changes, they offer unrelated descriptions of the effects of age on putatively independent mental functions such as memory, attention, imagery, perceptual discrimination, and language ability. These local system models, and the paradigms from which they are derived, are excellent analytic tools if we envisage the brain as a structure in which the functional processes necessary to carry out different tasks may be supported by anatomically and neurophysiologically distinct modules. That is, sub-systems subserving different mental abilities are independent of each other and have different functional architectures, so it is plausible that the process of biological aging of the brain may affect some of them earlier than others (Robbins *et al.* 1994, 1997). Local system models become unconvincing when we recognize that common language distinctions between different mental abilities such as memory and attention may simply be classifications of task demands rather than of the functional architectures of the subsystems by which these demands are met (Rabbitt 1997). There is growing recognition that the demands of apparently very disparate tasks may be carried out by systems with identical functional architectures (Kimberg and Farrah 1993) and that some of the putative system performance indices, such as inhibition or excitation, which have been taken over by cognitive gerontologists from mainstream cognitive psychology have dubious construct validity (Lowe and Rabbitt 1997).

Global, single-factor models have different problems. They assume that individual differences in a very wide variety of cognitive tasks (in the most extreme statements, in all cognitive tasks), which are consequent on general intellectual ability, or in cognitive aging, can be well represented by rank-ordering individuals in terms of a single, higher-order statistical construct such as Spearman's (1924) *g* which is derived by principal component analysis of scores from a range of different tasks such as intelligence tests. Such statistical procedures are, of course, very useful, but it is important to bear in mind that they are techniques of data analysis and not functional descriptions and, further, that they are exploratory rather than confirmatory. The discovery of marked shared variance between different tasks does not entail the radical, and logically unrelated, proposition that the particular task performance indices measured in these tasks, and incorporated into the analysis, must directly reflect some basic functional performance characteristic of the CNS which may be identified with an apparently objective construct, such as 'speed', which can thereby be supposed to determine levels of performance on all, or most, mental activities. Positive manifolds in such analyses may well occur because in this universe, all events, including those in psychological laboratories, take place in time, so that the only measures we have of people's efficiency are the times that they take to do things and the numbers of errors they make. Given that this is the way things are, it is hard to think of any performance index which we can obtain from any task that does not implicitly or directly measure durations of decisions, and is not affected by the times allowed to make them.

Our understanding of what can be measured in simple laboratory tasks determines whether we consider the distinction between global and local models sensible. All global models for individual differences in general mental abilities, childhood development (Anderson 1995), and cognitive aging (Salthouse 1985, 1991) have been based on laboratory tasks which have been deliberately designed to be so simple that all individuals perform indistinguishably close to the possible limits of accuracy. We can only measure differences between individuals in terms of the time that they take to make decisions. Correlations between levels of performance between such tasks, or between such tasks and years of age, or scores on intelligence tests do not, of course, necessarily mean that speed is a basic, functional performance characteristic in terms of which all mental abilities can be modelled. Still less can we assume from these, typically very modest, correlations that people who consistently make fast decisions differ from those who consistently make slow decisions in terms of the speed at which elementary processes in their CNSs take place. To decide whether this is the case we need additional and quite different, evidence; for example, whether individual differences in speed on different stages of these tasks have a direct, one-to-one, correspondence with more direct measures of the latencies of neural events. Where such corroborative evidence has been directly sought from evoked potentials, as by Reed (1993), or Reed and Jensen (1992), the evidence still seems to be tantalisingly incomplete: correlations are observed between intelligence test scores and evoked potential latencies, and between intelligence test scores and choice reaction times (CRTs), but, to our knowledge, the triangle of correlations has not been closed in any single experiment on the same group of people. We would argue that even were such closure to occur, arguments that speed is a fundamental property of the CNS would still not be sensible. Because all events occur in time, duration is inevitably one measure of the efficiency with which neural events occur in different people or kinds of animals, but it does not describe a property of the nervous system that entails such differences in efficiency. What we actually need to know are the functional properties of the cognitive or neural system that allow particular processes to be completed faster in some brains than in others. The response 'because they are faster' is a tautology, and more acceptable answers might be 'richer connections between units', 'changes in unit activation thresholds', 'changes in biochemistry at synapses', or, as in the case of comparisons between fast insects and slower mammals, 'radically different kinds of neurones and much shorter connections between them'. In terms of functional, computational, and neuropsychological models, speed, or for that matter accuracy, is not a fundamental system property but only one of many possible indices of measurement of system output. Speed is not a primitive characteristic of functional systems (cf. Salthouse, Chapter 2). We suggest that it is only a very primitive measurement of performance efficiency.

To illustrate that average CRTs or inspection times are neither the sole, the most irreducible, nor the most informative indices of performance efficiency we shall show that they provide insufficient descriptions of individual differences in performance, even on the simple tasks in which they are measured. Moreover, an alternative task-performance index, trial-to-trial variability, is also a stable individual difference characteristic that predicts performance not only across a wide range of CRT tasks but also in other tasks, such as the estimation and production of brief time intervals and the predictive synchronization of responses with anticipated events in which the determinant of individual differences in efficiency is variability rather than maximum possible decision speed. We show that knowledge of people's trial-to-trial variability gives us very useful information about individual differences in their performance which measurements of their average decision speeds alone cannot provide. We compare some functional models to illustrate that it is not useful, or even interesting, to consider either speed or performance variability, or both, as primitive properties that uniquely determine stable individual differences in performance. Finally we consider what this does for the dialectic of global vs local functional modelling of individual differences, and for the logic of functional models in general.

HOW INDIVIDUAL DIFFERENCES IN INFORMATION PROCESSING SPEED ARE MEASURED

The literature on individual differences in decision speed has been almost entirely based on means or medians computed from distributions of dozens, or hundreds, of CRTs. This is incompletely informative because distributions of CRTs have marked variance and skew, so that individuals' mean or median CRTs are much more powerfully determined by the number of unnecessarily slow responses that they make rather than by the fastest correct decisions of which they are capable (Rabbitt and Goward 1994; Rabbitt and Vyas 1969; Smith and Brewer 1995). The implications for models of individual differences are illustrated by Fig. 6.1, which compares distributions of 1000 successive CRTs, cumulated over ten runs of 100 signals and responses made on a four-choice RT task by each of two men with identical vocabulary test scores, one of whom (A), aged 19 years, scored 34 and the other (B), aged 73 years, scored 26 points on the Cattell and Cattell (1960) 'Culture Fair' (CF) intelligence test.

Both men responded equally accurately (A made 1.4% and B 1.2% errors). Fig. 6.1 shows that although their mean CRTs differed significantly by 84 ms, in this particular comparison, the fastest correct responses that they made did not.

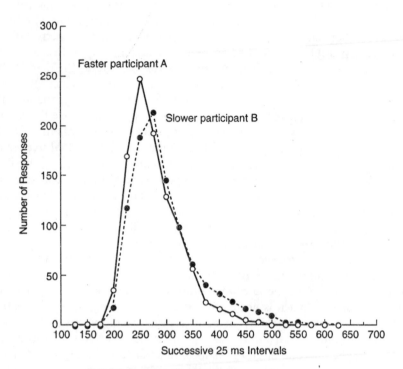

Fig. 6.1 Distributions of responses made by two participants on a four-choice reaction time task.

B's mean CRT was longer because his responses were much more variable and included many responses that were much slower than any made by A. On this evidence it would be as rational to conclude that A and B differ in terms of the trial-to-trial variability of their performance, or in their ability to control this variability, as in the maximum speed with which they can process information.

Any comparison between two deliberately selected individuals is, of course, merely illustrative. As another example, 40 people aged from 60 to 69 years, with CF scores between 26 and 39 points (mean = 32; SD = 8) and 40 aged from 70 to 81 years with CF scores between 11 and 25 (mean = 21; SD = 11) were each asked to make 100 correct responses in each of six different CRT tasks. Means and SDs of each individual's CRT distributions were computed (see Table 6.1). As usual, groups with higher CF scores had faster mean CRTs on all tasks. However SDs of CRTs were also significantly smaller for high than for low CF scorers. Empirically, SDs of CRT distributions are invariably found to increase linearly with their means so this difference between groups might simply reflect this general relationship. To adjust differences in variance for differences in mean CRTs, coefficients of variation (CVs, i.e., SD/mean; Howell 1992) were computed for each volunteer in each experiment and are also shown in Table 6.1. High CF scorers still showed significantly less within-session variability in all tasks.

This parallels recent demonstrations by Dywan and Segalowitz (1996, personal communication) that older children have faster mean CRTs than younger children mainly because their CRT distributions have smaller CVs. Such comparisons suggest that not only average speed but also moment-to-moment variability of performance may be stable performance characteristics of individuals, and may systematically vary with their developmental or involutional ages and their general intellectual ability as assessed by scores on pencil and paper intelligence tests. This can be modelled by assuming that the distribution of CRTs obtained from any individual during a single experimental run on any task can be considered as a single session sample from a stable 'latent' distribution of all of the CRTs that he or she may make during many different testing sessions spread over a period of days or weeks. It follows that as the standard error of any person's latent CRT distribution increases so must the

Table 6.1 Mean and standard deviation (ms) choice reaction time (CRT) and coefficients of variation (CV) across six tasks, for High and Low scorers on the Cattell and Cattell Culture Fair (CF) test

Task	CRT		CV Mean
	Mean	SD	
High CF scorers			
Two-choice CRT	346	41	0.13
Four-choice CRT	419	55	0.14
Six-choice CRT	481	68	0.14
Eight-choice CRT	530	81	0.15
Word categorization	650	112	0.17
Alphabet categorization	696	119	0.17
Low CF scorers			
Two-choice CRT	411	67	0.16
Four-choice CRT	507	91	0.18
Six-choice CRT	596	111	0.18
Eight-choice CRT	625	115	0.18
Word categorization	812	163	0.20
Alphabet categorization	828	174	0.21

Comparisons of means of individual means, SDs and CVs of choice reaction times produced by 40 High CF test scorers (26–39 points) and 40 Low CF test scorers (11–25 points) on six different tasks. In the CRT tasks participants responded to horizontally aligned illuminated squares on a computer monitor, pressing two to eight spatially correspondent keys on a console. In the word categorization task they distinguished between 4 semantic categories of nouns. In the alphabet categorisation task they distinguised between four subsets of six of the 24 letters from A through X, i.e. A through F; G through L; M through R, and S through X.

standard error of the distribution of the means of the independent samples of CRTs which are drawn from it during successive experimental sessions. That is, individuals whose CRTs are more variable during a single session (Within-session variance, WSV) must necessarily also show greater variance in mean CRTs across different sessions (Between-session variance, BSV). So if young children, elderly adults, and people with relatively low intelligence test scores are more variable from trial to trial during individual testing sessions, their mean CRTs must also vary more from session to session and from day to day than do the mean CRTs obtained from older children, young adults, and people with relatively high intelligence test scores.

TESTING WHETHER INDIVIDUAL VARIABILITY OF PERFORMANCE IS A STABLE INDIVIDUAL DIFFERENCE CHARACTERISTIC

Forty women and 21 men aged from 52 to 79 years (mean = 65.9; SD = 7.1) completed the CF intelligence test on which their scores ranged from 11 to 40 points (mean = 28.5; SD = 6.2). They were then given 36 weekly practice sessions on each of six different CRT tasks. Because the aim was to investigate differences in variability associated with age as well as those associated with intelligence test performance, volunteers were selected from three groups aged from 50 to 60, 61 to 70 and 71 to 79 years, who had been matched in terms of their average CF scores. Because performance is known to vary systematically with time of day (Blake 1967a), and the patterns of these diurnal changes are also known to differ characteristically between individuals (Blake 1967b), each volunteer was tested at the same one of four different times of day during the entire 36 weeks of practice, and these times (10.00, 12.00, 14.00, and 16.00 hours) were balanced across age and intelligence test score groups.

In all six tasks and during all 36 sessions participants with high CF scores (HCF group) had significantly faster mean CRTs and showed significantly lower variability in CRTs during individual experimental runs (WSV) than did those with relatively low CF scores (LCF group). After an initial advantage for the HCF individuals both groups performed equally accurately making less than 1.5% errors. The question was whether the HCF group showed less variability in mean CRTs from session to session (BSV) than the LCF group. Since practice markedly reduces mean CRTs from session to session, it was necessary to analyse data only from successive sessions across which no further improvement with practice was discernible. For both groups the last 10 of 36 sessions met this criterion.

For all tasks, volunteers' BSVs were positively and significantly correlated with their WSVs and negatively with their CF scores. In this sample, in which age groups had been deliberately matched in terms of CF scores, correlations between BSV or WSV and age were not significant. Individual differences in CF scores seem to pick up all individual differences in variance associated with age.

Because age was not a significant independent factor in determining CRT variability it was ignored in all subsequent analyses. Allocation of participants had ensured that their segregation into HCF and LCF groups did not affect balancing for time of day. The significant positive correlation between BSV and WSV supports the hypothesis that WSV is a stable individual performance characteristic that, necessarily, also expresses itself in terms of BSV. The new finding is that not only mean CRTs, but also WSVs and BSVs, correlate significantly with a measure of general intellectual ability. The next question was whether individual differences in BSVs can be entirely accounted for by corresponding individual differences in WSVs or whether variations in performance from session to session and from day to day are also determined by other factors independent of WSV.

The idea guiding this analysis was that each individual's WSV can be considered as a random sample from his or her latent CRT distribution which, therefore, can be modelled by summing the corresponding observed CRT distributions obtained on the ten sessions during which there was no evidence for improvement with practice. The process of sampling from this distribution during individual trials was then simulated by drawing, at random, 20 samples of 100 CRTs to represent the 20 single-session samples of CRTs actually obtained from that individual on that task during the final ten testing sessions.

Given the fact that latent CRT distributions were simulated by summing actual distributions of CRTs obtained during experimental runs, each participant's simulated mean CRTs and WSVs should be statistically indistinguishable from those which were actually observed during the experiment. Further, simulated mean CRTs and WSVs for HCF individuals should both be reliably less than for LCF individuals. This was so. However it is not logically necessary that simulated BSVs should be identical to observed BSVs. A finding that the simulated BSVs were identical to empirically observed BSVs would mean that there is no evidence that individual differences in observed BSVs are brought about by any factor other than corresponding differences in observed WSVs. A finding that observed BSVs were significantly larger than the simulated BSVs would mean that BSVs were partly determined by WSVs (as the correlations show to be the case) but also affected by some other factor that also varied systematically between individuals. For simulations for each and all volunteers observed BSVs were significantly larger than simulated BSVs. Thus individual differences in WSVs, from which simulated BSVs were derived, can account for most, but not for all, observed individual differences in BSVs. It follows that other state-changes from session to session must also have significantly contributed to variability of performance from day to day during the course of the experiment.

One possibility is that individuals' mean CRTs are also affected by prolonged state-changes, that is, they experience good or bad experimental sessions or days or even weeks which affect all of the tasks they undertake. Because volunteers completed six different tasks during each experimental session, it was possible to check whether performance on all tasks covaried across days. There was, indeed, significant covariance of performance across the six tasks across the ten weekly sessions during which no practice effects were evident. It seems that, in addition to BSV, which is a direct consequence of their characteristic WSVs, individuals also experience state changes that last at least as long as a one hour testing session, and which affect their levels of performance on all tasks that they may perform during that period.

SOME METHODOLOGICAL AND PRACTICAL CONSEQUENCES OF FINDINGS THAT INDIVIDUAL DIFFERENCES IN MEAN CRTs, IN WSVs, AND IN BSVs MAY BE STABLE CHARACTERISTICS ASSOCIATED WITH GENERAL INTELLECTUAL ABILITY

These findings identify an unacknowledged methodological problem not only for investigation of individual differences in performance associated with age and ability but also for a much earlier literature on circadian rhythms. It is well established that humans experience cyclical changes in efficiency during the course of each day (Colquhoun and Corcoran 1964). It is natural to ask whether patterns of diurnal variability change with age and many recent studies have undertaken to test this (e.g. Intons-Peterson *et al*. 1998). In our laboratory we have tried to elicit diurnal changes in CRTs in individuals aged between 60 and 80 years but only in a minority of experiments have we found evidence of circadian effects for older adults and, even when these were statistically reliable, their amplitudes were much smaller than those which are commonly reported for young adults. Since we now know that people with lower intelligence test scores (e.g. older adults) vary more from session to session, we must accept that this is likely to mask the true extent of their circadian variability in performance. It follows that unless intrinsic age differences in WSV and BSV are measured, and taken into consideration, circadian variability will appear to be absent or greatly reduced in samples with lower intelligence test scores, and so also in older samples.

There are wider methodological implications for earlier findings of individual differences in circadian variability. Many studies, exhaustively reviewed by Broadbent (1971), have found systematic differences both in the absolute extents and in the time courses of circadian fluctuations in performance shown by individuals who are classified as introverts and as extroverts in terms of their scores on the Maudesley Personality Inventory (MPI). Since MPI scores are known to be modestly, but robustly, correlated with scores on tests of general intelligence, it follows that this literature must be re-evaluated and earlier studies re-analysed or replicated to discover whether individual differences in circadian variability which have been attributed to introversion and extroversion can, instead, be attributed to differences in general intellectual ability.

It is also important to make the point that these methodological inconveniences follow from an advance in our practical understanding of human performance. Individuals who are more variable during one brief experimental session will, necessarily, vary more from session to session. Extended practice reduces variability within sessions, and so must, correspondingly, also reduce variability in average performance from session to session. In applied studies of human operators, in which day-to-day variability can matter a great deal, we now know that day-to-day variability can be well predicted by within-session variability. Our descriptions of human performance gain generality, detail and predictive power.

A different methodological issue, which is particularly important for cognitive gerontology, is that a sample of individuals who vary more from session to session with respect to themselves must also vary more with respect to each other on any single occasion on which they are compared. Meta-analyses of published data, such as that by Morse (1993), show that even on tasks such as memory tests, in which the measured performance index is errors rather than speed, between-individual variability is, indeed, typically greater in samples of elderly than of young adults. It has been assumed that a sufficient explanation for this is an increased incidence with population age of pathologies that affect mental ability which increases the differences between the most and least able individuals (Rabbitt 1981). Clearly this is not the whole story. The question of how much of the age-related variance between individuals is due to incidence of pathologies and how much to individual differences in rates of normal or usual aging is a basic issue in cognitive gerontology, and attempts to compute their relative contributions will be misleading unless they measure, and take into account, age-related increases in WSV and BSV.

It now appears that variability, like speed, is a stable characteristic of individuals that can be predicted by their scores on pencil and paper intelligence tests. It is important to note that this is more useful than a suggestion that we may possibly substitute one primitive for another, using variability rather than speed as a master index in terms of which to rank individuals. Measurements of variability tell us more about individuals than their mean response speeds alone and so, as we have pointed out above, give us some very useful extra practical information about them: they tell us about their extent of variability in average speed from session to session and, consequently, their variability in speed with respect to each other when they are compared on any single occasion. However, it can be argued that mean CRT and CRT variability may both directly reflect the same functional performance characteristics of the CNS; that is, in Salthouse's (Chapter 2, this volume) terminology they are equivalent indices of the same primitive functional property of the cognitive system, or even of the CNS. We examine the logic of this suggestion by comparing the way in which speed and variability have been related to each other in a variety of equally plausible current models for the functional decision processes underlying CRTs. We shall first use a different, empirical approach and see whether, in tasks that are very different from the CRT paradigms we have discussed, trial-to-trial variability in performance accuracy can be shown to be a stable individual difference characteristic which is independent of performance speed.

CRT tasks are deliberately designed to be as simple as possible in order to minimize the complexity of the functional processes whose durations they reflect. They measure the speed and accuracy with which individuals can identify signals and then choose and make appropriate responses to them. Such situations are very rare in the real world where it is unacceptably risky to live a long reaction time behind a rapidly changing environment. To gain an evolutionary edge creatures must predict what is going to happen next so as to anticipate and forestall, rather than simply to answer, events. For example, in order to identify a safe gap to cross a street through a dense, fast-moving traffic stream people must continually sample the trajectories of many objects rapidly moving at different speeds and predict their own positions relative to these during a future transit, the duration of which they must also correctly anticipate before they begin to act. We may assume that, like the functional processes underlying performance in CRT experiments, these more complex computations must be subject to moment-to-moment variability. The question is whether trial-to-trial variability in effecting such computations can be shown to be independent of the effects of the times available to make them.

VARIABILITY IN EFFECTING SPATIAL AND TEMPORAL SYNCHRONICITY OF FUTURE EVENTS

The point that variability in decision accuracy can be independent of decision speed was made by recording performance on a very simple video-game in which, on each trial, a 1 cm long tank appeared and remained stationary at one of four possible positions along a horizontal yellow line representing a flat desert. A 0.5 s 70 dB 1500 Hz tone provided a warning signal before each trial and, 1 s later, an aeroplane appeared on the left-hand margin of the monitor screen and proceeded on a linear flight path 12 cm above, and parallel to, the desert at one of three different speeds (5, 6, or 7 pixels per second). The task was to press a single button at the precise moment at which the aeroplane passed vertically above the tank. Immediately the button was pressed a bomb dropped vertically from the aeroplane, without transferred velocity, to the desert below. If the button was pressed too early an undershoot occurred and if too late an overshoot occurred, and the bomb exploded to the left or the right of the tank providing immediate feedback on the direction and extent of error. Note that since the aeroplane moved continuously, and since intervals between participants' initiations and completions of their key-presses had finite duration, effective bomb strikes were possible only if participants could learn to judge the speed of the aeroplane accurately enough to begin making their responses precisely one simple reaction time before it was due to transit the tank. The computer controlling the game logged tank position and aeroplane flight-path duration and speed on each trial, and calculated three different performance indices: the total numbers of hits and misses; the absolute size and sign (undershoot or overshoot) of each error; and the distribution (and so the mean, median, standard error, and standard deviation) of all bomb drops.

Two groups of older adults were matched on total scores on both parts of the Heim (1970) AH4 intelligence test. Thirty-eight, whose AH4 scores ranged from 11 to 36 points, were aged from 60 to 69 years (mean AH4 = 21; SD = 12) and 42, whose AH4 scores ranged from 12 to 35 points (mean = 22; SD = 10) were aged from 70 to 79 years. Each participant was given 30 trials on each of 12 conditions (four aeroplane flight-path lengths at each of three aeroplane speeds during each of ten, one-hour testing sessions one week apart). The results described below were obtained during the penultimate session.

Figure 6.2 shows averages of the SDs of bomb releases for older and younger groups at all 12 combinations of aircraft speed and flight-path length. Because the means of these distributions are not taken into consideration, these data points are not measures of aiming accuracy but rather of trial-to-trial consistency, or variability, in moments of bomb release. Differences in accuracy, computed as percentages of target hits, must be considered separately.

At very short aeroplane flight paths, participants did not have enough time to predict the moment when the aircraft would transit the target tank. Here the best they could do was to begin to respond as soon as they saw the aircraft on the left hand margin of the screen. At these shortest flight paths the task became, in effect, a simple RT task in which participants attempted to respond as rapidly as possible to a signal that appeared after a fixed fore-period. Under these circumstances most of their responses occurred too late (overshoots), so that accuracy was correspondingly low. However, in these cases the SDs of distributions of bomb strikes were also relatively small (at least for V6 and V7) because they represented, in effect, distributions of simple RTs to aircraft appearances.

At intermediate and long flight-path lengths, when the task was not just an analogue of a simple RT task, SDs of bomb strikes reduced as aircraft speed increased. Overall, the HCF group was significantly more accurate and less variable than the LCF group but the patterns of relationships between aircraft speed, flight-path length, and accuracy and variability of responses were very similar for both groups. Numbers of direct hits on the target tank changed consistently with SDs of bomb strikes, increasing with aeroplane speed and reducing with flight-path length. That is to say, beyond the lower limit to trajectory duration at which they could only produce simple reaction times, the less time that both older and younger people had to process information about the trajectory of the aircraft and compute the correct moment at which to make a response, the less variable and more accurate they became. It is certainly true that the younger participants, and those with higher CF scores could process information faster (and indeed a different experiment confirmed that they had significantly faster mean CRTs). However, as Fig. 6.2 shows, in this particular task, the greater variability and lower accuracy of older

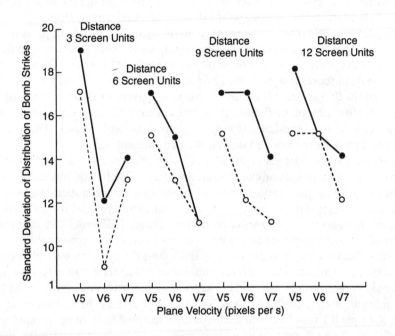

Fig. 6.2 Data from a video game task in which participants were required to release a bomb from a plane travelling at three different velocities (V5, V6, and V7 pixels per second) onto a tank located at one of four distances (3, 6, 9, and 12 screen units) from the point at the left hand side of the screen at which the plane begins its flight. The y-axis gives average standard deviations of bomb releases mades by groups of older (70–79) and younger (60–69) participants (solid and dashed lines, respectively).

participants could not be explained in terms of their slower information processing speeds alone.

The theme of this chapter is the logical relationship between the performance indices that we measure in laboratory tasks and the functional, or even neurophysiological models that we use to interpret patterns of relationships between these indices. This is particularly instructive in the case of the tanks and planes task because functional and neurophysiological models are much better developed in vision science than in other areas of psychology. Classic studies of movement perception show that the threshold for detecting whether a briefly presented object is moving or at rest steadily reduces with the temporal duration of the trajectory observed and with the brightness of the moving target (Liebowitz 1955). Because visual acuity declines with loss of retinal receptors, because tachistoscopic recognition thresholds increase with age, and because increasing opacity of the cornea, lens, and aqueous and vitreous humours reduces the amount of light that reaches the retina, it is also surprising that some investigators, such as Brown and Bowman (1987), should have found virtually no age differences in discrimination of the relative speed of moving objects. However Ball and Sekuler's (1986) finding that thresholds for discrimination of direction of movement are almost twice as great in older as in younger observers strongly suggests that some differences do indeed exist. In this particular task individuals' performance is limited by other, tightly specifiable factors. One is that, within known limits, the faster an object crosses the visual field, the stronger the signal it elicits from movement receptors. A second factor is that, although a long aircraft flight path potentially offers a more adequate sample of information from which to compute a prediction of the moment of its future transit of a particular point, it is likely that the earlier predictions are computed during an aircraft's trajectory the more difficult becomes the problem of estimating the precise interval of time after which the transit will occur and of initiating one's response so that it will be completed at the exact correct moment. If considered as a simple RT task, the tanks and planes game involves the problem of estimating the precise moment in time at which a signal (vertical coincidence of the tank and aeroplane) will occur after a warning signal (appearance of the aeroplane on the left hand side of the screen) has been perceived. Simple RTs are known to improve as the interval between warning signal and response signal (fore-period) increases from 50 to 500 ms, thereby allowing more time for optimal preparation, and then to decline as fore-periods further increase, and time-estimation begins to become more difficult and so more variable. By analogy, the longer the interval between the first appearance of the aeroplane and its crossing of the target, the harder it is to respond at the precise moment of transit. However, Fig. 6.2 shows that analogies with simple RT tasks do not provide a complete description of these results because variability of bomb release changes not only with the total time available to prepare and make a response, and so with the period over which anticipation must be controlled, but also with aeroplane speed and flight-path length, independently of the total time elapsed before target transit. The task also demands accurate estimation of aeroplane speed, prediction of its future position, and anticipatory initiation of a response at a moment which, allowing for one's own RT, will allow it to occur at precisely the right moment for bomb release. Variability in meeting these demands, and probably variability in one's own RT as a factor in this computation, evidently increases significantly with age and reduces with general intellectual ability.

We see that, in many tasks, while performance may improve with the time available to make decisions, in this simple simulation of some of the complex decisions that people make in everyday life, the average accuracy, and particularly the trial-to-trial variability, of their performance depends on other factors besides the maximum speed at which they can process information. It is recognized that in this task, as in most others, faster information processing speed may convey advantages. However, these results allow us to make two points. First, because models for movement perception are so well developed, they provide. more sophisticated frameworks for discussions of the possible functional, and neurophysiological aetiology of age differences than are available for other laboratory tasks on which authors such as Salthouse (1985, 1991, 1996 and Chapter 2, this volume) have based global models of aging. In the context of these more developed models, distinctions in terms of a single system performance parameter, information processing speed, are seen as crude and uninformative. The discussion shifts to possible parameters of individual difference, such as the relative strengths of signals from the movement receptors produced by targets moving at different speeds, and the numbers of retinal receptors available. These system parameters will, of course, help to determine decision speed, but attempts to quantify them solely in terms of their contributions to decision speed are obviously retrogressive. The second, more general methodological ·point is that this particular task does provide an empirical dissociation between the two task performance parameters that we were considering: the average time taken to make decisions and the average variability of the decisions made. These points are further illustrated by the results of a study by Wearden *et al.* (1997) comparing older and younger or more and less able individuals on four, even simpler, tasks in which they estimated and generated a time interval of 500 ms.

DIFFERENCES IN ACCURACY AND VARIABILITY OF TIME ESTIMATION

Wearden *et al.* (1997) compared older and younger volunteers with higher and lower CF scores on Temporal Generalization, Temporal Bisection, Threshold Determination, and Interval Production tasks. In all of these four different paradigms, participants' accuracy varied from trial-to-trial, providing distributions so that the average accuracy and the trial to trial variability of estimates could be separately computed and compared between age and CF groups. The pattern of individual differences was consistent across all four tasks: means of distributions of estimates varied little, or not at all, with age and CF scores, but variability of estimates markedly increased with age and reduced with CF score. Re-analyses of the data also found that individuals' variability on any one of these four tasks predicted their variability on all of the other three (values for *r* ranged from 0.35 to 0.54). Stepwise regression analyses showed that these relationships remained significant and, indeed, were not significantly reduced when individual values for mean accuracy of interval duration in each task were entered into the regression equation. It seems that degree of variability of time estimation is also a stable characteristic of individuals that can, independently of mean accuracy of temporal discrimination, significantly increase with age and fall with general intellectual ability.

Current functional models for time estimation assume that these performance indices are determined by the functional characteristics of systems of one or more 'clocks' or 'oscillators' (see reviews in Wearden and Penton-Voak 1995, and Wearden *et al.* 1997). A possible speculation is that the maximum speed of the 'pacemakers' of such clocks or oscillators, and so their finest possible temporal resolutions, is determined by the maximum rate of information processing in the CNS of which they are a part. If slowing of clock speed (i.e., a decrease in the number of pacemaker ticks occurring in unit time) varies with information processing rate and, for that reason, slows with age and increases with level of general intellectual ability, some changes in timing behaviour may also be expected. However, internal clocks that tick more slowly do not necessarily underestimate durations compared with those that operate at higher speeds since individuals may learn to re-calibrate behaviour to take account of this (e.g. some unit of time becomes identified with the completion of fewer ticks than before). Mathematical explorations of the effects of clock speed on the outputs of various plausible sorts of internal clocks show that clock slowing will certainly increase the variability, but not necessarily the average accuracy, of time judgements (Gibbon *et al.* 1984). Thus, in some plausible models, variability in time estimation will be functionally determined by clock speed and so related to information processing rate. However, even in these models the relationship between clock speed and information processing rate need not be straightforward. We might equally plausibly assume that individuals' internal clocks do not necessarily differ in terms of their average relative speeds (i.e., in terms of the maximum numbers of ticks that they make in unit time) but do differ in terms of the regularity with which their ticks occur. In this case clock regularity would be functionally independent of information processing speed.

It is important to note that this explanation is not arbitrarily generated without any theoretical or empirical grounding. Clocks or oscillators certainly have the property that they can run fast or slow, producing more or fewer signals per unit of time, but their most important property, which is quite independent of the sizes of the units into which they divide time, is their degree of moment-to-moment variability. As work by Brown and Vousden (1998), Brown *et al.* (1999), Henson and Burgess (1998), and others has shown, assumptions about the degree of regularity, the rate, and the number of oscillators we posit, allow us to fit a very wide range of well-described psychological phenomena, including serial position curves and relative frequencies with which different kinds of transposition errors occur in immediate serial recall, both in younger and older adults (Maylor *et al.* 1999). To claim that models of this kind are, fundamentally, only complex demonstrations that the relative speed of oscillators may simply be regarded as another functional instantiation of system information processing rate would be to throw away hard-won elegance and rigour.

It would also be retrogressive to use these models as illustrations of the fact that, because quite complex patterns of performance in immediate memory tasks can be derived from models of oscillator frequency and regularity and because, in some models, oscillator frequency can be directly related to information processing speed, it must necessarily follow that individual differences in memory efficiency and in CRTs and inspection times are fundamentally dependent on the same functional primitive, that is, information processing speed. To find modest correlations between levels of performance on tasks in which efficiency is measured in terms of average decision times and in memory tasks in which performance efficiency is measured in terms of errors, and to show that levels of performance on both kinds of tasks are modestly associated with performance in intelligence tests (Jensen 1985) or with differences in age (Salthouse 1985) are interesting observations that require explanation. To work out in detail models of how differences in one hypothetical system performance parameter, oscillator rate, can bring about differences in patterns of errors in memory tasks (Brown *et al.* 1999; Henson and Burgess 1998; Maylor *et al.* 1999), is a much more substantial and fruitful achievement precisely because it eschews pointless discussion of primitives to focus on patterns of underlying relationships that determine the fine details of performance across a variety of tasks. It also illustrates the kind of explanation that associations between performance on different tasks require.

The point is not to debate whether variability of time estimation is determined by clock regularity, which is a different primitive to clock speed, or whether it is directly determined by another primitive, information processing rate. It is rather to illustrate that while the average variability and the average accuracy of temporal interval judgements are things that we can independently measure, our assumptions as to how these measurements relate to the functional characteristics of the cognitive system, and of the brain, depend on the details of the models within which we work. Well-articulated models allow us to discuss the functional aetiology of age differences, or differences in general mental ability, in ways that generate alternative hypotheses, suggest experimental tests between them, and so gain new information about human performance. In this context, the argument as to whether the particular functional performance characteristics of the models we use are, or are not, primitive to age differences is not right or wrong but irrelevant because it does not raise any new questions that help us to explore functional or neurophysiological systems or even to obtain new information that is of use in applied cognitive gerontology.

FURTHER WAYS OF INVESTIGATING INDIVIDUAL DIFFERENCES IN VARIABILITY, INDEPENDENTLY OF DECISION SPEED

Since time-estimation experiments involve comparisons of duration, they are not ideal scenarios for investigating variability in performance independently of latency. Investigations of trial-to-trial variability within and between tasks can of course be carried out in a wide range of situations in which decisions are not time limited. An obvious field would be psychophysical judgements of absolute or relative differences in brightness, weight, size, loudness, etc. in tasks in which participants take as long as they need to respond. Correlations between variability between such tasks, the components of BSV that are contributed by WSV, and systematic individual differences in variability with age and intelligence test performance seem to be very fruitful fields for further work.

We shall consider below a range of functional models, derived from those in the literature on CRTs, which illustrate how performance variability and performance speed can be treated as separate and independent properties of the functional cognitive system or, alternatively, how each of these properties can be described as a direct derivation of the other.

HOW CAN EXISTING FUNCTIONAL MODELS EXPLAIN CONSISTENT INDIVIDUAL DIFFERENCES IN TRIAL-TO-TRIAL VARIABILITY IN CRTS?

To decide whether variability and average speed of performance on CRT tasks reflect the same or different performance characteristics of the CNS, let us first consider functional models for fast decisions. This turns out to be interesting since in some current models they derive from the same, and in others from quite different, assumptions about underlying functional processes.

Models in which individual differences in speed and variability are accounted for by distinct functional system performance characteristics

A simple functional model

Derived from Cerella (1985) and discussed by Rabbitt (1992), this model assumes that each signal that occurs during a CRT task activates the same chain of N successive information processing units which, acting in series, identify it, and then select and organize the execution of an appropriate response to it. Each successive unit has an operating time, t, so that observed CRTs will be a function of $N*t$. That is, CRTs will be slower for difficult tasks or discriminations which require chains of many units than for easier tasks or discriminations that require fewer units. Such a model can simply account for findings that mean CRTs from tasks of very different kinds and levels of difficulty are scaled by the same common factor whose magnitude is determined by the magnitudes of differences in age (Cerella 1985) or in fluid intellectual ability (Rabbitt 1996). If we suppose that old age or low ability slows the operating time for each unit by the same constant factor, M, across tasks of different levels of difficulty, mean CRTs for older or for less able people can be closely estimated from mean CRTs for younger or more able people simply by multiplying the latter by a single, empirically derived, age or ability constant, M.

However, as we have seen, to fit all of the data a model must also explain why distributions of CRTs vary widely about their means, and why this variance increases with age. This simplistic model can most easily account for this by assuming that the operating time, t, of each unit is not constant but varies from trial to trial. In this case the observed variance of individual CRTs, which are the summed operating times of all units, will directly reflect the unobservable variance of the termination times for individual units (see Rabbitt 1992). Even this very simple model can generate the prediction that age and general intellectual ability will markedly affect the variances as well as the means or distributions of CRTs in simple tasks. Note, however, that in order to do so it assumes that the factors that determine the variability of the operating time of each individual unit are functionally distinct from, and independent of, the factors that limit the maximum speed with which individual units can operate.

'First-past-the-post' models

Most current models for fast decisions are based on the assumption that they are made by neural networks in which inputs activate large numbers of units and connections between them. Outcomes of decision processes are seen in terms of competition between rival pathways that may terminate to offer different solutions for signal identification in CRT experiments, or to activate different traces in memory. Such competitions may be resolved in several different ways, for example, by a simple 'first-past-the-post horse-race', in which the first process to terminate captures the decision or in terms of a poll of outcomes of successively terminating processes which proceeds until a criterial value is reached. We shall suggest below that some variants of first-past-the-post models do allow us to account for individual differences in the average speeds, and in the trial-to-trial variability of decision times in terms of a single functional parameter: that is, lagging in the average latencies of the activation times of the individual units that comprise the pathways that race to capture the decision. However, it is necessary to stress that the first-past-the-post model is not the only plausible description, and that some poll models offer accounts in which mean decision times and variability of decision times are derived from quite distinct system performance parameters.

Criterion selection

Irrespective of mean decision speed, decision times will vary with the criterion adopted for assessment of evidence from the outcome of the poll of decisions. This can occur for at least two, logically distinct, reasons. First, adoption of a lax criterion which allows decisions to be based on the outcomes of only the earliest terminating processes will lead to faster average CRTs but, since fewer successively terminating processes are polled on each trial, the intervals between the termination times of the first and last polled processes will be relatively short, and trial-to-trial variability in decision times will be accordingly reduced.

Adoption of a cautious criterion, in which decisions are based on a larger, and so temporally more protracted, sample of successive terminations of processes will result in slower average CRTs. Because the intervals between the first and last processes polled will be longer, this will also result in greater trial-to-trial variability. Second, all models which invoke decision criteria also assume random shifts in these criteria from trial to trial or systematic changes in these criteria with practice (see reviews by Logan 1992; Luce 1986). In this case variations in trial-to-trial decision times may be determined by trial-to-trial criterion shifts which are functionally independent of process duration. In other words, individual differences in variability may be determined by individual differences in criterion selection and in criterion lability that are quite independent of individual differences in functional speed.

Decision capture

All models that assume that decisions are based on the outcome of only a subset of many concurrent processes must specify how the decision is captured. Whether we assume that evidence is accumulated as successive processes terminate until some decision criterion is reached, or that a single winning process is the first of many to terminate, the description remains incomplete until we specify why other concurrent processes are prevented from affecting the outcome. One option is to suppose that all processes compete to determine the outcome and that the most powerfully activated process wins this contest by successfully inhibiting all others (e.g. Grossberg 1982, 1987). On this assumption, both the average latency and the trial-to-trial variability of decisions will be determined by a performance parameter, overall differences in strength of inhibition between processes, which is functionally unrelated to decision speed per se. Individual differences in mean CRTs and in CRT variability can be modelled in terms of individual differences in efficiency of inhibition between units or processes rather than in terms of individual differences in the operating speed of decision pathways or of the units of which they are composed.

Speed–accuracy trade-off

A simple model proposed by Rabbitt and Vyas (1969) and more elegantly articulated and extended by Smith and Brewer (1995) derives from observations that, in any task, there is a limit to the speed with which individuals can make correct responses. Thus there is a range of CRTs, known as the speed–accuracy trade-off band, across which the probability of a correct decision reduces to chance as speed increases. The model assumes that individuals learn to optimize their performance in any CRT task by responding faster until they locate their speed–accuracy limit and by then tracking this limit as closely as possible. The more precisely they can do this, the fewer unnecessarily slow correct responses they will make, and so the smaller will be the variance and the skew of their CRT distributions.

In this model the position of a person's speed–accuracy trade-off limit is an index of the maximum speed with which the person can make reliable decisions. Incidentally, the speed–accuracy trade-off function is a much more rational and meaningful index of the limits to information processing rate than is mean CRT, since it is independent of the variability and skew of the distribution from which it is computed and takes into consideration not only the total numbers of errors that are committed but also their latencies relative to those of all correct responses. Further, Rabbitt and Banerji (1986) have empirically shown that the variance of CRT distributions may vary considerably without any apparent change in the intercepts and slopes of speed–accuracy trade-off functions. In other words, trial-to-trial variance in CRT may vary independently of the maximum speed at which individuals can make correct responses. One way to account for this is to suppose that the variability of individuals' CRTs from trial-to-trial does not depend on the maximum speed with which they can process information but rather on the precision with which they can actively and purposefully control their response speeds so as first to locate, and then to track their own speed–accuracy trade-off functions and so maximize speed and minimize errors. It is reasonable to suppose that individuals' efficiency at doing this may depend on the precision with which they can estimate, and reproduce, brief intervals of time. As Wearden *et al.* (1997) found, older age and poorer performance on intelligence tests have comparatively little effect on the average accuracy but do markedly increase the trial-to-trial variability of time-interval judgements.

Models in which average speed and variability of CRTs can be accounted for in terms of the same functional system performance characteristics

Models based on activation and selection of optimal decision pathways

Classes of more plausible and well-articulated models are discussed in excellent reviews by Luce (1986) and Townsend and Ashby (1983). For example, useful models have been based on the assumption that the identification of any event and selection of an appropriate response to it, is managed by the activation of one of a number of different possible pathways between units. An early instantiation of this idea by Crossman (1958) accounted for the characteristic power function improvement in decision times with practice by assuming that, early in practice, decisions may be made by any one of a sheaf of possible pathways, some of which are optimally short, because they comprise fewer information processing units and so terminate in decisions faster than others which are longer, and comprise more information processing units. Early in practice, pathways are selected more or less at random from trial to trial with the result that average decision times are slow with correspondingly large trial-to-trial variability. As practice continues optimal pathways are progressively selected and inefficient pathways are progressively discarded. Crossman (1958) neatly showed that this process could generate the logarithmic or power function reduction in mean CRTs and the directly correlated fall in trial-to-trial CRT variance that are actually observed when tasks are practised.

This allows us to see that if old age or low general intellectual ability lags all units by a constant (L), then each pathway will be lagged in proportion to the number (N) of units that it comprises $(L*N)$. Because pathways of different lengths may be selected on different experimental trials this will result in simple linear scaling of distributions of decision times (CRTs), with the obvious consequence that variances of CRT distributions will correspondingly increase. Linear scaling of CRT distributions by individual differences in age and ability is, in fact, just what is observed (Rabbitt and Maylor 1991).Thus, from individual differences in a single functional performance parameter, unit lag, it is possible to derive individual differences in the means and also in the variances of CRT distributions. Further, from hypothetical differences in unit lag we can also derive precise predictions of individual differences in the slopes and asymptotes of functions that describe the different, joint, rates of improvement with practice in mean CRTs and in CRT variability in older and younger or in more and less intelligent individuals. These exercises remain to be undertaken, and tested against empirical data.

Models based on comparison of memorial representations

Serial self-terminating decision models, such as that used by Sternberg (1969) to account for the results of experiments with his memory search paradigm, can be given wider applications in CRT models. For example, by analogy with Logan's (1992) instance theory we may suppose that memorial representations of all of the states between which discriminations must be made are serially scanned in order to find a match for a perceptual representation of a current input. Serial comparisons proceed until a match is found, when the process terminates in a decision. The order in which memorial representations of states are tested may vary from trial to trial with such factors as their relative recency of occurrence during the course of the experiment. The average number of comparisons which must be made before a match is found will increase with the number of different states which must be represented. Thus, mean decision times, and also the difference between the fastest and slowest matches that can be made (i.e., variance in decision times), will increase directly with the number of different memorial representations against which perceptual inputs must successively be compared (i.e., with the degree of choice between alternatives). Lagging of the system will therefore slow mean decision times for difficult decisions more than for easy decisions. This is, in fact, observed. Because each comparison will be lagged, slow decisions which occur after many serial comparisons have been made will be lagged more than fast decisions which occur after only a few comparisons have been made. The effect of increases in unit lag will be to multiply distributions of CRTs by a constant, producing the linear transformations of distributions of decision times which are, indeed, observed as a result of differences in age, general intellectual ability, and alcohol ingestion (e.g. Rabbitt and Maylor 1991).

SO WHERE DO WE GO FROM HERE?

We might hope that with careful thought we might come up with better alternative models and discover the right experimental questions to choose between them. We may have to face the possibility that this may not be possible from behavioural evidence alone. Townsend and Ashby (1983) have lucidly pointed out that it may well be that even when all possible task performance indices are measured and compared, patterns of relationships between them will be fitted equally well by a wide range of models that derive from quite distinct functional assumptions. A brilliant review of models for decision and learning processes by Page (1999) formally demonstrates that many models for CRTs and other decision processes that have been regarded as functionally distinct are, in fact, mathematically equivalent. This of course means that no patterns of data that we analyse in terms of these models can discriminate between them. Equally rigorous analyses of alternative models for behaviours other than the production of fast decisions is likely to reveal that this is a very general and insufficiently recognized problem in cognitive psychology and gerontology. It is very likely that we will have to learn to come to terms with the fact that comparisons of the means and distributions of decision times between different task conditions and individuals at different levels of practice will not, on their own, allow us to deduce the actual functional architecture of decision-making networks. In this context, speculations concerning whether individual differences in performance of CRT tasks with age or with general intellectual ability can be entirely described in terms of individual differences in the levels of one, or even two, primitive performance indices are seen as neither right, nor wrong, but beside the point.

It may well be possible to design batteries of tests on which composite scores efficiently predict performance on all, or most, cognitive skills. It may further be assumed that if several different batteries of this kind can be developed, and scores on these batteries obtained from large groups of people are factor-analysed, variance will be found to be best expressed in terms of a single, common factor which, with a nod to Spearman's g we might, if we choose, call 'gp(erformance)' and, further, that individuals' performance on a variety of different laboratory tasks can indeed be rank ordered in terms of values of this construct. Current work suggests that test batteries that only incorporate measures of decision speed, such as CRT or inspection time, would not do this very well. They would also have to include tests of learning, memory, and problem solving ability (Rabbitt and Yang 1996; Robbins *et al.* 1994, 1997). Such task-performance test batteries would be of practical use in applied cognitive gerontology since, even better than the intelligence tests from which they draw their rationale, they might guide selection of older individuals who can, and rejection of those who cannot, meet particular everyday demands, such as driving in fast busy traffic or learning to operate complex machinery. However attempts to identify *gp* with any single hypothetical functional characteristic of the cognitive system (such as information processing speed or moment-to-moment variability, still less with any neurophysiological characteristic of the brain such as synaptic conduction speed or level of neural random noise) would not be sensible or fruitful because a plurality of rival descriptions usually fit the case equally well. Cognitive gerontologists may do well to learn from the growing scepticism among psychometricians as to the value of derivation of constructs such as *g* (e.g. Detterman 1982, 1986).

SUMMARY

Both speed and variability of performance are stable characteristics of individuals; each of these indices yields useful empirical predictions about performance that the other, on its own, does not make. Thus, both indices are needed to fully describe individual differences in performance on laboratory tasks. It is useful to generate, and to empirically test, models that describe how relationships between these two indices alter with individual differences in age, general intellectual ability, and also with extended practice. This research agenda gains nothing from discussions as to whether speed, or variability, or both are, or are not, fundamental system performance characteristics whose values entirely determine competence on all, or most, cognitive tasks. As models improve it may well turn out to be possible to accept some particular, single system performance parameter as a summary index that predicts performance across a wide variety of different tasks. But this will only be useful if it has clear functional definitions in the context of tightly articulated models and simulations. If this can be done it is likely that useful hypothetical constructs to rank-order performance across wide ranges of tasks will not be directly reflected by particular raw performance indices such as means of variances of CRTs or inspection times, which can be directly measured in particular tasks, but will rather be more abstractly defined, higher-order mathematical entities analogous to 'system temperature' in connectionist models which are computationally derived, and tightly specifiable but which, when task outputs are examined, are 'hidden' in the sense that they are not directly reflected by any single performance index derived from any particular task, nor can they necessarily be derived from such indices in the same ways as psychometric constructs such as *g*. Parenthetically, it must be stressed that psychometric constructs such as *g* and higher-order statistical constructs are not conceptually identical. Psychometric constructs are theoretically neutral indices describing statistical patterns of relationships in variance on individuals' scores across a variety of tasks. Higher-order indices in connectionist and other systems are expressions of the results of patterns of relationships between elements in a fully described functional system. It is plausible that descriptions of system outputs can be analysed to yield factor structures which turn out to be quantitatively reflected in higher-order indices programmed into the system. The problem of 'bootstrapping' functional descriptions of systems from patterns of relationships between measured task performance indices can be tackled only by realizing that the conceptual structure of the models that we generate and test determines the status of the indices that we chose to measure and so the nature of the analyses that we undertake. Different models demand different analyses in which different measurable indices may emerge as statistical primitives. Lack of attention to this point led to the current comic situation in which single-factor models of intelligence, and of cognitive aging, while continuing to be of obsessive interest to the distinguished, scholarly, and talented investigators who propose them, are acknowledged, but not actually used by those who try to make progress at understanding relationships between behaviour and brain function.

REFERENCES

Anderson, M. (1995). Evidence for a single global factor of developmental change – too good to be true? *Australian Journal of Psychology*, **47**, 18–24.

Ball, K. and Sekuler, R. (1986). Improving visual perception in older observers. *Journal of Gerontology*, **41**, 176–182.

Blake, M. J. F. (1967a). Time of day effects on performance in a range of tasks. *Psychonomic Science*, **9**, 349–50.

Blake, M. J. F. (1967b). Relationship between circadian rhythm of body-temperature and introversion-extroversion. *Nature*, **199**, 1312.

Brand, C.R. and Deary, I. J. (1982). Intelligence and inspection time. In H. J. Eysenck (ed.), *A model for intelligence* (pp. 218–36). New York: Springer-Verlag.

Broadbent, D. E. (1971). *Decision and Stress*. Academic Press: New York.

Brown, B. and Bowman, K. J. (1987). Sensitivity to changes in size and velocity in older observers. *Perception*, **16**, 41–7.

Brown, G. D. A., Preece, T., and Hulme, C. (1999). Oscillator-based memory for serial order. *Psychological Review*. (In press).

Brown, G. D. A. and Vousden, J. I. (1998). Adaptive sequential behaviour: oscillators as rational mechanisms. In M. Oaksford and N. Chater (ed.), *Rational models of cognition* (pp. 165–93). Oxford: Oxford University Press.

Cattell, R. B. and Cattell, A. K. S. (1960). *Handbook for the Individual or Group Culture Fair Intelligence Test*. Champaign, IL: IPAT.

Cerella, J. (1985). Information processing rates in the elderly. *Psychological Bulletin*, **98**, 67–83.

Colquhoun, W. P. and Corcoran, D. W. J. (1964). The effects of time of day and social isolation on the relationship between temperament and performance. *British Journal of Social and Clinical Psychology*, **3**, 226–31.

Crossman, E. R. F. W. (1958). A theory of the acquisition of speed-skill. *Ergonomics*, **2**, 153–66.

Detterman, D. K. (1982). Does 'g' exist ? *Intelligence*, **6**, 99–108.

Detterman, D. K. (1986). Human intelligence is a complex system of separate processes.

In R. J. Sternberg and D. K. Detterman (ed), *What is intelligence?* (pp. 136–44). Norwood, NJ: Ablex.

Dywan, J. and Segalowitz, S. J. (1996). 'Source memory and ageing: ERP evidence for changes in attentional control'. unpublished manuscript.

Eysenck, H. J. (1986). The theory of intelligence and the psychophysiology of cognition. In R. J. Sternberg (ed.), *Advances in the psychology of human intelligence* (Vol. 3, pp. 232–48). Hillsdale, NJ: Lawrence Erlbaum.

Gibbon, J., Church, R. M., and Meck, W. H. (1984). Scalar timing in memory. In J. Gibbon and L. G. Allan (ed.), *Timing and time perception* (pp. 52–77). New York: New York Academy of Sciences.

Grossberg, S. (1982). *Studies of mind and brain.* NY: Reidel.

Grossberg, S. J. (1987). Competitive learning: from interactive activation to adaptive resonance. *Cognitive Science,* **11**, 23–63.

Hasher, L., Stoltzfus, E. R., Zacks, R. T., and Rypma, B. (1991). Age and inhibition. *Journal of Experimental Psychology: Learning, Memory and Cognition,* **17**, 163–9.

Henson, R. N. A. and Burgess, N. (1998). Representations of serial order. In J. A. Bullinaria, D. W. Glasspool, and G. Houghton (ed.), *Proceedings of the fourth neural computation and psychology workshop: connectionist representations* (pp. 283–300). London: Springer-Verlag.

Howell, D. C. (1992). *Statistical methods for psychology* (3rd edn., p 42). London: Duxbury Press.

Intons-Peterson, M. J., Rocchi, P., West, T., McLellan, K., and Hackney, A. (1998). Aging, optimal testing times, and negative priming. *Journal of Experimental Psychology: Learning, Memory, and Cognition,* **24**, 362–76.

Jensen, A. R. (1980). Chronometric analysis of mental ability. *Journal of Social and Biological Structures,* **3**, 181–224.

Jensen, A. R. (1985). The nature of the black–white difference in various psychometric tests. Spearman's hypothesis. *The Behavioral and Brain Sciences,* **8**, 193–219.

Jensen, A. R. and Whang, P. A. (1993). Reaction times and intelligence: a comparison of Chinese-American and Anglo-American children. *Journal of Biosocial Science,* **25**, 397–410.

Kimberg, D. Y. and Farrah, M. J. (1993). A unified account of impairments following frontal lobe damage: the role of working memory in complex organised behavior. *Journal of Experimental Psychology: General,* **122**, 411–28.

Liebowitz, H. W. (1955).The relation between the rate-threshold for the perception of movement and luminance for various durations of exposure. *Journal of Experimental Psychology,* **49**, 209–14.

Logan, G. D. (1992). Shapes of reaction-time distributions and shapes of learning curves: a test of the instance theory of automaticity. *Journal of Experimental Psychology: Learning, Memory and Cognition,* **18**, 883–914.

Lowe, C. A. and Rabbitt, P. M. A. (1997). Cognitive models of ageing and frontal lobe deficits. In P. M. A. Rabbitt (ed.), *Methodology of frontal and executive functions* (pp. 26–45). Hove, UK: Lawrence Erlbaum.

Luce, R. D. (1986). *Response times: their role in inferring elementary mental organisation.* Oxford: Oxford University Press.

Maylor, E. A., Vousden, J. I., and Brown, G. D. A. (1999). Adult age differences in short-term memory for serial order: data and a model. *Psychology and Aging.* (In press.)

Morse, C. K. (1993). Does variability increase with age? An archival study of cognitive measures. *Psychology and Aging*, **8**, 156–64.

Page, M. (1999). Connectionist models in psychology: a localist manifesto. *The Behavioral and Brain Sciences*. (In press.)

Parkin, A. J. and Walter, B. M. (1991). Aging, short-term memory and frontal dysfunction. *Psychobiology*, **19**, 175–9.

Parkin, A. J. and Walter, B. M. (1992). Recollective experience, normal aging, and frontal dysfunction. *Psychology and Aging*, **7**, 290–8.

Parkin, A. J., Yeomans, J., and Bindschaedler, C. (1994). Further characterization of the executive memory impairment following frontal-lobe lesions. *Brain and Cognition*, **26**, 23–42.

Rabbitt, P. (1981). Cognitive psychology needs models for changes in performance with old age. In A. D. Baddeley and J. Long (ed.), *Attention and performance IX* (pp. 323–40). Hillsdale, NJ: Lawrence Erlbaum.

Rabbitt, P. M. A. (1992). Many happy repetitions: a celebration of the 'Bertelson repetition effect', 1961 to 1991. In J. Allegria, D. Hollander, J. Junca de Morais, and M. Radeau (ed.), *Analytic approaches to human cognition* (pp. 313–30). Amsterdam: Elsevier.

Rabbitt, P. M. A. (1996). Do individual differences in speed reflect global or local differences in mental abilities? *Intelligence*, **22**, 69–88.

Rabbitt, P. M. A. (1997). Models for executive processes. In P. M. A. Rabbitt (ed.), *Methodologies for frontal and executive function* (pp. 6–30). Hove, UK: Lawrence Erlbaum.

Rabbitt, P. M. A. and Banerji, N. (1986). How does very prolonged practice affect decision speed? *Journal of Experimental Psychology: General*, **98**, 244–73.

Rabbitt, P. M. A. and Goward, L. (1994). Age, information processing speed and intelligence. *Quarterly Journal of Experimental Psychology*, **47A**, 741–60.

Rabbitt, P. M. A. and Maylor, E. A. (1991). Investigating models of human performance. *British Journal of Psychology*, **82**, 259–90.

Rabbitt, P. M. A. and Vyas, S. M. (1969). An elementary preliminary taxonomy for some errors in laboratory choice RT tasks. In A. Sanders (ed.), *Attention and performance III* (pp. 56–76). Amsterdam: North Holland.

Rabbitt, P. M. A. and Yang, Q. (1996). What are the functional bases of individual differences in memory ability? In D. Herrmann, C. Mc Evoy, C. Hertzog, P. Hertel and M. K. Johnson (ed.). *Basic and applied memory research. Theory in context.* (Vol. 1, pp. 127–59). Mahwah, NJ: Lawrence Erlbaum.

Reed, T. E. (1993). Effects of enriched (complex) environment on nerve conduction velocity: new data and implications for the speed of information processing. *Intelligence*, **17**, 461–74.

Reed, T. E. and Jensen, A. R. (1992). Conduction velocity in a brain-nerve pathway of normal adults correlates with intelligence level. *Intelligence*, **16**, 259–72.

Robbins, T. W., James, T., Owen, A. M., Sahakian, B. J., Mc Innes, L., and Rabbitt, P. M. A. (1994). CANTAB: a factor analytic study of a large sample of normal elderly volunteers. *Dementia*, **5**, 266–81.

Robbins, T. W., James, M., Owen, A. M., Sahakian, B. J., Mc Innes, L., and Rabbitt, P. M. A. (1997). A neural systems approach to the cognitive psychology of aging: studies with CANTAB on a large sample of the normal elderly population. In P. M. A. Rabbitt (ed.), *Methodology of frontal and executive function* (pp. 215–38). Hove, UK:

Lawrence Erlbaum.

Salthouse, T. A. (1985). *A cognitive theory of aging.* Berlin: Springer-Verlag.

Salthouse, T. A. (1991). *Theoretical perspectives on cognitive aging.* Hillsdale, NJ: Lawrence Erlbaum.

Salthouse, T. A. (1996). The processing-speed theory of adult age differences in cognition. *Psychological Review,* **103,** 403–28.

Smith, G. A. and Brewer, N. (1995). Slowness and age: speed-accuracy mechanisms. *Psychology and Aging,* **11,** 326–47.

Spearman, C. (1924). *The abilities of man.* London: Macmillan.

Sternberg, S. (1969). Memory scanning: mental processes revealed by reaction time experiments. *American Scientist,* **57,** 421–57.

Townsend, J. T. and Ashby, F. G. (1983). *Stochastic modelling of elementary psychological processes.* Cambridge: Cambridge University Press.

Vernon, P. A. (1983). Speed of information processing and intelligence. *Intelligence,* **7,** 53–70.

Vernon, P. A. (1985). Individual differences in general cognitive ability. In L. C. Hartledge and C. F. Telzner (ed.), *The neuropsychology of individual differences: a developmental perspective* (pp. 134–78). New York: Plenum.

Wearden, J. A. and Penton-Voak, I. S. (1995). Feeling the heat: body temperature and the rate of subjective time revisited. *Quarterly Journal of Experimental Psychology,* **48B,** 129–41.

Wearden, J. A., Wearden, A. J., and Rabbitt, P. M. A. (1997). Age and IQ effects on stimulus and response timing. *Journal of Experimental Psychology: Human Perception and Performance,* **23,** 239–51.

SEVEN

Determinants of age-related memory loss

ALAN J. PARKIN AND ROSALIND I. JAVA

The cognitive basis of age-related memory loss has become of increasing interest over the last ten years – not in the least, perhaps, because cognitive psychologists are themselves getting older and gaining first hand experience of the problem. The study of age-related memory loss can be characterized as one in which 'generalist' explanations have been sought. A generalist explanation, in this context, is one in which a specific deficit is explained as one consequence of a more general problem brought on by advancing years. Within the sphere of age-related memory loss there have been a number of generalist accounts (e.g. Hasher and Zacks 1988; Light 1991) and, in this chapter, we will focus on three: frontal lobe dysfunction, speed of processing, and fluid intelligence.

THE NATURE OF AGE-RELATED MEMORY LOSS

The characteristics of age-related memory loss are now fairly well documented. First, within the implicit/explicit dimension, there is abundant evidence that aging affects explicit rather than implicit memory tasks (Kausler 1994; Light *et al.* Chapter 9, this volume). Furthermore, where aging effects on an implicit task appear to have been found the impairment actually arises from deficits related to explicit mediation. Russo and Parkin (1993), for example, showed that an apparent age-related deficit on an implicit picture completion task arose because older subjects were less able to mediate completion via explicit recollection of the training procedure. Within the explicit domain free recall shows dramatic age-related loss whereas recognition is far less affected. Indeed, some studies have reported no age decline in recognition memory. However, caution must be observed in drawing conclusions about the relative insensitivity of recognition memory to age manipulations. A major problem is that recognition memory is a much easier task – partly because provision of copy cues reduces retrieval demands on explicit memory *per se*, and partly because copy cues provide a basis for implicit, familiarity-driven, components of recognition memory to exert a positive influence on identification accuracy. Another problem, often overlooked, is that aging can give rise to higher false alarm rates despite no age effect on hit rates (Parkin and Walter 1992).

FRONTAL LOBE DYSFUNCTION AND MEMORY

The frontal lobe (FL) theory of age-related memory loss stems from the purported similarity between the memory impairments shown by older people and those presented by patients with focal lesions of the frontal cortex and demonstrations that the frontal cortex is selectively vulnerable to the effects of age. The first study to raise the FL theory of age-related memory loss was by Craik *et al.* (1990) who showed that elderly subjects were impaired on source memory relative to fact memory. In addition, these authors showed that the extent of this source-memory impairment was correlated with older subjects' performance on tests of frontal lobe function. Parkin and Walter (1991) examined age-related declines in recall performance on the Brown–Peterson task and found that the extent of older subjects' impairments correlated with deficits shown on measures of frontal lobe function.

Parkin and Walter (1992) examined recognition performance in older people using what has been termed the 'recognition and conscious awareness' (RCA) task. In this task, devised originally by Endel Tulving and developed by Gardiner (1988), subjects make recognition judgements about previously studied items and, for each positive identification response, subjects are further required to make a 'remember–know' judgement – 'remember' (R) corresponds to a recognition response associated with a specific contextual recollection of the item's appearance in the study list whereas a 'know' (K) response is a decontextualized recognition of an item's familiarity. In a finding that has now been replicated a number of times, Parkin and Walter (1992) showed that recognition memory per se did not decline much with age (although there was a notable increase in false alarms by older subjects). There were, however, very marked changes in the subjective nature of recognition with older subjects producing far more K judgements relative to R judgements than their younger counterparts (see Light *et al.*, Chapter 9 this volume, for further discussion). An additional feature of the study was that the extent of the switch from R to K in the older subjects correlated with their performance on the Wisconsin Card Sorting Test (WCST).

These early reports have given rise to additional studies which confirm a relationship between frontal measures, age, and memory performance (see Parkin 1997*a*, and Perfect 1997 for recent reviews). For example, older subjects have been shown to have deficits in temporal discrimination which relate to frontal abilities (Parkin *et al.* 1995) and Glisky *et al.* (1995) have confirmed the relation between frontal function and source memory in older people. However, in his recent review, Perfect pointed out that studies exploring the relationship between frontal function and memory have tended to be only confirmatory in nature. Singling out the Parkin and Walter (1992) study he notes that these authors did not include measures reflecting other theoretical accounts of aging. As a result, the apparent relationship between memory and frontal factors, and hence the theoretical import of this relationship, might be undermined if this relationship were, itself, a function of something else. We will return to this point when we have considered two other approaches to the explanation of age-related memory loss.

GENERALIZED SPEED FACTOR

In an impressive array of studies Salthouse has put forward the view that a 'general speed factor' might explain, among other things, the effects of age on memory (e.g. Salthouse 1993a, 1993b, 1996). In essence the theory argues that age produces a generalized slowing of the brain which has widespread consequences for cognitive function, including memory. An example of this approach is provided by Salthouse's (1993a) study in which age-related deficits on tests of free recall and paired associate learning were first obtained followed by the demonstration that most of the age-related memory variance associated with these tests could be removed by partialling out generalized speed measures. One measure of speed was the Digit Symbol Substitution Test (DSST) of the WAIS-R (Wechsler 1987). The DSST comprises a code table showing the digits one to nine each paired with a symbol and rows of double boxes each with a digit in the top box and nothing in the lower box. The participants' task is to place the symbol appropriate to each digit in the blank box and the dependent variable is the number of symbols correctly inscribed in 90 seconds. It was found that DSST removed 73.4% of age-related memory variance when used as a covariate (for similar findings see Bryan and Luszcz 1996; Dunlosky and Salthouse 1996).

The influence of tasks such as DSST as determinants of age-related memory variance are impressive and lend heavy support to the idea that some general slowing of mental operations underlies the effect of aging on memory. However, the exact interpretation of why these powerful effects are observed depends, in turn, on what these tasks are measuring. Most commonly Salthouse (1996) has referred to these measures as ones of 'perceptual speed' – a definition that appears, principally, to dissociate the influence these tasks have on performance from any role that their motor components might exert on the pattern of cognitive decline. This latter point seems fair in the light of various lines of evidence indicating that the motor dimension of tasks such as DSST is not relevant to the moderating influence of its performance on age-related changes in memory cognition (e.g. Erber 1986; Salthouse et al. 1988). What is less clear, however, is what DSST is measuring beyond motor speed. Use of the term 'perceptual speed' to denote its cognitive characteristics implies that DSST is serving to measure some fundamental property of many cognitive operations – a fact endorsed by the alternative term 'general speed factor'. However, the evidence supporting this seems lacking and derives principally from face-validity arguments based on the apparent simplicity of the test itself. Thus, in a recent review Salthouse (1996) states: 'the tasks used to assess processing speed are so simple' (p. 423) and changes in the rate of performance reflect 'a slower speed of transmission along single ... or multiple pathways' (p. 425). Thus, there seems little doubt in Salthouse's mind that measurements such as DSST speed are tapping the efficiency of fundamentally simple processes.

There are good reasons to suppose that DSST is not just measuring relatively low level perceptual processes. First, there is the issue of a putative memory component arising from the possibility that DSST speed can be enhanced if the associations between the digits and symbols can be learned thus requiring less reference to the code table. A number of studies have reported that older subjects have poorer memory for digit–symbol pairs following DSST administration (Shuttleworth and Bode 1995). This could be attributable to a direct impairment in learning the associations or, because fewer digit symbols are processed, there are fewer opportunities to learn the pairs. A memory factor might therefore have some bearing on the speed at which subjects carry out DSST. In connection with this Chandler (personal communication) has shown that the shared variance between DSST speed and a group of memory measures (free recall and paired associate learning) is reduced by 18% when memory for the digit–symbol pairings is partialled out.

A second factor relates to intelligence. DSST is a subtest of the *Wechsler Adult Intelligence Scale-Revised* (WAIS-R; Wechsler 1987) and, as such, is presumably IQ sensitive. Standardization data from WAIS-R confirm this, showing that DSST has a correlation of 0.70 with performance IQ and 0.65 (table 16) with full scale IQ. However, one might argue that, given the emphasis on speed in many components of WAIS-R, this could reflect a general speed factor. This point can be countered by evidence that skill in encoding the symbols verbally enhances performance (Estes 1974) – a finding that may explain why women consistently outperform men on DSST (Snow and Weinstock 1990), and why DSST correlates 0.47 with the vocabulary component of WAIS-R (a subtest which is not time based).

FLUID INTELLIGENCE

Intelligence is usually defined as either 'crystallized' or 'fluid' depending on the task in question. Crystallized intelligence refers to knowledge that is invariant and it is typified by measures of language ability such as the Mill Hill Vocabulary Test (Raven 1982) and the National Adult Reading Test (NART; Nelson 1985). Fluid intelligence represents the ability to think flexibly and is best characterized by tests which measure problem solving such as AH4 (Heim 1968) and the performance subtests of the WAIS-R. There is good evidence that crystallized and fluid intelligence dissociate with age. Vocabulary remains either invariant with age or actually shows an improvement (e.g. Salthouse *et al.* 1996). In contrast fluid intelligence shows marked declines with age (e.g. Holland and Rabbitt 1990; Horn and Masunaga, Chapter 5, this volume).

Some researchers have proposed that there is a link between fluid intelligence and age-related memory loss – the argument being that memory is an activity which requires cognitive flexibility both at encoding and retrieval. As a result, any loss of cognitive flexibility would be sure to affect memory directly. A number of studies have provided direct support for this idea. Holland and Rabbitt (1990) showed that the specificity of autobiographical recall in older subjects was predicted by subjects' performance on AH4. Cockburn and Smith (1991) found that fluid intelligence reliably predicted the performance of older subjects on a short memory test that provided analogs of everyday activities. More recently, Bäckman and Wahlin (1995) showed that fluid intelligence influenced free and cued recall performance in elderly subjects and, in a study of dementia, Bäckman *et al.* (1994) showed that fluid intelligence predicted free recall performance beyond that predicted by severity of symptoms.

INTERIM CONCLUSION

The above review has indicated three sets of studies which, taken individually, provide good support for a particular generalist account of age-related memory loss. However, they echo Perfect's (1997) point about confirmatory bias in that no study sets out to test one generalist account against another. Thus frontal studies do not include measures of perceptual speed or fluid intelligence, perceptual speed studies have not considered fluid intelligence or frontal performance, and studies of fluid intelligence have not emphasized processing speed or frontal function as explanatory concepts. It seems intuitively unlikely that all three accounts are correct. In the following section we describe the results of an experimental study which meets the criticism of Perfect in that it embraces manipulations which enable all three of the above accounts of age-related memory loss to be evaluated within the same set of data.

EXPERIMENTAL DATA

In this section we present data obtained from 40 elderly and 20 younger subjects on tests of recall and recognition. We also present data on their performance across a range of tests reflecting frontal lobe function, speed of processing, and intelligence – both crystallized and fluid. From these data, by means of regression analysis, we examine which factors determine most age-related variance in memory performance and, from that point, consider which of the above accounts provides the most satisfactory explanation of age-related impairments in recall and recognition.

Subjects

The elderly group comprised 40 subjects, 20 'Young–Old' (YO) between the ages of 63 and 74, and 20 'Old–Old' (OO) between the ages of 75 and 88. Of these, there were 9 males and 11 females in the YO group and 8 males and 12 females in the OO group. Young control subjects were 10 male and 10 female subjects between the ages of 22 and 31. The elderly groups were all healthy and living independently in their own homes and were screened for dementia using the Mini-Mental State Exam (Folstein *et al.* 1989; cut-off score 25) and depression using the Geriatric Depression Scale (Brink *et al.* 1982). Details of the subjects are shown in Table 7.1. Age differences in crystallized intelligence differed to the advantage of the older groups with NART scores significantly higher for both YO and OO groups compared to the younger adults, $F(2,57) = 7.563$, $p = 0.0012$. In contrast younger subjects showed higher fluid intelligence, $F(2,57) = 78.95$, $p < 0.0001$, but AH4 scores did not differ between the two elderly groups.[1]

Design and Procedure

Memory tasks

We used two recall and two recognition tests. The study list for the recall tasks each comprised six sets of categorically related items, four in each, which are presented in six blocks, each comprising items from one category. There were two recognition tasks. The first of these, designated 'Sheet', comprised 40 target items and 40 distractors. The second recognition task, designated 'Single Probe', was similarly constructed using different materials. Study words for both recall and recognition were presented via a Macintosh 520 Powerbook computer screen at a rate of four seconds per item. Retention was tested immediately after presentation. For recall, subjects were first asked to write down a four-figure number, as a means of eliminating recency, and then write down as many of the words as they could remember in any order. In the Sheet recognition task, 40 targets and 40 distractors were printed on an A4 sheet of paper in three columns and subjects were asked to place a ring around any

Table 7.1 General characteristics of experimental groups

	Young		Young–Old		Old–Old	
	Mean	SD	Mean	SD	Mean	SD
Age	25.4	2.6	69.2	2.8	78.8	3.8
AH4	109.3	12.1	66.2	13.1	61.5	14.4
MMSE	–	–	29.2	0.7	29.2	1.1
NART	113.7	8.2	120.1	6.6	121.8	5.7

AH4 = Alice Heim (1968) verbal, logical, and spatial reasoning test;
MMSE = Mini-Mental State Examination;
NART = NART FSIQ = National Adult Reading Test Full Scale IQ.

1 All post hoc comparisons are based on Fisher's Protected LSD with a significance level of 0.05.

item they recognized from the study list. In the single probe test subjects saw a random sequence of targets and distractors on the Powerbook and had to indicate 'yes' or 'no' as to whether an item had appeared in the study list.

Frontal lobe tests

Subjects were given the WCST as modified by Nelson (1976). Subjects sort a set of stimulus cards into categories of shape, number and colour, according to a set of four reference cards. The first category sorted is scored as correct, and that category is maintained until six consecutive sorts are correct. The examiner then states 'the rules have now changed, I want you to find another rule'. Successful subjects figure out that there are only three sets of rules which are repeated once. Three fluency measures were given, FAS – a measure of letter fluency, and two tests of category fluency: the HOME test in which subjects generate as many items as possible corresponding to items in the home, and the FOOD test involving the generation of food items available in a supermarket (Parkin *et al.* 1995). All three measures are based on responses generated in one minute.

Tasks of perceptual speed

In order to relate directly to the work of Salthouse the digit symbol substitution subscale from the WAIS-R (DSST; Wechsler 1987) was employed (see earlier description). However, given concerns about what DSST might actually be measuring we also included a less ambiguous measure of perceptual speed, Digit Cancellation (DC). Our DC task is one that has been used in several studies involving tranquillizing and anticonvulsive drugs (e.g. Curran and Java 1993). Subjects cancel out 40 randomly set digits – in this case 4s – that are set within a block of 400 numbers, all between one and nine. The reliability of this test, as estimated by our successive administrations, is 0.71, which comes reasonably close to the typical figure cited for DSST reliability of around 0.84 (Lezak 1995). Our view is that this test meets the criterion of 'perceptual' far more than DSST. It makes little cognitive demand, has less of a motor component, and has a minimal memory load.

Results

Table 7.2 shows the memory performance of the three subject groups. The relation between performance on the two tests of recall was very high (0.742) so, for simplicity, the scores on the two tests are combined. There was a highly significant main effect of age, $F (2, 57) = 17.23$, $p < 0.0001$, with the younger subjects recalling significantly more than the two older groups who, in turn, did not differ. The recognition tests yielded three measures each, hits, false alarms, and a guessing corrected accuracy measure – hits minus false alarms (H-FA). These data are also shown in Table 7.2. For Sheet recognition there was a main effect of age on hits, $F (2,57) = 10.88$, $p < 0.0001$, false alarms, $F (2, 57) = 3.68$, $p = 0.03$, and on H-FA, $F (2, 57) = 8.81$ $p < 0.001$. For hits and H-FA the young group performed significantly better than either of the older groups who, in turn, did not differ. On false alarms, the only significant difference was between the young and OO groups. For single probe there was a main effect of age on hits, $F(2, 57) = 5.08$, $p = 0.009$, false alarms, $F(2, 57) = 5.45$, $p = 0.007$, and on H-FA, $F(2, 57) = 10.03$, $p < 0.0002$. Post hoc analysis of all three measures indicated that the young differed significantly from both older groups who, in turn, did not differ from one another.

Table 7.3 shows performance on the tests of frontal lobe function. For WCST the mean number of categories correctly sorted and the total number of errors are shown. The number of categories correctly completed differed significantly with age, $F(2,57) = 5.24$, $p = 0.0082$, as did the number of errors $F(2,57) = 10.42$, $p = 0.0001$. For categories sorted there was only a significant difference between the young and OO groups whereas, for errors, there was a significant difference between the young and both the YO and OO groups. For category fluency the scores on the HOME and FOOD test were highly correlated (0.715) so a combined score was used in this analysis. There was a main effect of age, $F(2, 57) = 8.26$, $p < 0.001$, with the younger group differing significantly from both older groups who, in turn, did not differ from each other. In contrast, there was no age difference on the FAS test, $F < 1$. This latter finding replicates other studies showing similar effects (e.g. Parkin and Java 1999; Salthouse *et al.* 1996) and supports Miller's (1984) contention that FAS is best considered a measure of verbal IQ (crystallized intelligence).

Table 7.4 summarizes the scores on tasks of perceptual speed. The effect of age on DSST was significant, $F(2,57) = 58.76$, $p < 0.0001$, with significant differences between the young group and each of the older groups who, in turn,

Table 7.2 Mean recall and recognition data for each age group

	Recall					
	Young		Young–Old		Old–Old	
	Mean	SD	Mean	SD	Mean	SD
Recall	36.1	6.4	26.6	4.1	23.9	9.3
Recognition hits						
Sheet	31.4	6.0	23.6	7.5	21.7	7.3
Probe	30.4	5.4	23.0	9.5	24.6	7.6
Recognition false alarms						
Sheet	1.1	1.3	2.7	2.7	3.5	3.8
Probe	2.2	2.2	2.3	2.6	5.7	5.6
Recognition (H–FA)						
Sheet	30.0	8.7	20.9	7.6	18.3	6.8
Probe	28.3	6.3	20.8	9.5	19.0	6.3

Sheet = sheet recognition; Probe = Single Probe recognition.

Table 7.3   Mean performance on tests of frontal lobe function by Young, Young–Old, and Old–Old groups

	Young		Young–Old		Old–Old	
	Mean	SD	Mean	SD	Mean	SD
WCSTc	6.0	0.0	5.6	1.0	4.9	1.4
WCSTe	1.3	1.2	8.3	7.4	11.7	11.7
FAS	49.5	14.6	51.3	10.9	47.7	11.6
CF	58.5	11.6	49.3	8.3	44.9	12.2

WCSTc = Categories on Wisconsin Card Sort Test; WCSTe = Errors on Wisconsin Card Sort Test; FAS = Letter Fluency; CF = Category Fluency.

Table 7.4   Performance on DSST and DC

	Young		Young–Old		Old–Old	
	Mean	SD	Mean	SD	Mean	SD
DSST (number correct)	68.3	10.4	48.2	7.8	36.1	9.6
DSST (errors)	0.0	0.0	0.0	0.0	0.2	0.5
DC (time in seconds)	64.8	15.1	68.9	12.1	84.0	20.9
DC (errors)	0.4	0.6	1.3	1.3	0.7	1.1

DSST = Digit Symbol Substitution Test (WAIS-R); DC = Digit Cancellation of 4s.

did not differ. Errors were also scored, but no significant differences in age were shown, $F(2,57) = 2.11, p = 0.13$. For DC there was again a significant effect of age $F(2,57) = 7.17, p = 0.0017$ but the only significant difference was between the young and the OO groups.

Regression analyses

Stepwise regressions were performed separately using each memory measure in turn as a dependent variable and age, frontal measures (excluding FAS), AH4, DSST (number correct), and DC (time in seconds) as independent variables. For recall, DSST was the most powerful predictor of performance, accounting for 58% of the variance. No other variable entered significantly into the model although additional variance attributable to WCST (7%) just missed conventional significance. For Sheet recognition, DSST was again the most powerful predictor of performance accounting for 28% of the variance. No other variable entered significantly into the model although additional variance attributable to WCST (5%) just missed conventional significance. A similar picture emerged with Single Probe recognition with DSST accounting for 36% of the variance. No other variable entered significantly into the model although the additional variance attributable to WCST (6%) again just missed conventional significance.

A particular focus of interest was the relationship between AH4 and DSST in relation to the age-related variance shown in the three dependent measures. To examine this, further regressions were carried out. In all, six regressions were carried out, two for each dependent variable. For each of these pairs of regressions one involved entering AH4, followed by DSST, followed by age, and the other involved DSST, followed by AH4, followed by age. For recall, entering AH4 first accounted for 41% of the variance, DSST added a further 18%, and age added 1%. Entering DSST first accounted for 58% of the variance, with AH4 adding 1% and age zero. For Sheet recognition (H-FA), AH4 entered first accounted for 15% of the variance, DSST a further 13%, and age an additional 2%. DSST entered first accounted for 28% of the variance, AH4 added zero, and age added a further 2%. For Single Probe recognition, AH4 entered first accounted for 20% of the variance, DSST accounted for a further 16%, and age added zero. DSST entered first accounted for 36% of the variance, AH4 added zero, and age added 1%.

The above regressions indicate that the variance associated with AH4 and the memory measures is totally subsumed by the variance associated with DSST and those measures. This might suggest that speed is the common factor linking AH4 and DSST. To examine this, a further set of regressions were carried out. There were three regressions involving entering AH4 first, followed by DC, followed by DSST. For recall, AH4 entered first contributed 41%, DC added 4%, and DSST a further 14%. For Sheet recognition, AH4 contributed 15%, DC zero, and DSST 15%. For Single Probe recognition, AH4 contributed 20%, DC zero, and DSST 19%. These data indicate that the additional amount of variance accounted for by DSST, once AH4 has been partialled out, does not appear to be related to perceptual speed. If this had been so we would have expected DC to make a significant independent contribution to the variance estimates in the absence of DSST.

DISCUSSION

The present data showed reliable age-related declines in recall and two forms of recognition memory. Age-related deficits in AH4, DSST, and DC performance were also shown. Using step-wise regression it was demonstrated that, for all three memory measures, DSST was the best predictor of performance and that no other independent variable entered significantly into the regression model – although there was some suggestion that WCST accounted independently for a small amount of additional variance.

At first sight these data seem to provide overwhelming support for the perceptual speed account of age-related memory loss in that aging did not share any additional variance with memory measures once the variance associated with DSST had been taken out – findings which therefore replicate and extend research principally carried out by Salthouse and his associates. However, while we cannot question the robust nature of these effects we can raise important doubts about their exact interpretation.

In the introduction we noted some *a priori* concerns about the use of DSST as an unambiguous measure of simple processing speed. In particular we raised doubts concerning Salthouse's (1996) recent assumption that DSST is one of a group of tasks whose apparent demands are so simple that they do not load on other cognitive factors. Data from our experiment cast doubt on this assumption. Additional regression analyses showed that introducing DC did not take out any variance in addition to that explained by AH4. However, when DSST was then added, further variance was taken out. This suggests that the additional variance accounted for by DSST cannot readily be interpreted in terms of the task's ability to measure elementary processing speed that may not have been picked up by the more complex AH4 test – if this had been the case then we would have expected DC to account for more variance than it did when DSST was not present in the model.

WHY IS DSST PEFORMANCE SO STRONGLY ASSOCIATED WITH AGE-RELATED MEMORY LOSS?

Despite the present findings, proponents of the perceptual speed hypothesis might wish to argue that the DC task is not an appropriate instrument for measuring processing speed. An argument based on face validity, the same basis by which DSST is accepted as a measure of processing speed, does not, however, provide an answer. By any yardstick DC is a more straightforward measure of perceptual speed – it is less complex than DSST in that it involves no attention switching, minimal motor demands, and has little, if any, memory load. In short, this task very much reflects the 'criterion ... that the tasks used [to measure perceptual speed] ... should be relatively simple, such that most of the individual differences in performance are attributable to how quickly one can carry out the relevant operations rather than to *variations in the amount of knowledge or in other cognitive abilities*' (Salthouse 1996, pp. 406–7, emphasis added). An alternative explanation is that DC is a less reliable measure than DSST; that is, that the uncontrolled variance associated with performance of this task is sufficient to mask any covariance with age-related memory variance. This seems highly unlikely given a test/re-test value of 0.71 for DC.

Our view, as suggested in the introduction, is that DSST is not as simple a task as has been suggested and, on *prima facie* grounds, does not meet the above selection criterion for simplicity. It is difficult, for example, to accept that a task that correlates 0.65 with full scale IQ and 0.70 with performance IQ is not, in some significant way, linked to processes associated with other cognitive abilities. Indeed we noted earlier that there is a memory factor associated with DSST performance and that verbal coding ability, as reflected in sex differences, also appears to determine how well people perform on DSST.

An alternative view, therefore, is that the relationship between DSST and age-related memory variance reflects the former's association with cognitive processes linked to the determination of IQ. Our study did not include measures from the WAIS (with the exception of the DSST) but we did use a measure of fluid intelligence, AH4. If we look at the recall data, the dependent measure showing the strongest effects of age, we see that AH4, when entered first into a regression, explains 41% of age-related variance with DSST accounting for an additional 18% as a second independent variable. Reversing the order of the variables, however, leaves DSST explaining 58% of the variance and AH4 explaining *no* additional variance. This relation also holds for both forms of recognition: thus age-related memory variance associated with AH4 is totally subsumed by that explained by DSST.

One explanation for the dominance of DSST as a determinant of age-related memory variance might be that it presents a 'cleaner' measure of fluid intelligence than AH4. Thus, despite the latter's more complex demands, DSST may tap into processing operations fundamental to the efficiency of higher-level cognitive abilities. We think this idea is unlikely on intuitive grounds and it also fails to square with further data we have collected examining the influences of DSST and AH4 on age-related variance in cognitive performance. In a parallel study, Parkin and Java (1999) examined the influence of AH4 and DSST on the performance of three frontal lobe tasks, WCST, Category Fluency, and Alternate Uses. There were large effects of age on all three tasks. However, introduction of AH4 rendered all age effects non-significant whereas DSST, although attenuating age effects as well, did not make any contribution to age-related variance beyond that associated with AH4. This result is difficult to explain on the basis that DSST loads more readily on to fluid intelligence than AH4.

DSST AS A MEASURE OF WORKING MEMORY

Kiriasic *et al.* (1996) examined the effects of age on declarative learning (e.g., learning a menu, or learning a spatial arrangement) when the effects of 'processing speed' and 'working memory' were partialled out. The former involved tasks such as meaning verification and simple addition, while the latter involved more complex tasks such as evaluating the correctness of a series of mathematical operations and measuring the outcome. The results were clear cut in that 'working memory capability was the major mediator of age-related differences in declarative learning' (p. 658). The contribution of processing speed was small, and its role as a mediator of age effects was subsumed under the influence of working memory capability.

There are obvious difficulties in making direct comparisons between the present results and those reported by Kiriasic *et al.*(1996) because very different tasks were used. However, the general proposal is that an explanation of the present data couched within the framework of working memory warrants consideration. An immediate problem, however, is what does one mean by 'working memory'? Used broadly, the term refers to a hypothetical memory mechanism which enables current information to be combined with stored information in order to produce some kind of output. Various formulations of this idea have been considered, such as Baddeley's (1986) *structural* approach, in which working memory comprises a central executive linked to input-specific storage components, and *capacity-based* approaches in which the centre of interest is the amount of information the putative memory mechanism can handle at any one time (Daneman and Carpenter 1980).

The present data do not speak to the contrasting ideas described above. Nonetheless it is possible, in a more general sense, to consider whether the presence of processing operations akin to the nature of supposed working memory systems may explain the strong influence that DSST performance has on age-related memory variance. All concepts of working memory emphasize the interactions between coding, storage, and output operations. As a cognitive task DSST potentially loads on all three factors because, in our view, performance of DSST can be enhanced by an individual's ability to code the symbols effectively, learn the associations between the digits and the symbols, and match a new number to the appropriate association in order to specify an output. Following this output the system must be 'cleared' ready to deal with the next digit in the table. In these 'working memory' terms DSST is far more complex than DC because, in the case of DC, there are no novel coding demands, there is no potential for associative learning, and only one response is involved throughout the task. In the case of DC, the determinant of performance is very much the speed of visual scanning, whereas in DSST the speed of performance reflects a combination of factors.

Our working hypothesis, therefore, is that DSST exerts such a strong influence on age-related memory variance because it is principally a measure of working memory as opposed to a task that measures processing speed *per se*. Thus in memory tasks such as recall and recognition, working memory processes can reasonably be assumed to be involved in both the encoding and storage of information. Working memory, as defined, must also be part of the cognitive machinery that individuals use in the performance of fluid intelligence tests, hence the lesser but significant association of AH4 with age-related memory variance in the absence of DSST as a factor.

CONCLUSION

Our aim at the outset was to examine which of three competing generalist accounts of aging and memory provided the best explanation of why memory declines with age. These theories were frontal lobe dysfunction, fluid intelligence and processing speed. The first of these gained no support from the data in that regression analyses failed to show any significant contribution of frontal variables once the effects of DSST had been partialled out. The frontal theory of aging and memory has certainly had considerable prominence in recent years but various demonstrations of associations between memory tasks and frontal lobe test performance have not included parallel assessments of more general single factors. Our own recent work (Parkin and Java, 1999) has also undermined the viability of assuming that age deficits in frontal function exist beyond any deficits subsumed under the well-demonstrated decline in fluid intelligence shown by elderly people. In the absence of any evidence to the contrary, it appears that an account of age-related memory impairment based on a direct association with frontal lobe dysfunction is inconsistent with the present data.

The second explanation, of a relation between fluid intelligence and age-related memory variance, also fails to gain support. Although AH4 did remove age-related memory variance this effect was totally subsumed by the effects of DSST. The strong influence of DSST as a determinant of aging and memory replicates a large number of previous studies. However, we have argued that a finding such as this should not be interpreted as support for a processing speed account of aging. At several points we have noted that the processing speed account of aging has been supported by making *a priori* assumptions about the apparent simplicity of tasks. Thus DSST has featured prominently because its overt demands have been considered so simple that performance can only be constrained by the speed at which the individual operates. We have argued against this assumption on several grounds, including the demonstration that a processing task which meets the face-validity criteria of apparent simplicity does not attenuate age effects to any significant extent.

This contribution ends on an inconclusive note. Having pitched three generalist accounts of aging and memory directly against one another we find that none of them provides a satisfactory account. This has led us to consider the idea that some form of working memory concept might be a more useful basis for explaining age deficits in memory, as expressed in the interaction between these deficits and the attenuating influence of DSST performance. Moreover, we consider that the present account reveals the inherent problems in developing a psychological theory based on assumptions about the relationship between task and process. As for the idea of working memory itself, this has been evoked as a basis for understanding cognitive aging before (e.g., Hasher and Zacks 1988; see Salthouse, Chapter 2, this volume, for discussion) but it remains to be seen whether the concept can be specified in sufficient detail to deal with age-related changes in memory.

ACKNOWLEDGEMENT

The work reported in this chapter was supported by a grant from The Wellcome Trust.

REFERENCES

Bäckman, L., Hill, R. D., Herlitz, A., Fratiglioni, L., and Winblad, B. (1994). Predicting episodic memory performance in dementia: is severity all there is? *Psychology and Aging*, **9**, 520–7.

Bäckman, L. and Wahlin, A. (1995). Influences of item organizability and semantic retrieval cues on word recall in very old age. *Aging and Cognition*, **2**, 312–25.

Baddeley, A. D. (1986). *Working memory*. Oxford: Oxford University Press.

Brink, T. L., Yesavage, J. A., Lum, O., Heersema, P. H., Adey, M., and Rose, T. S. (1982). Geriatric depression scale. *Clinical Gerontologist*, **1**, 37–43.

Bryan, J. and Luszcz, M. A. (1996). Speed of information processing as a mediator between age and free recall performance. *Psychology and Aging*, **11**, 3–9.

Cockburn, J. and Smith, P. T. (1991). The relative influence of intelligence and age on everyday memory. *Journal of Gerontology: Psychological Sciences*, **46**, P31–6.

Craik, F. I. M., Morris, L. W., Morris, R. G., and Loewen, E. R. (1990). Relations between source amnesia and frontal functioning in older adults. *Psychology and Aging*, **5**, 148–51.

Curran, H. V. and Java, R. I. (1993). Memory and psychomotor effects of oxcarbazepine in healthy human volunteers. *European Journal of Clinical Pharmacology*, **44**, 529–33.

Daneman, M. and Carpenter, P.A. (1980). Individual differences in working memory and reading. *Journal of Verbal Learning and Verbal Behavior*, **19**, 450–66.

Dunlosky, J. and Salthouse, T. A. (1996). A decomposition of age-related differences in multitrial free recall. *Aging, Neuropsychology, and Cognition*, **3**, 2–14.

Erber, J.T. (1986). Age-related effects on spatial contiguity and interference on coding performance. *Journal of Gerontology*, **41**, 641–4.

Estes, W. K. (1974). Learning theory and intelligence. *American Psychologist*, **29**, 740–9.

Folstein, M. F., Folstein, S. E., and McHugh, P. R. (1989). 'Mini-mental state'. *Journal of Psychiatric Research*, **12**, 189–98.

Gardiner, J. M. (1988). Functional aspects of recollective experience. *Memory and Cognition*, **16**, 309–13.

Glisky, E. L., Polster, M. R., and Routhieaux, B. C.. (1995). Double dissociation between item and source memory. *Neuropsychology*, **9**, 229–35.

Hasher, L. and Zacks, R. T. (1988). Working memory, comprehension, and aging. A review and a new view. In G. H. Bower (ed.), *The psychology of learning and motivation*, (Vol. 22, pp. 193-225). New York: Academic Press.

Heim, A. (1968). The AH4 test. Windsor, UK: NFER-Nelson.

Holland, C. A. and Rabbitt, P. M. A. (1990). Autobiographical text recall in the elderly: an investigation of a processing resource deficit. *Quarterly Journal of Experimental Psychology*, **42A**, 441–70.

Kausler, D. H. (1994). *Learning and memory in normal aging*. San Diego: Academic Press.

Kiriasic, K. C., Allen, G. L., Dobson, S. H., and Binder, K. S. (1996). Aging, cognitive resources, and declarative learning. *Psychology and Aging*, **11**, 658–70.

Lezak, M. D. (1995). *Neuropsychological assessment* (3rd edn.). New York: Oxford University Press.

Light, L. L. (1991). Memory and aging: four hypotheses in search of data. *Annual Review of Psychology*, **42**, 333–76.

Miller, E. (1984). Verbal fluency as a function of a measure of verbal intelligence and in relation to different types of cerebral pathology. *British Journal of Psychology*, **23**, 53–7.

Nelson, H. E. (1976). A modified card sorting test sensitive to frontal lobe defects. *Cortex*, *12*, 313–24.

Nelson, H. E. (1985). *National adult reading test (NART): test manual*. Windsor, UK: NFER-Nelson.

Parkin, A. J. (1997*a*). Normal age-related memory loss and its relation to frontal lobe function. In P. M. A. Rabbitt (ed.), *Methodology of frontal and executive control* (pp. 177–90). Hove, UK: Psychology Press.

Parkin, A. J. (1997*b*). *Memory and amnesia: an introduction* (2nd edn.). Oxford: Blackwells.

Parkin, A. J. and Java, R. I. (1999). Deterioration of frontal lobe function in normal aging: influences of fluid intelligence versus perceptual speed. (Submitted.)

Parkin, A. J. and Lawrence, A. (1994). A dissociation in the relation between memory tasks and frontal lobe tests in the normal elderly. *Neuropsychologia, 32*, 1523–32.

Parkin, A. J. and Walter, B. M. (1991). Aging, short-term memory, and frontal dysfunction. *Psychobiology, 19*, 175–9.

Parkin, A. J. and Walter, B. M. (1992). Recollective experience, normal aging, and frontal dysfunction. *Psychology and Aging, 7*, 290–8.

Parkin, A. J., Walter, B. M., and Hunkin, N. M. (1995). Relationships between normal aging, frontal lobe function, and memory for temporal and spatial information. *Neuropsychology, 9*, 304–12.

Perfect, T. J. (1997). Memory aging as frontal lobe dysfunction. In M. A. Conway (ed.), *Cognitive models of memory* (pp. 315–40). Hove, UK: Psychology Press.

Raven, J. C. (1982). *Revised manual for raven's progressive matrices and vocabulary scale.* Windsor, UK: NFER-Nelson.

Raz, N., Gunning, F. M., Head, D., Dupuis, J. H., McQuain, J., Briggs, S. D., Loken, W. J., Thornton, A. E., and Acker, J. D. (1997). Selective aging of the human cerebral cortex observed *in vivo*: differential vulnerability of the prefrontal gray matter. *Cerebral Cortex, 7*, 268–82.

Russo, R. and Parkin, A. J. (1993). Age differences in implicit memory: more apparent than real. *Memory and Cognition, 21*, 73–80.

Salthouse, T. A. (1993*a*). Speed mediation of adult age differences in cognition. *Developmental Psychology, 29*, 722–38.

Salthouse, T. A. (1993*b*). Influence of working memory on adult age differences in matrix reasoning. *British Journal of Psychology, 84*, 171–200.

Salthouse, T. A. (1996). General and specific speed mediation of adult age differences in memory. *Journal of Gerontology: Psychological Sciences, 51B*, P30–42.

Salthouse, T. A., Kausler, D. H., and Saults, J. S. (1988). Investigation of student status, background variables, and the feasibility of standard tasks in cognitive aging research. *Psychology and Aging, 3*, 29–37.

Salthouse, T. A., Fristoe, N. A., and Rhee, S. Y. (1996). How localized are age related effects on neuropsychological measures? *Neuropsychology, 10*, 272–85.

Shuttleworth, A. B. and Bode, S. G. (1995). Taking account of age-related differences on digit symbol and incidental recall for diagnostic purposes. *Journal of Clinical and Experimental Neuropsychology, 17*, 439–48.

Snow, W. G. and Weinstock, J. (1990). Sex differences among non-brain damaged adults on the Wechsler Adult Intelligence Scales. *Journal of Clinical and Experimental Neuropsychology, 12*, 873–86.

Wechsler, D. (1981). *Wechsler Adult Intelligence Scale.* New York: Psychological Corporation.

Wechsler, D. (1987). *Wechsler Memory Scale–Revised.* San Antonio, CA: Psychological Corporation.

EIGHT

Theoretical approaches to language and aging

DEBORAH M. BURKE, DONALD G. MACKAY, AND LORI E. JAMES

INTRODUCTION

Research on cognition and aging has developed rapidly over the past several decades, moving beyond its early focus on psychometric intelligence tests to encompass new experimental paradigms and theoretical frameworks from cognitive psychology and the neurosciences. Although the accumulation of empirical findings has overshadowed the development of theories for explaining the patterns of cognitive change in old age, specification of theories of cognitive aging has undergone recent progress (e.g. Bowles 1994; Byrne 1998; Hasher and Zacks 1988; MacKay and Burke 1990; Myerson *et al.* 1990; Salthouse 1996). In this chapter, we describe a detailed theory of cognitive aging, the Transmission Deficit hypothesis, comparing it to other theories and demonstrating its account of evidence relating aging and language. We start with evidence indicating that effects of aging on language comprehension versus production are asymmetric, a phenomenon that sets a boundary condition for theories of cognitive aging. Although theories of cognitive aging have in general focused on cognitive decrements, these asymmetries indicate that they must also account for domains of performance that are preserved in old age, such as language comprehension. We compare two classes of cognitive aging theories for explaining asymmetric effects of aging on language: information-universal and information-specific theories. Then we provide a detailed account within the Transmission Deficit model of how aging impacts three aspects of language production: tip-of-the-tongue experiences (TOTs), proper name recall, and retrieval of orthographic knowledge.

PATTERNS OF LANGUAGE PERFORMANCE IN NORMAL AGING

One empirical generalization that emerged from early research on cognitive aging was that language processing was spared in old age, especially when compared to the decline in 'fluid' intellectual abilities, such as remembering new information (e.g. Botwinick 1984). The last 20 years of research on aging and language, however, have revealed a more complex pattern, with asymmetric aging effects on input versus output processes. The input side of language includes perception of the letters and speech sounds that make up words, and retrieval of semantic and syntactic information about words and sentences. These input-side processes are frequently referred to as 'language comprehension', and they remain remarkably stable in old age, independent of age-linked declines in sensory abilities (Madden 1988) and memory for new information (Kemper 1992b; Light and Burke 1988; Tun and Wingfield 1993). Indeed, tasks highlighting comprehension processes, such as general knowledge and vocabulary tests, provided much of the data for earlier conclusions about age constancy in language processes. The output side of language involves retrieval of phonological and orthographic components of words and their production in speaking or writing. These output-side processes, commonly termed 'language production', do show age-related performance declines. In the next sections we present empirical evidence for these asymmetric effects of aging on language processes.

Language comprehension and aging

Aging has little effect on the representation of semantic knowledge as revealed, for example, by word associations (e.g. Burke and Peters 1986), script generation (e.g. Light and Anderson 1983) and the structure of taxonomic categories (Howard 1980; Mueller *et al.* 1980). Because comprehension involves mapping language onto existing knowledge structures, age constancy in the nature of these structures is important for maintaining language comprehension in old age. There is no age decrement in semantic processes in comprehension as measured via on-line techniques. Probably the most popular of these on-line measures is the semantic priming effect, the reduction in the time required to identify a target word, say, *TEACHER*, when it follows a semantically related word, for example *STUDENT*, rather than a semantically unrelated word, for example *GARDEN*. Even when participants cannot develop expectancies concerning related words or when the interval between prime and target is too brief for attentional effects, semantic priming effects can be attributed to automatic activation of meaning during perception of the prime word, and spread of excitation (priming) to semantic representations of related words, making them easier to activate. Thus, perception of *STUDENT* primes semantically related information, speeding recognition of *TEACHER*; and such semantic priming effects are at least as large in older as in young adults (e.g. Balota *et al.* 1992; Burke *et al.* 1987; see meta-analyses by Laver and Burke 1993 and Myerson *et al.* 1992). The same is true of mediated semantic priming effects, which are measured for prime words that are related to target words only through another *unpresented* word that is related to both prime and target, e.g. prime word: *LION* (related to mediating word: *TIGER*), target: *STRIPES*. For both young and older adults, recognition of *STRIPES* is faster following *LION*, rather than a completely unrelated word, an effect attributed to priming triggered by activation of *LION* and transmitted through *TIGER* to *STRIPES* (Bennett and McEvoy 1999). These mediated priming effects indicate how far priming spreads in semantic networks and provide further evidence for age constancy in transmission of semantic priming within a network.

Semantic priming effects also provide a measure of semantic processing during silent reading of sentences: participants identify the target word *BOOKS* more quickly and accurately in a common context (e.g. *The accountant balanced the BOOKS*) than in an uncommon context (e.g. *The train went over the BOOKS*; (see Madden 1988), and facilitation from common contexts is at least as large for older as for young adults (Burke and Yee 1984; Cohen and Faulkner 1983; Nebes *et al.* 1986; Stine and Wingfield 1994; Wingfield *et al.* 1994). There is also no age decrement in drawing correct inferences during reading or in specifying particular word meanings implied by the context (Burke and Harrold 1988; Burke and Yee 1984; Hamm and Hasher 1992; Light 1991; Light *et al.* 1991), except when working memory deficits intervene (e.g. Light and Capps 1986).

In a meta-analysis of age effects on direct and indirect measures of memory, Light *et al.* (Chapter 9, this volume) found that latency measures of repetition priming effects were age invariant while accuracy measures showed age-related declines in repetition priming effects. This disparity is theoretically interesting because general slowing models of cognitive aging predict larger repetition priming effects for older adults using latency measures because of older adults' longer overall latencies; if older adults are less responsive to repetition, as suggested by their smaller repetition effects on indirect measures involving accuracy, than on indirect measures involving latency, their increased latencies due to general slowing may compensate for smaller repetition effects so that the change in latency produced by repetition (priming effect) may appear to be age invariant.

This asymmetry in age effects for latency and accuracy measures does not hold for semantic priming effects. An informal comparison of effects in semantic priming studies showed that these effects were at least as large for old as for young adults, both with accuracy measures (e.g. Cohen and Faulkner 1983; Hutchinson 1989; Stine and Wingfield 1994; Wingfield *et al.* 1994; Wingfield *et al.* 1991) and latency measures (for meta-analysis, see Laver and Burke 1993). Thus repetition priming effects and semantic priming effects appear to be differently affected by age.

Studies using on-line techniques rule out a major confound inherent in off-line tasks that measure comprehension processes by examining what people remember about the meaning of sentences or paragraphs presented earlier. Age differences invariably appear in such off-line tasks (e.g. Hamm and Hasher 1992; Hartley 1988; Hartman and Hasher 1991), but have less to do with initial comprehension than with memory for the comprehended information (see, e.g., Burke 1997; Stine *et al.* 1996). Results of off-line studies seem to reflect an age-related deficit in remembering the link between comprehended information and its source or context. When episodic memory is factored out, evidence for age constancy in language comprehension and in the structure and retrievability of general knowledge is both strong and consistent (Burke 1997; Kemper 1992*b*; Light 1991; MacKay and Abrams 1996; MacKay and Burke 1990; Tun and Wingfield 1993).

Language production and aging

In contrast to the age constancy in comprehending word meaning, extensive experimental research shows age-related declines in retrieving a word corresponding to a meaning or a picture, and so do older adults' self reports. Older adults rated word finding failures and TOTs as cognitive problems that are both most severe and most affected by aging (Rabbitt *et al.* 1995; Ryan *et al.* 1994; Sunderland *et al.* 1986). Older adults rated retrieval failures for proper names as especially common (Cohen and Faulkner 1984; Martin 1986; Ryan 1992) and the most annoying, embarrassing, and irritating of their memory problems (Lovelace and Twohig 1990).

Older adults' performance in language production experiments confirms their self reports. Compared to young adults, older adults are slower and less accurate in producing names for definitions or pictures (e.g. Au *et al.* 1995; Bowles and Poon 1985; Nicholas *et al.* 1985; see Goulet *et al.* 1994 for a review). They also produce more ambiguous references and pronouns in their speech, apparently because of an inability to retrieve the appropriate nouns (e.g. Cooper 1990; Heller and Dobbs 1993; but see Glosser and Deser 1992). Speech disfluencies such as filled pauses and hesitations increase with age and may likewise reflect word retrieval difficulties (Cooper 1990; Kemper 1992*a*). Finally, TOT states increase with aging, one of the most dramatic instances of word finding difficulty in which a person is unable to produce a word although absolutely certain that they know it. Both naturally occurring (Burke *et al.* 1991) and experimentally induced TOTs (Brown and Nix 1996; Burke et al. 1991; James and Burke 1998; Maylor 1990*b*; Rastle and Burke 1996) increase with aging. As we discuss in detail below, word retrieval failures in young and especially older adults appear to reflect declines in access to phonological representations.

Evidence for age-linked declines in language production has come almost exclusively from studies of word retrieval. Recently, however, MacKay and Abrams (1998; MacKay *et al.* 1999) reported some important new age-related production deficits that were unanticipated in previous experimental studies and self report questionnaires: older adults made certain types of spelling errors[1] more often than young adults in written production, a sub-lexical retrieval deficit involving orthographic units. This decline occurred despite age equivalence in the ability to detect spelling errors and despite the higher vocabulary and education levels of older adults.

1 In particular, older adults more so than young adults misspelled irregularly-spelled letter combinations by regularizing them, for example, *calendar* → *calender*, and only the oldest older adults (over age 73) misspelled regularly-spelled combinations more often than young adults, for example *calendar* → *kalendar*.

The phonological/orthographic retrieval problem in old age is not due to deficits in formulating the idea to be expressed, but rather appears to reflect an inability to map a well defined idea or lexical concept onto its phonological and orthographic forms. Thus, unlike comprehension of word meaning, which seems to be well preserved in old age, retrieval at phonological and orthographic levels of representation declines with aging. This asymmetric pattern of aging effects for comprehension versus production provides fertile testing ground for theoretical accounts of cognitive aging, as we discuss next.

THEORIES OF COGNITIVE AGING

Comprehensive theories that can be applied to language and aging fall into two categories: information-universal and information-specific. In information-universal theories, the mechanism underlying cognitive aging is independent of the type or structure of the information being processed, unlike information-specific theories, where the type or structure of language units plays an important role in aging effects.

Information-universal theories

General slowing theories postulate aging effects that are independent of the type or structure of information being processed and represent the oldest and most extensively researched of the information-universal theories. Under general slowing theories, the speed of executing cognitive operations decreases with aging regardless of the task or the mental operations involved in the task (e.g. Birren 1965; Cerella *et al.* 1980; Myerson *et al.* 1990; Salthouse 1985, 1996). A variant of this general slowing assumption holds that age-related slowing remains constant across all tasks within a 'domain', but not across different task domains, for example, lexical versus spatial tasks (e.g. Cerella 1985; Lima *et al.* 1991).

General slowing assumptions are compatible with two types of empirical generalization. One is that across the lifespan, perceptual–motor reaction times correlate highly with errors in performance on a broad range of tasks involving new learning or speeded performance, for example, working memory, free recall, and verbal fluency tasks (e.g. Salthouse 1985). The second compatible generalization is that older adults are slower on many cognitive tasks regardless of the psychomotor requirements of the task. Indeed, some researchers have used Brinley plot analyses to argue for a universal general slowing factor. When older adults' mean latency is plotted as a function of young adults' mean latency in the same condition, regression analyses have revealed a consistent mathematical relationship between young and older adults' response latency for a variety of tasks (e.g. Cerella 1990; Lima *et al.* 1991; Myerson *et al.* 1992).

Salthouse (1996) proposed two mechanisms through which general slowing may cause errors and disrupt performance. First, some cognitive operations may be executed too slowly for successful completion in the available time, causing an increase in errors. Second, information from different sources may become available to a central processor so slowly that the earlier information has decayed or is no longer active by the time the later information arrives. As a result, cognitive operations that depend on the simultaneous availability of both sources of information can no longer be executed. This second mechanism would cause an age-linked increase in errors even for tasks without time constraints.

This and other general slowing theories must address two interrelated issues. One is that age-related slowing is universal in these theories, whereas deficits in language performance are not. General slowing theories require a principled basis for explaining the asymmetric effects of aging on the input vs output side of language, for example, the preserved detection of spelling errors and impaired production of correct spelling (MacKay *et al.* 1999), or the preserved interpretation of word meaning and impaired production of words (Burke *et al.* 1991; although see Salthouse, Chapter 2, this volume, for a general slowing account of asymmetric age effects). Explaining why some aspects of language remain intact in old age, even though older adults perform these tasks more slowly than young adults, provides a related challenge for general slowing theories. For example, even though older adults require more time to produce word associations than young adults, word association responses are identical in frequency and type across age (Burke and Peters 1986), an asymmetry that is unpredicted by general slowing theories.

The second issue that general slowing theories must address is methodological in nature and concerns the almost exclusive reliance on Brinley plots and regression analyses. With older adults' latency plotted as a function of young adults', several studies have reported a consistent linear function with a slope greater than 1.0 (e.g. Cerella *et al.* 1980; Lima *et al.* 1991; Madden 1989). However, this consistency in slope across conditions is in part a consequence of the insensitivity of regression techniques to variation across conditions (Fisher *et al.* 1995; Fisk and Fisher 1994; Perfect 1994). Moreover, conclusions about general slowing based on such analyses assume isomorphism between the processes that young and older adults use to perform the task, an assumption that has proven invalid (see Fisher *et al.* 1995; Rogers and Fisk 1991; Stine 1995). Finally, a growing number of Brinley-plot *exceptions* to a slowing factor greater than 1.0 require explanation: meta-analytic studies have reported old:young ratios approximating 1.0 for reading time (Stine 1995), for implicit memory tasks (see Light *et al.*, Chapter 9, this volume), and for semantic priming effects (Laver and Burke 1993; see also Fisk and Rogers 1991). Thus, the slowing factor exhibits considerable variation, even within a single domain such as verbal performance.

The *inhibition deficit* hypothesis is a rather different type of information-universal theory which assumes that aging weakens inhibitory processes associated with task-irrelevant information. That is, older adults are assumed to activate more irrelevant information than young adults and suppress less irrelevant information once it is activated, regardless of the type or structure of the irrelevant information. Under this hypothesis, aging impairs inhibition in all cognitive systems, including attention, memory, and language, and this disrupts use of relevant information (Hasher and Zacks 1988; Zacks and Hasher 1994, 1997). Studies showing greater behavioural interference for older than young adults in a variety of tasks have been cited as evidence for such age-related inhibitory deficits. For example, relative to young adults, older adults show more interference from the inconsistent colour baseword in the Stroop colour naming task (e.g. Spieler *et al.* 1996), and from superimposed, distracting words when reading sentences (Connelly *et al.* 1991) or processing pictures (Bowles 1994; Duchek *et al.* 1995).

However, inhibition has proven elusive as a theoretical concept because behaviourally defined inhibition (negative priming and Stroop interference effects) does not necessarily entail theoretical inhibition and alternative, non-inhibitory accounts have been offered for behavioural inhibition effects (e.g. Burke 1997; Dywan and Murphy 1996; Hartman 1995; Kieley and Hartley 1997; Wheeldon and Monsell 1994). Even for behaviourally defined inhibition, age differences have been consistently obtained neither for Stroop interference (Verhaeghen, Chapter 3, this volume) nor negative priming effects (e.g. McDowd 1997), and neither negative priming nor Stroop interference effects correlate well with other tasks showing age differences hypothesized to depend on inhibition (e.g. Christidis and Burke 1998; Kramer *et al.* 1994; Shilling and Rabbitt 1998; but see Kwong See and Ryan 1995).

Because of its information-universal nature, the inhibition deficit hypothesis is also incapable of explaining asymmetric effects of aging on input versus output processes. If, as Hasher and Zacks (1988) assume, inhibition is an essential component of both the comprehension and production of language, age decrements should occur for both. Because the incompatibility of inhibition deficit theory with age constancy in comprehension processes has been well documented (Burke 1997), we will focus here on an aspect of language production that does show age changes, and has been claimed to support the inhibition deficit hypothesis. This aspect is off-topic speech.

Verbosity, or the production of prolonged and redundant speech that is irrelevant to the current topic, increases with aging according to Arbuckle and Gold (1993) and Gold *et al.* (1988). The explanation offered by the inhibition deficit hypothesis is that older adults' reduced ability to inhibit irrelevant information makes it difficult or impossible for them to suppress thoughts that digress from the current speech topic, resulting in production of extraneous personal observations and unrelated information in their speech (Arbuckle and Gold 1993; Zacks and Hasher 1994). Two aspects of the empirical findings, however, challenge the inhibitory deficit explanation. First, age differences in off-topic speech are obtained in some contexts, for example, when describing autobiographical information (Arbuckle and Gold 1993; James *et al.* 1998) but not in others, for example when describing pictures (Cooper 1990; James *et al.* 1998) or when describing a vacation (Gould and Dixon 1993). Inasmuch as inhibitory deficits are information-universal, they should influence all speech and it is unclear how they can explain why older adults wander off-topic for some topics but not others.

A second problematic finding for the inhibition deficit hypothesis is that evaluative ratings are more favourable for older adults' than young adults' speech (e.g. James *et al.* 1998; Kemper *et al.* 1990). In James *et al.*, young and older raters read transcribed descriptions of autobiographical events and rated older adults' descriptions more positively than young adults', even though older adults strayed off topic more frequently than young adults. When the older speakers were divided into high- and low-verbosity groups based on the amount of off-topic speech they generated, ratings of the descriptions were more favourable for the high- than low-verbosity group. Thus, increased off-topic information appears to increase, not decrease, the communicative value of older adults' speech. This is paradoxical under the inhibition deficit model which claims that off-topic speech reflects a cognitive impairment. Deepening the paradox, older adults' off-topic speech also failed to impair performance on a problem solving task that required effective communication (Arbuckle *et al.*1998).

To explain these off-topic speech results, the inhibition deficit hypothesis must either modify its system-wide inhibitory decrement assumption, or specify additional mechanisms to account for the topic specificity and high communicative value of older adults' off-topic speech. Moreover, this new account must compete for parsimony with the hypothesis that young and older adults adopt different communicative goals when speaking (James *et al.* 1998). Under this pragmatic change hypothesis, older adults adopt the goal in autobiographical contexts of emphasizing the significance of their life experiences rather than the usual goal of imparting information concisely. This assumed age-related change in communicative goals explains both the more favourable evaluative ratings and the topic specificity of off-topic speech of older adults, and the pragmatic change hypothesis provides a simpler and more coherent account of age differences in off-topic speech than cognitive impairment accounts.

In sum, one of the challenges for future generations of information-universal theories is to explain why some language functions decline in old age but not others. As Salthouse (1996; Chapter 2, this volume) suggested, specific, local mechanisms, in addition to a general mechanism, may underlie the pattern of spared and impaired abilities in old age.

Information-specific theories

As a class, information-specific theories deal well with asymmetries in aging effects. However, some information-specific theories originated as descriptions of just such effects. For example, *Region-specific neural aging* hypotheses link the amount of age-related neurobiological change in specific areas of the brain to patterns of spared and impaired cognitive functions (e.g. Madden and Hoffman 1997; Moscovitch and Winocur 1992; Raz *et al.* 1993; West 1996). Although most region-specific neural aging hypotheses have focused on memory rather than language functions, the hypothesis that age-related increases in verbosity are linked to age-related, frontal lobe decrements (Arbuckle and Gold 1993; West 1996) is an exception.

The *transmission deficit* hypothesis is more general in nature, for example providing an account of age-linked slowing data (see MacKay and Burke 1990), and represents a quite different approach to developing an information-specific theory. Under the transmission deficit hypothesis, language perception and production depend on how fast and how much priming can be transmitted across the connections linking representational units, called nodes, in the language-memory system. Priming is a form of subthreshold excitation that prepares a node for activation, the basis for retrieving the information represented by the node (MacKay 1982, 1987). Because a node is selected for activation only if its priming level reaches a critical difference above that of other nodes in the same domain, the rate and amount of priming transmitted across connections between nodes is an important determinant of what information in memory becomes available. The rate of priming transmission depends on the strength of connections among nodes: connections become stronger with use (activation), and especially recent use, and weaken over time as a result of disuse. Aging is also postulated to weaken connection strength. Transmission deficits result when relevant connections become especially weak, but the functional effect of transmission deficits depends on the processes and architectures of specific memory systems in node structure theory (NST), which provides the framework for the transmission deficit hypothesis. This property enables the theory to account in a noncircular manner for the asymmetric effects of aging on language comprehension versus production (e.g. Burke *et al.* 1991; MacKay and Abrams 1996, 1998; MacKay and Burke 1990). By the same token, understanding this account requires a detailed look at the processes and architecture underlying language-memory systems in NST.

Like other current interactive activation models of language (e.g. Dell 1986; Dell *et al.* 1997; Levelt *et al.* 1991), NST postulates a vast network of interconnected nodes. Nodes are organized into a *semantic system* which represents the meanings of words and propositions, a *phonological system* which represents speech sounds and syllables, and an *orthographic system* which represents letters and other orthographic units. The hierarchical organization of nodes in NST clarifies differences between processes underlying the production versus comprehension of words (MacKay 1987). By way of illustration, consider the specific nodes in semantic, phonological, and orthographic systems in Fig. 8.1 for comprehending and producing a familiar word such as *star*. In comprehension, hearing or reading *star* transmits bottom-up priming via many orthographic and/or phonological nodes whose connections all converge onto a single lexical node (see Fig. 8.1). This convergence enables activation of the lexical node, which transmits priming to interconnected semantic nodes whose activation constitutes retrieval of word meaning. The converging characteristic of bottom-up connections for perception, for example, from phonological nodes to a lexical node, can offset a transmission deficit in any one connection. Moreover, transmission of priming within the semantic system is likewise aided by the many connections that link related concepts and produce convergent or summating priming at semantic nodes (Laver and Burke 1993). For example, although omitted from Fig. 8.1, many semantic propositions linked to *star* also link to each other (a theoretical definition of semantic similarity or overlap). A higher level propositional node representing the information that celestial bodies are a topic in astronomy would link *celestial bodies* to *astronomy* (a 'semantically similar' concept). Priming from *astronomy* to *celestial bodies* could therefore offset a deficit in transmission of priming from *star* to *celestial bodies*. More generally, the interconnected nature of semantic representations will offset a transmission deficit in any one connection within the semantic system.

In production, the idea or picture of a star, for example, activates semantic nodes which transmit priming top-down to the lexical node for *star*, and activating this lexical node transmits top-down priming simultaneously and divergingly to many phonological nodes (see Fig. 8.1). Retrieval of a word's phonology is complete only when nodes at the lowest level (i.e., phonological features) have been primed and then activated. These top-down connections for producing phonology are always one-to-one and this diverging characteristic of top-down connections increases their vulnerability to transmission deficits. Each phonological node must receive sufficient priming from its single top-down connection in order to become activated, without augmented priming from other phonological nodes which lack the interconnections of semantic nodes: a transmission deficit in a single top-down connection will prevent activation of that node. However, the converging characteristic of bottom-up connections for perception can offset a transmission deficit in any one connection. Receiving summated priming from many phonological connections, the appropriate lexical node will achieve sufficient priming in order to become activated despite a transmission deficit in any one connection. The asymmetry in the structure of bottom-up and top-down processes in NST means that the transmission deficit hypothesis predicts small or no aging effects for language comprehension tasks, but large age-linked deficits for production tasks, including word retrieval and the production of spelling.

Semantic priming effects further illustrate how the structure of connections within a memory system determines whether age-linked transmission deficits become manifest in behaviour. For example, the lexical nodes for *star* and *planet* are indirectly connected via shared semantic proposition nodes, for example, *is a celestial body*, *studied in astronomy*. Because of these shared links, activating the concept *star* in the semantic priming paradigm will prime the concept *planet*, enabling faster lexical decision times for this semantically

SEMANTIC SYSTEM

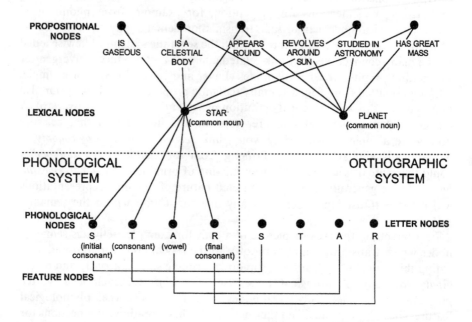

Fig. 8.1 Example memory representation of semantic, phonological, and orthographic information linked to the word *star*. Some semantic connections between *star* and *planet* are shown. Many nodes necessary for perceiving or producing these words have been omitted to simplify the figure.

related word. Why are there no age-related declines in semantic priming effects? First, under NST, priming summates over the multiple connections between highly related concepts like *star* and *planet*, and summation of priming reduces the effect of a transmission deficit in any single connection. Second, semantically related concepts such as *star* and *planet* are likely to have more indirect links for older than young adults because over the course of their (longer) lifetimes, older adults have acquired more general knowledge in the form of propositions such as, say, *stars and planets seem to move with the seasons*, and *stars affect the temperature of planets*. As a result of this enriched semantic network, more connections will link semantically related concepts in the memory systems of older than young adults. Priming will therefore converge across these additional, parallel connections and summate to a greater extent for older than young adults. As a result, semantic priming effects will be at least as large for older adults relative to young adults (see Laver and Burke 1993).

Summary

All of the theories reviewed above are in the early stages of development. All can explain some aspects of available data on language performance and aging, but all are in need of further development and tests that focus not on confirming results, but on points of theoretical weakness. These points of weakness are perhaps clearest in the case of information-universal theories which have concentrated on cognitive decline in old age and therefore require additional mechanisms to account for the pattern of preserved cognitive functions, for example, in language comprehension but not language production. Such differential aging patterns come built into information-specific theories such as the transmission deficit hypothesis, but it is too soon to tell how this theory will fare with direct empirical tests.

In the next sections, we describe in greater detail the transmission deficit account of age deficits in language production. According to this theory, production deficits occur when nodes that represent information essential to production fail to activate because of weak connections that impair transmission of priming. Such transmission deficits are due to aging, frequency, and recency of use, but whether or not they become manifest depends on the architecture of connections within phonological and orthographic systems. We demonstrate how this account applies to age differences in three domains of language production: the tip-of-the-tongue experience, proper name retrieval, and spelling or orthographic retrieval.

TRANSMISSION DEFICITS AND TIP-OF-THE-TONGUE STATES

The TOT experience represents a pure phonological retrieval deficit. Because of this, it has provided an important source of information for developing models of speech production, for example by indicating that retrieval of lexical and semantic information precedes retrieval of phonological information in speech production (e.g. Burke *et al.* 1991; Dell 1986; Levelt 1989; MacKay 1987; Miozzo and Caramazza 1997). TOTs are equally important for developing models of cognitive aging, for example by indicating age deficits in phonological but not semantic retrieval processes.

The transmission deficit hypothesis postulates that TOTs reflect a deficit in the transmission of priming to phonological nodes representing the target word (Burke *et al.* 1991; MacKay and Burke 1990; Rastle and Burke 1996). A TOT occurs when a lexical node becomes activated via top-down priming, giving access to semantic information about the target word, but some of its phonological information remains inaccessible because transmission deficits weaken connections to its phonological nodes, preventing activation. Rarely and not-recently activated nodes have weakened connections, explaining why TOT targets tend to be low frequency words that have not been recently used or encountered (Burke *et al.* 1991; Cohen and Faulkner 1986; Harley and Bown 1998; Rastle and Burke 1996; see Brown 1991, for a review). Why are phonological nodes more susceptible to transmission deficits than semantic or lexical nodes? In general, phonological nodes are hierarchically linked via only a single top-down connection and so receive a single source of priming without the possibility of summation across multiple connections, as typically occurs within the semantic system.

The transmission deficit hypothesis also explains why partial phonological information and related alternate words come to mind during the majority of TOT experiences (Brown 1991). Only some of the phonological nodes for producing the target word may be suffering a transmission deficit due to aging or infrequent and non-recent use of the target word. Some subset of the remaining phonological nodes may in fact become activated, providing a basis for partial phonological recall. Persistent alternates also arise when some (but not all) phonological nodes suffer transmission deficits. For example, in a study of naturally occurring TOTs, the persistent alternate *charity* was repeatedly retrieved instead of the TOT target *chastity*, and under the model this was because some of the phonological nodes for *chastity* received sufficient priming for activation (e.g. the initial ch), transmitting bottom-up priming to the lexical node for *charity* (Burke *et al.* 1991). Priming was sufficient for *charity* to be selected for activation and awareness because *charity* was not suffering transmission deficits. Consistent with this, alternate words tend to share phonology with the TOT targets (Brown and McNeill 1966; Burke *et al.* 1991).

The transmission deficit hypothesis predicts the finding that older adults experience more TOT states than young adults because aging reduces connection strength, thereby increasing the probability of transmission deficits which, in the phonological system, are likely to cause retrieval failure. Reduced transmission of phonological priming also predicts that older adults will access less phonological information about the target and fewer persistent alternates, as has been repeatedly observed (Burke *et al.* 1991; Cohen and Faulkner 1986; Maylor 1990*a*).

An alternative account of TOTs is that persistent alternates cause the TOT by 'blocking' retrieval of the target word. Despite its popularity, this inhibition hypothesis has little empirical support. Jones (1989; Jones and Langford 1987; see also Maylor 1990*a*) reported that TOTs increased with prior presentation of words phonologically related to the target word, and argued that this increase simulated the blocking effect of persistent alternates. However, Perfect and Hanley (1992) and Meyer and Bock (1992) demonstrated that Jones' effect reflected a failure to counterbalance materials and that prior presentation of phonologically related words increased correct responding, a finding consistent with the transmission deficit account, but not an inhibition account of TOT states (James and Burke 1998; Meyer and Bock 1992).

At least one effect of aging on TOTs is also inconsistent with blocking accounts. Age-related inhibitory deficits should *reduce* the inhibitory effect of an alternate word on the target, so that older adults should suffer *fewer* TOTs than young adults, but the opposite occurs. Perhaps, however, inhibition is unidirectional, occurring only for the irrelevant information that comes to mind during an attempt to retrieve a target word, so that older adults' decreased ability to suppress irrelevant associations or competing words would increase interference with target retrieval, thereby causing the observed age-linked increase in TOTs (Hartman and Hasher 1991; Hasher and Zacks 1988; Zacks and Hasher 1994). This being the case, however, older adults should report more alternate words that come to mind persistently during a TOT than young adults, but in fact they report fewer alternate words and less partial phonological information (Burke *et al.* 1991; Cohen and Faulkner 1986; Maylor 1990*a*). Contrary to this inhibition deficit account of the age-related increase in TOTs, older adults do not report that their minds teem with alternate words, but that their minds simply go blank (Burke *et al.* 1991; Cohen and Faulkner 1986). Nevertheless, the blocking model of TOTs has retained its popularity (Brown 1991), perhaps a tribute to the power of the subjectively experienced correlation between TOTs and alternate words.

Phonological priming effects on TOTs in young and older adults

What is the evidence that TOTs reflect phonological but not semantic deficits? The phenomenology of TOTs is that the meaning and syntactic category of the target word is available, but not the phonological word form (e.g. Brown 1991). This has been corroborated in the laboratory where, for example, participants report alternate words in the same syntactic category as the target with greater than chance probability (Burke *et al.* 1991), and speakers of Italian can accurately report the grammatical gender for an unavailable TOT target (Miozzo and Caramazza 1997). The effectiveness of different types of cues to a TOT word also attests to the availability of semantic information in TOT states: resolution of TOTs is unaffected by semantic cues such as an alternative photograph of a person but is aided by phonological cues such as the initial letter(s) of the target word (e.g. Brennen *et al.* 1990), a phonologically related word, or a sound pattern with the same number of 'syllabic peaks' and stress pattern as the target (Kozlowski 1977; Meyer and Bock 1992).

The transmission deficit model makes clear predictions on how to eliminate transmission deficits in the phonological system and thus improve word retrieval, and we tested these predictions in a series of experiments. Under NST, recent activation strengthens the connections among nodes, increasing the amount of priming transmitted across the connections and reducing transmission deficits which cause TOTs. Therefore, prior processing of phonological segments of a word should increase the word's retrievability and decrease the likelihood of suffering a TOT for that word. These priming effects occur implicitly under the model, and do not require awareness of the prime–target relation. In a repetition priming paradigm, Rastle and Burke (1996) manipulated the type of processing involved in a prior processing task with target words that were the answers to subsequent general knowledge questions. Prior processing of target phonemes reduced TOTs and increased correct recall, and additional semantic processing had no effect on this priming effect. This supports the hypothesis that frequency and recency of target processing influence the likelihood of TOTs, and that the retrieval failure occurs at the phonological level, although a lexical level effect can also be expected with full repetition of the target word.

James and Burke (1998) eliminated lexical level effects by presenting words in the prior processing task (rating 'pronunciation difficulty') that were phonologically similar, but not identical to, the target. When participants first processed five words that were phonologically similar to the target (e.g. *eucalyptus*, *infidelity*, and *pessimism* for the subsequently presented target, *euphemism*), interspersed among five unrelated words to prevent attempts to use the prime words as cues to the target in an explicit conscious search, TOTs decreased relative to when all ten words were phonologically unrelated to the target. These priming effects clearly occurred at a phonological rather than lexical level because primes and targets were always different words. A second experiment demonstrated effects of processing phonologically related words *following* occurrence of a TOT. The TOT-inducing questions were presented first, and when participants reported a TOT, they rated pronunciation difficulty of ten words that were either all unrelated to the target or half unrelated and half phonologically related. Then, when the TOT question was presented again, the probability of a correct answer, that is, retrieval of the TOT target, increased after processing related compared to unrelated words. These effects occurred without awareness of prime–target relatedness because the participants could not identify which prime words were related to the target and which were not.

These findings suggest a solution to the puzzle of how TOT targets come 'spontaneously' to mind in everyday life when a person is no longer actively trying to resolve a TOT: phonologically similar words occurring inadvertently in the environment (e.g. on TV, radio, or in conversation or internal speech) could activate phonological components of the target that were previously unavailable because of transmission deficits. The TOT target then 'pops up', a resolution that will be experienced as spontaneous because there is no awareness of the relationship between the prime word and TOT target.

Neither repetition priming nor phonological priming produced larger effects for older than young adults in the just discussed paradigms. This is consistent with the transmission deficit hypothesis if the transmission deficits that precipitate TOTs are comparable in severity for young and older adults, except that older adults simply suffer more transmission deficits, yielding more frequent TOTs. Moreover, if older adults tend to have multiple transmission deficits underlying the TOT for a single word, this would explain why older adults report less partial information when in the TOT state.

Interestingly, however, an age-by-prime condition interaction emerges with a homophone priming technique (Burke *et al.* 1998). Spoken homophones, for example *burr* and *Burr*, share identical phonological nodes but their lexical and semantic representations differ (Burke *et al.* 1998; Valentine *et al.* 1995). Figure 8.2 illustrates aspects of the representation of the proper name and common noun homophone *burr*. The lexical nodes for *burr* (common noun) and *Burr* (proper name) connect to identical phonological nodes, so that production of burr(common noun) should improve retrieval of *Burr* (proper name). To test this prediction, participants performed two tasks on alternate trials: a sentence completion task where participants completed a phrase with a single word (e.g. she sells sea shells at the sea ___) and a picture naming task involving famous persons. The name of the person in the picture naming task was either a homophone of the word in the sentence completion task two trials earlier (e.g. [Dinah] *Shore* following *shore*) or unrelated to the earlier word (e.g. [Cary] Grant following *shore*). Overall, older adults produced fewer correct names and more TOTs than young adults in picture naming. However, there was an age-by-prime condition interaction: prior production of a homophone reduced TOTs and increased correct naming of the picture, but only for older adults. Indeed, the homophone priming condition eliminated age differences in naming and TOTs.

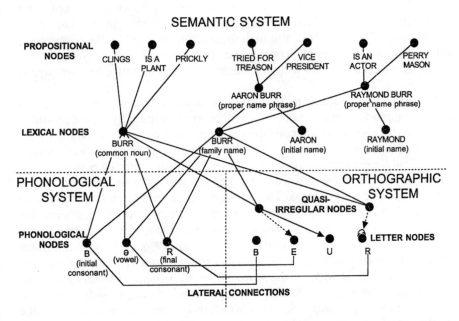

Fig. 8.2 A sample of nodes and connections in the semantic, phonological, and orthographic systems representing the proper name *Burr* and its homophone, the common noun *burr*. Broken top-down links indicate inhibitory connections, and solid top-down links indicate excitatory connections (see text for explanation).

In sum, the transmission deficit hypothesis can account for established characteristics of the TOT state, including its increase with age. Considerable evidence also supports the corollary hypothesis that TOTs are pure phonological retrieval deficits. However, additional research is needed to better understand phonological effects of priming on TOTs. Because the relation between phonological priming effects and aging has implications for the nature of age-linked transmission deficits, identifying the conditions determining whether and when priming effects increase with aging is an important goal for future research.

TRANSMISSION DEFICITS AND RETRIEVAL OF PROPER NAMES

Several sources of evidence indicate that proper name retrieval is disproportionately impaired in old age: proper names are more difficult to retrieve than other information about people, such as their occupation (Cohen and Burke 1993; Valentine *et al.* 1996; Young *et al.* 1985), especially for older adults (James 1997). Burke *et al.* (1991) found that proper names accounted for more than half the TOTs reported in a diary study, and most were names of acquaintances or famous people, rather than, for example, place names or movie titles. Older adults also reported that remembering proper names deteriorates with aging and represents their most disturbing cognitive problem (Cohen and Faulkner 1984; Lovelace and Twohig 1990), although these self reports may reflect the greater importance of remembering proper names, or even the absence of synonyms for proper names, rather than a special retrieval problem relative to other words (Maylor 1997).

The transmission deficit hypothesis predicts that retrieval deficits should be more common for proper names than other words, especially for older adults. To illustrate this prediction, compare the representations of *Burr* (family name) and *burr* (common noun) in Fig. 8.2. Only a single top-down connection links *Burr* (family name) to the memory representation for a specific person, unlike *burr* (common noun) which receives many top-down connections from inter-related semantic propositions. The transmission of priming to the lexical node for *Burr* (family name) depends primarily on that single connection, whereas for *burr* (common noun) priming can summate over the many connections from related concepts (Burke *et al.* 1991; Valentine *et al.* 1996; cf. Burton and Bruce 1992; and Cohen 1990). Thus, one locus of proper name retrieval deficits is in activating the lexical node for the proper name. Consistent with this hypothesis, Bredart and Valentine (1998) showed that cartoon characters with meaningful proper names (e.g. *Grumpy*, *Scrooge*), which receive connections from semantic nodes as well as name-phrase nodes, were correctly named more often and with fewer TOTs than characters with arbitrary proper names (e.g. *Aladdin*, *Peter Pan*) which only receive connections from name-phrase nodes. A second locus of proper name retrieval deficits, as for TOTs in general, is the single top-down connections to phonological nodes, which render proper names especially vulnerable to transmission deficits, causing increased proper name TOTs.

Consistent with these predictions, several sources of evidence suggest that older adults are especially impaired in proper name recall. In naming famous faces, correct responses included both first and last names more often for young than older adults (Maylor 1998) and latencies for older adults were disproportionately slower for naming, but not for semantic decisions concerning occupation or fame (Maylor and Valentine 1992; but see Maylor 1997). In a task where participants named pictures of famous people, older adults reported more proper name TOTs than young adults (Burke *et al.* 1998; Maylor 1990*b*). However, the age-related increase in proper name TOTs in these studies may simply reflect the general age-related increase in TOTs for all types of words: the studies failed to compare young and older adults' TOTs for names versus other types of information.

In the experimental study of Burke *et al.* (1991), names of famous people were the only class of words with significantly more TOT responses for older adults than young adults. In fact, 33% of older adults' TOTs were for names of famous people, compared to only 20% for young adults, which indicates an age-linked increase in proper name TOTs while controlling for the increased TOTs for older adults across all word types. However, an analysis of TOTs as a proportion of unrecalled words in Burke *et al.* indicated an age-linked increase in TOTs for three classes of words: famous people, object nouns, and verbs and adjectives, inconsistent with a specific age-related impairment in proper name retrieval. Thus, the Burke *et al.* study does not unequivocally demonstrate that TOTs for names are especially frequent in older adults.

Rastle and Burke (1996), however, found disproportionate age-related increases in TOTs for proper names compared to common nouns: older adults reported more TOTs for common nouns than young adults, but the age difference was twice as large for proper name TOTs. Moreover, the same pattern also emerged in an analysis of TOTs as a proportion of unrecalled words: older adults experienced more TOTs than young adults for both common and proper nouns, but the age difference in TOTs was twice as large for proper as for common names.

Studies comparing age differences in retrieval of proper names versus other types of biographical information about a person have yielded equivocal results. James (1997) tested predictions of the transmission deficit model for age differences in TOTs for proper names versus other words. Participants saw pictures of famous people and attempted to write down the full name and specific occupation of people whose faces they found familiar, indicating TOT states for names or occupations. There were no age differences in correct responses for names or occupations. TOTs for occupations were rare for both young and older adults, occurring for only 2% of the pictures for each age group. TOTs for names, however, occurred more frequently for older adults (17% of familiar pictures) than young adults (11% of familiar pictures). These

findings are consistent with the prediction that proper names are more susceptible to retrieval failure than other types of biographical information, and especially so for older adults, but TOTs for occupations were at floor in this study,
and therefore the results must be interpreted cautiously.

Maylor (1997) recently argued that age differences in correct recall of proper
names versus semantic information about a person indicate that older adults
are *not* disproportionately impaired on proper name retrieval. Reanalysing data
from Maylor (1990*b*) on 50-, 60-, and 70-year olds, she reported age-related
declines in correct recall of semantic information about a familiar famous
person and in correct recall of the name of the famous person, given that correct
semantic information was recalled. The age difference was *not* statistically
greater for names than for semantic information, and although numerically
the age difference for names was twice as large as for semantic information, this
may reflect ceiling effects in recall of semantic information. In a task requiring
identification of famous people from their voices, Maylor (1997) eliminated
ceiling effects and reported equivalent differences between participants in their
50s and 60s and participants in their 70s and 80s in recall of semantic information and in recall of names.

In sum, proper names are more difficult to recall than other semantic
information about a person, but whether older adults show relatively greater
deficits for proper names than young adults depends on the measure. Conditional probabilities for recalling proper names versus semantic information
reveal no disproportionate decline in proper name retrieval, at least between the
ages of 50 and 85 years. TOTs, however, show larger age differences for proper
names than other types of words. Clearly, more research is needed on this issue.

TRANSMISSION DEFICITS AND ORTHOGRAPHIC KNOWLEDGE

Two contrasting classes of theories have been developed to explain how young
adults map orthography onto phonology, allowing them to pronounce a word
they read (and by extension, to spell a word they hear). One class, known as
parallel distributed processing (PDP) theories, represents orthographic knowledge in terms of connection strengths or weights within a complex, highly
interactive network involving large numbers of excitatory and inhibitory connections for each word, without rules of any kind for representing either regularly or irregularly spelled words (see, e.g., Plaut *et al.* 1996). The second class
of theories, known as 'dual route' theories, postulates two routes from orthography to pronunciation (e.g. Coltheart *et al.* 1993). One is an indirect route
from orthography-to-phonology-to-semantics-to-pronunciation that incorporates grapheme-to-phoneme correspondence rules. These rules are categorical
in nature and translate orthography into phonology for regularly spelled words,
that is, words whose speech sounds follow the most common orthography-to-
pronunciation pattern in the lexicon, for example, *bunt*, *punt*, and *hunt*. The

second route leads directly from orthography to semantics, bypassing phonology on the input side. This 'direct route' makes no use of rules of any kind, and translates orthography into phonology for irregularly spelled words, that is, words that contain one or more speech sounds that follow a unique or uncommon orthography-to-pronunciation pattern. For example, *bush* and *push* are irregularly spelled because the [U] in these words is pronounced in an uncommon way.

The NST and transmission deficit hypothesis represent a hybrid PDP–dual route theory for perceiving and producing orthographic information. As with bottom-up processes for speech perception, perceiving orthography differs in fundamental ways from the top-down processes for producing orthography, and these differences give rise to age-linked asymmetries between perception versus production. Like phonological nodes, orthographic nodes are part of a hierarchically organized network: letter nodes in the orthographic system are connected laterally to phonological nodes, relating spellings to their most common sounds, an indirect route that can be used for regularly spelled components of words (MacKay and Abrams 1998). Figure 8.1 shows these lateral connections for the regularly spelled word *star*.

Unlike dual route theories, NST focuses on speech sounds and letters rather than words as the unit of analysis in defining 'regular spelling': a speech sound in a word is regularly spelled if it follows the most common spelling pattern for that speech sound in the lexicon, but is irregularly spelled if it follows a unique or uncommon spelling pattern. For example, the speech sounds /ər/ in *cooker* is regularly spelled because most words, for example, *worker, baker, amber*, follow the same spelling pattern, but /ər/ is irregularly spelled in the word *burr* because /ər/ is spelled [UR] in only a few words, for example, *fur, duration*. The double [R] in *burr* is also irregular because most words, for example, *fur, duration*, spell /r/ with a single [R].

Lateral connections in NST suffice to correctly spell the regularly spelled aspects of an irregularly spelled word, but to spell the irregularly spelled aspects, a 'quasi-irregular node' must be activated to introduce the irregularly spelled letters and to prevent intrusion of the regular spelling pattern. Figure 8.2 shows the quasi-irregular nodes and lateral connections for spelling the word *burr* in the orthographic system of NST (omitting nodes within the muscle movement systems for handwriting and typing). The lexical nodes representing *burr* (both common noun and proper noun) are connected top-down to a node in the orthographic system that represents the fact that *burr* spells /ə/ as [U]. This quasi-irregular node is connected top-down via an inhibitory connection (represented by a broken line) to the letter [E], the usual spelling, and via an excitatory connection to the letter [U]. As a result, activating this quasi-irregular node inhibits the letter [E] to counteract the lateral connections for regular spelling, and enables activation of the letter [U] to correctly spell /ə/ as [U]. This same quasi-irregular node also becomes activated when spelling, writing, or typing the small number of other words that spell /ə/ as [U], ergo the term quasi-irregular. The lexical nodes representing *burr* are connected to a second quasi-irregular node that represents the fact that *burr* spells /r/ irregularly as [RR]. This quasi-irregular node blocks (represented by the broken line) the self inhibition (represented by the loop) that follows activation of the node for [R] (see MacKay 1987), allowing [R] to be doubled.

Aging and retrieval of orthographic knowledge

We now examine theoretical effects of age-linked transmission deficits on orthographic retrieval in NST. Older adults will be especially likely to misspell irregularly spelled English words because nodes critical to the correct spelling depend on a single connection within the network. For example, in spelling burr, the activated lexical node can only contribute top-down priming to the quasi-irregular nodes in Fig. 8.2 via a single connection. Consequently, deficits in transmission of priming across that one connection to each quasi-irregular node will reduce the likelihood of activation. One possible consequence of a transmission deficit is that the wrong quasi-irregular node becomes activated: because only the most-primed quasi-irregular node can be activated at any point in time, the wrong quasi-irregular node may be activated in error if a transmission deficit prevents the appropriate quasi-irregular node from achieving most-primed status. In short, the transmission deficit hypothesis predicts that older adults will sometimes misspell irregularly spelled words by applying the quasi-irregular pattern for some other irregularly spelled word.

A second possible consequence of transmission deficits is that no quasi-irregular node achieves sufficient priming to become activated, so that the regular spelling pattern predominates. For example, if the quasi-irregular nodes are not activated in spelling the word *burr*, the letter [E] will not be inhibited, the letter [U] will not be activated, and the [R] will not be doubled, so that *burr* will be misspelled *ber*, following the pattern represented by the lateral connections for spelling this phoneme in most English words (see Fig. 8.2). In short, the transmission deficit hypothesis predicts that older adults will misspell irregularly spelled words as regularly spelled.

Misspellings due to age-linked transmission deficits are much less likely for the regularly than irregularly spelled aspects of words under NST. The lateral, phonology-to-orthography connections for spelling regularly spelled letters are used with extremely high frequency over the course of a lifetime, a factor that will offset transmission deficits. By comparison, irregularly spelled components receive relatively little practice because they occur in only a few irregularly spelled words, and even irregularly spelled words generally contain more regularly than irregularly spelled components. Thus, the lateral connection for spelling /b/ as [B] may be activated many times a day when typing, writing or spelling the many regularly-spelled English words that contain /b/, and the many irregularly spelled words that contain one or more regularly spelled /b/s. By contrast, the single connections linking *burr* to each of its quasi-irregular nodes are unique to the word burr (see Fig. 8.2), and only transmit priming when writing, typing, or spelling the word *burr*. Similarly, the single connection linking a quasi-irregular node to a letter, say, [U], is only activated when writing, typing, or spelling the small number of words that spell /ə/ as [U], for example, *fur*. The frequency difference between regularly versus irregularly spelled letters predicts that older adults will exhibit a greater deficit in spelling irregularly than regularly spelled letters. Nonetheless, the lateral connections that link phonological nodes to the orthographic nodes for representing regular spelling constitute a single source of priming that should ultimately succumb to age-linked transmission deficits under the transmission deficit hypothesis, so that very old adults will eventually exhibit a deficit in spelling regularly as well as irregularly spelled aspects of words.

NST also predicts that aging will have disproportionately greater effects on production of orthographic patterns than on perception of orthographic patterns. The reason is that bottom-up priming converges in a way that offsets age-linked transmission deficits, so that aging will impair production of orthographic patterns more so than perception. Theories that do not postulate fundamental differences between perception and production processes, such as information-universal theories, and attribute cognitive aging to a single factor, for example, general slowing, do not make this asymmetric prediction, and can only explain age-linked asymmetries between perception versus production in terms of experimental artifact, for example, differences in stimuli, participant characteristics, or difficulty of the perception versus production tasks (see Salthouse, Chapter 2, this volume).

MacKay *et al.* (1999) developed a paradigm for comparing the perception versus production of spelling patterns, and their results provide clear and dramatic support for the age-linked asymmetry prediction of NST. Young and older adults with normal or corrected-to-normal vision saw on a computer monitor briefly presented words that they knew would be either correctly spelled or deliberately misspelled (in unspecified ways). The misspellings were created by adding or substituting a single letter in a word, for example *elderly* misspelled as *elderdly*. Participants had two tasks. The first was a perception task: to respond 'right' to indicate correct spelling or 'wrong' to indicate incorrect spelling. The second, immediately subsequent task involved production: participants wrote out the spelling of the word, exactly as presented on the screen.

Results of the perception task indicated that recognizing spelling patterns did not decline with age for either correctly or incorrectly spelled words (see Fig. 8.3, left panel). That is, perception of spelling patterns remained constant in old age, consistent with the frequently observed small or nonexistent age effects for other aspects of language perception discussed earlier. However, age declines did occur in the production task. Older adults correctly reproduced the incorrectly spelled words significantly less often than young adults ($p = 0.02$), even when both groups indicated awareness that these stimuli were misspelled

(Fig. 8.3, right panel). Older adults also correctly reproduced correctly spelled words significantly less often than young adults ($p = 0.02$), even when the words had high frequency of use, and even when they had indicated awareness in the immediately prior perception task that the stimuli were correctly spelled (right panel). These age-related declines in spelling production cannot be explained in terms of 'memory load' and indicate that information about the orthography of words becomes more difficult to retrieve with age, consistent with the NST prediction and with declines discussed earlier for retrieval of phonology in spoken language production.

MacKay *et al.* (1999) also showed that the age-linked asymmetries in Fig. 8.3 were specific to the task factor (perception versus production) rather than general in nature: not every factor that affects the detection and retrieval of misspellings exhibits the same interaction with either age or task. Specifically, letter repetition strongly influenced the detection and retrieval of misspellings for both young and older adults: repeated-letter misspellings, for example,

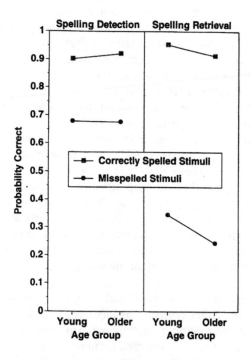

Fig. 8.3 Probability of correct detection (left panel) for young and old adults, and conditional probability of correct retrieval given correct perception (right panel) for correctly spelled and misspelled stimuli (from MacKay *et al.* 1999).

elderdly, were harder to detect, and if detected, were harder to recall, than unrepeated-letter misspellings, for example, *elderkly*. However, these 'repetition deficits' did not exhibit age-linked asymmetries: effects of repetition were symmetric or equivalent in magnitude for young and older adults in both the detection and retrieval tasks.

MacKay and Abrams (1998) examined aging effects on correct spelling of auditorily presented words. NST predicts that both young and older adults will misspell auditorily presented low frequency words more often than high frequency words because word frequency covaries with recency and frequency of node activation, two factors that offset transmission deficits (see, e.g., Burke *et al.* 1991). A related prediction is that errors will tend to involve irregularly spelled letters more often than regularly spelled letters for both high and low frequency words, due to the greater frequency of regularly than irregularly spelled components. The third prediction concerns two types of misspellings: same-pronunciation errors versus different-pronunciation errors. Same-pronunciation errors are pronounceable in the same way as the original, correctly spelled word because they follow the phonology-to-orthography pattern found in the majority of English words. For example, 97% of English words spell /i/ as [I], and only 3% spell /i/ as [Y] as in *cyst* (Barry 1994), so that *cist* is a same-pronunciation misspelling of *cyst*. By contrast, different-pronunciation errors cannot be pronounced in the same way as the correctly spelled word because their phonology-to-orthography pattern is unique or found in few other English words, for example *sausage* misspelled as *sasuage*. Under NST, same-pronunciation errors will be more common than different-pronunciation errors for both irregularly and regularly spelled letters in misspelled words because same-pronunciation links have greater frequency than different-pronunciation links.

MacKay and Abrams (1998) presented a tape recorded series of 'difficult-to-spell' English words to young (age 17–23 years), older (age 60–71 years), and very old participants (age 73–88 years). Half the words were relatively common in English, for example *rhythm*, *spontaneous*, and half were relatively rare, for example *chauffeur*, *pageant*. The participants' task was to write each word down at their own pace during a 20-second interval between words. The instructions encouraged accurate spelling and de-emphasized response speed. To rule out explanations based on age-linked sensory or perceptual deficits, perceptual errors (where a word was mispelled as some other phonologically similar word) were excluded from all analyses reported here.

The results replicated the age-related decline in correct spelling in MacKay *et al.* (1999) with several refinements: misspellings increased with age, especially for high frequency words, and this pattern of age differences remained when differences in vocabulary were factored out in covariate analyses shown in Fig. 8.4 (left ordinate). Low frequency words were correctly spelled less often than high frequency words, and correct spelling decreased with aging for both high and low frequency words, consistent with NST predictions (Fig. 8.4). However, the relatively greater age difference for high than low frequency words was not consistent with NST, but almost certainly arose because the young adults were unfamiliar with many of the low frequency words. Consistent with this hypothesis, same-pronunciation errors on the low frequency, irregularly spelled words were especially common for young adults (Fig. 8.4, right ordinate) as if they had reverted to 'spelling by sound', a default strategy for spelling unknown words.

Also apparent in Fig. 8.4 (right panel), is the finding that the older and oldest adults made more different-pronunciation errors, for example *calendor*, than young adults in spelling both high and low frequency words, and the older and oldest adults made more same-pronunciation errors, for example *calender*, than young adults in spelling high frequency words, both findings consistent with NST.

The age-linked decline in spelling ability was not due to a general slowing factor, even one embedded within a connectionist architecture resembling NST, because the words were spoken slowly, participants were instructed to stop and restart the tape recorder if they needed more time, and they wrote down the words at their own pace, with response speed de-emphasized in the instructions. Even the sophisticated 'processing-speed theory' of Salthouse (1996) seems incapable of explaining the data. In processing-speed theory, general slowing degrades cognitive performance because the products of earlier processing are no longer available when later processing requires those products (the simultaneity mechanism). However, decaying processing products are difficult to imagine in this task: written spelling retrieval runs off rapidly letter by letter from left to right in a word, and products of earlier processing are available on the page.

Nor can the age-linked decline in spelling ability be explained by embedding an inhibition deficit hypothesis within the cognitive architecture of NST. If inhibitory but not excitatory connections exhibit age-linked impairment (e.g. Hasher and Zacks 1988; Zacks and Hasher 1994), then failure of an inhibitory link (see Fig. 8.2) might cause an age-linked increase in same-pronunciation errors, but not also an age-linked increase in different-pronunciation errors, contrary to present data. The similarities between age-linked declines in orthographic and phonological retrieval (reviewed earlier) are also difficult to explain under an inhibition deficit hypothesis.

More refined analyses in MacKay and Abrams (1998) that used letters rather than words as the dependent measure indicated that the older and oldest adults were especially likely to misspell irregularly spelled letters relative to young adults, with no age-linked difference in the probability of misspelling regularly spelled letters. However, the very oldest adults exhibited deficits in spelling regularly spelled letters, consistent with the NST claim that even the frequently used lateral connections representing regular spelling constitute a single source of priming that eventually succumbs to age-linked transmission deficits. That is, regularly spelled letters involve a one-to-one lateral connection in NST (see Fig. 8.1 and 8.2), and one-to-one connections are especially susceptible to age-linked

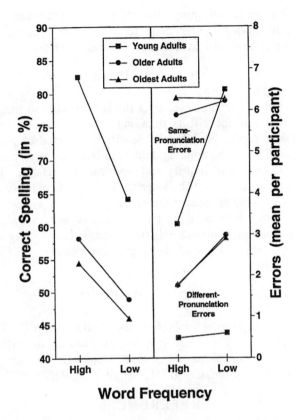

Fig. 8.4 Mean per cent correct spelling per participant (adjusted with Nelson-Denny scores as covariate; left ordinate), and mean number of same-pronunciation and different-pronunciation errors per participant (adjusted with Nelson-Denny scores as covariate; right ordinate) for young, older and oldest adults spelling high and low frequency words (N = 40) (from MacKay & Abrams 1998).

transmission deficits, but because these lateral phonology-to-orthography connections receive so much use, effects of transmission deficits in these extremely strong connections only became evident in the oldest adults.

Another letter-level finding was that the oldest adults produced more same-pronunciation misspellings than did young adults for irregularly spelled letters, consistent with the NST prediction that the most likely outcome of transmission deficits in connections to or from quasi-irregular nodes is a same-pronunciation misspelling. The oldest adults also made more different-pronunciation errors than the young and older adults when spelling regularly spelled letters, but these misspellings involve an additional process under NST, namely inappropriate activation of a quasi-irregular node. That is, for the oldest adults, transmission deficits may have reduced priming delivered to the appropriate nodes, so that an inappropriate quasi-irregular node received more priming and became activated, giving rise to these different-pronunciation errors.

CONCLUSIONS

Experimental evidence accumulated over the last 20 years strongly supports a general asymmetry in the effects of aging on language perception versus production. Older adults exhibit clear deficits in retrieval of phonology and orthography, with no corresponding deficits in language perception and comprehension, independent of sensory and new learning deficits. This emerging pattern presents a fundamental challenge for theories of cognitive aging, which must explain why some aspects of the language memory system are so much more vulnerable to effects of aging than others. A decremental approach to theory construction that addresses only the deficits in cognitive aging and leaves unspecified the mechanisms underlying preserved cognitive functions is no longer a viable option.

ACKNOWLEDGEMENT

This research was supported by NIA grants AGO8835 to D.M. Burke and AGO97705 to D.G. MacKay. Correspondence concerning this article should be sent to Deborah Burke, Department of Psychology, 550 Harvard Avenue, Pomona College, Claremont, CA 91711. E-mail: DBURKE@POMONA.EDU

REFERENCES

Arbuckle, T. Y. and Gold, D. P. (1993). Aging, inhibition, and verbosity. *Journal of Gerontology: Psychological Sciences*, **48**, P225–32.

Arbuckle, T. Y., Pushkar, D., Nohara-LeClair, M., Basevitz, P., and Peled, M. (1998, April). *Variation in off-topic verbosity in relation to conversational context.* Poster session presented at the Seventh Cognitive Aging Conference, Atlanta, GA.

Au, R., Joung, P., Nicholas, M., Obler, L. K., Kass, R., and Albert, M. L. (1995). Naming ability across the adult life span. *Aging and Cognition*, **2**, 300–11.

Balota, D. A. and Ferraro, F. R. (1993). A dissociation of frequency and regularity effects in pronunciation performance across young adults, older adults, and individuals with senile dementia of the Alzheimer type. *Journal of Memory and Language*, **32**, 573–92.

Balota, D. A, Black, S., and Cheney, M. (1992). Automatic and attentional priming in young and older adults: reevaluation of the two process model. *Journal of Experimental Psychology: Human Perception and Performance*, **18**, 489–502.

Barry, C. (1994). Spelling routes (or roots or rutes). In G. D. A. Brown and N. C. Ellis (ed.), *Handbook of spelling: theory, processes and intervention* (pp. 27–49). Chichester: Wiley.

Bennett, D. J. and McEvoy, C. L. (1999). Mediated priming in younger and older adults. *Experimental Aging Research*. (In press.)

Birren, J. E. (1965). Age changes in speed of behavior: its central nature and physiological correlates. In A. T. Welford and J. E. Birren (ed.), *Behavior, aging and the nervous system* (pp. 191–216). Springfield, IL: Thomas.

Botwinick, J. (1984). *Aging and Behavior*. New York: Springer.

Bowles, N. L. (1994). Age and rate of activation in semantic memory. *Psychology and Aging*, **9**, 414–29.

Bowles, N. L. and Poon, L. W. (1985). Aging and retrieval of words in semantic memory. *Journal of Gerontology*, **40**, 71–7.

Bredart, S. and Valentine, T. (1998). Descriptiveness and proper name retrieval. *Memory*, **6**, 199–206.

Brennen, T., Baguley, T., Bright, J., and Bruce, V. (1990). Resolving semantically-induced tip-of-the-tongue states for proper nouns. *Memory and Cognition*, **18**, 339–47.

Brown, A. S. (1991). A review of the tip-of-the-tongue experience. *Psychological Bulletin*, **109**, 204–23.

Brown, A. S. and Nix, L. A. (1996). Age-related changes in the tip-of-the-tongue experience. *American Journal of Psychology*, **109**, 79–91.

Brown, R. and McNeill, D. (1966). The 'tip of the tongue' phenomenon. *Journal of Verbal Learning Behavior*, **5**, 325–37.

Burke, D. M. (1997). Language, aging and inhibitory deficits: evaluation of a theory. *Journal of Gerontology: Psychological Sciences*, **52B**, P254–64.

Burke, D. M. and Harrold, R. M. (1988). Automatic and effortful semantic processes in old age: experimental and naturalistic approaches. In L. L. Light and D. M. Burke (ed.), *Language, memory and aging* (pp. 100–16). New York: Cambridge University Press.

Burke, D. and Peters, L. (1986). Word associations in old age: evidence for consistency in semantic encoding during adulthood. *Psychology and Aging*, **4**, 283–92.

Burke, D. M. and Yee, P. L. (1984). Semantic priming during sentence processing by young and older adults. *Developmental Psychology*, **20**, 903–10.

Burke, D., White, H., and Diaz, D. (1987). Semantic priming in young and older adults: Evidence for age-constancy in automatic and attentional processes. *Journal of Experimental Psychology: Human Perception and Performance*, **13**, 79–88.

Burke, D. M., MacKay, D. G., Worthley, J. S., and Wade, E. (1991). On the tip of the tongue: what causes word finding failures in young and older adults. *Journal of Memory and Language*, **30**, 542–79.

Burke, D. M., Austin, A., and Kester, J. (1998, April). *Repetition priming with homographs: age interactions in production of proper names*. Paper presented at the Seventh Cognitive Aging Conference, Atlanta.

Burton, A. M. and Bruce, V. (1992). I recognize your face but I can't remember your name: a simple explanation? *British Journal of Psychology*, **83**, 45–60.

Byrne, M. D. (1998). Taking a computational approach to aging: the SPAN theory of working memory. *Psychology and Aging*, **13**, 309–22.

Cerella, J. (1985). Information processing rates in the elderly. *Psychological Bulletin*, **98**, 67–83.

Cerella, J. (1990). Aging and information-processing rate. In J. E. Birren and K. W. Schaie (ed.), *Handbook of cognitive aging*, (3rd edn. pp. 201–21). New York: Academic Press.

Cerella, J., Poon, L. W., and Williams, D. M. (1980). Age and the complexity hypothesis. In L. W. Poon (ed.), *Aging in the 1980s: psychological issues* (pp. 332–40). Washington: American Psychological Association.

Christidis, P. and Burke, D.M. (1998, April). *Under what conditions does aging affect Stroop interference?* Poster session presented at the Seventh Cognitive Aging Conference, Atlanta, GA.

Cohen, G. (1990). Why is it difficult to put names to faces? *British Journal of Psychology*, **81**, 287–97.

Cohen, G. and Burke, D. M. (1993). A review of memory for proper names. Memory, **1**, 249–64.

Cohen, G. and Faulkner, D. (1983). Word recognition: age differences in contextual facilitation effects. *British Journal of Psychology*, **74**, 239–51.

Cohen, G. and Faulkner, D. (1984). Memory in old age: 'good in parts'. *New Scientist*, **11**, 49–51.

Cohen, G. and Faulkner, D. (1986). Memory for proper names: age differences in retrieval. *British Journal of Developmental Psychology*, **4**, 187–97.

Coltheart, M., Curtis, B., Atkins, P., and Haller, M. (1993). Models of reading aloud: dual-route and parallel-distributed-processing approaches. *Psychological Review*, **100**, 589–608.

Connelly, S. L., Hasher, L., and Zacks, R. T. (1991). Age and reading: the impact of distraction. *Psychology and Aging*, **6**, 533–41.

Cooper, P. V. (1990). Discourse production and normal aging: performance on oral picture description tasks. *Journal of Gerontology: Psychological Sciences*, **45**, P210–14.

Dell, G. S. (1986). A spreading-activation theory of retrieval in sentence production. *Psychological Review*, **93**, 283–321.

Dell, G. S., Burger, L. K., and Svec, W. R. (1997). Language production and serial order: A functional analysis and a model. *Psychological Review*, **104**, 123–47.

Duchek, J. M., Balota, D. A., Faust, M. E., and Ferraro, F. R. (1995). Inhibitory processes in young and older adults in a picture-word task. *Aging and Cognition*, **2**, 156–67.

Dywan, J. and Murphy, W. E. (1996). Aging and inhibitory control in text comprehension. *Psychology and Aging*, **11**, 199–206.

Fisher, D. L., Fisk, A. D., and Duffy, S. A. (1995). Why latent models are needed to test hypotheses about the slowing of word and language processes in older adults. In P. A. Allen and T. R. Bashore (ed.), *Age differences in word and language processing* (pp. 1–29). Amsterdam: Elsevier.

Fisk, A. D. and Fisher, D. L. (1994). Brinley plots and theories of aging: the explicit, muddled, and implicit debates. *Journal of Gerontology: Psychological Sciences*, **49**, P81–9.

Fisk, A. D. and Rogers, W. A. (1991). Toward an understanding of age-related memory and visual search effects. *Journal of Experimental Psychology: General*, **120**, 131–49.

Glosser, G. and Deser, T. (1992). A comparison of changes in macrolinguistic and microlinguistic aspects of discourse production in normal aging. *Journal of Gerontology: Psychological Sciences*, **47**, P266–72.

Gold, D., Andres, D., Arbuckle, T., and Schwartzman, A. (1988). Measurements and correlates of verbosity in elderly people. *Journal of Gerontology: Psychological Sciences*, **43**, P27–33.

Gould, O. N. and Dixon, R. A. (1993). How we spent our vacation: Collaborative storytelling by young and older adults. *Psychology and Aging*, **8**, 10–17.

Goulet, P., Ska, B., and Kahn, H. J. (1994). Is there a decline in picture naming with advancing age? *Journal of Speech and Hearing Research*, **37**, 629–44.

Hamm, V. P. and Hasher, L. (1992). Age and the availability of inferences. *Psychology and Aging*, 7, 56–64.

Harley, T. A. and Bown, H. E. (1998). What causes a tip-of-the-tongue state? Evidence for lexical neighbourhood effects in speech production. *British Journal of Psychology*, 89, 151–74.

Hartley, J. (1988). Aging and individual differences in memory for written discourse. In L. L. Light and D. M. Burke (ed.) *Language, memory and aging* (pp. 36–57). New York: Cambridge University Press.

Hartman, M. (1995). Aging and interference: evidence from indirect memory tests. *Psychology and Aging*, 10, 659–69.

Hartman, M. and Hasher, L. (1991). Aging and suppression: memory for previously irrelevant information. *Psychology and Aging*, 6, 587–94.

Hasher, L. and Zacks, R.T. (1988). Working memory, comprehension, and aging: a review and a new view. In G.H. Bower (ed.), *The psychology of learning and motivation* (Vol. 22, pp. 193–225). San Diego: Academic Press.

Heller, R. B. and Dobbs, A. R. (1993). Age differences in word finding in discourse and nondiscourse situations. *Psychology and Aging*, 8, 443–50.

Howard, D. V. (1980). Category norms: a comparison of the Battig and Montague (1960) norms with the responses of adults between the ages of 20 and 80. *Journal of Gerontology*, 35, 225–31.

Hutchinson, K. M. (1989). Influence of sentence context on speech perception in young and older adults. *Journal of Gerontology: Psychological Sciences*, 44, P36–44.

James, L.E. (1997). *Memory for proper names in young and older adults.* Unpublished doctoral dissertation, Claremont Graduate University, Claremont, CA.

James, L. E. and Burke, D. M. (1998). *Phonological priming effects on word retrieval and tip of the tongue experiences in young and older adults.* (Manuscript submitted for publication.)

James, L. E., Burke, D. M., Austin, A., and Hulme, E. (1998). Production and perception of verbosity in young and older adults. *Psychology and Aging*, 13, 355–67.

Jones, G.V. (1989). Back to Woodworth: role of interlopers in the tip of the tongue phenomenon. *Memory and Cognition*, 17, 69–76.

Jones, G.V. and Langford, S. (1987). Phonological blocking in the tip of the tongue state. *Cognition*, 26, 115–22.

Kemper, S. (1992a). Adults' sentence fragments: who, what, when, where, and why. *Communication Research*, 19, 444–58.

Kemper, S. (1992b). Language and aging. In F. I. M. Craik and T. A. Salthouse (ed.), *The handbook of aging and cognition* (pp. 213–70). Hillsdale, NJ: Lawrence Erlbaum.

Kemper, S., Rash, S., Kynette, D., and Norman, S. (1990). Telling stories: the structure of adults' narratives. *European Journal of Cognitive Psychology*, 2, 205–28.

Kieley, J. M. and Hartley, A. A. (1997). Age-related equivalence of identity suppression in the Stroop color-word task. *Psychology and Aging*, 12, 22–9.

Kozlowski, L. T. (1977). Effects of distorted auditory and of rhyming cues on retrieval of tip-of-the-tongue words by poets and nonpoets. *Memory and Cognition*, 5, 477–81.

Kramer, A. F., Humphrey, D. G., Larish, J. F., Logan, G. D., and Strayer, D. L. (1994). Aging and inhibition: beyond a unitary view of inhibitory processing in attention. *Psychology and Aging*, 9, 491–512.

Kwong See, S. T. and Ryan, E. B. (1995). Cognitive mediation of adult age differences in language performance. *Psychology and Aging*, 10, 458–68.

Laver, G. D. and Burke, D. M. (1993). Why do semantic priming effects increase in old age? A meta-analysis. *Psychology and Aging*, **8**, 34–43.

Levelt, W. J. M. (1989). *Speaking: from intention to articulation*. Cambridge, MA: MIT Press.

Levelt, W. J. M., Schriefers, H., Vorberg, D., Meyer, A. S., Pechmann, T., and Havinga, J. (1991). The time course of lexical access in speech production: a study of picture naming. *Psychological Review*, **98**, 122–42.

Light, L. L. (1991). Memory and aging: four hypotheses in search of data. *Annual Review of Psychology*, **42**, 333–76.

Light, L. L. and Anderson, P. A. (1983). Memory for scripts in young and older adults. *Memory & Cognition*, **11**, 435–44.

Light, L. and Burke, D. (1988). Patterns of language and memory in old age. In L. Light and D. Burke (ed.), *Language, memory and aging* (pp. 244–71). New York: Cambridge University Press.

Light, L. L., and Capps, J. L. (1986). Comprehension of pronouns in young and older adults. *Developmental Psychology*, **22**, 580–85.

Light, L. L., Valencia-Laver, D., and Zavis, D. (1991). Instantiation of general terms in young and older adults. *Psychology and Aging*, **6**, 337–51.

Lima, S. D., Hale, S., and Myerson, J. (1991). How general is general slowing? Evidence from the lexical domain. *Psychology and Aging*, **6**, 416–25.

Lovelace, E. A. and Twohig, P. T. (1990). Healthy older adults' perceptions of their memory functioning and use of mnemonics. *Bulletin of the Psychonomic Society*, **28**, 115–18.

Luce, P. A., Pisoni, D. B., and Goldinger, S. D. (1990). Similarity neighborhoods of spoken words. In G.T.M. Altmann (ed.), *Cognitive models of speech processing* (pp. 122–47). Cambridge, MA: MIT Press.

McDowd, J. M. (1997). Inhibition in attention and aging: paradigms lost? *Journal of Gerontology: Psychological Sciences*, **52B**, P265–73.

MacKay, D. G. (1982). The problems of flexibility, fluency, and speed-accuracy trade-off in skilled behavior. *Psychological Review*, **89**, 483–506.

MacKay, D. G. (1987). *The organization of perception and action: a theory for language and other cognitive skills*. New York: Springer-Verlag.

MacKay, D. G. and Abrams, L. (1996). Language, memory and aging: distributed deficits and the structure of new versus old connections. In J. E. Birren and W. K. Schaie (ed.), *Handbook of the psychology of aging* (4th edn. pp. 251–65). San Diego: Academic Press.

MacKay, D. G. and Abrams, L. (1998). Age-linked declines in retrieving orthographic knowledge: empirical, practical and theoretical implications. *Psychology and Aging*, **13**, 647–62.

MacKay, D. G. and Burke, D. M. (1990). Cognition and aging: new learning and the use of old connections. In T. M. Hess (ed.), *Aging and cognition: knowledge organization and utilization* (pp. 213–63). Amsterdam: North-Holland.

MacKay, D. G., Abrams, L., and Pedroza, M. J. (1999). Aging on the input versus output side: theoretical implications of age-linked asymmetries between detecting versus retrieving orthographic knowledge. *Psychology and Aging*, **14**, 3–17.

Madden, D. J. (1988). Adult age differences in the effects of sentence context and stimulus degradation during visual word recognition. *Psychology and Aging*, **3**, 167–72.

Madden, D. J. (1989). Visual word identification and age related slowing. *Cognitive Development*, **4**, 1–29.

Madden, D. J. and Hoffman, J. M. (1997). Application of positron emission tomography to age-related cognitive changes. In K. R. R. Krishnan and P. M. Doraiswamy (ed.), *Brain imaging in clinical psychiatry* (pp. 575–613). New York: Dekker.

Martin, M. (1986). Ageing and patterns of change in everyday memory and cognition. *Human Learning*, **5**, 63–74.

Maylor, E. A. (1990*a*). Age, blocking and the tip of the tongue state. *British Journal of Psychology*, **81**, 123–34.

Maylor, E. A. (1990*b*). Recognizing and naming faces: aging, memory retrieval and the tip of the tongue state. *Journal of Gerontology: Psychological Sciences*, **45**, P215–25.

Maylor, E. A. (1997). Proper name retrieval in old age: converging evidence against disproportionate impairment. *Aging, Neuropsychology, and Cognition*, **4**, 211–26.

Maylor, E. A. (1998). Retrieving names in old age: short- and (very) long-term effects of repetition. *Memory and Cognition*, **26**, 309–19.

Maylor, E. A. and Valentine, T. (1992). Linear and nonlinear effects of aging on categorizing and naming faces. *Psychology and Aging*, **7**, 317–23.

Meyer, A. S. and Bock, K. (1992). The tip-of-the-tongue phenomenon: blocking or partial activation? *Memory & Cognition*, **20**, 715–26.

Miozzo, M. and Caramazza, A. (1997). Retrieval of lexical-syntactic features in tip-of-the-tongue states. *Journal of Experimental Psychology: Learning, Memory and Cognition*, **23**, 1410–23.

Moscovitch, M. and Winocur, G. (1992). The neuropsychology of memory and aging. In F. I. M. Craik and T. A. Salthouse (ed.), *The handbook of aging and cognition* (pp. 315–72). Hillsdale, NJ: Lawrence Erlbaum.

Mueller, J. H., Kausler, D. H., Faherty, A., and Oliveri, M. (1980). Reaction time as a function of age, anxiety, and typicality. *Bulletin of the Psychonomic Society*, **16**, 473–6.

Myerson, J., Hale, S., Wagstaff, D., Poon, L. W., and Smith, G. A. (1990). The information-loss model: a mathematical theory of age-related cognitive slowing. *Psychological Review*, **97**, 475–87.

Myerson, J., Ferraro, F. R., Hale, S., and Lima, S. D. (1992). General slowing in semantic priming and word recognition. *Psychology and Aging*, **7**, 257–70.

Nebes, R. D., Boller, F., and Holland, A. (1986). Use of semantic context by patients with Alzheimer's disease. *Psychology and Aging*, **1**, 261–9.

Nicholas, M., Obler, L., Albert, M., and Goodglass, H. (1985). Lexical retrieval in healthy aging. *Cortex*, **21**, 595–606.

Perfect, T. J. (1994). What can Brinley plots tell us about cognitive aging? *Journal of Gerontology: Psychological Sciences*, **49**, P60–4.

Perfect, T. J. and Hanley, J.R. (1992). The tip-of-the-tongue phenomenon: do experimenter-presented interlopers have any effect? *Cognition*, **45**, 55–75.

Plaut, D. C., McClelland, J. L., Seidenberg, M. S., and Patterson, K. (1996). Understanding normal and impaired word reading: computational principles in quasi-regular domains. *Psychological Review*, **103**, 56–115.

Rabbitt, P., Maylor, E., McInnes, L., Bent, N., and Moore, B. (1995). What goods can self-assessment questionnaires deliver for cognitive gerontology? *Applied Cognitive Psychology*, **9**, S127–52.

Rastle, K. G. and Burke, D. M. (1996). Priming the tip of the tongue: effects of prior processing on word retrieval in young and older adults. *Journal of Memory and Language*, 35, 586–605.

Raz, N., Torres, I. J., Spencer, W. D. and Acker, J. D. (1993). Pathoclysis in aging human cerebral cortex: evidence from in vivo MRI morphometry. *Psychobiology*, 21, 151–60.

Rogers, W. A. and Fisk, A. D. (1991). Age-related differences in the maintenance and modification of automatic processes: arithmetic Stroop interference. *Human Factors*, 33, 45–56.

Ryan, E. B. (1992). Beliefs about memory changes across the adult life span. *Journal of Gerontology: Psychological Sciences*, 47, P41–6.

Ryan, E. B., See, S. K., Meneer, W. B., and Trovato, D. (1994). Age-based perceptions of conversational skills among younger and older adults. In M. L. Hummert, J. M. Wiemann, and J. N. Nussbaum (ed.), *Interpersonal communication in older adulthood* (pp.15–39). Thousand Oaks, CA: Sage.

Salthouse, T. A. (1985). *A theory of cognitive aging*. Amsterdam: North-Holland.

Salthouse, T. A. (1996). The processing-speed theory of adult age differences in cognition. *Psychological Review*, 103, 403–28.

Shilling, V. and Rabbitt, P. (1998, April). *Performance of older adults across several measures of Stroop interference*. Poster session presented at the Seventh Cognitive Aging Conference, Atlanta, GA.

Spieler, D. H., Balota, D. A., and Faust, M. E. (1996). Stroop performance in normal older adults and individuals with senile dementia of the Alzheimer's type. *Journal of Experimental Psychology: Human Perception and Performance*, 22, 461–79.

Stine, E. A. L. (1995). Aging and the distribution of resources in working memory. In P. A. Allen and T. R. Bashore (ed.), *Age differences in word and language processing* (pp. 171–86). Amsterdam: Elsevier.

Stine, E. A. L. and Wingfield, A. (1994). Older adults can inhibit high-probability competitors in speech recognition. *Aging and Cognition*, 1, 152–7.

Stine, E. A. L., Soederberg, L. M., and Morrow, D. G. (1996). Language and discourse processing through adulthood. In F. Blanchard-Fields and T. M. Hess (ed.) *Perspectives on cognitive change in adulthood and aging* (pp. 255–90). New York: McGraw-Hill.

Sunderland, A., Watts, K., Baddeley, A. D., and Harris, J. E. (1986). Subjective memory assessment and test performance in the elderly. *Journal of Gerontology*, 41, 376–84.

Thomas, J. C., Fozard, J. L., and Waugh, N. C. (1977). Age-related differences in naming latency. *American Journal of Psychology*, 90, 499–509.

Tun, P. A. and Wingfield, A. (1993). Is speech special? Perception and recall of spoken language in complex environments. In J. Cerella, W. Hoyer, J. Rybash, and M. L. Commons (ed.) *Adult information processing: limits on loss* (pp. 425–57). San Diego: Academic Press.

Valentine, T., Moore, V., and Bredart, S. (1995). Priming productions of people's names. *The Quarterly Journal of Experimental Psychology*, 48A, 513–35.

Valentine, T., Brennen, T., and Bredart, S. (1996). *The cognitive psychology of proper names: on the importance of being Ernest*. London: Routledge.

West, R. L. (1996). An application of prefrontal cortex function theory to cognitive aging. *Psychological Bulletin*, 120, 272–92.

Wheeldon, L. R. and Monsell, S. (1994). Inhibition of spoken word production by priming a semantic competitor. *Journal of Memory and Language*, 33, 332–56.

Wingfield, A., Aberdeen, J. S., and Stine, E. A. L. (1991). Word onset gating and linguistic context in spoken word recognition by young and elderly adults. *Journal of Gerontology: Psychological Sciences*, **46**, P127–9.

Wingfield, A., Alexander, A. H., and Cavigelli, S. (1994). Does memory constrain utilization of top-down information in spoken word recognition? Evidence from normal aging. *Language and Speech*, **37**, 221–35.

Young, A. W., Hay, D. C., and Ellis, A. W. (1985). The face that launched a thousand slips: Everyday difficulties and errors in recognizing people. *British Journal of Psychology*, **76**, 495–523.

Zacks, R. T. and Hasher, L. (1994). Directed ignoring: inhibitory regulation of working memory. In D. Dagenbach and T.H. Carr (ed.) *Inhibitory processes in attention, memory, and language* (pp. 241–64). San Diego: Academic Press.

Zacks, R. T. and Hasher, L. (1997). Cognitive gerontology and attentional inhibition: a reply to Burke and McDowd. *Journal of Gerontology: Psychological Sciences*, **52B**, P274–83.

NINE

Dual-process theories of memory in old age

LEAH L. LIGHT, MATTHEW W. PRULL, DONNA J. LA VOIE, AND MICHAEL R. HEALY

INTRODUCTION

Contemporary theories of memory often posit two processes, recollection and familiarity, that subserve recall and recognition (Atkinson and Juola 1974; Hintzman 1986; Humphreys *et al.* 1989; Jacoby and Dallas 1981; Mandler 1980; Raaijmakers and Shiffrin 1992). Recollection (or in some models, recall) is typically characterized as conscious or intentional and as attention demanding, whereas familiarity is thought to be unconscious and to have relatively low attentional requirements. In most two-process models, recollective processes involve conscious remembering of particular aspects of a prior episode, such as perceptual details, spatial or temporal information, the source of information, or thoughts and feelings that accompanied the episode. Even single-process theories of recognition (e.g. Hintzman 1988; Ratcliff *et al.* 1995) acknowledge the crucial role played by contextual information in determining the similarity between current experiences and memories of earlier events. Moreover, reality monitoring, separating fact from fantasy, requires memory for contextual details as well as thoughts and feelings accompanying particular experiences (Johnson *et al.* 1993).

Several lines of evidence suggest that age-related deficits in recall and recognition stem from reduced efficiency in recollection, while familiarity-based mechanisms are relatively preserved. In this chapter, we critically evaluate this dual-process hypothesis. We begin with a brief summary of relevant findings from a diversity of sources and then consider in depth the three major paradigms that have been used to dissociate recollection and familiarity in young and older adults. These are (a) direct vs indirect measures of memory, (b) the process dissociation procedure developed by Jacoby (1991), and (c) the remember/know technique developed by Tulving (1985) and Gardiner (1988). Our goal is not merely to review the literature, but to place findings with respect to aging in the context of current theoretical debates about the nature of memory constructs and appropriate models for indices of these constructs. We end with recommendations for future directions for research in this area.

EVIDENCE FOR A DISSOCIATION BETWEEN
RECOLLECTION AND FAMILIARITY IN OLD AGE

The existence of age differences in direct measures of memory that require conscious recollection seems incontrovertible. Adults over 60 report more problems with memory (Cutler and Grams 1988), experience less perceived control over memory functions (Dixon and Hultsch 1983), and, in fact, show age-related declines in memory. Older adults score lower on laboratory based memory tasks such as recall and recognition (for reviews see Craik and Jennings 1992; Light 1991), on batteries of tasks designed to emulate memory in everyday life (West *et al.* 1992; Kirasic *et al.* 1996), and on standardized tests designed for use in neuropsychological assessment (Salthouse *et al.* 1996). Negative correlations between age and episodic memory tasks requiring recollection are greater in adults over 50 years of age (mean weighted correlation = −0.23), but are found even in adults under 50 (mean weighted correlation = −0.15) (Verhaeghen and Salthouse 1997).

Older adults also have poorer memory for contextual information. When asked about particulars of earlier experiences, older adults report fewer details than young adults. Summaries of the literature on this topic may be found elsewhere (Kausler 1991; Light 1991, 1996). A few illustrative examples are offered here. Hashtroudi *et al.*(1990) asked young and older adults to carry out some scripted activities (e.g. packing a picnic basket) and to imagine carrying out others that were described to them in detail. The recall protocols of older adults contained fewer mentions of colours, nonvisual sensory information (touch, sounds, and smells), spatial references, and actions, though there were no age differences in number of words, ideas, or mentions of people. In studies in which they are asked about particular details of events, older adults are less apt to remember whether a word appeared in the most recent of a series of lists or in an earlier one (Kliegl and Lindenberger 1993), whether they learned a fact in an experimental setting or knew it before (McIntyre and Craik 1987), whether they had already carried out a particular act (Koriat *et al.* 1988), or which orienting tasks they performed for particular items during study (Brigham and Pressley 1988).

Although it is unlikely that any measures of memory are process pure (Jacoby 1991), it is reasonable to assume that recollective processes that depend on contextual information are most heavily involved in recall, with recognition having a larger familiarity component, and indirect measures of memory that do not solicit deliberate recollection having the largest contribution from familiarity. This assumption is consonant with the frequent observation that when test cues are held constant, age differences are small to nil on indirect memory tests but large for cued recall (e.g. Light and Albertson 1989; Light and Singh 1987). It also predicts the ordering of effect sizes for age differences in recall, recognition, and priming obtained in meta-analyses. Verhaeghen *et al.* (1993) reported mean weighted effect sizes of 0.99 for list recall, 0.91 for paired-associate recall, and 0.67 for prose recall. Similarly, La Voie and Light (1994) obtained mean weighted effect sizes of 0.50 for recognition memory and 0.97 for recall. Spencer and Raz (1995) found mean effect sizes of 0.58 and 0.87 for content and context, respectively, suggesting that memory for context is disproportionately affected in old age.[1] In contrast to these findings for direct measures of memory, the mean weighted effect size for a collection of 39 studies using indirect measures of memory was 0.30 in La Voie and Light's meta-analysis.

Findings from numerous other paradigms also comport well with the hypothesis that aging is accompanied by impairment of recollection and relative sparing of familiarity-based mechanisms. For instance, older adults are more influenced by misleading information presented after they have witnessed a series of events (Cohen and Faulkner 1989). They are more likely to believe incorrectly that a particular scene was watched in a videotape, when in fact that scene was depicted in a photograph they subsequently viewed (Schacter et al. 1997). After studying lists of items associated with target concepts, older adults often have higher false alarms for the target concepts than young adults, a form of memory illusion (Koutstaal and Schacter 1997; Norman and Schacter 1997; Tun et al. 1998). Older adults are more likely to call a previously seen nonfamous name 'famous' on seeing it later (Bartlett et al. 1991; Dywan and Jacoby 1990; Jennings and Jacoby 1993), a kind of source memory error; interestingly, encouraging older adults to use relatively strict criteria in making fame judgements can reduce such errors to the level of young adults (Multhaup 1995).

Jacoby (1999) has also identified a particularly striking ironic effect of repetition on memory in young and older adults. After seeing a list in which some words appeared one, two, or three times and then hearing a second list of words, participants took a recognition test on which they were asked to respond 'old' only to words they had heard. For young adults, exclusion of seen words improved as a function of repetition but the opposite was true for older adults, implicating an age-related deficit in the use of contextual information to oppose enhanced familiarity due to repetition. Evidence from response–signal methodology, in which the amount of time participants have to make judgements is

---

1 Such a conclusion must be viewed with some caution, because the studies included in the meta-analysis examined memory for contextual information contingent on memory for content. Even if memory for content and for context were equally affected by aging, we would expect to find larger age differences for context than for content on recognition memory tasks – getting a content item correct by chance requires one guess on a recognition test, but getting both content and context correct by chance takes two guesses. Nonetheless, there are now several studies that have systematically equated memory for content in young and older adults (e.g. Chalfonte and Johnson 1996; Kliegl and Lindenberger 1993; Schacter et al. 1994b) and still report age differences in memory for contextual information, though equating young and old on content memory does not invariably produce this outcome (e.g. Bayen and Murnane 1996).

varied and accuracy is plotted as a function of available processing time, suggests that for young adults retrieval of familiarity information is faster than retrieval time for list discrimination (e.g. Hintzman *et al.* 1998). Although response–signal methodology has not been used to compare the rise times of young and older adults for recognition and list discrimination over the very short intervals (mostly less than a second) typically used in such studies, Jacoby (1999) has shown that young adults show ironic effects of repetition similar in form to those shown by older adults when the time available for responding is short (a 750 ms deadline) but not long (a response deadline of 750 ms after a waiting period of 1250 ms); the negative effect of repetition was reduced for older adults when deadlines were very long (2750 ms after a 1250 ms waiting period).

Opposition methodology, in which feelings of familiarity lead to incorrect responses in the absence of contextual information, yields separate estimates of familiarity and recollection within a single paradigm (Jennings and Jacoby 1993, 1997). To preview the more detailed discussion to follow, we simply note here that estimates of recollection show age differences favouring the young, but estimates of familiarity (assuming that recollection and familiarity are independent) are age invariant. Finally, in the remember/know paradigm, participants do not merely designate test items as previously presented or new, but also judge whether they recollect specific details about the circumstances in which they originally encountered list words ('remember' judgements) or just 'know' that they were presented, presumably because the item feels familiar. Remember judgements decrease with age whereas know judgements typically remain constant or increase (e.g. Parkin and Walter 1992; Perfect and Dasgupta 1997).

All of these findings are consistent with principles associated with dual-process views of recognition that distinguish between a recollection process that declines with advanced age and a familiarity process that is relatively unaffected. We turn now to a more detailed analysis of studies of indirect measures of memory in old age, process dissociation procedures, and the remember/know paradigm.

INDIRECT MEASURES OF MEMORY: AN UPDATED META-ANALYSIS

Graf and Schacter (1985) differentiated between two broad classes of indirect measures of memory, those involving memory for words or objects that have pre-existing memory representations (item priming) and those involving memory for new connections or for novel stimuli (associative priming). Roediger and his colleagues (e.g. Srinivas and Roediger 1990) have suggested a further distinction between priming tasks that are largely perceptual in nature and those that are primarily conceptual. The former include tasks such as perceptual identification and word stem or word fragment completion that are not sensitive to variations in levels of processing (semantic vs nonsemantic orienting tasks) at study but are influenced by changes in the format of presentation (e.g. from auditory to visual) between study and test. The latter include tasks such as category exemplar generation and answering general knowledge questions that are sensitive to levels of processing during encoding but not to changes in format between study and test.

Age differences are usually, though not always, unreliable in studies of both item and associative priming. For example, nonsignificant age differences have been observed for perceptual priming tasks such as word identification (Light and Kennison 1996a), word stem completion (Light and Singh 1987), word fragment completion (Light *et al.* 1986), and for conceptual priming tasks such as exemplar generation (Light and Albertson 1989) and answering general knowledge questions (Small *et al.* 1995). Although statistically reliable age differences are sometimes obtained on both perceptual and conceptual item priming tasks (e.g. Grober *et al.* 1992; Small *et al.* 1995), such findings are not consistently obtained despite the fact there is often a numerical advantage for young adults. Because older adults have difficulty in forming new connections (see Kausler 1994, for a review), it might be anticipated that age differences would be obtained on associative priming even if none were found for item priming. However, the data are not consistent here either (e.g. Howard *et al.* 1991; Light *et al.* 1995).

This is a situation that calls for a more systematic and quantitative integration. Meta-analysis provides tools for aggregating results across experiments, taking account of the fact that studies vary in sample size and in the paradigms used to investigate priming. There have, in fact, been two prior meta-analyses of this literature. As noted earlier, La Voie and Light (1994) obtained a reliable mean weighted effect size of 0.304 for a corpus of 41 effect sizes; this effect size was reliably smaller than that for either recognition and recall. Mitchell (1993) concluded from a meta-analysis of picture priming studies that age differences were absent for this class of materials. However, neither meta-analysis was comprehensive. Mitchell included only picture priming studies and the inclusion criteria for La Voie and Light (1994) were somewhat narrow, excluding tasks using nonverbal materials, conceptual priming tasks, and tasks for which only one experiment had been reported in the literature. Moreover, the numbers of effect sizes falling into particular categories (e.g. item priming or associative priming) were rather small, decreasing confidence in conclusions about the absence of reliable partitions of effect sizes within the corpus. In the relatively few years since the publication of these meta-analyses, many additional articles have reported studies of indirect measures of memory in young and older adults. These studies have been reviewed recently by Fleischman and Gabrieli (1998) who reported head counts of significant and nonsignificant age differences in a large variety of tasks. Fleischman and Gabrieli (1998) did not, however, carry out a quantitative meta-analysis. We have now completed an elaborated update of our 1994 meta-analysis.[2]

We constrained our analyses to published studies. Doing so gives all readers the same access to the entire collection of studies for purposes of verifying our results and evaluating the adequacy of individual investigations. Although the general practice is to include all available studies in a meta-analysis in the interest of offsetting possible biases against publication of research that does not yield statistically significant outcomes, with repetition priming studies of young and older adults what is of interest is the possibility of dissociations between direct and indirect measures. Bias against nonsignificant results should not be an issue here, because it is precisely findings of age differences on direct measures and no age differences on indirect measures that is of theoretical interest when evidence for dissociation is sought. Similarly, the presence in our corpus of a number of studies with reliable age differences favouring the young on priming tasks suggests that there is little bias against findings inconsistent with the dissociation hypothesis. Moreover, to detect an effect size of 0.20 with power of 0.80 and an alpha of 0.05 requires sample sizes of 393 per group for a two-sample design. We doubt that authors who carry out studies of this magnitude would suppress their results, whichever side of the debate they favoured! Overall, then, we believe that there is little cause for worry about the 'file drawer problem' (Rosenthal 1991). Table 9.1 gives the 95 effect sizes that were included in the analysis.

The chief measure of interest in the meta-analysis was the age difference in the amount of priming that occurred on an indirect memory task. The amount of priming that can occur on a task is defined as the difference between indirect test performance and baseline test performance. Although

2   The methodology employed in this meta-analysis was modelled after that in our previous work (La Voie and Light 1994; Light and La Voie 1993). In addition to studies included in those analyses, we used four methods to locate additional studies comparing young and older adults: (a) manual search of journals known to publish research on indirect measures of memory in old age; (b) review of references from identified studies; (c) computerized searches of *PsycLIT*, *Dissertation Abstracts International*, and *Social Science Citation Index*; and (d) letters or e-mail queries sent to researchers who have published findings on indirect measures of memory in old age, requesting that they send us their unpublished findings. The key terms used for the database search were *repetition priming*, *memory and aging*, *implicit memory*, and *episodic memory*. The time period covered by this search was 1986 to 1997.

The following periodicals were searched: *Aging, Neuropsychology, and Cognition; American Journal of Psychology; Behavioral Neuroscience; Brain; Brain and Cognition; Brain and Language; Cahiers de Psychologie Cognitive; Canadian Journal of Experimental Psychology; Cognitive Neuropsychology; Consciousness and Cognition; Cortex; European Journal of Experimental Psychology; Experimental Aging Research; International Journal of Neuroscience; Journal of Experimental Psychology: Learning, Memory, and Cognition; Journal of Experimental and Clinical Neuropsychology; Journal of Cognitive Neuroscience; Journal of Gerontology: Psychological Sciences; Journal of the International Neuropsychological Society; Journal of Memory and Language; Memory; Memory and Cognition; Neuropsychologia; Neuropsychology; Psychobiology; Psychological Medicine; Psychological Research; Psychological Science; Psychology and Aging; Psychonomic Bulletin and Review; Quarterly Journal of Experimental Psychology;* and *Swiss Journal of Psychology.*

interest has recently begun to develop in negative consequences of experiences (i.e., costs rather than benefits, see Ratcliff and McKoon 1997), with the exception of subjective judgements we included only tasks in which priming is defined in positive terms – that is, in which experience produces either a faster response or an increase in the frequency of some response. In contrast to our previous analyses, the present meta-analyses include studies that used both linguistic and nonlinguistic and pictorial materials. In addition, studies met the following criteria:

1.   The indirect memory measure was a repetition priming task, that is, the task measured changes in speed, accuracy, or response bias as a consequence of exposure to previously encountered stimuli. The tasks included anagram solution, answering general knowledge questions, auditory and visual word identification, category exemplar generation, credibility judgements, homophone spelling, item recognition, lexical decision, mirror reading, object decision, picture fragment completion, picture naming, ratings of likability, rhyme generation, semantic classification, sentence completion, Turkish word reading, word association, word fragment completion, word/nonword naming, word stem completion, text rereading, and nonword/word pair naming.

2.   The comparison groups for each study consisted of at least one group of young adults (18–40 years old) and a group of healthy, community-dwelling older adults (aged 60 + years old). In studies with more than one group of older adults, data from each group were combined and compared to the young adult data. If a study included other comparison groups (e.g. middle-aged adults) data from these groups were not included. Table 9.1 lists the studies included in the meta-analyses, together with the tasks used in each, the sample sizes of young and older adults, and the method used to compute an effect size.

Published studies often do not provide the information needed to compute an effect size for a meta-analysis. Thus, when necessary, we requested supplementary information from authors.[3] Effect sizes for each study were calculated for the reported age difference in priming. In some cases it was possible to compute this statistic directly from the means and standard deviations reported in the original study, using the formula for the standardized effect size g as reported in Hedges and Olkin (1985):

$$g = \frac{(\bar{Y}^E - \bar{Y}^C)}{s} \tag{9.1}$$

3   The authors are grateful to the following investigators who generously provided us with additional information needed to compute effect sizes (often at short notice): D. M. Burke, F. R. Ferraro, D. Friedman, R. Habib, M. Hartman, M. Isingrini, R. Java, R. Knight, P. Maki, C. Manning, T. Meulemans, L. Monti, S. Mutter, B. Ober, D. Park, R. Russo, M. Schugens, D. Spieler, D. Swick, C. Wiggs.

where $\bar{Y}^E$ is the mean priming score for the young, $\bar{Y}^C$ is the mean priming score for the old, and s is the pooled sample standard deviation. When the appropriate means and standard deviations were not reported, effect sizes were calculated from the appropriate F, t, or r statistics, using conversion formulas given in Wolf (1986).

Occasionally, researchers reported priming scores for two or more experimental conditions, creating the possibility for these studies to contribute more than one effect size to the meta-analysis. Because these scores generally included the same people tested in more than one condition, the calculated effect sizes for these priming scores would not be independent. Hence, separate effect sizes were calculated for each condition within an experiment whenever possible, and then an average effect size (arithmetic mean) for the entire experiment was obtained. In eight instances, a study included more than one task or more than one type of stimulus material; for these studies, separate effect sizes were computed for each task type or stimulus type.[4] Overall, the meta-analysis included 95 effect sizes, based on the responses of 5904 research participants (2590 young adults and 3314 older adults).

The effect sizes calculated according to the procedures just outlined provide biased estimates of true effect sizes, so a correction factor (Hedges 1984) was applied to the g values to provide the unbiased estimate of effect sizes, d; here N is the sum of the sample sizes of young and older adults.

$$d \cong \left(1 - \frac{3}{4N - 9}\right)g \tag{9.2}$$

The effect size obtained from this calculation was used to compute an effect size variance and standard deviation for each study (as outlined in Hedges and Olkin 1985, p. 86). The effect size standard deviation was used to calculate a 95% confidence interval for each calculated effect size, using the following formula:

$$95\% \text{ confidence interval} = d \pm (C_{\alpha/2})(s_d) \tag{9.3}$$

where $C_{\alpha/2}$ is the two-tailed critical value of the standard normal distribution (here 1.96) and s_d is the estimated effect size standard deviation. When the confidence interval includes 0, d is not significant at the $p = 0.05$ level. When the confidence interval does not include 0 then d is significant (i.e., there is an age difference in repetition priming).

We had two goals in carrying out the meta-analysis. The first was to determine whether it makes sense to describe our corpus by using a single effect size value. Thus, we began our data analysis using procedures outlined in Hedges and Olkin (1985) for calculating the homogeneity of effect sizes across experiments. The statistic Q_T has a chi-square distribution with k-1 degrees of freedom (with k

---

4 The following studies contributed two effect sizes each: Geva *et al.* 1997; Jelicic *et al.* 1996; Maki and Knopman 1996; Ober *et al.* 1991; Schugens *et al.* 1997; Small *et al.* 1995; Wiggs and Martin 1994 (Experiments 1 and 2); Winocur *et al.* 1996.

Table 9.1 Experiments included in the meta-analysis together with relevant meta-analytic statistics

Experiment	Task	Procedure for effect size calculation	n Young	n Old	d	95% confidence interval	
						Lower limit	Upper limit
Abbenhuis et al. 1990, Experiment 2	Visual word identification (single words)	Standardized mean difference for priming scores averaged across high and low frequency items	11	11	0.680	-0.180	1.539
Balota and Ferraro 1996[a]	Lexical decision	Standardized mean difference for priming averaged across words for yes responses	48	39	-0.047	-0.470	0.376
Chiarello and Hoyer 1988	Visual word completion	Conversion of F for age difference in priming collapsed across encoding conditions and delays	36	36	0.657	0.182	1.131
Davis et al. 1990, Experiment 1	Homophone spelling	Conversion of Age x Item Status F	45	21	0.808	0.272	1.344
Davis et al. 1990, Experiment 2	Visual word stem completion	Standardized mean difference for priming scores for two youngest and three oldest age groups	47	62	1.099	0.693	1.505
Dick et al. 1989, Experiment 1[b]	Visual word stem completion	Standardized mean difference for read condition averaged across encoding conditions for Trial 1	24	24	-0.191	-0.758	0.376
Friedman et al. 1994	Visual word stem completion	Standardized mean difference for priming averaged across encoding conditions	20	20	0.389	-0.236	1.015
Geva et al. 1997	Word fragment completion	Standardized mean difference for priming averaged across encoding condition and fragment type	12	12	0.421	-0.388	1.230
Geva et al. 1997	Visual word stem completion	Standardized mean difference for priming averaged across encoding condition	12	12	0.172	-0.629	0.974
Gibson et al. 1993, Experiments 2A, 2B	Visual word stem completion	Standardized mean differences for priming score averaged across encoding conditions and test format (same/different) for Experiments 2A, 2B	32	56	0.258	-0.178	0.695
Habib et al. 1996	Word fragment completion	Standardized mean difference for priming averaged across encoding conditions, study modality, and test modality	20	20	0.581	-0.052	1.213
Hartman 1995, Experiment 1	Sentence completion	Standardized mean difference for priming averaged across target type	24	24	0.151	-0.416	0.717

Study	Task	Measure					
Hartman 1995, Experiment 2	Sentence completion	Standardized mean difference for priming averaged across encoding conditions and target type	40	40	-0.065	-0.504	0.373
Hartman 1995, Experiment 3 unexpected vs Experiment 4	Sentence completion	Standardized mean difference for priming averaged across target type (select unexpected target condition)	24	24	0.100	-0.466	0.666
Hartman and Dusek 1994, Experiment 1	Sentence completion	Standardized mean difference for priming averaged across target type	56	44	0.097	-0.298	0.492
Hartman and Hasher 1991	Sentence completion	Standardized mean difference for priming averaged across target type	44	24	0.048	-0.449	0.546
Hasher et al. 1997, Experiment 1	Sentence completion	Standardized mean difference for priming averaged across conditions	24	24	-0.471	-1.044	0.103
Hasher et al. 1997, Experiment 2	Sentence completion	Standardized mean difference for priming averaged across conditions	24	24	0.055	-0.511	0.621
Hashtroudi et al. 1991, Experiment 1a[c]	Reading inverted words	Standardized mean difference for Trial 2 priming conditions equating young and old on baseline performance	20	20	0.140	-0.480	0.760
Hashtroudi et al. 1991, Experiment 2a[d]	Partial word identification	Standardized mean difference for Trial 2 priming conditions equating young and old on baseline performance	30	10	0.192	-0.525	0.909
Howard 1988, Delay study	Item recognition	Conversion of Age x Item Status F	16	16	0.271	-0.425	0.967
Howard 1988, Experiment 1	Homophone spelling	Standardized mean difference for priming scores	12	12	0.952	0.108	1.797
Howard 1988, Experiment 2	Homophone spelling	Standardized mean difference for priming scores averaged across delay conditions	24	24	0.361	-0.210	0.931
Howard 1988, Experiment 3	Homophone spelling	Standardized mean difference for priming scores averaged across delay conditions	24	24	-0.113	-0.679	0.453
Howard 1988, Two Proposition study	Item recognition	Conversion of Age x Item Status F	36	36	0.213	-0.250	0.676
Howard et al. 1986, Experiment 1	Item recognition	Conversion of age and per cent priming effect r	32	32	0.219	-0.273	0.710
Howard et al. 1986, Experiment 2	Item recognition	Conversion of age and per cent priming effect r	32	32	0.811	0.302	1.321
Howard et al. 1991, Experiment 1	Visual word stem completion	Conversion of priming effect t	20	20	1.088	0.424	1.752

Study	Task	Measure	N1	N2			
Howard et al. 1991, Experiment 2	Visual word stem completion	Conversion of priming effect t	20	20	0.143	-0.478	0.764
Howard et al. 1991, Experiment 3	Visual word stem completion	Conversion of priming effect t	24	24	0.389	-0.182	0.960
Hultsch et al. 1991	Visual word stem completion	Standardized mean difference for priming scores	96	203	0.441	0.196	0.686
Isingrini et al. 1995	Category exemplar generation	Standardized mean difference for priming scores for youngest and two oldest age groups	40	80	0.037	-0.343	0.416
Java 1992	Anagram solution	Standardized mean difference for priming averaged across encoding conditions	16	16	0.003	-0.690	0.696
Java 1996	Word association	Standardized mean difference for priming averaged across encoding conditions	20	20	0.152	-0.469	0.773
Java and Gardiner 1991, Experiment 1	Visual word stem completion	Standardized mean difference for priming scores averaged across encoding conditions	16	16	0.270	-0.426	0.966
Java and Gardiner 1991, Experiment 2[e]	Visual word stem completion	Standardized mean difference for priming scores averaged across encoding conditions	16	16	0.283	-0.414	0.979
Jelicic et al. 1996	Category exemplar generation	Conversion of age difference in priming t	24	24	0.598	0.019	1.176
Jelicic et al. 1996	Word fragment completion	Conversion of age difference in priming t	24	24	0.136	-0.430	0.703
Kazmerski et al. 1995	Semantic classification of pictures	Standardized mean difference for Trial 1 vs Trial 2 RTs for same items (no new baseline)	16	8	-0.613	-1.479	0.253
Light and Albertson 1989	Category exemplar generation	Conversion of Age x Item Status F	32	33	0.343	-0.147	0.833
Light and Kennison 1996a, Experiment 1	Visual word identification (single words)	Standardized mean difference for priming scores	24	24	0.230	-0.338	0.798
Light and Kennison 1996a, Experiment 2	Visual word identification (forced choice)	Standardized mean difference for priming scores	32	32	-0.230	-0.721	0.262
Light and Kennison 1996a, Experiment 3	Visual word identification (forced choice)	Standardized mean difference for priming scores	24	24	0.234	-0.333	0.802
Light and Kennison 1996a, Experiment 5	Visual word identification (forced choice)	Standardized mean difference for priming scores averaged across encoding conditions for standard instructions only	24	24	0.330	-0.239	0.900

Study	Task	Description	N	N			
Light et al. 1996, Experiment 1	Nonword naming	Conversion of Age x Item Status F	16	16	-0.071	-0.764	0.622
Light et al. 1996, Experiment 2	Nonword naming	Conversion of Age x Item Status F averaged across encoding conditions	48	48	0.095	-0.305	0.495
Light et al. 1996, Experiment 3	Nonword naming	Conversion of Age x Item Status F averaged across encoding conditions	36	36	0.039	-0.424	0.501
Light et al. 1995, Experiment 1	Nonword naming	Standardized mean difference for priming scores averaged across unique and repeated conditions	18	18	-0.042	-0.695	0.612
Light et al. 1995, Experiment 2	Nonword naming	Standardized mean difference for priming scores averaged across presentation frequencies of 2, 4, 8	18	18	-0.125	-0.779	0.529
Light et al. 1995, Experiment 3	Nonword naming	Standardized mean difference for priming scores averaged across test delays	18	18	0.017	-0.636	0.671
Light et al. 1992, Experiment 1[f]	Visual word identification (single words)	Standardized mean difference for priming scores averaged across encoding conditions and test modality	32	32	0.343	-0.151	0.836
Light et al. 1992, Experiment 2[g]	Auditory word identification	Standardized mean difference for priming scores averaged across test modality	32	32	-0.101	-0.591	0.390
Light and Prull 1995, Experiment 1	Word naming	Standardized mean difference for priming scores (New - (FA + DA)/2)	24	24	-0.203	-0.770	0.364
Light and Prull 1995, Experiment 2	Word naming	Standardized mean difference for priming scores (New - (FA + DA + H)/3)	48	48	0.018	-0.382	0.418
Light and Singh 1987, Experiment 1	Visual word stem completion	Conversion of Age x Item Status F	32	32	0.322	-0.171	0.815
Light and Singh 1987, Experiment 2	Visual word stem completion	Conversion of Age x Item Status F	16	16	0.528	-0.177	1.233
Light and Singh 1987, Experiment 3[h]	Partial word identification	Conversion of Age x Item Status F	32	32	0.411	-0.084	0.906
Light et al. 1986	Word fragment completion	Conversion of Age x Item Status F	32	32	0.308	-0.184	0.801
Maki and Knopman 1996	Category exemplar generation	Standardized mean difference for priming averaged across encoding conditions	16	16	0.269	-0.427	0.965
Maki and Knopman 1996	Rhyme generation	Standardized mean difference for priming averaged across encoding conditions	16	16	0.127	-0.567	0.821

Study	Task	Description	n	n			
Manning et al. 1997	Visual word stem completion	Standardized mean difference for priming scores	24	23	0.407	-0.170	0.985
McCauley et al. 1996	Visual word stem completion	Standardized mean difference, averaged across lists and imagery conditions	24	32	2.710	1.980	3.440
Meulemans and Van der Linden 1995, Experiment 1[i]	Story rereading	Conversion of Age x Trial (1 vs 2) F averaged across story	16	16	-0.082	-0.776	0.611
Meulemans and Van der Linden 1995, Experiment 2[j]	Rereading grammatical but meaningless text	Conversion of Age x Trial (1 vs 2) F averaged across story	16	16	0.466	-0.236	1.168
Mitchell 1989	Picture naming	Standardized mean difference in priming scores aggregated across lags	48	48	0.177	-0.224	0.578
Monti et al. 1996	Category exemplar generation	Standardized mean difference for priming averaged across encoding conditions	24	24	0.003	-0.562	0.569
Monti et al. 1997	Scrambled text rereading	Conversion of Age x Trial 1 (1 vs 2) x Passage type (same-random vs different-random) F—logarithmic reading times	18	18	-0.149	-0.803	0.505
Mutter et al. 1995, Experiment 1	Credibility judgment	Conversion of Age x Item Status F	40	40	-0.363	-0.805	0.079
Nilsson et al. 1989[k]	Lexical decision	Standardized mean difference for episodic priming scores averaged across encoding conditions for weak and strong pairs	10	10	-0.466	-1.354	0.422
Nyberg et al. 1996	Visual word stem completion	Standardized mean difference for priming for youngest and five oldest groups	100	500	0.323	0.108	0.539
Ober et al. 1991[l]	Lexical decision	Conversion of Age x Item Status F averaged across Experiments 2, 4, 6	20	19	0.023	-0.604	0.651
Ober et al. 1991[m]	Word naming	Conversion of Age x Item Status F averaged across Experiments 1, 3, 5	21	19	0.008	-0.613	0.628
Park and Shaw 1992[n]	Visual word stem completion	Standardized mean difference for priming averaged across encoding conditions for stem lengths 3 and 4 for all Ss	143	144	0.138	-0.093	0.370
Rastle and Burke 1996	General knowledge questions	Conversion of Age x Item Status F for know responses	30	30	0.162	-0.345	0.669
Rose et al. 1986	Homophone spelling	Conversion of Age x Item Status F	16	16	1.175	0.424	1.925

Study	Task	Description					
Russo and Parkin 1993	Picture fragment completion	Standardized mean difference for priming for young full attention and old groups	24	24	0.804	0.216	1.392
Schacter et al. 1994a, Experiment 1	Auditory word stem completion	Standardized mean difference in priming scores aggregated over encoding and voice conditions	48	48	0.955	0.532	1.378
Schacter et al. 1994a, Experiment 3	Auditory word identification	Standardized mean difference in priming scores averaged over voice conditions	24	24	0.152	-0.414	0.719
Schacter et al. 1992, Experiment 2	Object decision	Standardized mean difference in priming scores for possible objects only	32	32	-0.330	-0.823	0.164
Schugens et al. 1997	Mirror reading	Standardized mean difference for priming (unique vs repeated triads in second session) for two youngest and oldest group only	20	10	-0.397	-1.163	0.368
Schugens et al. 1997	Visual word stem completion	Standardized mean difference for priming for two youngest groups and oldest group only	20	10	0.926	0.132	1.720
Small et al. 1995	General knowledge	Standardized mean difference for priming	82	321	-0.016	-0.259	0.226
Small et al. 1995	Visual word stem completion	Standardized mean difference for priming	82	321	0.329	0.086	0.572
Spieler and Balota 1996, Experiment 1	Word naming	Conversion of Age x Trials (1 vs 2) x Target type (repeated targets vs consistent pairs) F	32	32	-0.046	-0.536	0.444
Spieler and Balota 1996, Experiment 2	Word naming	Conversion of Age x Trials (1 vs 2) x Target type (repeated targets vs consistent pairs) F	32	32	0.645	0.143	1.148
Swick and Knight 1997	Lexical decision	Standardized mean difference for priming (for words only)	9	9	-0.688	-1.638	0.263
Titov and Knight 1997	Visual word stem completion	Standardized mean difference for priming	30	30	0.897	0.366	1.428
Wiggs 1993	Likability rating	Standardized mean difference for 0 vs 1 frequency conditions	16	16	0.489	-0.214	1.192
Wiggs and Martin 1994, Experiment 1	Turkish word naming	Standardized mean difference for priming averaged over font type and study-test font constancy	16	16	1.010	0.274	1.746
Wiggs and Martin 1994, Experiment 2	Turkish word naming	Standardized mean difference for priming averaged over font type and study-test font constancy	32	32	0.716	0.210	1.222
Wiggs and Martin 1994, Experiment 1	Word naming	Standardized mean difference for priming averaged over font type and study-test font constancy	16	16	-0.014	-0.707	0.679

Word pairs and triads				
Item recognition	Latency	Associative	Other	Other
Lexical decision	Latency	Associative	Other	Other
Mirror reading	Latency	Other	Other	Other
Word naming	Latency	Associative	Other	Other
Visual word stem completion	Other	Associative	Other	Other
Sentence and Text Materials				
Credibility judgements	Other	Other	Other	Other
Meaningless text rereading	Latency	Other	Other	Other
Scrambled text rereading	Latency	Associative	Other	Other
Story rereading	Latency	Other	Other	Other

equal to the number of effect sizes included in the analysis). The analysis of the 95 published studies produced an initial $Q_T(94) = 203.74, p < 0.05$. Removing six outliers (Davis *et al.* 1990, Experiment 2; Howard *et al.* 1991, Experiment 1; McCauley *et al.* 1996; Rose *et al.* 1986; Schacter *et al.* 1994a, Experiment 1; Titov and Knight 1997) produced a homogeneous set of 89 effect sizes, $Q_T(88) = 109.21, p > 0.05$. The mean weighted effect size $(d+)$ is 0.185, with a 95% confidence interval from 0.133 to 0.237. Because the confidence interval for our overall estimate of effect size does not include 0, we can reject the hypothesis that there are no age differences in repetition priming. This result is consistent with the results of our previous meta-analyses, though the value of $d+$ here is smaller than the $d+$ of 0.304 reported by La Voie and Light (1994).

Finding homogeneity of effect sizes after eliminating just over 6% of values suggests that no partitioning of effect sizes is needed. The frequency distribution shown in Fig. 9.1 also reveals that the distribution of effect sizes, though positively skewed, is unimodal, again suggesting that a single distribution is involved. Nevertheless, examination of Table 9.1 and Fig. 9.1 reveals a considerable range of effect sizes in the corpus, from –0.688 (Swick and Knight 1997) to 2.710 (McCauley *et al.* 1996). Moreover, there is considerable theoretical interest in

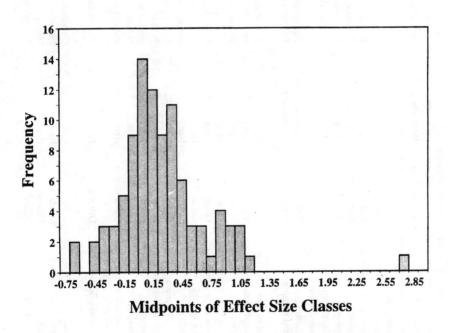

Fig. 9.1 Frequency distribution of 95 effect sizes. After removing six outliers, the mean weighted effect size for the remaining studies was 0.185, with a 95% confidence interval from 0.133 to 0.237.

Table 9.2 Task classifications for meta-analysis

Materials/tasks	Latency/other	Item/associative	Conceptual/perceptual	Production/identification	Competition
Nonverbal materials					
Likability rating	Other	Other	Other	Other	Other
Picture fragment completion	Other	Item	Perceptual	Identification	High
Object decision	Other	Other	Perceptual	Identification	Low
Picture naming	Latency	Item	Perceptual	Identification	High
Semantic classification	Latency	Item	Unknown	Identification	Low
Verbal, not meaningful					
Nonword naming	Latency	Associative	Perceptual	Identification	Low
Turkish word naming	Latency	Associative	Perceptual	Identification	Low
Single words					
Auditory word identification	Other	Item	Perceptual	Identification	High
Auditory word stem completion	Other	Item	Perceptual	Production	High
Anagram solution	Other	Item	Perceptual	Production	High
Category exemplar generation	Other	Item	Conceptual	Production	High
General knowledge questions	Other	Item	Conceptual	Production	High
Homophone spelling	Other	Item	Unknown	Production	High
Lexical decision	Latency	Item	Perceptual	Identification	Low
Partial word identification	Other	Item	Perceptual	Identification	High
Reading inverted words	Other	Item	Perceptual	Identification	High
Rhyme generation	Other	Item	Perceptual	Production	High
Sentence completion	Other	Item	Unknown	Production	High
Visual word identification (single words)	Other	Item	Perceptual	Identification	Low
Visual word identification (forced choice)	Other	Item	Perceptual	Identification	Low
Word association	Other	Item	Conceptual	Production	High
Word fragment completion	Other	Item	Perceptual	Production	Low
Word naming	Latency	Item	Perceptual	Identification	Low
Word stem completion	Other	Item	Perceptual	Production	High

Study	Measure	Description	n	n			
Wiggs and Martin 1994, Experiment 2	Word naming	Standardized mean difference for priming averaged over font type and study-test font constancy	32	32	-0.249	-0.741	0.243
Wiggs et al. 1994	Turkish word naming	Standardized mean difference for reading times of words presented 1 vs 3 times	15	15	-0.059	-0.775	0.657
Winocur et al. 1996[o]	Visual word stem completion	Standardized mean difference for priming	29	24	0.309	-0.235	0.853
Winocur et al. 1996[p]	Word fragment completion	Standardized mean difference for priming	29	24	0.097	-0.444	0.638

[a] Data from Old-Old participants were not included due to an error.
[b] Data from Generate condition were not requested from authors for La Voie and Light (1994).
[c] Categorized as perceptual identification in La Voie and Light (1994).
[d] Categorized as perceptual identification in La Voie and Light (1994).
[e] Only the Read condition was included in La Voie and Light (1994).
[f] Only the same modality test condition was included in La Voie and Light (1994).
[g] Only the same modality test condition was included in La Voie and Light (1994).
[h] Categorized as perceptual identification in La Voie and Light (1994).
[i] No new baseline condition was included.
[j] No new baseline condition was included.
[k] Only weak pairs were included in La Voie and Light (1994).
[l] The same participants were tested in all experiments. The number of participants included in each analysis varied slightly from experiment to experiment. The smallest *n*s are tabled.
[m] The same participants were tested in all experiments. The number of participants included in each analysis varied slightly from experiment to experiment. The smallest *n*s are tabled.
[n] Only unaware participants were included in La Voie and Light (1994).
[o] Only community dwelling older adults were included.
[p] Only community dwelling older adults were included.

determining whether some types of tasks yield larger effect sizes. For these reasons, we felt it appropriate to pursue the second goal of the meta-analysis, namely partitioning the set of effect sizes to determine whether there is a way to explain the variability in their magnitudes. These analyses are outlined below.

Each analysis began with a partitioning of the 95 published studies included in the initial overall meta-analysis along the grouping dimensions to be tested.[5] As was the case in the overall analysis, the first step entailed an estimate of the homogeneity of effect sizes by calculating Q_T. In addition, two other estimates were calculated: (a) an estimate of the homogeneity of effect sizes within each partitioned class, Q_W, with $k - p$ degrees of freedom (with k = number of effect sizes, and p = number of partitions) and (b) an estimate of between-class homogeneity, Q_B, with $p - 1$ degrees of freedom. A nonsignificant Q_W indicates that an appropriate categorical model has been fitted to the data. If Q_W is significant, it indicates a lack of homogeneity within classes. There are two ways to deal with a significant Q_W. The first option is to continue partitioning studies until homogeneity is achieved; the second is to seek outliers within classes. Because each of our partitions addressed a particular research question, we opted to examine each class for outliers whenever a significant Q_W was obtained. Q_B provides an index of the extent to which effect sizes differ across classes. This procedure is analogous to the partitioning of variance in the analysis of variance, with Q_W and Q_B providing independent estimates of the within-class and between-class fits to the data. In general, an appropriate categorical model exists when both Q_T and Q_B are significant, and Q_W is nonsignificant (Hedges and Olkin 1985, p. 157).

The first analysis, more empirically motivated, investigated the possibility that effect sizes vary across types of stimulus material. The remaining analyses were more theory guided. We asked whether effect sizes varied in magnitude as a function of dependent variable (latency vs other measures), whether the task involved item priming or associative priming, whether the task could be classified as perceptual or conceptual, whether the task involved identification or production, and whether the response involved high or low competition. (See Table 9.2 for a guide to task classification.) The rationale for each of these analyses is provided below.

Materials analysis

In this analysis, we asked if there were any age differences in priming for different types of testing materials. As noted above, Mitchell (1993) found no age differences in picture priming studies, whereas La Voie and Light (1994) reported a nonzero effect size for linguistic materials. Studies were assigned to one of five classes: (1) nonverbal materials (i.e., pictures, possible objects, ideograms); (2) verbal, but not meaningful materials (i.e., nonwords and Turkish

---

5   All 95 effect sizes were included, rather than only the 89 effect sizes that entered into the overall weighted mean effect size because it is not possible to determine a priori if a given effect size will be an outlier in a particular analysis.

words); (3) single words; (4) word pairs and triads; (5) larger linguistic units (sentences, stories, scrambled or semantically meaningless text). See Table 9.3 for a list of tasks included in each class.

The initial analysis of this data set indicated a lack of homogeneity within classes, Q_W (90) = 195.57. We identified three outliers for the single words category (Davis *et al.* 1990, Experiment 2; McCauley *et al.* 1996; Schacter *et al.* 1994*a*, Experiment 1), one outlier for the word pairs and triads category (Howard *et al.* 1991, Experiment 1), and one in the picture category (Russo and Parkin 1993). Excluding these five studies from the analysis produced homogeneity of effect sizes within each class, all *ps* > 0.10. However, at this juncture there was still not homogeneity of effect sizes, Q_T (89) = 118.46, *p* < 0.05, and the overall within-class homogeneity statistic also remained statistically significant, Q_W (85) = 111.05. The between-class statistic was also not significant, Q_B (4) = 7.41. Although in other instances we deleted additional cases to achieve a nonsignificant Q_W, we did so only when the homogeneity statistic within a class fell between 0.05 < *p* < 0.10, to avoid overfitting the model. Here, all within-group homogeneity *p*-values were 0.10 or greater, suggesting that heterogeneity in effect sizes is simply not well explained by differences in materials. The effect sizes and 95% confidence intervals for the five materials categories are given in Table 9.3. For ease of reference, Table 9.3 also includes effect sizes for individual tasks subsumed under the five major groupings.

One criticism that can be levelled against any meta-analysis is inclusion of studies that employ a wide variety of testing measures in examining a particular phenomenon so that it is not clear that all measures index the same construct. A quick look at Table 9.3 indicates that there are indeed different patterns of age-related performance across tasks, with some having negative effect sizes (lexical decision), some having effect sizes hovering about zero (answering general knowledge questions, sentence production, nonword naming), and some being sizable and positive (homophone spelling). The remaining analyses address the question of whether differences across tasks are systematic.

Response type: latency vs other dependent variables

Our next question was whether age differences in priming are different for studies involving latencies and for those using other response measures. Older adults are known to be slower than young adults on almost all cognitive tasks (Salthouse 1996; Verhaeghen and Salthouse 1997). General slowing theory predicts that priming effects will be larger for older adults than for younger adults on tasks using response latency measures as the dependent variable; this prediction arises because older adults are generally slower on baseline measures, so that similar proportions of priming in young and older adults may translate into larger absolute priming scores for older adults. Thus, it is possible that the mean effect size for latency measures will be smaller than that for other dependent variables or even that it will reverse direction. We

Table 9.3 Effect sizes for classes of materials and experimental paradigms

Materials/tasks	N	d	95% confidence interval	
			Lower limit	Upper limit
Nonverbal materials	4	-0.006	-0.276	0.264
Likability rating	1	0.489	-0.214	1.192
Picture fragment completion	1	0.804	0.216	1.392
Object decision	1	-0.330	-0.823	0.164
Picture naming	1	0.177	-0.224	0.578
Semantic classification	1	-0.613	-1.479	0.253
Verbal, not meaningful	9	0.174	-0.016	0.364
Nonword naming	6	0.014	-0.210	0.237
Turkish word naming	3	0.590	0.230	0.950
Single words	63	0.208	0.150	0.267
Auditory word identification	2	0.008	-0.363	0.379
Auditory word stem completion	1	0.955	0.532	1.378
Anagram solution	1	0.003	-0.690	0.696
Category exemplar generation	5	0.209	-0.018	0.437
General knowledge questions	2	0.017	-0.202	0.236
Homophone spelling	4	0.754	0.434	1.075
Lexical decision	3	-0.104	-0.434	0.225
Partial word identification	2	0.340	-0.067	0.748
Reading inverted words	1	0.140	-0.480	0.761
Rhyme generation	1	0.127	-0.567	0.821
Sentence completion	7	0.000	-0.189	0.189
Visual word identification (single words)	3	0.355	0.013	0.697
Visual word identification (forced choice)	3	0.077	-0.234	0.388
Visual word stem completion	17	0.336	0.242	0.430
Word association	1	0.152	-0.469	0.773
Word fragment completion	5	0.281	0.020	0.541
Word naming	5	-0.086	-0.320	0.149
Word pairs and triads	10	0.262	0.083	0.440
Item recognition	4	0.379	0.119	0.640
Lexical decision	1	-0.466	-1.355	0.422
Mirror reading	1	-0.397	-1.163	0.368
Visual word stem completion	3	0.508	0.153	0.863
Word naming	2	0.291	-0.060	0.642
Sentence and text materials	4	-0.124	-0.418	0.170
Credibility judgements	1	-0.363	-0.805	0.079
Rereading grammatical but meaningless text	1	0.466	-0.236	1.168
Scrambled text rereading	1	-0.149	-0.803	0.505
Story rereading	1	-0.082	-0.776	0.611

The entries in Table 9.3 are effect sizes and mean weighted effect sizes after removing outliers for the materials analysis and for separate analyses for outliers for each task. The number of cases given for tasks within each materials class may therefore not sum to the number of tasks for that category. In the meta-analysis using materials as the partitioning variable, there were five outliers (one for nonverbal materials, three for single words, and one for word pairs and triads). Without excluding outliers, the mean weighted effect sizes and confidence intervals would be 0.135 (-0.110 to 0.381) for nonverbal materials, 0.258 (0.199 to 0.316) for single words, and 0.317 (0.145 to 0.489) for word pairs and triads. Three effect sizes were outliers within particular tasks, two for visual word stem completion with single words and one for homophone spelling. Without removing outliers, the effect sizes and associated confidence intervals would be 0.412 (0.320 to 0.504) for visual word stem completion and 0.544 (0.265 to 0.822) for homophone spelling.

therefore divided studies into two groups, placing reaction time tasks in one group and all other tasks in the other.[6] At the final step, after excluding five outliers, $Q_T(89) = 117.69$, $p = 0.02$, $Q_W(88) = 109.56$, $p = 0.06$, and $Q_B(1) = 8.13$, $p < 0.01$. This analysis indicates that there are reliable differences in effect sizes for latency and other measures, as predicted by general slowing theory. The effect sizes were $d_{LAT}+ = 0.072$, with a confidence interval from -0.034 to 0.178, and $d_{OTHER}+ = 0.249$, with a confidence interval from 0.187 to 0.311.

For the 40 studies entering into the response type analysis in La Voie and Light (1994), the outcome was different, with no reliable difference in effect sizes for latency and accuracy measures. The larger corpus in the present analysis permitted a more powerful test of the response measure variable and netted a difference between these classes of measures. Interestingly, Laver and Burke (1993) reported a similar phenomenon for semantic priming studies, though their conclusion has been challenged (Hale and Myerson 1995). It is not clear whether our findings should be interpreted as evidence for age stability in repetition priming with latency measures, or whether it should be taken as evidence for reduced priming in old age. On the assumption that there is general slowing, a larger priming effect should be seen in older adults than in younger adults, but this result did not obtain.

Priming type: item vs associative

Indirect measures of memory can be classified as involving item priming or associative priming. Item priming tasks involve memory for words that have pre-existing memory representations, whereas associative priming tasks tap memory for new connections or for novel stimuli for which there are no previously existing memory representations (Graf and Schacter 1985). Older adults are known to experience greater impairment on direct measures of

---

6   To achieve homogeneity in the 'other' category, it was necessary to exclude four outliers (Davis *et al.* 1990, Experiment 2; McCauley *et al.* 1996; Schacter *et al.* 1994a, Experiment 1; Mutter *et al.* 1995); once we did so $Q_{OTHER}(60) = 77.20$, $p < 0.07$. Although the latency effect sizes were initially homogeneous, we deleted one study (Howard *et al.* 1986, Experiment 2) because doing so achieved overall homogeneity within groups leaving the *p*-values for homogeneity within classes fairly close; an alternative scheme, deleting Howard *et al.* 1991 (Experiment 1) from the other category would have achieved the same goal, but with greater overfitting.

memory that involve formation of new associations. For example, age differences are generally larger on the hard (unrelated) paired associates on the Wechsler Memory Scale than on the easy (related) pairs (e.g. Botwinick and Storandt 1974). Thus, it might be expected that effect sizes for associative priming would be greater than those for item priming (MacKay and Abrams 1996; MacKay and Burke 1990). Contrary to this prediction, La Voie and Light (1994) reported no difference in the effect sizes for these two classes of priming tasks, with the effect size for associative priming (0.276) actually slightly less than that for item priming (0.319).

To further address the question of whether the magnitude of the age difference in repetition priming is larger for associative priming studies as compared to item priming studies, we partitioned our studies along priming type. For the purposes of this analysis, we treated the following tasks as item priming: anagram solution, perceptual identification (both auditory and visual, and carried out with or without noise or visual degradation), word stem completion, word fragment completion, picture fragment completion, exemplar generation, general knowledge, word naming, lexical decision, picture naming, semantic classification, sentence completion, homophone spelling, and word association. Within the class of associative priming tasks, we included nonword naming, Turkish word naming, item recognition, reading scrambled text, lexical decision with word pairs, word stem completion with word pairs, and reading word triads.[7] Object decision and likability judgement tasks were excluded because they involved novel visual materials, but it is unclear whether new associations must be formed to perform the tasks. The credibility judgement task involved entire sentences but resisted classification. Story rereading and mirror reading were excluded because it is not possible to tell, given the design of the research, whether priming is due to processes involving repetition of single words or larger units. (Monti et al. (1997) was clearly an associative priming task and was so classified.)[8] The final fit statistics were $Q_T(83) = 101.13$, $p < 0.09$, $Q_W(82) = 101.03$, $p < 0.08$, and $Q_B(1) = 0.10$. The value of $d+$ is 0.205, CI = 0.150 to 0.261, for item priming, and 0.224, CI = 0.094 to 0.354, for associative priming.

---

7   Placement of the nonword and Turkish word naming tasks in the associative priming group reflects a theoretical decision on our part. We believe that these tasks involve the formation of new connections (see also Bowers 1994). However, Dorfman (1994) has argued that priming involving pseudowords is not mediated by formation of new connections.

8   In the initial step of this analysis the unclassifiable tasks were included as an 'other' category. There was a significant $Q_W(92) = 194.61$, indicating a lack of homogeneity of effect sizes across partitions. An examination of the individual within-class fit statistics indicated that the group containing unclassifiable tasks was homogeneous, $Q_{OTHER}(5) = 7.92$, with $d_{OTHER}+ = -0.125$, and a confidence interval from -0.367 to 0.118, while the other two classes were heterogeneous. Because the 'other' category is not of interest here, we omitted it from further consideration. Three item priming effect sizes proved to be outliers: Davis et al. (1990, Experiment 2); McCauley et al. (1996); Schacter et al. (1994a, Experiment 1). Removing these produced a homogeneous group of studies within the item priming category, $Q_{ITEM}(65) = 82.14$, p < 0.08. In the associative category, Howard et al. (1991, Experiment 1) was an outlier; removing this study left $Q_{ASSOC}(18) = 25.39$, p = 0.11. At this juncture, $Q_W(83) = 107.54$, p = 0.04. To produce within group homogeneity, Titov and Knight (1997) was deleted from the item category.

Not only did the item and associative classes not reliably differ (as indicated by the near zero value of the between-class statistic), but also the overall fit statistic was not reliable. This outcome invites the conclusion that there are no differences in the magnitude of effect sizes for age differences in repetition priming across item and associative priming studies, the same conclusion reached by La Voie and Light (1994). It is, however, important to keep in mind that the dependent variable for the majority of tasks classed as associative priming here was latency, whereas there is a mix of dependent variables for item priming tasks. Thus, such a conclusion should be viewed with caution.

Conceptual vs perceptual priming

The next analysis explored potential differences in effect sizes for age differences in priming on conceptual and perceptual tasks. There have been recent sugges-tions that older adults have relatively unimpaired priming on perceptual tasks, while showing reduced conceptual priming (Jelicic 1995; Rybash 1996). To examine this issue, we took as our point of departure the suggestion by Blaxton (1989) and Srinivas and Roediger (1990) that measures of memory, whether direct or indirect, are conceptual if they are insensitive to changes of format between study and test (e.g. from visual to auditory modalities or from pictures to words) but are affected by levels of processing manipulations at encoding; in contrast, tasks that show the opposite pattern (sensitivity to format change but not to encoding task) are said to be perceptual in nature. Generally following the scheme of Roediger and McDermott (1993) and Fleischman and Gabrieli (1998), we classified word association, exemplar generation, and answering general knowledge questions as conceptual tasks, and perceptual identification, lexical decision, picture naming, word/nonword naming (including inverted word naming), Turkish word naming, object decision, partial word identification, picture fragment completion, rhyme generation (see Maki and Knopman 1996), word fragment completion, word stem completion, and anagram solution tasks as perceptual tasks. The status of the sentence completion, homophone spelling, and semantic classification tasks is ambiguous, although intuitively these would seem to require conceptual processing at test; these were placed in an 'un-known' category for the present purposes. All other tasks were classed as 'other' for the initial steps of the analysis and we present results for this cate-gory for information purposes only. For this analysis, and those that follow, interest centres on tasks that involved single-unit stimuli only. Text rereading probably involves both conceptual and perceptual processing (e.g. Carr *et al.* 1989; Tardif and Craik 1989) and the determination of priming type for tasks involving linguistic units of two or more words is not clear for some paradigms (e.g. Goshen-Gottstein and Moscovitch 1995*a, b*; Poldrack and Cohen 1997). Moreover, questions have been raised as to whether some allegedly associative priming tasks may yield priming only for participants who engage in deliberate recollection (e.g. Bowers and Schacter 1990; McKone and Slee 1997). The classification schema yielded 8 effect sizes in the conceptual category, 58 in the perceptual category, 13 in the unknown group, and 16 in the 'other' group.

As in the previously reported analyses on this corpus of 95, the initial Q_T (94) = 203.74. The conceptual priming category had no outliers, Q_{CON} (7) = 5.18, and $d_{CON}+$ = 0.112, with a confidence interval from -0.041 to 0.265. Each of the remaining categories had outliers. Three outliers (Davis et al. 1990, Experiment 2; McCauley et al. 1996; Schacter et al. 1994a, Experiment 1) were deleted from further analysis in the perceptual category, yielding $d_{PER}+$ = 0.226, with a confidence interval from 0.161 to 0.291. The unknown grouping had a single outlier, Rose et al. (1986); removing this effect size left $d_{UN}+$ = 0.101, with a confidence interval from -0.056 to 0.258. In the 'other' category, Mutter et al. (1995) was an outlier; without this study, the category was homogeneous with a $d_{OTHER}+$ = 0.287, and a confidence interval from 0.133 to 0.441. At this step of the analysis, we focused attention on the difference between the conceptual and perceptual categories. Confining the analysis to these two groups yielded Q_T (62) = 71.84, Q_W (61) = 70.04, and Q_B (1) = 1.80, all $p > 0.05$.

The conceptual priming category in the just-described analysis included only a small number of effect sizes. Although there have been no studies that we know of that manipulate modality at input and test or level of processing during study, it seems unlikely that sentence completion can be accomplished in the absence of semantic processing at test. Similarly, both semantic verification and homophone spelling tasks appear to require access to word meaning. These are the three tasks that were included in the 'unknown' category above. For exploratory purposes, we computed a contrast pitting the perceptual category against the conceptual and unknown categories (see Hedges and Olkin 1985, p. 159). The value of the contrast was -0.239, with a confidence interval ranging from -0.493 to 0.016. This contrast just misses being statistically significant, with a difference in the opposite direction from that predicted by Jelicic (1995) and Rybash (1996).

This contrast suggests that the outcome of the meta-analysis depends on which tasks are classified as perceptual and which are classified as conceptual. This problem is not unique to our meta-analysis. Jelicic's (1995) review treated as conceptual tasks both homophone spelling, for which our effect size was indeed rather large at 0.754, and exemplar generation, which, with an effect size of 0.209 here, was close to our overall weighted mean effect size of 0.185. Also, initial inclusion of homophone spelling as a conceptual task would probably have changed the outcome of our analysis. Rybash (1996) included under the rubric of conceptual-item priming tasks homophone spelling, word fragment completion, and word-stem completion; the latter two are more often treated as perceptual priming tasks (e.g. Roediger et al. 1992), and (as discussed below), the status of the former may be impossible to determine.

Task classification using the conceptual/perceptual dichotomy is in general not a trivial undertaking. Consider first some of the other tasks in our 'unclassified' group. Vriezen et al. (1995) argue that semantic classification tasks share properties with perceptual priming tasks in that the same perceptual information is presented at study and test (i.e., the word is repeated) but also resemble conceptual priming tasks in that semantic or conceptual information must be accessed. These investigators found that priming in semantic verification is quite sensitive to the nature of encoding tasks used, but did not vary with a change in format from pictures to words between study and test, suggesting that semantic verification is indeed conceptually driven. Nonetheless, semantic verification tasks have been found to be unresponsive to manipulations of attention or level of encoding at study and to shifts between modalities at study and test (Gabrieli *et al.* in press; Light *et al.* 1999; Vaidya *et al.* 1999). Thus, experimental paradigms that meet the intuitive criterion that they involve access to semantic information may not meet the operational definition for conceptual priming tasks.

Homophone spelling presents a different classificatory dilemma. In this task, participants hear one member of word pairs that sound alike (e.g. *cell* vs *sell*), but have different meanings, in contexts biasing one of these meanings. Later, they are asked to spell the words. Priming is defined as an increased probability of spelling the homophone in accordance with the biased meaning. It may not be possible, even in principle, to apply the criteria proposed by Roediger and his colleagues to this task. The reason for this is that the encoding task requires attention to word meaning and the test requires auditory presentation. Thus, neither manipulation of level of processing at encoding nor variation in test modality is straightforward.

Moreover, the operational definitions of conceptual and perceptual tasks may not be useful. For instance, in a meta-analysis Brown and Mitchell (1994) found that all of the tasks they included showed numerically more priming when the orienting task was semantic rather than nonsemantic. Some individual studies have also shown significant benefits for semantic processing (e.g. Challis and Brodbeck 1992) in allegedly perceptual tasks. Anagram solution is sensitive to modality switches and also shows small effects of levels of processing and generation at study (Srinivas and Roediger 1990). And, as noted above, it is becoming increasingly evident that the encoding requirements of purportedly conceptual tasks are not identical across tasks (e.g. Cabeza 1994; Light *et al.* 1999). Finally, tasks that meet the operational definitions of perceptual and conceptual tasks do not always behave in expected ways with respect to other variables (see, e.g., Rajaram 1998).

In short, it does not appear likely that adopting either simple intuitive schemata or empirical criteria proposed for classifying tasks as perceptual rather than conceptual will prove fruitful for explaining the heterogeneity of effect sizes obtained in studies of priming in young and older adults. The present state of classificatory disarray simply renders attempts to apply this dichotomy too arbitrary for most purposes. Moreover, there are relatively few studies at present that have examined conceptual priming across age, reducing the power of any meta-analysis to detect a difference between perceptual and conceptual tasks, however defined.

Production vs nonproduction tasks

Gabrieli and his colleagues have proposed that priming tasks can be classified in another way, namely as identification vs generation (Gabrieli *et al.* 1994) or as identification vs production (Fleischman and Gabrieli 1998). Gabrieli *et al.* (1994) characterize the distinction between identification and generation in this way in discussing priming tasks on which patients suffering from Alzheimer's disease (AD) show spared and compromised performance:

AD patients appear to have intact magnitudes of priming on tasks that demand the identification of the stimulus that is before them, whether the stimulus is pictorial (an object) or verbal. Perceptual identification of briefly presented words or pseudowords, identification of incomplete pictures, and lexical decision share the property that they require stimulus identification, and AD patients have been found to show normal magnitudes of priming on these tasks. Conversely, AD patients have reduced priming on generation tasks demanding retrieval from semantic memory that cannot be guided by identification alone. To perform word completion, AD subjects must do more than identify the three-letter stem before them. They must generate a response by retrieving an entry in long-term memory on the basis of a cue (the word stem). AD patients also show reduced repetition priming when the test-phase generation task is the retrieval of the semantically related word to a presented cue word (pp. 98–99).

Fleischman and Gabrieli (1998, p. 93) speak of *identification* tasks as requiring 'test phase identification of an item or *verification* of an attribute of an item, as opposed to the production of an item.' While claiming that tasks may not be process pure, they offer as examples of identification the following: word identification, lexical decision, picture naming, and category exemplar verification. Tasks exemplifying production include word stem completion, word association, and category exemplar generation. Word fragment completion is said to present an ambiguous case – it requires production but may, especially if there is only a single solution, 'depend relatively more than word-stem completion on identifying patterns of letters than on producing words.' Gabrieli *et al.* (in press) have suggested that identification tasks have lower attentional requirements than production tasks and that they are for this reason differentially spared in Alzheimer's disease (but see Light *et al.* (1999) for a different perspective). Evidence is mixed as to whether dividing attention during the study phase in either direct or indirect measures of memory produces a greater effect on memory for older than for younger adults (see Anderson *et al.* (1998) and Light and Prull (1995) for reviews). Nonetheless, we thought it potentially informative to pursue the identification/production grouping in our corpus of effect sizes.

We began with the criteria formulated by Fleischman and Gabrieli (1998) and designated word stem completion, word fragment completion, word association, exemplar generation, rhyme generation, homophone spelling, anagram solution, general knowledge questions, and sentence completion as production tasks. Object decision, picture naming, picture fragment completion, semantic classification, perceptual identification (including perceptual identification under degraded conditions and inverted word reading), lexical decision, word naming, nonword naming, and Turkish word naming tasks were treated as identification tasks. This classification scheme gave us a corpus of 79 effect sizes. We did not include the likability or credibility judgement tasks or tasks involving more than a single stimulus. The judgement tasks did not seem to fit the classificatory schema. Item recognition involves deciding if a word was previously presented and also did not neatly fit the grouping system.[9] The final homogeneity statistics were $Q_T(75) = 98.94$, $p = 0.03$, $Q_W(74) = 92.31$, $p = 0.07$, and $Q_B(1) = 6.63$, $p = 0.01$ The production task effect sizes were small to medium, $d_{PROD} + = 0.251$, with a 95% confidence interval from 0.183 to 0.319, while the identification task $d_{IDENT} +$ was smaller, 0.094, with a 95% confidence interval from -0.004 to 0.192.

There was some disagreement among the present authors as to classification of some tasks as production and identification. Gabrieli *et al.* (in press) treated picture naming as an identification task. However, after considerable discussion, we concluded that the identification/production classification criteria as reported in Fleischman and Gabrieli (1998) are ambiguous regarding certain tasks. Specifically, picture fragment completion and picture naming can be considered to be production tasks because they require access to, and production of, a word's pronunciation from meaning for a response to be made. That is, it is unclear whether in naming pictures, access to labels or phonology proceeds directly from the picture without access to meaning in the same way that word naming does (see Johnson *et al.* 1996, for a discussion of stages in picture naming). We reclassified these two tasks as production tasks, and reanalysed the same set of 79 effect sizes. Once again, identification tasks were homogeneous, $Q_{IDENT}(29) = 32.16$, $d_{IDENT} + = 0.068$, with a CI of -0.034 to 0.170. The production group was initially heterogeneous, with $Q_{PROD}(48) = 125.15$. Deleting the same three outlying studies created homogeneity, $Q_{PROD}(45) = 57.63$, $d_{PROD} + = 0.256$, CI = 0.188 to 0.324. The final homogeneity statistics were $Q_T(75) = 98.94$, $p = .03$, $Q_W(74) = 89.79$, $p = 0.10$, and $Q_B(1) = 9.15$, $p < 0.01$. Thus, both analyses led to the same conclusion.

Consistent with findings by Gabrieli *et al.* (in press) and Gabrieli *et al.* (1994) for Alzheimer's disease, we found reduced or no age differences for identification tasks. Still, the inability of the classificatory scheme to incorporate several indirect measures of memory and our own difficulty in applying the Fleischman and Gabrieli (1998) criteria suggest the need for further refinement of this classificatory scheme and more careful definition of the nature of identification

9   The initial analysis indicated a lack of homogeneity of effect sizes across studies and within classes, $Q_T(78) = 173.14$ and $Q_W(77) = 160.21$. The production group lacked homogeneity of effect sizes, $Q_W(46) = 122.02$, though the identification group was homogeneous, $Q_W(31) = 38.19$. Three studies in the production group were identified as outliers (Davis *et al.* 1990, Experiment 2; McCauley *et al.* 1996; Schacter *et al.* 1994a, Experiment 1) and excluded from further analyses, yielding a new $Q_W(43) = 54.12$.

and production. We might also note that the identification category includes a higher proportion of studies using latency measures than does the production category. Indeed, in our first cut of tasks for the present analysis, none of the production tasks involved latency measures. We have already seen that the mean effect size for latency studies is smaller than that for other types of responses in the entire corpus of 95 studies, and the same is true for the reduced corpus considered here ($d+$ for latencies = 0.041, 95% CI = -0.086 to 0.168), so there is a potential confound here.

High vs low response competition

All of the tasks initially grouped as production tasks share another feature. With the exception of single-solution word fragments, they permit more than a single response at test. This observation suggests an additional dichotomy for priming tasks, namely whether response competition is high or low. This classificatory schema is hinted at in work from the Gabrieli laboratory (Fleischman and Gabrieli 1998; Gabrieli et al. 1994), has been suggested as potentially informative by Toth (1998), and is in keeping with current theorizing that older adults suffer from a deficit in inhibitory processing (Hasher and Zacks 1988; Zacks and Hasher 1997). Although there has been a great deal of research directed at confirmation (or disconfirmation) of the inhibitory deficit hypothesis, relatively little of the priming research has been motivated by this goal. There are nonetheless a few relevant investigations, most of which (for reasons discussed below) were not included in the meta-analysis.

Using the word stem completion task, Nyberg et al. (1997) varied the number of letters that serve as cues (two vs three) and the size of the search space (three or fewer vs ten or more possible completions for the word stem). Only older adults (mean age = 77) were tested. Although significance tests are not reported for differences in priming among conditions, priming was numerically smaller in the 2–10 condition (0.06) than in the remaining conditions (0.15, 0.13, and 0.17, for the 3–10, 3–3, and 2–3 conditions, respectively), offering some support for the view that having more possible responses lowers priming, at least for cases in which the word stem cues have only two letters. Because only older adults were tested, however, it is unclear whether response competition and age would interact, with older adults more affected by search set size. It is not at all certain that this would occur given that Park and Shaw (1992) varied the number of letters offered as cues in a word stem completion task, thereby effectively varying search set size (giving more letters in the cue reduces the set of solutions), but did not obtain an interaction in priming scores between age and number of letters in the cue.

A similar logic was used by McEvoy et al. (1995) in a word association task. In the conditions of interest, words studied by young and older participants had large or small cue set sizes (number of associates). When asked to generate the first associate that came to mind, both young and old were more likely to generate previously studied items with small cue set sizes than those with large cue set sizes, though the effect was stronger for the old, suggesting a larger effect of response competition. Unfortunately, this study used word association norms for young adults as a baseline and, hence, was not included in the meta-analysis. Mitchell (1989), in a study of priming in picture naming, used stimuli that varied in codability (the extent to which the same name was given to the picture in a normative sample). Although there was no report of an interaction between codability and age in magnitude of priming scores, the pattern of means suggests no difference in priming for highly codable pictures, but a trend towards an age effect for the less codable pictures.

Nevertheless, there are findings less supportive of the competition hypothesis. Studies of word stem completion generally utilize word stems for which there are many possible completions and the completion chosen for study is typically not among the most frequent of these. Word fragment completion, on the other hand, usually involves items with single (or very few) completions. Despite claims of sizable age differences in the former task and no age differences in the latter one, Table 9.3 suggests that the effect sizes for the two tasks are not all that different, 0.336 for the former and 0.281 for the latter, and that their confidence intervals overlap. Also, Light and Kennison (1996a) found no evidence that older adults were more disadvantaged than young adults in a single stimulus or forced-choice perceptual identification task in which some of the test words were orthographically similar to study words. Under such conditions (but see below), it might be expected that these incorrect solutions might adversely affect identification of words (and this does occur) and that the effects might be stronger for older adults if increased competition among potential responses is more of a problem, but this did not occur.[10]

To examine this issue, we classified all priming tasks involving single unit stimuli (i.e., the first three groupings in Table 9.3) that did not involve ratings tasks as high or low in competition; the effect sizes included here were the same as those included in the production vs identification analysis. For the present grouping, low competition tasks included word fragment completion, perceptual identification, word naming, nonword naming, naming Turkish words, lexical decision, semantic verification, and object decision. High competition tasks included word stem completion, word association, homophone spelling, degraded word identification (either visual or auditory, and including inverted word reading), exemplar generation, picture naming, picture fragment completion, anagram solution, general knowledge questions, rhyme generation, and

---

,10   Hartman and Hasher and their colleagues (Hartman and Dusek 1994; Hartman and Hasher 1991; Hartman 1995; Hasher *et al.* 1997) have reported a series of studies using a sentence completion task as the test. At study, participants are asked to generate a word as the ending for a high cloze sentence but the expected word does not appear as the target to be remembered. Under these conditions, older adults are more likely to generate the to-be-ignored completion at test. The precise meaning of this result is in dispute (see exchange by Hartman 1995, and Hasher *et al.* 1997). For our purposes, the crucial point is that response competition at test was not directly varied, so these studies are not germane to the analysis at hand.

sentence completion.[11] There were 79 effect sizes included in the initial step of the analysis.

At the first step of the analysis, $Q_T(78) = 173.14$ and $Q_W(77) = 160.68$, both $ps < 0.05$. The low competition grouping was homogeneous at this point, $Q_{LOW}(29) = 33.73$, but the high competition grouping was not $Q_{HIGH}(48) = 126.95$. Elimination of three outliers (Davis *et al.* 1990, Experiment 2; McCauley *et al.* 1996; Schacter *et al.* 1994a, Experiment 1) rectified this problem, $Q_{HIGH}(45) = 58.55$. At this juncture, $Q_T(75) = 98.94$, $p < 0.05$, $Q_W(74) = 92.28$, $p > 0.05$, and $Q_B(1) = 6.66$, $p < 0.01$. The values of $d+$ were 0.086 for the low competition category and 0.248 for the high competition category, with 95% confidence intervals of -0.018 to 0.190 and 0.180 to 0.315, respectively.

The results of the meta-analysis therefore suggest that there may indeed be a larger effect size for high competition tasks. We nonetheless offer our usual caveat for interpreting this result. The meta-analysis is only as good as the classification scheme and we have reason to question this one, just as we have had reason to question other dichotomies offered above. We believe that classification of tasks as high or low in response competition is not straightforward. We included picture naming in the high competition class because more than one response is possible for some pictures. However, as discussed above, pictures vary in their codability, so response competition can be varied within a single task here as well. Similarly, perceptual identification of briefly presented words was classed as low in competition. However, words vary in whether their pronunciation is regular or irregular (cf. *hint* vs *pint*) and in the size of their neighbourhoods (the number of words that can be created by changing a single letter). Neighbourhood size is known to affect a variety of tasks (see Andrews 1997, for a review). Ratcliff and McKoon (1997) have recently shown that neighbourhood size affects accuracy of identifying studied words. In auditory word perception, information comes in sequentially and therefore the precise word that is being presented is not known until more than the initial phonemes have been encoded; this observation has led to the development of the cohort theory of auditory word identification (Marslen-Wilson 1987). To the best of our knowledge the role of cohort size in priming in auditory word identification tasks has not been studied. In word fragment completion, study of words that are orthographically similar to target fragments leads to intrusion of studied words, a result suggesting response competition in this task as well (Smith and Tindell 1997). Thus, the classificatory task is not so obvious as it might seem at first glance. It might well be better to abandon the enterprise of assigning tasks

---

11 The rationale for assigning some tasks to the high competition group may not be immediately obvious. Degraded word identification (including listening to words in noise) and picture fragment completion are tasks that may initially afford a variety of solutions though only one is ultimately correct (Bruner and Potter 1964; also see Snodgrass and Hirshman 1991). We therefore decided to include them among the high competition tasks. Readers with different views on these or other tasks may consult Table 9.3 to get a general sense of the consequences of moving tasks from category to category or dropping some from the analysis.

to classes in favour of focusing on individual tasks, varying properties of the stimuli that impinge on response competition. This would certainly be possible within perceptual identification (neighbourhood size, cohort size, regularity of spelling), word stem and word fragment completion (single vs multiple solutions), word association (small vs large numbers of associations), and category exemplar generation (small vs large categories). Experiments exploring this issue are currently underway in our laboratory.

What have we learned from the meta-analysis? We submit that three conclusions are warranted by our findings.

First, after discarding only six outliers, the mean weighted effect size for age differences on indirect measures of memory is 0.185 and has a mean confidence interval that does not encompass zero. This outcome supports our earlier claim (La Voie and Light 1994) that performance on this class of memory measures, while not age invariant, is nevertheless substantially less impaired than that on recognition and recall. This pattern of results is consistent with the two-process view that priming studies have a larger contribution from familiarity than from recollection and that familiarity is relatively preserved in old age.[12]

Second, we have identified some factors that may moderate age differences in indirect measures of memory as well as some that probably do not. Effect sizes did not vary systematically as a function of class of materials or as a function of whether tasks were classified as item or associative. Effect sizes were, however, smaller for studies using latency measures than for other measures (chiefly response probability or accuracy). They were also reliably smaller for tasks involving identification rather than production and for tasks with less rather than more potential response competition. In evaluating these findings, it is important to keep in mind the fact that most identification tasks that have been studied have response latency as their dependent variable and that is also true for low competition tasks. Hence, further work will be needed to disentangle the confounds inherent in these classification schemes.

Third, our focus has been on broad issues such as whether, in the aggregate, studies of indirect memory do or do not show age differences and whether age differences, when they occur, are greater for one class of tasks rather than another. The classification schemes we used for this purpose are quite broad and there has been little discussion of specific theoretical models for particular priming tasks. It is unlikely that the processes underlying the heterogeneous collection of paradigms subsumed under the rubric of indirect measures of memory are all the same. Hence, progress in understanding possible age differences in performance on indirect measures of memory is likely to be accelerated when specific models of both tasks and cognitive aging are formulated. Two

12 Although some authors have reported reasonable reliability for priming measures (e.g. Hultsch *et al.* 1991), others have reported dismally low reliability values (e.g. Park *et al.* 1996). It is conceivable that the lack of age differences on priming tasks is due to the poor psychometric properties of these tasks, a possibility that has yet to be fully explored. Process dissociation, however, may yield more reliable estimates (Salthouse *et al.* 1997).

examples will serve to drive home this point. Rastle and Burke (1996; see also Burke *et al.*, Chapter 8, this volume) have found that prior exposure to answers to general knowledge questions reduces reports of tip-of-the-tongue experiences to a similar extent in young and older adults. Although answering general knowledge questions fits criteria for a conceptual processing task, Rastle and Burke (1996) argue that the observed benefit is due to priming of the phonological representation of the correct answer to a question. Labelling the general knowledge task as conceptual tends here to de-emphasize the mechanisms involved in priming. In our own laboratory, we have explored negative effects of prior experience on perceptual identification, making predictions based on Ratcliff and McKoon's (1997) counter model. This model provides an explanation for a number of findings in the perceptual identification literature in terms of bias effects resulting from inhibitory processes operative at test; in opposition to inhibitory deficit models of cognitive aging, we have found little difference in the costs and benefits of prior exposure on perceptual priming in young and older adults (Light and Kennison 1996a). Initial interest in studying indirect measures of memory in populations of older adults was sparked by the possibility that dissociations would be observed between direct and indirect measures of memory in adulthood, thereby producing evidence that age-related memory changes are not ubiquitous. The results of our meta-analysis and the two examples offered above suggest strongly that simply searching for dissociations is unlikely to yield a complete description of factors underlying patterns of spared and impaired memory in older adults.

PROCESS DISSOCIATION PROCEDURE

It has long been understood that neither direct nor indirect measures of memory are process pure, raising the possibility that age differences observed in priming tasks reflect nothing more than episodic contamination (e.g. Howard 1988; Light and Albertson 1989; Light and Singh 1987; Schacter *et al.* 1994a). There is no fool-proof way to eliminate this problem in priming tasks. One strategy has been to report results separately for individuals who claim, on post-experimental questionnaires, to have deliberately guessed previously studied items and for individuals who deny doing so (e.g. Light and Albertson 1989; Light and Kennison 1996a). However, the validity of post-experimental questionnaires as tools for assessing deliberate contamination is uncertain (see the exchange between Light and Kennison 1996a, b and McKoon and Ratcliff 1996, for discussion). Priming tasks also do not permit separate estimates of familiarity and recollection as these operate simultaneously during particular mnemonic activities. Process dissociation procedures developed by Jacoby (1991) may provide a means of obtaining such estimates. Of course, process dissociation procedures generally involve recall and recognition tasks and their instructions invoke deliberate recollection, whereas it is one of the defining features of priming tasks that their instructions do not. Hence, conclusions drawn from process dissociation tasks can only inform our understanding of familiarity processes in priming tasks (and vice versa) to the extent that both tap the same underlying mechanisms. It is not clear that this is always the case (Wagner *et al.* 1997). Nevertheless, process dissociation procedures may provide a window into more automatic aspects of memory.

In general (though not invariably), the process dissociation procedure uses two tests, inclusion and exclusion, to estimate the contributions of recollection and familiarity to performance. Recollection, or R, has been described as a consciously controlled process involving retrieval of episodic details from memory (Jacoby 1991). In contrast, familiarity, or F, represents an unconscious or automatic process that produces a feeling of 'oldness'. Jacoby and his colleagues have also used the terms 'automatic process' and 'habit' to refer to the second of these components of memory (e.g. Hay and Jacoby 1996; Jacoby *et al.* 1993). For instance, in recognition memory an inclusion test requires participants to make positive judgements to items studied under particular conditions (e.g. say 'yes' to words previously seen or heard). Positive responses on the inclusion test are thought to reflect independent contributions of recollection and familiarity, or p (yes/inclusion) = R + F (1 − R). On an exclusion test, however, instructions request participants to avoid making positive responses to items from one source (e.g. say 'yes' to heard items but not seen items). The extent to which positive responses are made to items that should be excluded (despite instructions to avoid doing so) is taken as an index of familiarity in the absence of recollection, or p (yes/exclusion) = F (1 − R). Recollection can be estimated directly as the difference between p (yes) when trying to versus not trying to respond positively to items from a given class, R = p (yes/inclusion) − p (yes/exclusion). A value of R can then be substituted in the formula for exclusion and terms in that formula can be rearranged to solve for the familiarity term, F = p (yes/exclusion)/(1 − R).

To date, applications of process dissociation methodology to aging have included recognition memory (Jacoby 1999; Jennings and Jacoby 1993, 1997; Rybash and Hoyer 1996; Titov and Knight 1997), fame judgements (Jennings and Jacoby 1993), word stem completion (Jacoby *et al.* 1996; Rybash *et al.* 1998; Salthouse *et al.* 1997), and cued recall (Hay and Jacoby 1999). In the fame judgement task, participants initially rate a mixed list of famous and nonfamous people's names for fame, then read a list of nonfamous names, and finally take exclusion and inclusion tests. For the former test, they are told (correctly) that none of the just read names is that of a famous person, so that remembering that a name was read is diagnostic of fame; for the latter test, they are erroneously told that all read names were of famous persons. In word stem completion, exclusion instructions request participants to complete word stems (e.g. MOT__) with words they have not studied whereas inclusion instructions request completion of the stem with an old word if one can be remembered or with the first word that comes to mind if one cannot be remembered. Hay and Jacoby (1999) have used cued recall to study action slips. In the action slip experiments, responses are made typical or atypical by an initial training phase in which some associatively related pairs are presented with different probabilities to establish 'habits' of varying strength. Subsequently, participants are given paired-associate lists for study and test. On congruent trials, participants study items that were presented more frequently in the study phase; on incongruent trials, the less frequent items are to be learned. For incongruent trials, habit and familiarity are in opposition. Table 9.4 presents estimates of recollection and familiarity garnered from these studies. As is clear from the entries, aging is associated with declines in R (often quite sizable) but age constancy in F is the rule.

Table 9.4 Estimates of recollection and familiarity from process dissociation procedures

Source	Task	Recollection		Familiarity	
		Young	Old	Young	Old
Hay and Jacoby (1999, Exp. 1)	Action slips				
	Nondistinctive condition	0.44	0.29	0.72	0.72
	Distinctive condition	0.60	0.30	0.70	0.72
Jacoby (1996, Exp. 4)	Recognition				
	1×, long deadline	0.38	0.21	0.45	0.38
	1×, extra-long deadline	–	0.20	–	0.44
	3×, long deadline	0.67	0.33	0.57	0.62
	3×, extra-long deadline	–	0.49	–	0.58
Jacoby et al. (1996)	Word stem completion	0.44	0.16	0.46	0.46
Jennings and Jacoby (1993, Exp. 1)	Fame judgement	0.60	0.31	0.33	0.39
Jennings and Jacoby (1993, Exp. 2)	Forced choice recognition				
	Read condition	0.19	0.07	0.63	0.57
	Anagram condition	0.64	0.43	0.64	0.65
Jennings and Jacoby (1997)	Recognition				
	Lag = 3	0.90	0.71	0.64	0.67
	Lag = 12	0.83	0.51	0.66	0.74
Rybash et al. (1998)	Word stem completion for novel associations				
	Same context	0.59	0.27	0.14	0.20
	Different context	0.42	0.13	0.12	0.20
Salthouse et al. (1997)	Word stem completion	0.31	0.24	0.30	0.28
Titov and Knight (1997)	Recognition	0.49	0.27	0.53	0.57

The studies represented in Table 9.4 have generated single estimates of R and F for particular experimental conditions. However, it is also possible to obtain multiple estimates of R and F in recognition by analysing inclusion and exclusion performance across multiple levels of confidence, or criteria. Yonelinas (1994), for example, had participants study short and long word lists, followed by inclusion and exclusion tests. For each test, participants were asked to make confidence ratings on a 1 to 6 point scale whose endpoints were 'sure it was new' and 'sure it was old', respectively. Given such ratings, hits and false alarms can be plotted on a receiver operating characteristic (ROC). An ROC curve is constructed by plotting cumulative hits (y-axis) as a function of cumulative false alarms (x-axis). The first point of the ROC, at the bottom left, represents items given the highest level of confidence (6) that an item is old. The second point along the curve represents items given this rating or the next highest rating (i.e., a 6 or a 5). ROCs therefore provide a picture of recognition performance across different levels of confidence that test items are old. When Yonelinas (1994) applied the process dissociation formulas to performance at each level of confidence, he found support for the idea that R can be best described as a discrete, threshold-like process (i.e., it occurs or doesn't occur), whereas F is best characterized as a continuous, graded process that conforms reasonably well to assumptions of Gaussian models of signal detection theory.

Estimating recognition components in this fashion provides a more complete assessment of R and F because performance is analysed across the entire decision space, rather than relying on single points to estimate F. None of the studies in Table 9.4 has applied an ROC analysis to the memory performance of young and older adults. It is conceivable, therefore, that familiarity in young and older adults may be similar when a single value of F is obtained, but a different picture may emerge when the entire decision space is analysed. This appears to be the case for amnesia. Although Verfaellie and Treadwell (1993; but see Roediger and McDermott 1994, for a critique) found differences in R but not F between amnesic patients and controls, Yonelinas *et al.* (1998) analysed ROCs from amnesic patients and controls and found that amnesics were impaired in both components of recognition. In the Yonelinas *et al.* (1998) study, participants did not perform an exclusion task; an ROC was constructed from a standard recognition test procedure. To estimate R and F based on formulas described in Yonelinas *et al.* (1995), a search algorithm was used in which values of R and F were adjusted to produce the best fitting curve through the points in the ROC. In these ROC-based analyses, familiarity is expressed in units of d' and this is the value that was reduced in amnesia, along with the estimate of R.

We obtained a copy of the algorithm used by Yonelinas *et al.* (1998) and applied it to the recognition ROCs of young (mean = 21 years) and older (mean age = 71 years) women in a study by Harkins *et al.* (1979).[13] This study

13   We are grateful to Andrew Yonelinas for sharing his program with us.

is the only one that we are aware of that reported full recognition ROCs separately for young and older adults. We used the program DataThief to estimate the values for each of the points in the ROCs.[14]

A reconstruction of the ROCs based on these point estimates appears in Fig. 9.2. The numerical estimates used to create these ROCs are given in Table 9.5. Unsurprisingly, recollection decreased from 0.435 for young adults to 0.265 for older adults, a reduction of 39%. This result is consistent with previous studies suggesting that recollection declines significantly with advancing age. However, contrary to expectation from previous process dissociation studies, estimates of familiarity (in d' units) were reduced as well, declining from d' = 0.655 for the young to d' = 0.357 to the older adults, a 45% reduction.

Our analysis should be regarded as suggestive, rather than conclusive, for several reasons. First, the results from inclusion/exclusion studies are remarkably consistent in their outcomes and we have applied the ROC analysis to a single experiment. Obviously, replication with other data sets is needed. Second, our ROC-based analysis is somewhat limited because we could not obtain the ROC values in Harkins *et al.* (1979) directly from the raw data but needed to estimate them. Third, it is possible that the discrepancy between results obtained in the 'standard' inclusion/exclusion method reported in the literature and the ROC-based decomposition reflect peculiarities in each type of analysis. If so, the age difference in familiarity that we found may not be real, but may simply reflect an idiosyncrasy in the ROC algorithm. Still, this analysis suggests that applying process dissociation procedures to young and older adults may not yield uniform outcomes. This procedure may sometimes reveal age invariance in automatic, nonconscious forms of memory, but sometimes it may not (see also Rybash *et al.* 1998, pp. 20–1). In this sense, the process dissociation procedure and indirect tests of memory share something in common when they are applied to young and older adults; namely, they can lead to variable outcomes.

Despite the consistency of outcomes from the inclusion/exclusion procedure shown in Table 9.4, some caution is needed in drawing conclusions about aging from results of studies using process dissociation equations to estimate familiarity. First, alternative accounts of the processes involved in inclusion and exclusion tests of recognition memory have been offered. For example, R may reflect whatever information is retrieved from memory that permits individuals to successfully perform inclusion and exclusion tasks (e.g. I remember that this test item was in the list I saw and not the list I heard, so this item should be excluded). F, in contrast, may reflect the contribution of other retrieved episodic information that does not permit successful discrimination in an exclusion task (e.g. I remember that I studied this information earlier but not whether it was seen or heard). An even more extreme position holds that

---

14 DataThief is a Macintosh shareware program that reads in scanned graphs and recovers X and Y coordinates for selected points. The program is available at the following URL address: http://archives.math.utk.edu/software/mac/graphingAids/DataThief.

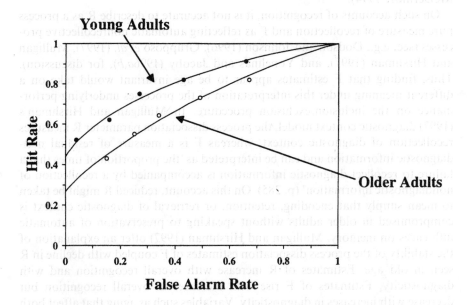

Fig. 9.2   ROC curves for young and older women in Harkins *et al.* (1979) as estimated using a process dissociation algorithm.

Table 9.5 Estimated cumulative proportion of 'yes' responses in Harkins *et al.* (1979)

	Confidence category					
	Definitely old					Definitely new
	6	5	4	3	2	1
Young						
Hits	0.52	0.62	0.75	0.82	0.91	1.00
False Alarms	0.04	0.16	0.27	0.43	0.66	1.00
Older						
Hits	0.43	0.55	0.64	0.73	0.82	1.00
False Alarms	0.15	0.25	0.34	0.49	0.67	1.00

the inclusion/exclusion paradigm, at least as applied to recognition, reduces to a source discrimination task (Buchner *et al.* 1997; see also Roediger and McDermott 1994).

On such accounts of recognition, it is not accurate to describe R as a process pure measure of recollection and F as reflecting automatic nonrecollective processes (see, e.g., Dodson and Johnson (1996), Grupposo *et al.* (1997), Mulligan and Hirshman (1997), and Yonelinas and Jacoby (1996*a,b*), for discussion). Thus, finding that F estimates appear to be age invariant would take on a different meaning under this interpretation of the processes underlying performance on the inclusion/exclusion procedure. In Mulligan and Hirshman's (1997) diagnostic context model, the process dissociation parameter R measures recollection of diagnostic context, whereas F is a measure of residual non-diagnostic information and can be interpreted as 'the proportion of times that a failure to recollect diagnostic information is accompanied by a recollection of nondiagnostic information' (p. 285). On this account, reduced R might be taken to mean simply that encoding, retention, or retrieval of diagnostic context is compromised in older adults without speaking to preservation of automatic influences on memory. Mulligan and Hirshman (1997) offer an explanation of the stability of the process dissociation estimates of F coupled with decline in R seen in old age. Estimates of R increase with overall recognition and with diagnosticity. Estimates of F rise with increases in overall recognition but decrease with increases in diagnosticity. Variables such as aging that affect both overall recognition and diagnosticity have opposing effects on F, resulting in little change in this parameter with increased aging. Craik (cited in Roediger and McDermott 1994) has been credited with the observation that process dissociation procedures used in recognition are uninformative about familiarity processes if inclusion and exclusion tests simply tap source monitoring.

The role accorded to context in two-process accounts of memory varies considerably from model to model (as suggested earlier). In the process dissociation approach of Jacoby and his colleagues, memory for contextual information would be crucial in mnemonic tasks involving opposition. Recollection or conscious memory depends on pitting memory for contextual information against familiarity or habit. In simulations of process dissociation using SAM, a global matching model that typically assumes a single process for recognition, Ratcliff *et al.* (1995) found it necessary to include a recall process as well as a global matching process based on familiarity. However, in SAM it is familiarity that receives a contribution from a context-matching parameter, whereas in Jacoby's treatment of process dissociation contextual information can have effects on both recollection and familiarity (Jacoby 1996; Jacoby *et al.* 1997). Thus, again, interpretation of age effects depends on the precise assumptions made by particular models. The constructs of recollection (or recall) and familiarity vary from model to model and conclusions about age constancy and change in these constructs can only be drawn within the boundaries of a given model. To date, attempts to fit data from young and older adults on a variety of models with different assumptions have been sorely lacking. This is clearly an area ripe for investigation.

Second, there has been controversy as to whether the assumptions for deriving estimates of R and F in recognition are reasonable. These have been both theoretical and methodological. On the theoretical side, debate has centred on the question of whether the relationship between R and F is one of independence, exclusivity, or redundancy (Joordens and Merikle 1993). The exclusivity assumption is not, on the face of it, plausible (but see the discussion of the remember/know (R/K) procedure below) because it assumes that when an item is recalled by exercise of the conscious process it cannot be familiar as well. Thus, the two most plausible assumptions are independence and redundancy; with the latter formulation, conscious influences are a subset of unconscious influences.

Estimates of recollection or conscious influences of memory are the same under both independence and redundancy assumptions. However, under the redundancy assumption, F would simply be equal to the proportion of words called old (ignoring guessing). Jacoby *et al.* (1997) have summarized a number of arguments on behalf of the independence assumption. These include (a) the fact (discussed above) that a number of variables have been shown to have different effects on estimates of familiarity and recollection and that the nature of these effects makes good intuitive sense (though intuition is arguably not the most stringent scientific criterion); (b) the fact that when care is taken to avoid episodic contamination in priming studies, some variables have similar effects on priming and familiarity; and (c) the fact that applying an independence correction to familiarity estimates obtained in remember/know tasks (see below) causes certain paradoxes in the data to vanish (but see Rajaram and Roediger 1997, for a different interpretation of some of these). This debate is ongoing (e.g. Buchner *et al.* 1997; Curran and Hintzman 1995, 1997; Hirshman 1998; Jacoby *et al.* 1994; Jacoby *et al.* 1997; Richardson-Klavehn *et al.* 1996). What is important for us at this time is to keep in mind that a different conclusion about the stability of estimates of F across age would be forced if the relationship between conscious and unconscious processes were one of redundancy rather than independence. Older adults often score well below younger adults on p (yes/inclusion), which serves as an estimate of familiarity under the redundancy assumption. Hence, adherents of the redundancy model would argue that both recollection and familiarity are impaired in old age.

On the methodological side, questions have been raised about the need to include base rates in the estimation procedure because estimates of R and F can be inaccurate when base rates differ across inclusion and exclusion conditions, especially when they differ across different groups (Buchner *et al.* 1995; Graf and Komatsu 1994). Young and old do not always have the same base rates. Indeed, on standard recognition tests, hit rates are often lower in older adults while false alarm rates are higher, an example of the mirror effect (e.g. Glanzer *et al.* 1993). Thus, sensitivity to base rate issues is needed in applying process dissociation methodology with participants of different ages. This does not, of course, render the procedure unusable (unless there is no consensus on methods to correct for base rate inequality), but it does mean that comparison of estimates across studies requires attention to whether the estimates have all been derived using the same measures for dealing with any base rate differences across conditions or groups. We might note, in this context, that the ROC-based analysis of Harkins *et al.* (1979) above used the model described by Yonelinas *et al.* (1995); that model was specifically designed to incorporate response biases (or base rate differences) across inclusion and exclusion tasks. So this criticism applies primarily to the 'classic' process dissociation procedure.

Third, despite arguments to the contrary above, it is not clear that familiarity estimates obtained in process dissociation procedures tap the same familiarity or fluency processes thought to be implicated in indirect measures of memory. Recollection and familiarity can be functionally dissociated in recognition memory experiments. Experimental treatments that reduce recollection but leave familiarity intact include speeded responding (Toth 1996), list length (Yonelinas 1994), and amnesia (Verfaellie and Treadwell 1993; but see Roediger and McDermott 1994). Some researchers have suggested that familiarity reflects a perceptually driven process (Jacoby and Dallas 1981; Mandler 1980; Yonelinas *et al.* 1995). Because perceptual priming is affected by study-phase variations of perceptual processing, but is relatively insensitive to study-phase conceptual processing, it may be hypothesized that similar perceptual processes should underlie perceptual priming and familiarity. However, estimates of F are often sensitive to manipulations of conceptual processing such as generation of items during the study phase (Jacoby 1991), levels of processing (Toth 1996), and picture/word manipulations (Wagner *et al.* 1997). Such manipulations do not typically affect perceptual priming in the same way or to the same extent (but see previous discussion of this subject), so it does not appear that process dissociation estimates of familiarity measure the same processes that mediate performance in perceptual priming tasks. Familiarity, as well as recollection, appears to be more sensitive to manipulations of conceptual processing than to perceptual processing.

REMEMBER/KNOW JUDGEMENTS

The process dissociation procedure estimates recollection and familiarity through application of formulas embodying assumptions about these processes and their relationship to data obtained from inclusion and exclusion tasks. The remember/know procedure (Tulving 1985), however, assesses the states of awareness that accompany positive recognition judgements. Thus, it does not estimate directly the postulated underlying processes of recollection and familiarity but purportedly taps their products. In a remember/know recognition task, participants make positive judgements for items that they believe were studied (i.e., say 'yes' to an old item). When such responses are made, individuals are requested to make a second decision between two alternatives – remember and know – based on the conscious experiences that led them to make the positive recognition judgement in the first place. A remember response is appropriate when elements of the original study experience are recollected (e.g. I recognize the word *automobile* because I remember thinking about my car when I studied it). A know response is appropriate when study-phase contextual details are not retrieved from memory, yet the test item feels sufficiently familiar to warrant a positive response (e.g. the word *barrel* seems familiar, so I must have studied it earlier). Although the remember/know procedure is designed to measure states of awareness rather than the processes presumed to mediate those states, researchers have often treated remember and know judgements as reflecting relatively pure measures of underlying processes of recollection and familiarity, respectively. To the extent that remembering and knowing reflect recollection and familiarity, results from remember/know and process dissociation tasks can be compared directly (e.g. Wagner *et al.* 1997).

Results from many studies suggest that remember and know judgements can be dissociated (see Rajaram and Roediger 1997, for a recent review). Indeed, many variables have been shown to affect remember but not know judgements, including long relative to short study-to-test delays, deep relative to shallow encoding, elaborative rehearsal relative to maintenance rehearsal, divided attention relative to full attention, low relative to high frequency words, and generating study items relative to reading them (Gardiner 1988; Gardiner and Java 1990; Gardiner and Parkin 1990; Gardiner *et al.* 1994; Tulving 1985). In contrast, variables such as visual pattern masking, gradual revealing of computer-fragmented test items, and maintenance rehearsal relative to elaborative rehearsal, exert their effects on know but not remember judgements (Gardiner *et al.* 1994; LeCompte 1995; Rajaram 1993). These dissociations between remember and know judgements have led to the proposition that remember and know judgements reflect the operation of two separate processes that contribute to recognition judgements (Gardiner 1988; Gardiner and Java 1990). The precise nature of these two processes is as yet not fully understood. Although early studies suggested that remember judgements are sensitive to variables that affect the extent of conceptual processing, whereas know judgements are supported by perceptually driven mechanisms, more recent evidence suggests that this is not the case (e.g. Dewhurst and Conway 1994; Rajaram 1998). Rather, it appears that remember and know judgements are influenced by both types of processing. Rajaram (1998) has suggested that recollection is affected by conceptual and perceptual salience and know responses by perceptual and conceptual fluency.

Studies of remember/know judgements in young and older adults have been fairly consistent in showing age-related declines in recognition based on remember judgements, but they have been inconsistent in their outcomes with regard to recognition based on knowing (see Table 9.6). For example, Parkin and Walter (1992) reported that aging was associated with reductions in remember responses and with increases in know responses. The same pattern was also observed in two experiments by Perfect *et al.* (1995, Experiments 1 and 2B). However, in a set of cued-recall experiments, Mäntylä (1993) found no change in the rate of know judgements despite age-related declines in remember judgements. This result is not peculiar to recall, inasmuch as a similar outcome has been observed in recognition tests (Java 1996; Perfect and Dasgupta 1997). Finally, Perfect *et al.* (1995, Experiment 2A) reported a significant age decline in know judgements. Thus, all three possible outcome patterns – age-related increases, age constancy, age-related decreases – have been obtained for know judgements.

To examine the question of whether age differences occur for remember and know judgements, we tabulated the remember and know hit and false alarm rates for each experiment represented in Table 9.6 for which complete data were available.[15] Across the ten studies with complete recognition data, the overall (unweighted) mean hit and false alarm rates for young adults were 0.77 and 0.08, respectively; the corresponding values for older adults were 0.63 and 0.13. Taking the difference between hits and false alarms as a summary measure of performance, the values are 0.69 and 0.50, respectively. Thus, young adults exhibited superior recognition performance, reflected in more hits and fewer false alarms, the typical pattern. For remember judgements, the average hit and false alarm rates were 0.56 and 0.02 for young adults, and 0.35 and 0.05 for older adults. Taking the difference between hits and false alarms, we get 0.54 for young adults and 0.30 for older adults. Thus, for remember judgements there is again an age difference, with young adults producing more hits and fewer false alarms than older adults. For know judgements, however, there is a different outcome. The mean hit and false alarm rates for young adults were 0.21 and 0.06 and for older adults they were 0.28 and 0.07. The difference between hits and false alarms for the know judgements is thus 0.15 for the young and 0.21 for the older adults. It therefore appears that, in this analysis, a dissociation is obtained between remember and know judgements. Remember judgements decline with advanced age, but know judgements may increase somewhat.

This analysis, however, assumes a particular relationship between the processes underlying remember and know judgements, namely one of exclusivity, such that a given item can be remembered or known, but not both (Gardiner and Parkin 1990). As discussed earlier, Jacoby and his colleagues argue for independence of the R and F processes estimated in the process dissociation equations they have developed. Under the assumption of independence, in contrast to that of exclusivity, items can be both remembered and known. Accordingly,

---

15 Because most studies used recognition tests, we did not include the cued-recall study of Mäntylä (1993). The requirement that a young group be tested also prevented inclusion of data from Maylor (1995). When hit and false alarm rates were presented graphically in published studies, we contacted the authors of these studies directly to obtain exact values; we thank Tim Perfect for furnishing us with hit and false alarm rates.

Table 9.6 Proportions of remember and know judgements given by young and older adults in recognition memory tests

Study	Recognition		Remember		Know		Know H (IRK)
	H	FA	H	FA	H	FA	
Fell (1992)							
Young, repetition	0.76	—[a]	0.57	—	0.19	—	0.44
Young, association	0.97	—	0.90	—	0.07	—	0.70
Old, repetition	0.79	—	0.24	—	0.55	—	0.72
Old, association	0.96	—	0.91	—	0.05	—	0.56
Jacoby et al. (1996)							
Young	0.78	—	0.56	—	0.22	—	0.50
Old	0.68	—	0.35	—	0.33	—	0.47
Java (1996) [b]							
Young	0.25	0.02	0.16	0.00	0.08	0.01	0.11
Old	0.17	0.02	0.10	0.00	0.08	0.01	0.08
Mark and Rugg (1998) [c]							
Young	0.84	0.05	0.64	—	0.19	—	0.54
Old	0.84	0.10	0.64	—	0.20	—	0.56
Norman and Schacter (1997, Exp. 1)							
Young, no explanation	0.79	0.08	0.53	0.01	0.26	0.07	0.55
Young, explanation	0.79	0.07	0.54	0.01	0.25	0.06	0.54
Old, no explanation	0.73	0.15	0.51	0.05	0.22	0.10	0.45
Old, explanation	0.76	0.16	0.55	0.10	0.21	0.06	0.47
Parkin and Walter (1992, Exp. 1)							
Young	0.77	0.05	0.52	0.01	0.25	0.04	0.52
Old	0.66	0.10	0.20	0.01	0.46	0.09	0.58
Parkin and Walter (1992, Exp. 2)							
Young	0.80	0.07	0.37	0.02	0.43	0.05	0.68
Old	0.67	0.09	0.12	0.02	0.55	0.07	0.62
Perfect and Dasgupta (1997) [d]							
Young	0.92	0.08	0.74	0.02	0.17	0.06	0.69

Old	0.71	0.19	0.48	0.08	0.23	0.10	0.45

Perfect et al. (1995, Exp. 1)							
Young	0.76	0.10	0.53	0.05	0.23	0.05	0.49
Old	0.71	0.10	0.18	0.07	0.53	0.03	0.65
Perfect et al. (1995, Exp. 2a)							
Young, shallow	0.76	0.05	0.40	0.00	0.36	0.05	0.60
Young, deep	0.97	0.02	0.68	0.01	0.29	0.01	0.91
Old, shallow	0.54	0.08	0.34	0.03	0.20	0.05	0.30
Old, deep	0.77	0.03	0.69	0.02	0.08	0.01	0.26
Perfect et al. (1995, Exp. 2b)							
Young	0.86	0.03	0.76	0.01	0.10	0.02	0.42
Old	0.64	0.11	0.25	0.03	0.39	0.08	0.52
Schacter et al. (1997, Exp. 1) [e]							
Young, once	0.89	0.11	0.83	0.02	0.06	0.10	0.38
Young, thrice	0.86	0.09	0.77	0.02	0.08	0.07	0.40
Old, once	0.78	0.16	0.70	0.02	0.08	0.13	0.29
Old, thrice	0.76	0.15	0.68	0.06	0.08	0.08	0.23
Schacter et al. (1997, Exp. 2) [e]							
Young	0.84	0.22	0.62	0.04	0.23	0.17	0.62
Old	0.59	0.34	0.43	0.19	0.16	0.15	0.30

[a] Dashed lines indicate values not provided by authors.
[b] Values averaged across postexplicit and postimplicit conditions.
[c] Absolute Remember and Know proportions estimated from values given in tables.
[d] Values averaged across word and nonword conditions.
[e] Values averaged across shown and not shown conditions.

proponents of the process dissociation procedure have criticized the exclusivity assumption in remember/know studies, and have proposed that an independence assumption be used in its stead (Jacoby *et al.* 1997; Yonelinas and Jacoby 1995).

To determine whether a reanalysis of the data in Table 9.6, assuming independence, would yield results similar to those we found when exclusivity was assumed, we carried out a reanalysis of these data. Following the 'independence remember know' or IRK procedure outlined by Yonelinas and Jacoby (1995), we converted each know rate into an estimate of familiarity (F) by dividing the know rate by one minus the remember hit rate, $F = K/(1 - R)$. When these estimates are averaged across experiments, we now get evidence for an age-related decline in know responding. For young adults, the familiarity estimate is 0.52, and for older adults it is 0.42. The overall false alarm rates, to which the familiarity estimates are usually compared (cf. Yonelinas and Jacoby 1995), are 0.08 for young adults and 0.13 for older adults. The difference between the familiarity estimate and the recognition false alarm rate is 0.44 for young adults and 0.29 for older adults. As was the case for estimates of R and F using process dissociation, the conclusion we draw here is that age differences in know judgements will depend on the relationship assumed between processes underlying remember and know judgements. Taken together, the priming meta-analysis, the ROC analysis of process dissociation (assuming independence), and the analysis of remember/judgements (also assuming independence) converge on the conclusion that automatic, nonconscious forms of memory decline with age. On the other hand, the process dissociation studies using recognition memory and other tasks support a conclusion of age stability in these processes, a conclusion also supported by the R/K results obtained under the assumption of exclusivity of states of awareness.

Two further cautionary notes about the use of the remember/know paradigm to dissect age differences in recollection and familiarity should be sounded. First, although know judgements are thought to reflect familiarity processes, such judgements, like remember judgements, assign items to the category of previously studied materials. Thus, at some level both must tap recollection, though know judgements reflect an absence of detailed memory for context. Hence, while remember judgements are presumably given only for cases in which recollection is accompanied by details of the acquisition event, know judgements reflect cases in which detailed information about acquisition is missing (cf. Mulligan and Hirshman 1997). By this account, know judgements would not yield pure estimates of familiarity in the absence of recollective experience.

The second concern is more serious. It has been suggested that apparent dissociations between processes underlying remember and know judgements can also be handled by signal detection models that assume a single memory process (Donaldson 1996; Hirshman and Master 1997; Inoue and Bellezza 1998). If so, age differences, or the lack thereof (depending on assumptions), in the remember/know paradigm would be uninformative about the adequacy of dual-process models in accounting for age differences in memory. We begin by discussing the model briefly and then discuss its applicability to studies of remember/know judgements in young and older adults.

Donaldson's (1996) SDT remember/know model assumes a single continuum that represents familiarity or memory 'strength'. Distributions corresponding to old and new items are placed along this continuum. A study phase increases the strength of items in the study list, effectively shifting the old item distribution to the right of the new item distribution. Recognition decisions are made by placing a criterion along this continuum; items whose strength is relatively low and that fall to the left of the criterion are called 'new'. Items whose strength is relatively high and fall to the right of the criterion are called 'old'. Old and new distributions overlap somewhat, so some new items are incorrectly called old, and some old items are incorrectly called new. So far, this describes a standard signal detection model of memory. The unique feature of the SDT remember/know model, however, is the incorporation of a second criterion that is placed to the right of the old/new criterion. The second criterion is used to determine remember/know judgements. Items that fall to the right of the second criterion are given remember judgements, items that fall between the two criteria are given know judgements (see Donaldson 1996, for details).

According to the model, dissociations between remember and know judgements can be understood simply in terms of the placement of the two criteria. To see how this works, consider two old distributions, with the distribution lower on the familiarity axis representing shallow encoding and the distribution higher on the familiarity axis representing deep encoding. Deep encoding produces more 'old' responses than shallow encoding and also yields more 'remember' judgements regardless of the placement of the criteria. However, the relative frequency of know judgements for deep and shallow encoding conditions depends on the placement of the criteria. When the criteria are conservative, deeply encoded items should receive more know judgements than shallowly encoded items as well. Thus, with conservative responding, both remember and know judgements are greater for deep encoding. However, as the criteria are relaxed, and positive responses are given more freely, the situation is not constant for know judgements. For fairly neutral criteria, the area between the two criteria (i.e., the items falling in the 'know' range), is about the same for the distributions of deeply and shallowly encoded items. This then produces a situation in which a variable affects remember but not know judgements, a single dissociation. If criteria are especially liberal, know judgements will be more frequent following shallow encoding than following deep encoding, yielding a double dissociation between remember and know judgements.

Can Donaldson's (1996) model account for the observed remember/know dissociations in young and older adults? Because the model assumes that the amount of know memory is related to the placement of the old/new criterion, we considered the possibility that the assortment of effects that have been observed for know judgements simply reflects age differences in criterion placement. Assume that the distribution lower on the familiarity axis represents older adults and the distribution higher on the familiarity axis represents young adults. If young and older adults maintain equally strict criteria, the predicted outcome is that know judgements should decline with age (as observed by Perfect *et al.* 1995, Experiment 2A). This is because the area between the two criteria is smaller for older than for younger adults. When criteria are relaxed somewhat, the predicted outcome is that aging is associated with no net change in rates of know responding (a result reported by Java 1996, and by Perfect and Dasgupta 1997). When young and older adults' criteria are very liberal, then aging should be associated with an increase in know responding.

This analysis, while superficially plausible, encounters some difficulties. First, in the studies that report sizably greater know values for older adults than for young adults, the overall recognition criteria for the two age groups were not particularly liberal. The recognition criterion measure B''_D was 0.70 for young adults and 0.65 for older adults in Parkin and Walter (1992, Experiment 1); the corresponding values for the second experiment in that study were 0.54 and 0.67. In Perfect *et al.* (1995), the B''_D values were 0.48 and 0.57 for young and older adults in Experiment 1 and the corresponding values were 0.68 and 0.64 for Experiment 2B. Second, and potentially more serious, is the concern that Donaldson's (1996) analysis is simply inappropriate when experimental conditions involve between-groups comparisons, though Donaldson included such comparisons in his meta-analysis. In the present situation, for instance, labelling the two distributions as young and older adults ignores the placement of new distributions (which are apt to differ across groups) and begs the question of how the criterion is set and by whom. When experimental manipulations are within-participant, it makes sense to talk about an observer (rememberer) who sets the criterion, but when experimental variables are manipulated across conditions, there is no single observer whose criterion can be raised or lowered. Hence, our conclusion is that, regardless of whether Donaldson is correct in asserting that remember and know responses reflect different criteria, we do not believe that his model can accommodate between-group designs without further development.

The appropriateness of Donaldson's (1996) analysis of the remember/know judgement task has been challenged on other grounds as well. There is some question as to whether specific numerical estimates are always as predicted (Gardiner and Gregg 1997; Gardiner *et al.* 1997). It is also worth noting in this context that global models of memory that began by invoking only a single process for recognition have found it necessary to postulate additional processes (Clark and Gronlund 1996; Rajaram and Roediger 1997) and that states of awareness associated with remember and know judgements appear to be dissociable electrophysiologically (e.g. Duzel *et al.* 1997). What is even more crucial for our purposes is that estimates of familiarity obtained from experiments using remember/know judgement tasks depend critically on the assumptions made about the relation between processes of recollection and familiarity as measured in these tasks. Assuming that they are mutually exclusive generally yields results in accord with the idea that age differences are large in recollection and small or nonexistent in familiarity, whereas applying a correction that is based on an assumption of independence between processes yields more equivocal results.

CONCLUSIONS

Our goal in this chapter has been to review and evaluate the ability of models of memory that postulate distinct contributions of recollection and familiarity to accommodate findings regarding age-related changes in memory from early to later adulthood. To this end, we have surveyed the literature dealing with three approaches to dissociations between preserved and impaired processes, namely the use of paradigms that measure priming of recently presented information, process dissociation procedures using opposition methodology, and the remember/know paradigm. In the remaining paragraphs, we briefly summarize our findings.

Our meta-analysis of priming studies yielded a mean weighted effect size of 0.185, with a confidence interval ranging from 0.133 to 0.237. Although this value is somewhat smaller than that reported by La Voie and Light (1994), the conclusion that older adults demonstrate less priming than young adults is reinforced by the present result. The fact remains, however, that age differences in priming tasks are considerably smaller than age differences in recall and recognition reported in meta-analyses by La Voie and Light (1994), Spencer and Raz (1995), and Verhaeghen *et al.* (1993). Thus, the disparity in effect sizes for indirect and direct measures of memory supports two process theories of memory to the extent that processes involved in these classes of tasks map onto familiarity and recollection in the hypothesized manner, a point to which we return below. Nonetheless, additional findings from the meta-analysis indicate that the story may not be as simple as it appears.

Despite the fact that homogeneity of effect sizes was achieved by discarding only 6 of 95 values, exploratory analyses suggest that effect sizes are not uniform across all priming tasks. Tasks employing latency as the dependent variable yielded no age differences in priming whereas those involving other measures produced reliable differences. Classifying tasks as conceptual or perceptual did not sort effect sizes into those that produced age differences and those that did not, but two other classificatory schemata did yield intriguing results, namely those involving distinctions between production and identification tasks and those separating tasks into those thought to involve higher and lower levels of response competition at test. These two classificatory schemata, however, suffer from a confounding of class of task with dependent variable, with identification tasks and lower competition tasks typically involving latency measures and production and higher competition tasks generally using response probability measures. Moreover, we found that applying classificatory schemata to assign tasks to categories was often not straightforward on conceptual grounds. To sort out these confounds, we recommend that future research decouple tasks from dependent variables (latency vs probability) by developing new task variants that permit an assessment of whether age differences on indirect measures of memory are dependent-variable specific or whether they vary with other characteristics of tasks. Given problems in the subjectivity of assigning tasks to categories we also urge manipulation of experimental variables such as response competition within, rather than across, tasks and we have described some ways in which this might be done. Once the requisite studies have been carried out, we expect that it will prove necessary to refine conclusions about the extent to which overarching conclusions about age differences on indirect measures of memory are present or absent by referring to more task-specific processes that are spared and impaired.

Examination of findings from process dissociation opposition methodology and remember/know paradigms sometimes produces results in accord with two-process theories of memory, but this is not invariably the case. By and large, studies estimating the contributions of recollection and familiarity to memory on the assumption that these processes are independent have led to the conclusion that aging reduces recollection but that the more unconscious or automatic familiarity component is age invariant. An exception to this finding comes from estimating recollection and familiarity from ROC curves on the assumption that the former entails a dichotomous decision whereas the latter is a continuous variable estimated using signal detection procedures (Yonelinas *et al.* 1998). For the one available data set permitting the use of this technique, we observed declines in parameters estimating both recollection and familiarity. Moreover, if recollection and familiarity are assumed to be redundant, rather than independent, it is necessary to conclude that both familiarity and recollection are age-sensitive processes.

A similar situation obtains for the remember/know paradigm. There is solid evidence from this paradigm as well that aging is accompanied by declines in recollection. Conclusions about familiarity mechanisms presumed to underlie know judgements, however, depend on the assumptions made about the relation between recollection and familiarity. When the processes subserving remember and know judgements are assumed to be mutually exclusive, the findings, though variable from study to study, in general comport reasonably well with age invariance in familiarity. However, when estimates of familiarity are obtained from know judgements by applying a correction assuming independence, the picture is far less clear and leaves open the possibility that familiarity is age sensitive.

In short, basing conclusions about the aging of memory on numerical estimates of parameters identified with particular processes such as recollection and familiarity must be conditional on the plausibility of the assumptions needed to compute these parameters. We would argue, nonetheless, that the behavioural outcomes of process dissociation and remember/know studies are consistent with two-process theories of memory. This is especially true for paradigms using Jacoby's (1991) opposition methodology in which recollection of details of prior episodes is pitted against an increased sense of familiarity occasioned by experiencing those episodes. However, as discussed above, whether the two processes supported by experimental findings should be labelled recollection and familiarity or something else, such as diagnostic and nondiagnostic context (Mulligan and Hirshman 1997), remains an open question. The implications of alternate interpretations for aging remain unexplored (but see Johnson *et al.* 1993).

It has often been assumed that the processes called 'familiarity' and 'recollection' operate in identical ways in recall, recognition, and priming tasks (e.g. Gardiner 1988; Jacoby and Dallas 1981; Mandler 1980; Wagner *et al.* 1997), though the contribution of familiarity would be least in recall and greatest in priming and the reverse would be true for recollection. This assumption of transsituational identity of processes has also been fundamental for two-process accounts of memory change in old age (e.g. La Voie and Light 1994). Nonetheless, considerable evidence is accruing that this assumption may be untenable. For instance, Wagner *et al.* (1997) have shown that familiarity-based explicit recognition in the inclusion/exclusion and remember/know procedures increases with conceptual processing at study, whereas priming in a perceptual identification task was greater when study and test modalities matched. It has been assumed that the familiarity underlying perceptual priming is perceptual in nature and it would therefore be expected that, if the familiarity processes subserving recognition and perceptual priming were identical, familiarity-based recognition should also be greater when study and test modalities match, but this did not occur. Neuroanatomic evidence also argues against transsituational identity of familiarity processes. Patient M. S., who has impaired visual repetition priming due to a right occipital cortex lesion, demonstrates intact overall recognition and intact familiarity-based recognition (as estimated using an inclusion/exclusion task), neither of which would be expected if the same familiarity mechanism is involved in both priming and recognition (Gabrieli *et al.* 1995; Wagner *et al.* 1998). We believe that the finding of dissociable familiarity processes in direct and indirect measures of memory argues strongly that we need to pursue multifarious approaches to the study of familiarity processes in old age to determine whether there is a convergence of results across classes of tasks.

ACKNOWLEDGEMENTS

The authors are grateful to Consuelo Bingham-Mira for assistance in preparation of this article. The research reported here was supported in part by NIA Grants R37 AG02452 to L. L. Light and F32 AG05750 to M. W. Prull.

REFERENCES

References marked with an asterisk indicate studies included in the meta-analysis.

*Abbenhuis, M. A., Raaijmakers, W. G. M., Raaijmakers, J. G. W., and van Woerden, G. J. M. (1990). Episodic memory in dementia of the Alzheimer type and in normal aging: similar impairment in automatic processing. *Quarterly Journal of Experimental Psychology*, **42A**, 569–83.

Anderson, N. D., Craik, F. I. M., and Naveh-Benjamin, M. (1998). The attentional demands of encoding and retrieval in younger and older adults: I. Evidence from divided attention costs. *Psychology and Aging*, **13**, 405–23.

Andrews, S. (1997). The effect of orthographic similarity on lexical retrieval: resolving neighborhood conflicts. *Psychonomic Bulletin & Review*, **4**, 439–61.

Atkinson, R. C. and Juola, J. F. (1974). Search and decision processes in recognition memory. In D. H. Krantz, R. C. Atkinson, R. D. Luce, and P. Suppes (ed.), *Contemporary developments in mathematical psychology, Vol. 1: Learning, memory, and thinking* (pp. 243–93). San Francisco, CA: W. H. Freeman

*Balota, D. A. and Ferraro, F. R. (1996). Lexical, sublexical, and implicit memory processes in healthy young and older adults and in individuals with dementia of the Alzheimer type. *Neuropsychology*, **10**, 82–95.

Bartlett, J. C., Strater, L., and Fulton, A. (1991). False recency and false fame of faces in young adulthood and old age. *Memory & Cognition*, **19**, 177–88.

Bayen, U. J. and Murnane, K. (1996). Age and the use of perceptual and temporal information in source memory tasks. *Psychology and Aging*, **11**, 293–303.

Blaxton, T. A. (1989). Investigating dissociations among memory measures: support for a transfer-appropriate processing framework. *Journal of Experimental Psychology: Learning, Memory, and Cognition*, **15**, 657–68.

Botwinick, J. and Storandt, M. (1974). *Memory, related functions, and age*. Springfield, IL: Thomas.

Bowers, J. S. (1994). Does implicit memory extend to legal and illegal nonwords? *Journal of Experimental Psychology: Learning, Memory, and Cognition*, **20**, 534–49.

Bowers, J. S. and Schacter, D. L. (1990). Implicit memory and awareness. *Journal of Experimental Psychology: Learning, Memory, and Cognition*, **16**, 404–16.

Brigham, M. C. and Pressley, M. (1988). Cognitive monitoring and strategy choices in younger and older adults. *Psychology and Aging*, **3**, 249–57.

Brown, A. S. and Mitchell, D. B. (1994). A reevaluation of semantic versus nonsemantic processing in implicit memory. *Memory & Cognition*, **22**, 522–41.

Bruner, J. S. and Potter, M. C. (1964). Interference in visual recognition. *Science*, **144**, 424–5.

Buchner, A., Erdfelder, E., Steffens, M. C., and Martensen, H. (1997). The nature of memory processes underlying recognition judgments in the process dissociation procedure. *Memory & Cognition*, **25**, 508–17.

Buchner, A., Erdfelder, E., and Vaterrodt-Plunnecke, B. (1995). Toward unbiased measurement of conscious and unconscious memory processes within the process dissociation framework. *Journal of Experimental Psychology: General*, **124**, 137–60.

Cabeza, R. (1994). A dissociation between two implicit conceptual tests supports the distinction between types of conceptual processing. *Psychonomic Bulletin & Review*, **1**, 505–8.

Carr, T. H., Brown, J. S., and Charalambous, A. (1989). Repetition and reading: perceptual encoding mechanisms are very abstract but not very interactive. *Journal of Experimental Psychology: Learning, Memory, and Cognition*, **15**, 763–78.

Chalfonte, B. L. and Johnson, M. K. (1996). Feature memory and binding in young and older adults. *Memory & Cognition*, **24**, 403–16.

Challis, B. H. and Brodbeck, D. R. (1992). Level of processing affects priming in word fragment completion. *Journal of Experimental Psychology: Learning, Memory, and Cognition*, **18**, 595–607.

*Chiarello, C. and Hoyer, W. J. (1988). Adult age differences in implicit and explicit memory: time course and encoding effects. *Psychology and Aging*, **3**, 358–66.

Clark, S. E. and Gronlund, S. D. (1996). Global matching models of recognition memory: how the models match the data. *Psychonomic Bulletin & Review*, **3**, 37–60.

Cohen, G. and Faulkner, D. (1989). Age differences in source forgetting: effects on reality monitoring and on eyewitness testimony. *Psychology and Aging*, **4**, 10–17.

Craik, F. I. M. and Jennings, J. M. (1992). Human memory. In F. I. M..Craik and T. A. Salthouse (ed.), *The handbook of aging and cognition* (pp. 51–110). Hillsdale, NJ: Lawrence Erlbaum.

Curran, T. and Hintzman, D. L. (1995). Violations of the independence assumption in process dissociation. *Journal of Experimental Psychology: Learning, Memory, and Cognition*, **21**, 531–47.

Curran, T. and Hintzman, D. L. (1997). Consequences and causes of correlations in process dissociation. *Journal of Experimental Psychology: Learning, Memory, and Cognition*, **23**, 496–504.

Cutler, S. J. and Grams, A. E. (1988). Correlates of self-reported everyday memory problems. *Journal of Gerontology: Social Sciences*, **43**, S82–90.

*Davis, H. P., Cohen, A., Gandy, M., Colombo, P., VanDusseldorp, G., Simolke, N., and Romano, J. (1990). Lexical priming deficits as a function of age. *Behavioral Neuroscience*, **104**, 288–97.

Dewhurst, S. A. and Conway, M. A. (1994). Pictures, images, and recollective experience. *Journal of Experimental Psychology: Learning, Memory, and Cognition*, **20**, 1088–98.

*Dick, M. B., Kean, M.-L., and Sands, D. (1989). Memory for internally generated words in Alzheimer-type dementia: breakdown in encoding and semantic memory. *Brain and Cognition*, **9**, 88–108.

Dixon, R. A. and Hultsch, D. F. (1983). Structure and development of metamemory in adulthood. *Journal of Gerontology*, **38**, 682–8.

Dodson, C. S. and Johnson, M. K. (1996). Some problems with the process-dissociation approach to memory. *Journal of Experimental Psychology: General*, **125**, 181–94.

Donaldson, W. (1996). The role of decision processes in remembering and knowing. *Memory & Cognition*, **24**, 523–33.

Dorfman, J. (1994). Sublexical components in implicit memory for novel words. *Journal of Experimental Psychology: Learning, Memory, and Cognition*, **20**, 1108–25.

Duzel, E., Yonelinas, A. P., Mangun, G. R., Heinze, H.-J., and Tulving, E. (1997). Event-related brain potential correlates of two states of conscious awareness in memory. *Proceedings of the National Academy of Science*, **94**, 5973–8.

Dywan, J. and Jacoby, L. L. (1990). Effects of aging on source monitoring: differences in susceptibility to false fame. *Psychology and Aging*, **5**, 379–87.

Fell, M. (1992). Encoding, retrieval and age effects on recollective experience. *Irish Journal of Psychology*, **13**, 62–78.

Fleischman, D. A. and Gabrieli, J. D. E. (1998). Repetition priming in normal aging and Alzheimer's disease: a review of findings and theories. *Psychology and Aging*, **13**, 88–119.

*Friedman, D., Snodgrass, J. G., and Ritter, W. (1994). Implicit retrieval processes in cued recall: implications for aging effects in memory. *Journal of Clinical and Experimental Neuropsychology*, **16**, 921–38.

Gabrieli, J. D. E., Keane, M. M., Stanger, B. Z., Kjelgaard, M. M., Corkin, S., and Growdon, J. H. (1994). Dissociations among structural-perceptual, lexical-semantic, and event-fact memory systems in Alzheimer, amnesic, and normal subjects. *Cortex*, **30**, 75–103.

Gabrieli, J. D. E., Fleischman, D. A., Keane, M. M., Reminger, S. L., and Morrell, F. (1995). Double dissociation between memory systems underlying explicit and implicit memory in the human brain. *Psychological Science*, **6**, 76–82.

Gabrieli, J. D. E., Vaidya, C. J., Stone, M., Francis, W. S., Thompson-Schill, S. L., Fleischman, D. A. *et al.* Convergent behavioral and neuropsychological evidence for a distinction between identification and production forms of repetition priming. *Journal of Experimental Psychology: General.* (In press.)

Gardiner, J. M. (1988). Functional aspects of recollective experience. *Memory & Cognition*, **16**, 309–13.

Gardiner, J. M. and Gregg, V. H. (1997). Recognition memory with little or no remembering: implications for a detection model. *Psychonomic Bulletin & Review*, **4**, 474–9.

Gardiner, J. M. and Java, R. I. (1990). Recollective experience in word and nonword recognition. *Memory & Cognition*, **18**, 23–30.

Gardiner, J. M. and Parkin, A. J. (1990). Attention and recollective experience in recognition memory. *Memory & Cognition*, **18**, 579–83.

Gardiner, J. M., Gawlick, B., and Richardson-Klavehn, A. (1994). Maintenance rehearsal affects knowing, not remembering; elaborative rehearsal affects remembering, not knowing. *Psychonomic Bulletin & Review*, **1**, 107–10.

Gardiner, J. M., Richardson-Klavehn, A., and Ramponi, C. (1997). On reporting recollective experiences and "direct access to memory." *Psychological Science*, **8**, 391–4.

*Geva, A., Moscovitch, M., and Leach, L. (1997). Perceptual priming of proper names in young and older normal adults and a patient with prosopanomia. *Neuropsychology*, **11**, 232–42.

*Gibson, J. M., Brooks, J. O., III, Friedman, L., and Yesavage, J. A. (1993). Typography manipulations can affect priming of word stem completion in older and younger adults. *Psychology and Aging*, **8**, 481–9.

Glanzer, M., Adams, J. K., Iverson, G. J., and Kim, K. (1993). The regularities of recognition memory. *Psychological Review*, **100**, 546–67.

Goshen-Gottstein, Y. and Moscovitch, M. (1995a). Repetition priming for newly formed and preexisting associations: perceptual and conceptual influences. *Journal of Experimental Psychology: Learning, Memory, and Cognition*, **21**, 1229–48.

Goshen-Gottstein, Y. and Moscovitch, M. (1995b). Repetition priming effects for newly formed associations are perceptually based: evidence from shallow encoding and format specificity. *Journal of Experimental Psychology: Learning, Memory, and Cognition*, **21**, 1249–62.

Graf, P. and Komatsu, S. (1994). Process dissociation procedure: Handle with caution! *European Journal of Cognitive Psychology*, **6**, 113–29.

Graf, P. and Schacter, D. L. (1985). Implicit and explicit memory for new associations in normal and amnesic subjects. *Journal of Experimental Psychology: Learning, Memory, and Cognition*, **11**, 501–18.

Grober, E., Gitlin, H. L., Bang, S., and Buschke, H. (1992). Implicit and explicit memory in young, old, and demented adults. *Journal of Clinical and Experimental Neuropsychology*, **14**, 298–316.

Gruppuso, V., Lindsay, D. S., and Kelley, C. M. (1997). The process-dissociation procedure and similarity: defining and estimating recollection and familiarity in recognition memory. *Journal of Experimental Psychology: Learning, Memory, and Cognition*, **23**, 259–78.

*Habib, R., Jelicic, M., and Craik, F. I. M. (1996). Are implicit memory deficits in the elderly due to differences in explicit memory processes? *Aging, Neuropsychology, and Cognition*, **3**, 264–71.

Hale, S. and Myerson, J. (1995). Fifty years older, fifty percent slower? Meta-analytic regression models and semantic context effects. *Aging and Cognition*, **2**, 132–5.

Harkins, S. W., Chapman, C. R., and Eisdorfer, C. (1979). Memory loss and response bias in senescence. *Journal of Gerontology*, **34**, 66–72.

*Hartman, M. (1995). Aging and interference: evidence from indirect memory tests. *Psychology and Aging*, **10**, 659–69.

*Hartman, M. and Dusek, J. (1994). Direct and indirect memory tests: what they reveal about age differences in interference. *Aging and Cognition*, **1**, 292–309.

*Hartman, M. and Hasher, L. (1991). Aging and suppression: memory for previously relevant information. *Psychology and Aging*, **6**, 587–94.

Hasher, L. and Zacks, R. T. (1988). Working memory, comprehension, and aging: a review and a new view. In G. H. Bower (ed.), *The psychology of learning and motivation* (Vol. 22, pp. 193–225). San Diego: Academic Press.

*Hasher, L., Quig, M. B., and May, C. P. (1997). Inhibitory control over no-longer-relevant information: adult age differences. *Memory & Cognition*, **25**, 286–95.

Hashtroudi, S., Johnson, M. K., and Chrosniak, L. D. (1990). Aging and qualitative characteristics of memories for perceived and imagined complex events. *Psychology and Aging*, **5**, 119–26.

*Hashtroudi, S., Chrosniak, L. D., and Schwartz, B. L. (1991). Effects of aging on priming and skill learning. *Psychology and Aging*, **6**, 605–15.

Hay, J. F. and Jacoby, L. L. (1996). Separating habit and recollection: memory slips, process dissociations, and probability matching. *Journal of Experimental Psychology: Learning, Memory, and Cognition*, **22**, 1323–35.

Hay, J. F. and Jacoby, L. L. (1999). Separating habit and recollection in young and elderly adults: effects of elaborative processing and distinctiveness. *Psychology and Aging*, **14**, 122–34.

Hedges, L. R. (1984). Advances in statistical methods for meta-analysis. In J. W. Yeaton and P. M. Wortman (ed.), *Issues in data synthesis* (pp. 25-42). San Francisco: Jossey-Bass.

Hedges, L. R. and Olkin, I. (1985). *Statistical methods for meta-analysis*. San Diego: Academic Press.

Hintzman, D. L. (1986). 'Schema abstraction' in a multiple-trace memory model. *Psychological Review*, **93**, 411–28.

Hintzman, D. L. (1988). Judgments of frequency and recognition memory in a multiple-trace memory model. *Psychological Review*, **95**, 528–51.

Hintzman, D. L., Caulton, D. A., and Levitin, D. J. (1998). Retrieval dynamics in recognition and list discrimination: further evidence of separate processes of familiarity and recall. *Memory & Cognition*, **26**, 449–62.

Hirshman, E. (1998). On the logic of testing the independence assumption in the process-dissociation procedure. *Memory & Cognition*, **26**, 857–9.

Hirshman , E. and Master, S. (1997). Modeling the conscious correlates of recognition memory: reflections on the remember-know paradigm. *Memory & Cognition*, **25**, 345–51.

*Howard, D. V. (1988). Implicit and explicit assessment of cognitive aging. In M. L. Howe and C. J. Brainerd (ed.), *Cognitive development in childhood: progress in cognitive development research* (pp. 3–37). New York: Springer-Verlag.

*Howard, D. V., Heisey, J. G., and Shaw, R. J. (1986). Aging and the priming of newly learned associations. *Developmental Psychology*, **22**, 78–85.

*Howard, D. V., Fry, A. F., and Brune, C. M. (1991). Aging and memory for new associations: direct versus indirect measures. *Journal of Experimental Psychology: Learning, Memory, and Cognition*, **17**, 779–92.

*Hultsch, D. F., Masson, M. E. J., and Small, B. J. (1991). Adult age differences in direct and indirect tests of memory. *Journal of Gerontology: Psychological Sciences*, **46**, P22–30.

Humphreys, M. S., Bain, J. D., and Pike, R. (1989). Different ways to cue a coherent memory system: a theory for episodic, semantic, and procedural tasks. *Psychological Review*, **96**, 208–33.

Inoue, C. and Bellezza, F. S. (1998). The detection model of recognition using know and remember judgements. *Memory & Cognition*, **26**, 299–308.

*Isingrini, M., Vazou, F., and Leroy, P. (1995). Dissociation of implicit and explicit memory tests: effects of age and divided attention on category exemplar generation and cued recall. *Memory & Cognition*, **23**, 462–7.

Jacoby, L. L. (1991). A process dissociation framework: separating automatic from intentional uses of memory. *Journal of Memory and Language*, **30**, 513–41.

Jacoby, L. L. (1996). Dissociating automatic and consciously controlled effects of study/test compatibility. *Journal of Memory and Language*, **35**, 32–52.

Jacoby, L. L. (1999). Ironic effects of repetition: measuring age-related differences in memory. *Journal of Experimental Psychology: Learning, Memory, and Cognition* **25**, 3–22.

Jacoby, L. L. and Dallas, M. (1981). On the relationship between autobiographical memory and perceptual learning. *Journal of Experimental Psychology: General*, **110**, 306–40.

Jacoby, L. L., Toth, J. P., and Yonelinas, A. P. (1993). Separating conscious and unconscious influences of memory: measuring recollection. *Journal of Experimental Psychology: General*, **122**, 139–54.

Jacoby, L. L., Toth, J. P., Yonelinas, A. P., and Debner, J. A. (1994). The relationship between conscious and unconscious influences: independence or redundancy? *Journal of Experimental Psychology: General*, **123**, 216–19.

Jacoby, L. L., Jennings, J. M., and Hay, J. F. (1996). Dissociating automatic and consciously controlled processes: implications for diagnosis and rehabilitation of memory deficits. In D. J. Herrmann, C. McEvoy, C. Hertzof, P. Hertel, and M. K. Johnson (ed.), *Basic and applied memory research: theory in context.* (Vol. 1, pp. 161–93). Mahwah, NJ: Lawrence Erlbaum.

Jacoby, L. L., Yonelinas, A. P., and Jennings, J. M. (1997). The relationship between conscious and unconscious (automatic) influences: a declaration of independence. In J. D. Cohen and J. W. Schooler (ed.), *Scientific approaches to consciousness* (pp. 13–47). Mahwah, NJ: Lawrence Erlbaum.

*Java, R. I. (1992). Priming and aging: evidence of preserved memory function in an anagram solution task. *American Journal of Psychology*, **105**, 541–8.

*Java, R. I. (1996). Effects of age on state of awareness following implicit and explicit word-association tasks. *Psychology and Aging*, **11**, 108–11.

*Java, R. I. and Gardiner, J. M. (1991). Priming and aging: further evidence of preserved memory function. *American Journal of Psychology*, **104**, 89–100.

Jelicic, M. (1995). Aging and performance on implicit memory tasks: a brief review. *International Journal of Neuroscience*, **82**, 155–61.

*Jelicic, M., Craik, F. I. M., and Moscovitch, M. (1996). Effects of ageing on different explicit and implicit memory tasks. *European Journal of Cognitive Psychology*, **8**, 225–34.

Jennings, J. M. and Jacoby, L. L. (1993). Automatic versus intentional uses of memory: aging, attention, and control. *Psychology and Aging*, **8**, 283–93.

Jennings, J. M. and Jacoby, L. L. (1997). An opposition procedure for detecting age-related deficits in recollection: telling effects of repetition. *Psychology and Aging*, **12**, 352–61.

Johnson, M. K., Hashtroudi, S., and Lindsay, D. S. (1993). Source monitoring. *Psychological Bulletin*, **114**, 3–28.

Johnson, C. J., Paivio, A., and Clark, J. M. (1996). Cognitive components of picture naming. *Psychological Bulletin*, **120**, 113–39.

Joordens, S. and Merikle, P. M. (1993). Independence or redundancy? Two models of conscious and unconscious influences. *Journal of Experimental Psychology: General*, **122**, 462–7.

Kausler, D. H. (1991). *Experimental psychology, cognition, and human aging* (2nd edn.). New York: Springer-Verlag.

Kausler, D. H. (1994). *Learning and memory in normal aging.* San Diego: Academic Press.

*Kazmerski, V. A., Friedman, D., and Hewitt, S. (1995). Event-related potential repetition effect in Alzheimer's patients: multiple repetition priming with pictures. *Aging and Cognition*, **2**, 169–91.

Kirasic, K. C., Allen, G. L., Dobson, S. H., and Binder, K. S. (1996). Aging, cognitive resources, and declarative learning. *Psychology and Aging*, **11**, 658–70.

Kliegl, R. and Lindenberger, U. (1993). Modeling intrusions and correct recall in episodic memory: adult age differences in encoding of list context. *Journal of Experimental Psychology: Learning, Memory, and Cognition*, **19**, 617–37.

Koriat, A., Ben-Zur, H., and Sheffer, D. (1988). Telling the same story twice: output monitoring and age. *Journal of Memory and Language*, **27**, 23–39.

Koutstaal, W. and Schacter, D. L. (1997). Gist-based false recognition of pictures in older and younger adults. *Journal of Memory and Language*, **37**, 555–83.

Laver, G. D. and Burke, D. M. (1993). Why do semantic priming effects increase in old-age? A meta-analysis. *Psychology and Aging*, **8**, 34–43.

La Voie, D. J. and Light, L. L. (1994). Adult age differences in repetition priming: a meta-analysis. *Psychology and Aging*, **9**, 539–53.

LeCompte, D. C. (1995). Recollective experience in the revelation effect: separating the contributions of recollection and familiarity. *Memory & Cognition*, **23**, 324–34.

Light, L. L. (1991). Memory and aging: four hypotheses in search of data. *Annual Review of Psychology*, **42**, 333-76.

Light, L. L. (1996). Memory and aging. In E. L. Bjork and R. A. Bjork (ed.), *Memory* (pp. 443-90). San Diego: Academic Press.

*Light, L. L. and Albertson, S. A. (1989). Direct and indirect tests of memory for category exemplars in young and older adults. *Psychology and Aging*, **4**, 487–92.

*Light, L. L. and Kennison, R. F. (1996a). Guessing strategies, aging, and bias effects in perceptual identification. *Consciousness and Cognition*, **5**, 463–99.

Light, L. L. and Kennison, R. F. (1996b). Guessing strategies in perceptual identification: a reply to McKoon and Ratcliff. *Consciousness and Cognition*, **5**, 512–24.

Light, L. L. and La Voie, D. (1993). Direct and indirect measures of memory in old age. In P. Graf and M. E. J. Masson (ed.), *Implicit memory: new directions in cognition, development, and neuropsychology* (pp. 207–30). Hillsdale, NJ: Lawrence Erlbaum.

*Light, L. L. and Prull, M. W. (1995). Aging, divided attention, and repetition priming. *Swiss Journal of Psychology*, **54**, 87–101.

*Light, L. L. and Singh, A. (1987). Implicit and explicit memory in young and older adults. *Journal of Experimental Psychology: Learning, Memory, and Cognition*, **13**, 531–41.

*Light, L. L., Singh, A., and Capps, J. L. (1986). Dissociation of memory and awareness in young and older adults. *Journal of Clinical and Experimental Neuropsychology*, **8**, 62–74.

*Light, L. L., La Voie, D., Valencia-Laver, D., Albertson Owens, S. A., and Mead, G. (1992). Direct and indirect measures of memory for modality in young and older adults. *Journal of Experimental Psychology: Learning, Memory, and Cognition*, **18**, 1284–97.

*Light, L. L., LaVoie, D., and Kennison, R. (1995). Repetition priming of nonwords in young and older adults. *Journal of Experimental Psychology: Learning, Memory, and Cognition*, **21**, 327–46.

*Light, L. L., Kennison, R. F., Prull, M. W., La Voie, D., and Zuellig, A. (1996). One-trial associative priming of nonwords in young and older adults. *Psychology and Aging*, **11**, 417–30.

Light, L. L., Prull, M. W., and Kennison, R. F. *Divided attention, aging, and priming in exemplar generation category verification.* (Manuscript submitted for publication.)

*McCauley, M. E., Eskes, G., and Moscovitch, M. (1996). The effect of imagery on explicit and implicit tests of memory in young and old people: a double dissociation. *Canadian Journal of Experimental Psychology*, **50**, 34–40.

McEvoy, C. L., Holley, P. E., and Nelson, D. L. (1995). Age effects in cued recall: sources from implicit and explicit memory. *Psychology and Aging*, **10**, 314–24.

McIntyre, J. S. and Craik, F. I. M. (1987). Age differences in memory for item and source information. *Canadian Journal of Psychology*, **41**, 175–92.

MacKay, D. G. and Abrams, L. (1996). Language, memory, and aging: distributed deficits and the structure of new-versus-old connections. In J. E. Birren and K. W. Schaie (ed.), *Handbook of the psychology of aging.* (4th ed., pp. 251–65). San Diego: Academic Press.

MacKay, D. G. and Burke, D. M. (1990). Cognition and aging: a theory of new learning and the use of old connections. In T. M. Hess (ed.), *Aging and cognition: knowledge organization and utilization* (pp. 213–64). Amsterdam: North Holland.

McKone, E. and Slee, J. A. (1997). Explicit contamination in 'implicit' memory for new associations. *Memory & Cognition*, **25**, 352–66.

McKoon, G. and Ratcliff, R. (1996). Separating implicit from explicit retrieval processes in perceptual identification. *Consciousness and Cognition*, **5**, 500–11.

*Maki, P. M. and Knopman, D. S. (1996). Limitations of the distinction between conceptual and perceptual implicit memory: a study of Alzheimer's disease. *Neuropsychology*, **10**, 464–74.

Mandler, G. (1980). Recognizing: the judgment of previous occurrence. *Psychological Review*, **87**, 252–71.

*Manning, C. A., Parsons, M. W., Cotter, E. M., and Gold, P. E. (1997). Glucose effects on declarative and nondeclarative memory in healthy elderly and young adults. *Psychobiology*, **25**, 103–8.

Mäntylä, T. (1993). Knowing but not remembering: adult age differences in recollective experience. *Memory & Cognition*, **21**, 379–88.

Mark, R. E. and Rugg, M. D. (1998). Age effects on brain activity associated with episodic memory retrieval: an electrophysiological study. *Brain*, **121**, 861–73.

Marslen-Wilson, W. D. (1987). Functional parallelism in spoken word-recognition. *Cognition*, **25**, 71–102.

Maylor, E. A. (1995). Remembering versus knowing television theme tunes in middle-aged and elderly adults. *British Journal of Psychology*, **86**, 21–5.

*Meulemans, T. and Van der Linden, M. (1995). Aging and text-specific implicit memory. *Psychologica Belgica*, **35**, 227–39.

*Mitchell, D. B. (1989). How many memory systems? Evidence from aging. *Journal of Experimental Psychology: Learning, Memory, and Cognition*, **15**, 31–49.

Mitchell, D. B. (1993). Implicit and explicit memory for pictures: multiple views across the lifespan. In P. Graf and M. E. J. Masson (ed.), *Implicit memory: new directions in cognition, development, and neuropsychology* (pp. 171–90). Hillsdale, NJ: Lawrence Erlbaum.

*Monti, L. A., Gabrieli, J. D. E., Reminger, S. L., Rinaldi, J. A., Wilson, R. S., and Fleischman, D. A. (1996). Differential effects of aging and Alzheimer's disease on conceptual implicit and explicit memory. *Neuropsychology*, **10**, 101–12.

*Monti, L. A., Gabrieli, J. D. E., Wilson, R. S., Beckett, L. A., Grinnell, E., Lange, K. L., and Reminger, S. L. (1997). Sources of priming in text rereading: intact implicit memory for new associations in older adults and in patients with Alzheimer's disease. *Psychology and Aging*, **12**, 536–47.

Mulligan, N. W. and Hirshman, E. (1997). Measuring the bases of recognition memory: an investigation of the process-dissociation framework. *Journal of Experimental Psychology: Learning, Memory, and Cognition*, **23**, 280–304.

Multhaup, K. S. (1995). Aging, source, and decision criteria: when false fame errors do not occur. *Psychology and Aging*, **10**, 492–7.

*Mutter, S. A., Lindsey, S. E., and Pliske, R. M. (1995). Aging and credibility judgment. *Aging and Cognition*, **2**, 89–107.

*Nilsson, L.-G., Backman, L., and Karlsson, T. (1989). Priming and cued recall in elderly, alcohol intoxicated and sleep deprived subjects: a case of functionally similar memory deficits. *Psychological Medicine*, **19**, 423–33.

Norman, K. A. and Schacter, D. L. (1997). False recognition in younger and older adults: exploring the characteristics of illusory memories. *Memory & Cognition*, **25**, 838–48.

*Nyberg, L., Backman, L., Erngrund, K., Olofsson, U., and Nilsson, L.-G. (1996). Age differences in episodic memory, semantic memory, and priming: relationships to demographic, intellectual, and biological factors. *Journal of Gerontology: Psychological Sciences*, **51B**, P234–40.

Nyberg, L., Winocur, G., and Moscovitch, M. (1997). Correlation between frontal lobe functions and explicit and implicit stem completion in healthy elderly. *Neuropsychology*, **11**, 70–6.

*Ober, B. A., Shenaut, G. K., Jagust, W. J., and Stillman, R. C. (1991). Automatic semantic priming with various category relations in Alzheimer's disease and normal aging. *Psychology and Aging*, **6**, 647–60.

*Park, D. C. and Shaw, R. J. (1992). Effect of environmental support on implicit and explicit memory in younger and older adults. *Psychology and Aging*, **7**, 632–42.

Park, D. C., Smith, A. D., Lautenschlager, G., Earles, J. L., Frieske, D., Zwahr, M., and Gaines, C. L. (1996). Mediators of long-term memory performance across the life span. *Psychology and Aging*, **11**, 621–37.

Parkin, A. J. and Walter, B. M. (1992). Recollective experience, normal aging, and frontal dysfunction. *Psychology and Aging*, **7**, 290–8.

Perfect, T. J. and Dasgupta, Z. R. R. (1997). What underlies the deficit in reported recollective experience in old age? *Memory & Cognition*, **25**, 849–58.

Perfect, T. J., Williams, R. B., and Anderton-Brown, C. (1995). Age differences reported in recollective experience are due to encoding effects, not response bias. *Memory*, **3**, 169–86.

Poldrack, R. A. and Cohen, N. J. (1997). Priming of new associations in reading time: what is learned? *Psychonomic Bulletin & Review*, **4**, 398–402.

Raaijmakers, J. G. and Shiffrin, R. M. (1992). Models for recall and recognition. *Annual Review of Psychology*, **43**, 205–34.

Rajaram, S. (1993). Remembering and knowing: two means of access to the personal past. *Memory & Cognition*, **21**, 89–102.

Rajaram, S. (1998). The effects of conceptual salience and perceptual distinctiveness on conscious recollection. *Psychonomic Bulletin & Review*, **5**, 71–8.

Rajaram, S. and Roediger H. L., III. (1997). Remembering and knowing as states of consciousness during retrieval. In J. D. Cohen and J. W. Schooler (ed.), *Scientific approaches to consciousness* (pp. 213–40). Mahwah, NJ: Lawrence Erlbaum.

*Rastle, K. G. and Burke, D. M. (1996). Priming the tip of the tongue: effects of prior processing on word retrieval in young and older adults. *Journal of Memory and Language*, **35**, 586–605.

Ratcliff, R. and McKoon, G. (1997). A counter model for implicit priming in perceptual word identification. *Psychological Review*, **104**, 319–43.

Ratcliff, R., Van Zandt, T., and McKoon, G. (1995). Process dissociation, single-process theories, and recognition memory. *Journal of Experimental Psychology: General*, **124**, 352–74.

Richardson-Klavehn, A., Gardiner, J. M., and Java, R. I. (1996). Memory: task dissociations, process dissociations and dissociations of consciousness. In G. Underwood (ed.), *Implicit cognition* (pp. 85–158). New York: Oxford University Press.

Roediger, H. L., III and McDermott, K. B. (1993). Implicit memory in normal human subjects. In F. Boller and J. Grafman (ed.), *Handbook of neuropsychology* (Vol. 8, pp. 63–131). Amsterdam: Elsevier.

Roediger, H. L., III and McDermott, K. B. (1994). The problem of differing false-alarm rates for the process dissociation procedure: comment on Verfaellie and Treadwell (1993). *Neuropsychology*, **8**, 284–8.

Roediger, H. L., III, Weldon, M. S., Stadler, M. L., and Riegler, G. L. (1992). Direct comparison of two implicit memory tests: word fragment and word stem completion. *Journal of Experimental Psychology: Learning, Memory, and Cognition*, **18**, 1251–69.

*Rose, T. L., Yesavage, J. A., Hill, R. D., and Bower, G. H. (1986). Priming effects and recognition memory in young and elderly adults. *Experimental Aging Research*, **12**, 31–7.

Rosenthal, R. (1991). *Meta-analytic procedures for social research* (rev. edn.). Newbury Park, CA: Sage.

*Russo, R. and Parkin, A. J. (1993). Age differences in implicit memory: more apparent than real. *Memory & Cognition*, **21**, 73–80.

Rybash, J. M. (1996). Implicit memory and aging: a cognitive neuropsychological perspective. *Developmental Neuropsychology*, **12**, 127–79.

Rybash, J. M. and Hoyer, W. J. (1996). Process dissociation procedure reveals age differences in unconscious influences on memory for possible and impossible objects. *Aging, Neuropsychology, and Cognition*, **3**, 251–63.

Rybash, J. M., Santoro, K. E., and Hoyer, W. J. (1998). Adult age differences in conscious and unconscious influences on memory for novel associations. *Aging, Neuropsychology, and Cognition*, **5**, 14–26.

Salthouse, T. A. (1996). The processing-speed theory of adult age differences in cognition. *Psychological Review*, **103**, 403–28.

Salthouse, T. A., Fristoe, N., and Rhee, S. H. (1996). How localized are age-related effects on neuropsychological measures? *Neuropsychology*, **10**, 272–85.

Salthouse, T. A., Toth, J. P., Hancock, H. E., and Woodard, J. L. (1997). Controlled and automatic forms of memory and attention: process purity and the uniqueness of age-related influences. *Journal of Gerontology: Psychological Sciences*, **52B**, P216–28.

*Schacter, D. L., Cooper, L. A., and Valdiserri, M. (1992). Implicit and explicit memory for novel visual objects in older and younger adults. *Psychology and Aging*, **7**, 299–308.

*Schacter, D. L., Church, B. A., and Osowiecki, D. M. (1994a). Auditory priming in elderly adults: impairment of voice-specific implicit memory. *Memory*, **2**, 295–323.

Schacter, D. L., Osowiecki, D., Kaszniak, A. W., Kihlstrom, J. F., and Valdiserri, M. (1994b). Source memory: extending the boundaries of age-related deficits. *Psychology and Aging*, **9**, 81–9.

Schacter, D. L., Koutstaal, W., Johnson, M. K., Gross, M. S., and Angell, K. E. (1997). False recognition induced by photographs: a comparison of older and younger adults. *Psychology and Aging*, **12**, 203–15.

*Schugens, M. M., Daum, I., Spindler, M., and Birbaumer, N. (1997). Differential effects of aging on explicit and implicit memory. *Aging, Neuropsychology, and Cognition*, **4**, 33–44.

*Small, B. J., Hultsch, D. F., and Masson, M. E. J. (1995). Adult age differences in perceptually based, but not conceptually based implicit tests of memory. *Journal of Gerontology: Psychological Sciences*, **50B**, P162–70.

Smith, S. M. and Tindell, D. R. (1997). Memory blocks in word fragment completion caused by involuntary retrieval of orthographically related primes. *Journal of Experimental Psychology: Learning, Memory, and Cognition*, **23**, 355–70.

Snodgrass, J. G. and Hirshman, E. (1991). Theoretical explorations of the Bruner-Potter (1964) interference effect. *Journal of Memory and Language*, **30**, 273–93.

Spencer, W. D. and Raz, N. (1995). Differential effects of aging on memory for content and context: a meta-analysis. *Psychology and Aging*, **10**, 527–39.

*Spieler, D. H. and Balota, D. A. (1996). Characteristics of associative learning in younger and older adults: evidence from an episodic priming paradigm. *Psychology and Aging*, **11**, 607–20.

Srinivas, K. and Roediger, H. L., III. (1990). Classifying implicit memory tests: category association and anagram solution. *Journal of Memory and Language*, **29**, 389–412.

*Swick, D. and Knight, R. T. (1997). Event-related potentials differentiate the effects of aging on word and nonword repetition in explicit and implicit memory tasks. *Journal of Experimental Psychology: Learning, Memory, and Cognition*, **23**, 123–42.

Tardif, T. and Craik, F. I. M. (1989). Reading a week later: perceptual and conceptual factors. *Journal of Memory and Language*, **28**, 107–25.

*Titov, N. and Knight, R. G. (1997). Adult age differences in controlled and automatic memory processing. *Psychology and Aging*, **12**, 565–73.

Toth, J. P. (1996). Conceptual automaticity in recognition memory: levels-of-processing effects on familiarity. *Canadian Journal of Experimental Psychology*, **50**, 123–38.

Toth, J. P. (1998, April). *Aging and priming: current status and future directions*. Paper presented at the Cognitive Aging Conference, Atlanta, GA.

Tulving, E. (1985). Memory and consciousness. *Canadian Psychology*, **26**, 1–12.

Tun, P. A., Wingfield, A., Rosen, M. J., and Blanchard, L. (1998). Response latencies for false memories: gist-based processes in normal aging. *Psychology and Aging*, **13**, 230–41.

Vaidya, C. J., Gabrieli, J. D. E., Keane, M. M., Monti, L. A., Gutierrez-Rivas, H., and Zarella, M. M. (1997). Evidence for multiple mechanisms of conceptual priming on implicit memory tests. *Journal of Experimental Psychology: Learning, Memory, and Cognition*, **23**, 1324–43.

Verfaellie, M. and Treadwell, J. R. (1993). Status of recognition memory in amnesia. *Neuropsychology*, **7**, 5–13.

Verhaeghen, P. and Salthouse, T. A. (1997). Meta-analyses of age-cognition relations in adulthood: estimates of linear and nonlinear age effects and structural models. *Psychological Bulletin*, **122**, 231–49.

Verhaeghen, P., Marcoen, A., and Goossens, L. (1993). Facts and fiction about memory aging: a quantitative integration of research findings. *Journal of Gerontology: Psychological Sciences*, **48**, P157–71.

Vriezen, E. R., Moscovitch, M., and Bellos, S. A. (1995). Priming effects in semantic classification tasks. *Journal of Experimental Psychology: Learning, Memory, and Cognition*, **21**, 933–46.

Wagner, A. D., Gabrieli, J. D. E., and Verfaellie, M. (1997). Dissociations between familiarity processes in explicit recognition and implicit perceptual memory. *Journal of Experimental Psychology: Learning, Memory, and Cognition*, **23**, 305–23.

Wagner, A. D., Stebbins, G. T., Masciari, F., Fleischman, D. A., and Gabrieli, J. D. E. (1998). Neuropsychological dissociation between recognition familiarity and perceptual priming in visual long-term memory. *Cortex*, **34**, 493–511.

West, R. L., Crook, T. H., and Barron, K. L. (1992). Everyday memory performance across the life span: effects of age and noncognitive individual differences. *Psychology and Aging*, **7**, 72–82.

*Wiggs, C. L. (1993). Aging and memory for frequency of occurrence of novel, visual stimuli: direct and indirect measures. *Psychology and Aging*, **8**, 400–10.

*Wiggs, C. L. and Martin, A. (1994). Aging and feature-specific priming of familiar and novel stimuli. *Psychology and Aging*, **9**, 578–88.

*Wiggs, C. L., Martin, A., and Howard, D. V. (1994). Direct and indirect measures of frequency monitoring in young and elderly adults. *Aging and Cognition*, **1**, 247–59.

*Winocur, G., Moscovitch, M., and Stuss, D. T. (1996). Explicit and implicit memory in the elderly: evidence for double dissociation involving medial temporal- and frontal-lobe functions. *Neuropsychology*, **10**, 57–65.

Wolf, F. M. (1986). *Meta-analysis: quantitative methods for research synthesis*. Beverly Hills, CA: Sage.

Yonelinas, A. P. (1994). Receiver-operating characteristics in recognition memory: evidence for a dual-process model. *Journal of Experimental Psychology: Learning, Memory, and Cognition*, **6**, 1341–54.

Yonelinas, A. P. and Jacoby, L. L. (1995). The relation between remembering and knowing as bases for recognition: effects of size congruency. *Journal of Memory and Language*, **34**, 622–43.

Yonelinas, A. P. and Jacoby, L. L. (1996a). Noncriterial recollection: familiarity as automatic, irrelevant recollection. *Consciousness and Cognition*, **5**, 131–41.

Yonelinas, A. P. and Jacoby, L. L. (1996b). Response bias and the process dissociation procedure. *Journal of Experimental Psychology: General*, **125**, 422–34.

Yonelinas, A. P., Regehr, G., and Jacoby, L. L. (1995). Incorporating response bias in a dual-process theory of memory. *Journal of Memory and Language*, **34**, 821–35.

Yonelinas, A. P., Kroll, N. E. A., Dobbins, I., Lazzara, M., and Knight, R. T. (1998). Recollection and familiarity deficits in amnesia: convergence of remember-know, process dissociation, and receiver operating characteristic data. *Neuropsychology*, **12**, 323–39.

Zacks, R., and Hasher, L. (1997). Cognitive gerontology and attentional inhibition: a reply to Burke and McDowd. *Journal of Gerontology: Psychological Sciences*, **52B**, P274–83.

Index

acculturation knowledge
  age-related improvement 128, 129, 131, 144
  definition 127
  interdependence among abilities of intelligence 141–3
accuracy data
  differences in 174–6, 206, 207
  indirect memory measurement 257–9
  iso-accuracy state traces 60–7
  iso-temporal state traces 74–9
  mean accuracies 51
  performance accuracy 25, 51, 74–5
  psychometrics 74–9, 129–43
  problems 76–9
  speed–accuracy trade-off model 5, 179–80
  time–accuracy functions 50–80
  variability in effecting synchronicity 170–4
action slips 272
age-related memory loss *see* memory loss
age x complexity interactions 4
age x task interactions 4
all-slow hypothesis 136
Alzheimer's disease 264
amnesia 278
anagrams 244, 254, 258, 260, 261, 263, 267
  process dissociation procedures 272
analogies 133, 144
analysis of covariance 28
analysis of variance *see* ANOVA approach
ANOVA approach 2, 3–7, 13, 74, 75, 76, 77
  and macro approach 24
apprehension–retention limits 146–7
architects 150
arithmetic *see* mental arithmetic
Armed Forces Qualification Tests 129
associative priming 241, 242

indirect memory task 256, 259–61
  see also priming
attention
  age-related decline 143
  as cognitive primitive 39–40
  divided attention ability 42
  divided attention costs 5
  inhibition deficit hypothesis 210
  and macro approach 23
  see also general cognitive slowing
auditory processing 268
  definition 127–8
auditory word identification *see* word identification
automatic processing 71
  and micro approach 22
average age effect 76–7
  see also meta-analysis

balance 34
baselines 6
  conditions 77–8, 94
  differences 4–6
  P(speed) 123–4
  speed 94, 95, 98, 100, 107
    implications 114
baseline tasks *see* control tasks
behavioural data 10, 14, 79–80, 125
  inhibition deficit hypothesis 209–11, 216–17
  see also time–accuracy functions
between-session variance 166–9
block design 19–20
blood pressure 35, 44
  and shared influence outcomes 34–5
brain damage 36
  frontal lobe dysfunction 16, 189–90, 195, 196, 200–1

see also focal brain damage;
  neuroanatomy
Brinley plots 6, 12–13, 51, 56, 99
  and common slowing 118, 136, 137, 138,
    208, 209
  criticisms 52
  iso-accuracy state traces 60
  iso-temporal state traces 67, 71, 76
  varieties 51
broad visualization *see* visual processing
Brown-Peterson task 189

cars 10
category exemplar generation 244, 264
Cattell and Cattell Culture Fair test 165
causation
  and correlational approach 10
  and mediational models 12, 29
  and shared influence analysis 31
central nervous system 9
  oscillators 175
  and shared influence outcomes 35
chess (game) 145, 146, 147, 149
choice reaction time tests 135, 162, 163,
    163–9, 183
  consistent individual differences 177–82
  models 182
  processing speed measurement 163–6
  see also reaction times
chronocentric slowing 94–9, 104, 151
  coefficients 121–2
  common 97, 115
  definition of model 90
  influence of 95–9, 107–9
  model 94–9, 101, 106, 110–12
  and performance 112–14
  response time 88–9, 90
  type 94, 116
  see also general slowing
chronological age 28
chronological slowing
  definition of model 90
  model of 91–4
  response time 88–9
  task-specific 104–6, 107, 116
  types 87, 91
  see also general slowing
chronometric tests 140, 141
chunking 147
clocks 175

cognitive primitives 9, 16
  alternative types 45
  and measurement indices 160
  and mediational models 29
  and neuroanatomical changes 43–4
  and performance 10
  processing efficiency 39–40
  and shared influence models 29, 38
cognitive slowing *see* general slowing
cognitive speed *see* processing speed
commonality analysis 29
'common cause model' 31
common factor of speed hypothesis 136
competition, high vs low response in
    indirect memory task 266–70
computation 42
concentration 42, 43, 142
  age-related decline 143
concept formation 133
'conceptual localization' 22
conceptual priming 241, 242
  indirect memory task: updated meta-
    analysis 256, 261–3
construct mediation approach 40–3, 139
contamination *see* task purity
context memory 53
controlled processing 22
control tasks 88, 95
  and common slowing 115–16
  Stroop effect 55
coordinative arithmetic, age differences
    65–6
correct decision speed, definition 128
correlation analyses 3, 7–10, 13
  and causation 10
  general chronological slowing 100, 116,
    118
  processing speed as intelligence
    theory 140
creativity 131
credibility judgments 244, 255, 258
criterion selection 178–9
criterion tasks 88, 94, 95, 98, 100, 111, 112,
    115, 116
  P(shared) 107, 115
  P(speed) 107, 123–4
  summary 118
crossword solving 149
crystallized intelligence *see* acculturation
    knowledge

cultural knowledge *see* acculturation
    knowledge

decision capture models 179
decision processes models 182
decision speed *see* processing speed
declarative learning 199
deductive reasoning, and expertise 146, 150
dementia 192
dendritic branching 43
diastolic blood pressure 35
Digit Cancellation test 190–1, 200
    and age-related memory loss 198–9
    recall and recognition experiment 194,
        196–8
Digit Symbol Substitution Test 190–1
    and age-related memory loss 198–9
    measurement of working memory
        199–200
    recall and recognition experiment 196–9
dissociations 2
    generalized speed factor 190
    levels-of-dissociation framework 64–7, 79
    and micro approach 22
    process dissociation procedures 270–8
    recollection and familiarity in old
        age 239–41
    in rejection of dull hypothesis 3–7
    remember/know judgements 279, 283
distractibility 143
divided attention
    ability 42
    costs 5
domains of cognition 2–3
    age-related change 209, 212–14, 220, 239,
        242
    general language slowing 208
double dissociations *see* dissociations
dual-process theories of memory 16, 238–88
dual route theories 222
dull hypothesis 1–17

elaborative encoding 37
empirical epistemology 53
encoding performance 3, 5, 58, 143, 263
    age differences 3–4, 67, 191
    elaborative 37
episodic contamination *see* task purity
episodic memory 19–20, 53, 54, 55
    age-related decline 131–3, 206

importance of processing speed 56
iso-accuracy traces 65, 67
and life-long experience 74
recall 68–71, 74, 90
and shared influence analysis 36
time-accuracy 59
see also tip-of-the-tongue states
esoteric analogies 144
evolution 170
exclusion tests 271, 274
exemplar generation 242, 260, 261, 262, 267
experimental perspectives 21
expertise
    intelligence theory 15, 144–51
    and recall 72–4
explicit memory 22, 189

fame judgement task 271
familiarity 238, 286–8
    dissociation between recollection
        and 239–41
    process dissociation procedures 270–8
    remember/know judgements 278–9
figural relations 133
financial planning, and expertise 145, 149
first-past-the-post models 178
fluency 8, 131
fluency of retrieval from long-term storage
    see tertiary storage and retrieval
fluid reasoning 130
    age-related decline 128, 133, 142, 150,
        192
    and age-related memory loss 191–2, 201
    definition 127
    interdependence among abilities of
        intelligence 141, 142
    processing speed and 192–4
focal brain damage 36
    see also brain damage
FOOD test 194
forward-span memory tests 133–4, 146
free recall 19–20, 190
frequency-of-occurrence 71–2
frontal lobe dysfunction 16, 189–90, 195,
    196, 200–1
    processing speed and 192–4, 195
functional neurons 43

Ga *see* auditory processing
g-auditory *see* auditory processing

Gc *see* acculturation knowledge
general chronological slowing 99, 104
  model 100
  theory of intelligence 135, 136–9
general cognitive slowing 87, 99
  language theory 208–9
  theories 50, 135
  see also attention; macro approaches;
    processing speed; working memory
generalized speed factor 190–1
general knowledge, indirect memory
    measurement 244, 254, 258, 260,
    261, 267, 270
general models *see* global models
general slowing
  and aging 87
  common factors 88, 95
  and control tasks 115–16
  and language theories 208–15, 257
  task-specific 87, 104, 118
  see also chronocentric slowing;
    chronological slowing; general
    cognitive slowing
generation priming *see* production priming
Geriatric Depression Scale 193
Gf *see* fluid reasoning
Gf-Gc theory 126–44
Glm *see* tertiary storage and retrieval
global models 3, 14, 16, 79, 80, 139, 160, 174
  all-slow hypothesis 136
  'common cause model' 31
  and mediational models 30
  and memory 189, 192, 200–1
  null hypothesis 52
  problems 161, 192
  and systematic relations model 26
  see also shared influence analysis
GO (game) 145, 149
Gq *see* quantitative knowledge
g-quantitative *see* quantitative knowledge
grip strength 44
  and shared influence outcomes 34, 35
Gs *see* processing speed
Gv *see* visual processing

hearing 34
hierarchical regression 10, 12
  analysis 30, 36
  and macro approach 24
  and mediational models 28, 29

HOME test 194
homophones 218–9, 219
  indirect memory measurement 244, 254,
    258, 260, 262, 263, 267
human performance *see* performance
hypothesized variables 28

identification priming
  indirect memory task 264–6
  see also priming
implicit memory 22, 189
inclusion tests 271, 274
independence of variables 24–5, 31–6, 37,
    128
  see also interdependence of variables;
    shared influence analysis
individual performance *see* performance
inductive reasoning 19–20
  and shared influence analysis 36
  see also reasoning
information processing speed *see* processing
    speed
information-specific theories of
    language 211–5
information-universal theories of
    language 208–11
inhibition 80, 161, 270
  as cognitive primitive 39–40
  as construct in mediation of age-related
    influences 42
  Stroop effect 55
inhibition deficit hypothesis 209–11,
    216–17, 266
  and spelling ability 228
initiation 39–40
intelligence
  expertise development theory 144–51
  interdependence among abilities 141–3
  major capabilities 127–8
  nature of 125–6
  and neural speed 135
  processing speed theory 139–41
  slowing with age theory 136–9
interactionism 52–3, 79, 80
interdependence of variables 141–3
  see also independence of variables
iso-accuracy state traces 60–7
iso-temporal state traces 67–79
  equations 66, 68
  psychometrics 74–9

issue isolationism 53, 55
Italian speakers, and tip-of-tongue states
    217
item priming 241, 242
    indirect memory task 256, 259–61
    see also priming
item recall *see* episodic memory
item recognition 244, 255, 258, 260
iterative tasks 110, 113

knowledge 8
    general 244, 254, 258, 260, 261, 267, 270

language 16, 204–30
    comprehension and aging 205–7
    information-specific theories 211–15
    information-universal theories 208–11
    inhibition deficit hypothesis 210
    node-structure theory 212–14
    processing and aging 204–5
    production 207–8
    theories 208–15
    transmission deficit hypothesis 212,
        215–30
latency measures 53, 54, 55, 65, 67, 76–9
    indirect memory measurement 257–9,
        266, 269, 286
    mean latencies 51, 54
    repetition priming effects 206
    response 4, 6–7, 54
latent models 117
    summary 118
latent variables *see* hypothesized variables
learning, declarative 199
letter comparison 19–20
    and shared influence outcomes 35, 42
letter fluency test 194
letter series 42, 43, 142
levels-of-dissociation framework 64–7,
    79–80
lexical decision 244, 254, 255, 258, 260, 261,
    264, 265, 267
lexical processing 53, 59
    nodes 215–20
likability 244, 254, 258
list length 278
list recall 72, 75, 76
    from episodic memory 70–1
local models 2, 13, 14, 16, 161
    and mediational models 30

problems 161
    and systematic relations model 26
longitudinal changes in individuals 24
    and mediational models 29
long-term memory *see* tertiary storage and
        retrieval
long-term working memory 7
    apprehension-retention limits 147
    and expertise 146, 149, 150, 152
    method of working 148
lower limb strength 34

macro approaches 21, 23–5, 90
    comparison with micro approaches 23
    new investigative methods needed 45
    summary of results 36–7
    see also general cognitive slowing;
        psychometrics
'magical number seven plus or minus
    two' test 133, 146
maintained abilities 15, 133
manifest variables *see* observed variables
mathematical reasoning 35
    see also mental arithmetic
matrices 133, 142
Maudesley Personality Inventory 168
mean accuracies 51
meaningless text rereading 255, 258
mean latencies 51
measurement indices 160–84
    local and global models 160–3
mediational models 28–30
    comparison with shared influences
        models 36, 37
    limitations 29–30
        common factors 34–5
medical diagnosis, and expertise 145, 149
memorial representation models 181–2
memory 8
    capacity 9, 10
    conclusions 269–70
    dual-process theories 16, 238–88
    global models 189, 192, 200–1
    implicit 22, 189
    inhibition deficit hypothesis 210
    measurement
        and aging 191, 206, 239–41
        indirect: updated meta-analysis 206,
            241–70
    and micro approach 22

region-specific neural aging
    hypotheses 211–12
time-accuracy functions 58
see also working memory
memory loss
    age-related determinants 188–201
        fluid intelligence 191–2, 201
        frontal lobe dysfunction 189–90, 195,
            196, 200–1
        generalized speed factor 190–1
        recall and recognition experiment
            192–7
    characteristics 188
    and digit Symbol Substitution Test 198–9
    processing speed and 192–4
Memory for Names 130–1
mental arithmetic 53
    iso-accuracy traces 65–6
    systematic relation method 25
    time-accuracy functions 58, 79
    see also mathematical reasoning
mental rotation 133
meta-analysis 17, 53, 55, 76
    indirect measures of memory 206, 241–70
    measurement domains 53–4
    memory and measurement of aging 206
    recall for frequency-of-occurrence 71–2
    recall from episodic memory 68–71
    see also average age effect
metaphors 133
method of loci 72–4
metric units 50
    different domains 53
    systematic relation method 25, 26
    see also psychometrics; time-accuracy
        functions
micro approaches 21–3, 50, 90
    comparison with macro approaches 23
Mill Hill Vocabulary Test 191
Mini-Mental State Exam 193
mirror reading 244, 255, 258
molar models 117
motivation 39–40, 43
motor speed 5–6, 39–40
movement perception 170–4
multiple-partialling procedures 142
myelin sheathing 43

National Adult Reading Test 191
negative priming 53

networks 10
    loss of connections 9
neural speed *see* processing speed
neuroanatomy 43
    and familiarity 288
    regional age-related effects 44
    region-specific neural aging
        hypotheses 211–12
    and shared influence outcomes 34, 37
    see also brain damage
nodes
    lexical processing 53, 59, 215–20
    node-structure theory 16, 212–14, 220
        orthographic retrieval 224–30
    as parallel distributed processing
        theory 223
    transmission deficit hypothesis 212
non-iterative tasks 110, 114
nonproduction priming *see* identification
    priming
nonword naming 244, 254, 258, 260, 261,
    265
null hypothesis
    adaptation 76–9
    global models 52
    rejection 1–2, 80
numeracy 35

object assembly 19–20
object decision 244, 254, 258, 261, 267
observed variables 28
off-topic speech 210–11
    region-specific neural aging
        hypotheses 212
opposition methodology 241, 288
optimal decision pathways models 180–1
orthographic systems of nodes 208, 212–14,
    222, 223
    and tip-of-tongue states 215–20
    transmission deficits 224–30
oscillators 175
outliers 26, 257, 262, 269
output performance 3–4

paired-associate recall 190
    from episodic memory 70–1, 76
paired associates 19–20
parallel distributed processing theories
    222–3
parallelism 51–2, 79

parameters 27
part correlation analsysis 29
partial correlation 28
path analytical techniques 3, 10
  and common slowing 118
  criticisms 11
pattern comparison 19–20
  and shared influence outcomes 35
perceptual grouping 39–40
perceptual priming 241, 242
  indirect memory task 256, 261–3, 265,
    267, 268, 270
perceptual speed 8, 19, 42, 190, 197
  memory tests 194, 195
  nature of 39
  see also processing speed
performance 3–4
  age differences 1–2, 192
  and chronocentric slowing 112–4
  individual variability testing 166–8,
    168–70
    independent of performance
      speed 177–82
  and micro approach 22
performance accuracy 74–5
  Brinley plots 51
  systematic relation method 25
personality 131
  Maudesley Personality Inventory 168
phonological systems of nodes 208, 212–14,
    215–20, 222
  and tip-of-tongue states 215–20, 220–1
  priming effects 217–20
piano playing 150
pictures 207
  completion or naming 188, 244, 254, 258,
    260, 261, 264, 265, 267, 268
power measures 142
practice, and development of
    expertise 148–50
primary memory, importance of processing
    speed 56
priming 53
  associative priming 241
  indirect memory task 241–70
  phonological priming effects on tip-of-
    tongue states 217–20
  process dissociation procedure 270–8
  transmission deficit hypothesis 212
  see also associative priming;

identification priming; item priming;
    production priming; semantic priming
primitives *see* cognitive primitives
principal components analysis 30
process dissociation procedures 270–8
processing
  as construct in mediation of age-related
    influences 42
  controlled 22
  iso-accuracy state traces 60–4
  and micro approach 22
  parallelism 51–2, 79
processing efficiency
  age-related differences 51
  cause or consequence of age-related
    differences 43–4
  potential primitives 39–40
processing resources 9
  and macro approach 23
processing speed 9, 10, 15, 162–3
  age-related decline 16, 128, 133, 134–5,
    150
  and age-related memory loss 194–8, 198,
    201
  and cognititve aging 56, 79
  and declarative learning 199
  definition 127
  dynamic and asymptotic effects 59
  and fluency measures 131
  generalized speed factor 190–1
  as intelligence theory 126, 135, 139–41
  interdependence among abilities of
    intelligence 141, 142
  and learning 199
  and macro approach 23, 37
  measurement 163–6, 174, 190–1, 198
  and investigation of individual differences
    in variability 176–7
  as mediating factor 56
  and mediational models 28–9
  and processing efficiency 39–40, 43
  and shared influence models 37, 38
  and spelling ability 228
  see also general cognitive slowing;
    perceptual speed
process-specific cognitive slowing 87, 109–
    14, 115, 116
  model 109–10
  summary 118
production priming

indirect memory task 264–6
  high vs low response 266–70
  see also priming
prolonged speech 210–11
pronunciation errors 227–8
proper names
  and aging 207
  transmission deficit hypothesis 219–20,
    220–2
proportionate costs 5–6
prose memory 54
prose recall, from episodic memory 70–1, 76
P(shared) 123–4
  chronocentric slowing 113
  definition 98–9
  general chronological slowing 100–4, 117
  task-specific chronological slowing 107–9
P(speed) 123–4
  chronocentric slowing 112
  definition 95–8
  general chronological slowing 100–4, 117
  task-specific chronological slowing 107–9
psychometrics 21, 204
  accuracy data 76–9, 80
  accuracy tests 163–83
  chronometric tests 140, 141
  group-comparison research 50, 54
  iso-temporal state traces 74–9
  see also macro approaches; metric units
purity of tasks *see* task purity

quantitative knowledge, definition 128

reaction times 53, 76, 137–8
  tests 135
  see also choice reaction time tests
reading
  mirror reading 244, 255, 258
  National Adult Reading Test 191
  span 42
reasoning 8, 37
  age-related decline 133
  and expertise 145, 146
  importance of processing speed 56
  systematic relation method 25
  see also fluid reasoning; inductive
    reasoning
recall
  Brown-Peterson task 189
  experiment 192–7

frequency-of-occurrence 71–2
  from episodic memory 68–71, 74, 80
  over periods of time 130–1
  process dissociation procedures 270–8
  recollection 238
  role of expertise 72–4
  and shared influence outcomes 35
  see also recollection
recognition 11, 189
  experiment 192–7
  familiarity 238
  process dissociation procedures 270–8
recollection 238, 286–88
  dissociation between recollection and
    familiarity 239–41
  process dissociation procedures 270–8
  remember/know judgements 278–9
  see also recall
redundant speech 210–11
region-specific neural aging
  hypotheses 211–12
regression analyses
  in Brinley plots 12
  and general slowing theories 209
  multiple 3
  problems 10–12
  and shared influence analysis 36
regularity 27
reliability 54
  and micro approach 22
  processing speed as intelligence
    theory 140
  and shared influence models 31
remember/know judgements 241, 278–86,
  287
repetition
  effect on memory 240–1
  indirect memory measurement 244, 259,
    260
response
  indirect memory task, high vs low
    response 266–70
  latencies 4, 6–7, 54
response time 3, 5, 12
  chronological and chronocentric
    slowing 88–9, 91–4, 96, 99
  P(speed) 95–8
  variability in decision accuracy 171, 173
rhyme decision 244, 254, 258, 261, 267
rule-based behaviour 7

sample size 54
  and cognitive slowing models 102–4, 107–9
  construct mediation approach 42
  and mediational models 29, 30
  processing speed as intelligence theory 140
  and shared influence analysis 36, 42
SAR *see* short term apprehension and retrieval
scrambled text rereading 255, 258, 260
script generations 205
self-monitoring explanation 80
semantic classification 244, 254, 258, 260, 262, 267
semantic memory 58
semantic priming 205, 206
  see also priming
semantic systems of nodes 212–14
  and tip-of-tongue states 215–20, 222
sensitivity
  and micro approach 22
  process dissociation procedures 277–8
  and shared influence models 31
sensory acuity 39–40, 44
sentence completion 244, 254, 258, 260, 268
sequential arithmetic, age differences 65–6
series completion 19–20
series comprehension 133
Shakespeare, William 51, 56
shared influence analysis 30–6
  'common cause model' 31
  outcomes 31–4
  processing speed theory of intelligence 141
  responsibility for influences 37–43
  see also global models; independence of variables
short term apprehension and retrieval 130
  age-related decline 128, 133, 150
  apprehension-retention limits 146–7
  definition 127
  interdependence among abilities of intelligence 141
  measurement 133–4
short-term working memory 7, 130–1, 133, 134
  and expertise 146
simultaneity mechanism 80
slowing *see* general slowing

spatial ability 56, 170–4
spatial visualization 19–20, 150
  and shared influence analysis 36
speed *see* processing speed
speed-accuracy trade-off model *see* time-accuracy method
speeded responding 278
spelling 16, 132
  aging and retrieval of orthographic knowledge 224–30
  errors and aging 207
  homophones, indirect memory measurement 244
spontaneous organization 37
standard deviation 7
state trace analysis 59–79
Sternberg search paradigm 3–4
storage 42
  performance 3–4
  see also tertiary storage and retrieval
story retelling, indirect memory measurement 255, 258
strategy 39–40, 43
Stroop effect 53, 54–5, 210
structural equation models 30–1, 37
sustained attention 39–40
switching attention 39–40
syllogisms 133
synchronicity 170–4
systematic relation method 25–7
  limitations 26–7
systolic blood pressure 35

tactile sensitivity 34
task analysis
  age *x* complexity interactions 4
  age *x* task interactions 4
  and micro approach 21
  and shared influence analysis 37
task complexity 4–5, 7
task performance *see* performance
task purity 7
  and causation 10
  and micro approach 22–3
  process dissociation procedure 270–8
task-specific chronological slowing 104–6, 116
  model 105–6, 107
task-specific cognitive slowing 80, 87, 104
  summary 118

tertiary storage and retrieval
  age-related improvement 128, 129, 144
  definition 127
  and expertise 146
  interdependence among abilities of
    intelligence 141
  measurement 130–1
  see also storage
text rereading 244
time-accuracy functions 56–80
  estimation differences 174–6
  iso-accuracy state traces 60–7
  iso-temporal state traces 67–79
  meta-analysis 54
  models for age differences 60–4
  suitability 55
  in young adults 56–7
  see also behavioural data; metric units
time-accuracy method
  advantages 57
  levels-of-dissociation framework 64–7
  speed-accuracy trade-off model 5, 179–80
time estimation, differences in 174–6
tip-of-the-tongue states 16
  age-related decline 207, 270
  transmission deficit hypothesis 215–20
  see also episodic memory
topology 133
transmission deficit hypothesis 204, 212,
    215–30
  as parallel distributed processing
    theory 223
TSR *see* tertiary storage and retrieval
Turkish word reading 244, 254, 258, 260,
    261, 265, 267
typing 150

unique models *see* local models

variables
  in mediation of age-related influences on
    cognition 42
  and mediational models 28
  observed, and mediational models 28
  and shared influence analysis 30
Venn diagrams 8
verbosity 210–11
  region-specific neural aging
    hypotheses 212

video game task 170–4
vigilance 143
visibility of aging process 51
visual acuity 34, 35
visual degradation factors 5
visual processing, definition 127
visual word identification *see* word
    identification
vocabulary 144
vulnerable abilities 133

Wechsler Adult Intelligence Scales 129,
    191, 194, 199
Wisconsin Card Sort Test 7, 19–20, 189,
    194, 196, 199
wisdom 125
within-session variance 166–9
Woodcock-Johnson Psycho-Educational
    Battery-Revised 129, 130, 144
word associations
  and aging 205, 209
  indirect memory measurement 244, 254,
    255, 258, 260, 261, 262, 264, 266–7, 267,
    268
  tests 131
word finding, and aging 207
word identification 242
  indirect memory measurement 244, 254,
    258, 264
word scanning, age differences 59, 66–7
word stem completion
  indirect memory measurement 266, 267,
    269
  process dissociation procedures 272
working memory
  as construct in mediation of age-related
    influences 42
  and declarative learning 199
  and macro approach 23, 37
  measurement 199–200
  and mediational models 29
  and processing efficiency 39–40, 43
  and reasoning 133
  and shared influence models 37
  tertiary storage retrieval
    measurement 130
  see also general cognitive slowing; long-
    term working memory; memory; short-
    term working memory